FIRES
OF
ROME

FIRES

OF

ROME

JESUS
AND THE
EARLY CHRISTIANS
IN THE
ROMAN EMPIRE

John Hagan

Rauson Group LLC

ISBN 978-0-9820828-1-2

LCCN 2009942127

Proofreading services provided by Victoria Brouillette.
Acknowledgments: Peter Kirby, earlychristianwritings.com; ccel.org.
Contact: 2313 L-S, #138, San Antonio, Texas 78230;

Cover: Rock of the Tomb of Jesus, Church of the Holy Sepulcher

Table of Contents

Maps/Graphics

Introduction

And now I say unto you, Refrain from these men, and let them alone: for
if this counsel or this work be of men, it will be overthrown: but if it is of
God, ye will not be able to overthrow them; lest haply ye be found even
to be fighting against God. (Acts 5:38-9)

Early Christianity cannot be fully understood through early
Christian writings alone-one must have a strong grounding in
ancient Roman and Jewish history. It is for this purpose that *Fires
of Rome* and *Year of the Passover* were written.

To connect the religious sources with the secular and make
sense of it all, a time line has to be created. This was done in *Year
of the Passover*, and will be continued in *Fires of Rome*. The early
Christian sources are full of fascinating characters who also are
found in the pages of secular works. Studying them is the key to
the accurate dating of Christian events.

The completed time lines follow in table format.

In *Year of the Passover*, it was determined that Jesus was born in
either 12 or 11 B.C., and was crucified in A.D. 36. This gave Jesus
an eight-year Ministry and making him in his late 40's at the time
of his crucifixion. John the Baptist, six months older than Jesus,
was arrested in late A.D. 34, and executed in early A.D. 35. The
Tetrarch Herod Antipas married his niece Herodias in A.D. 32,
and was defeated in war by King Aretas IV of Nabotea in late
A.D. 35, and so on.

Year of the Passover also identified a central but little-known
individual in the crucifixion drama — Roman General Lucius
Vitellius. Vitellius was the most powerful man in the eastern
Roman Empire at that time, and was a key factor in Jesus'
execution.

Fires of Rome begins with preparatory chapters on the physical layout of ancient Jerusalem and the Second Temple. Jewish historian Flavius Josephus describes both in detail. Combining what Josephus says with modern Archeology reveals important insights into the Jerusalem of Jesus' time and what is seen today.

The events surrounding Jesus' crucifixion are then detailed over the next several chapters, after which the struggles of the early Christian Church are chronicled–to include the martyrdom of Stephen, the Nazarene persecutions in Jerusalem, the epiphany of Saul, the adventures of the Apostles, and the continuing involvement of the Temple High Priesthood in later Christian persecutions. The final five chapters deal with the fall of the Caesars and the disastrously ill-fated Jewish revolt of A.D. 66. Christians even today ascribe that disaster to the Jews' crucifixion of Jesus and persecution of the Nazarenes.

In *Fires of Rome,* many of the biographies started in *Year of the Passover* are concluded, as well as new and relevant historical figures introduced. A major focus is on Paul the Apostle, one of the most unusual and energetic men of his time or any other. Other Jewish figures are also studied, such as King Agrippa I, Agrippa II, Egyptian Governor Tiberius Alexander, historian Flavius Josephus, and several of the Second Temple High Priests. The Roman emperors of that era are also included, as well as many of Judea's quasi-criminal Roman procurators.

Both *Year of the Passover* and *Fires of Rome* were prospective, secular undertakings. There was no particular religion, philosophy, or dogma that I wanted supported–or debased. Logical connections and reasonable conclusions were made based on the facts that were found. Admittedly, I could not resist, at times, speculation of a more extreme nature. Purposefully, they were set off in sections prefaced "Interlude" as a warning to the reader!

As with *Year of the Passover, Fires of Rome* cannot be more accurate than the sources upon which it relies. For this reason, only the most veracious of written sources are used–scholarly works on the subject written after the fall of the Roman Empire are ignored. Even among those earlier works, most are dismissed as being either biased, derivative, or outright fabrications. Selections from the remaining accepted references are reproduced liberally to support important conclusions and to give a flavor to the times.

Relatively few historical manuscripts written in the first century A.D. are extant apart from the Christian. In the accepted methodology of critical analysis, a potential reference source is completely discarded if it is demonstrated to have any errors. But provable errors occur in even in the "best" of ancient source manuscripts. For that reason, unfortunately, both *Year of the Passover* and *Fires of Rome* can never truly pass critical muster. It is admitted at the outset, then, that the conclusions drawn in these works cannot be anything other than speculative. But that does not mean they are necessarily false!

The people of antiquity were intelligent and capable. They were our progenitors, after all, and with the added burden of having to survive and function in a far more challenging age. Technical advances have made modern life easier, to be sure, but it has not made the human animal any more intelligent.

There are universal ethical, moral, and social issues that men and societies of every age must deal with. In that respect, "civilized" society has changed little over the past 2,000 years–or 10,000 years. Modern man can–and should–learn from ancient history.

	Roman Events	12 B.C.- A.D. 34	Christian Events

Roman Events	12 B.C.- A.D. 34	Christian Events
	12 B.C. ?	Birth year of Jesus
Tiberius is in his fifteenth year of rule	A.D. 28	John the Baptist rises to fame as a prophet, possibly baptizes Jesus
Livia dies, the widow of Augustus Caesar and the protector of the Herod family in Rome	A.D. 29	
Attempted coup fails by Sejanus. Proscriptions and chaos reigns in Rome for years	Oct A.D. 31	
Herod Agrippa leaves Rome. Herodias weds Herod Antipas in Galilee. Pharaelis flees to Nabotea.	Spring A.D. 32	
Herod Philip marries Salome, Herodias' daughter	Summer A.D. 32	
Herod Philip dies. Tiberius delays award of his kingdom	Jan A.D. 34	
Pilate unveils aqueduct project, riots ensue.	Spring A.D. 34	Jesus drives out the merchants in the Second Temple at the Passover in Jerusalem
Parthia challenges Rome in Armenia. Parthian nobles approach Tiberius for help	Summer A.D. 34	

xii

	Roman Events	A.D. 34-36	Christian Events

Roman Events	A.D. 34-36	Christian Events
Tiberius orders Vitellius to Syria to stop Parthian aggression, ? orders Herod Antipas to invade Nabotea.	Dec A.D. 34	
	Jan A.D. 35	John the Baptist is arrested by Herod Antipas as Antipas prepares for war
	Feb A.D. 35	John the Basptist is beheaded by Antipas, Jesus retreats north
	April A.D. 35	Jesus celebrates the Passover in the hills of the Decapolis
Vitellius successfully stops Parthia's attempted takeover of Armenia Herod Antipas continues to prepare his army for an invasion of Nabotea	Summer A.D. 35	Jesus introduces communion ceremony in Capernaum, loses many followers
Herod Antipas' army is defeated by Aretas'.	Late Summer A.D. 35	
Tiberius orders Vitellius to invade Nabotea and avenge Antipas' defeat	Fall A.D. 35	Jesus returns to Jerusalem for the feast of the Tabernacles
	Dec A.D. 35	Jesus revists John the Baptist's camp by the Jordan
Vitellius arrives in Jerusalem for the Passover after Jesus' crucifixion, Ciaiphas removed	Spring A.D. 36	Lazarus ressurrected Crucifixion of Jesus early in the Passover

xiii

Roman Events	A.D. 36-54	Christian Events
	Summer A.D. 36	Miracle of the Tongues Stephen stoned on the orders of High Priest Jonathan
Pilate sends force to destroy Samaritan religious leader And his followers	Fall A.D. 36	Saul of Tarsus has a vision of Jesus on the road to Damascus
Vitellius removes Pilate as Procurator. Tiberius dies. Jonathan removed as High Priest.	Spring A.D. 37	
	A.D. 39	Saul of Tarusus, now known as Paul, returns to Jerusalem
Caius assasinated, Claudius assumes power.	A.D. 41	Agrippa the Great gains Judea, James the disciple is executed.
	A.D. 42	Agrippa the Greal arrests Peter who later escapes
Agrippa the Great dies	A.D. 44	
Rebellion in Judea. Quadrtus sends Cumanus, High Priest Ananias, and others to Rome for trail	A.D. 51	
Felix appointed Produrator, Gallio appointed Proconsul of Achaea	A.D. 52	
	A.D. 53	Christian summit meeting in Jerusalem with Paul attending
	A.D. 54	Paul's trial before Gallio

Roman Events	A.D. 56-70	Christian Events
Felix arranges the murder of ex-High Priest Jonathan in the Second Temple courtyard	A.D. 56	
	A.D. 58	Paul the Apostle on trial before the Sanhedrin in Jerusalem, imprisoned in Caesarea by Felix
Festus appointed Procurator High Priest Ismael demands Paul's execution	A.D. 60	Paul the Apostle extradited to Rome by Festus
Ismael resigns as High Priest, joins Poppea's salon in Rome	A.D. 61	Paul arrives in Rome and set free
Festus dies suddenly	A.D. 62	Ananus convenes Sanhedrin, James and other Christians executed in Jerusalem
Josephus in Rome, meets Poppea, ? Nero, ?Ismael, and ??Paul	A.D. 63	Acts end with Paul in Rome.
	July A.D. 64	Persecutions in Rome. Deaths of Paul, Peter, and hundreds of Christians
Jewish revolt begins	A.D. 66	
Vespasian subdues much Judea, Galilee	A.D. 67-8	
Nero Commits Suicide	June A.D. 68	
Year of the Four Emperors. Vespasian, gains power in December of A.D. 69	A.D. 69	
Destruction of Jerusalem and the Second Temple	Oct A.D. 70	

Early First Century A.D. Roman East

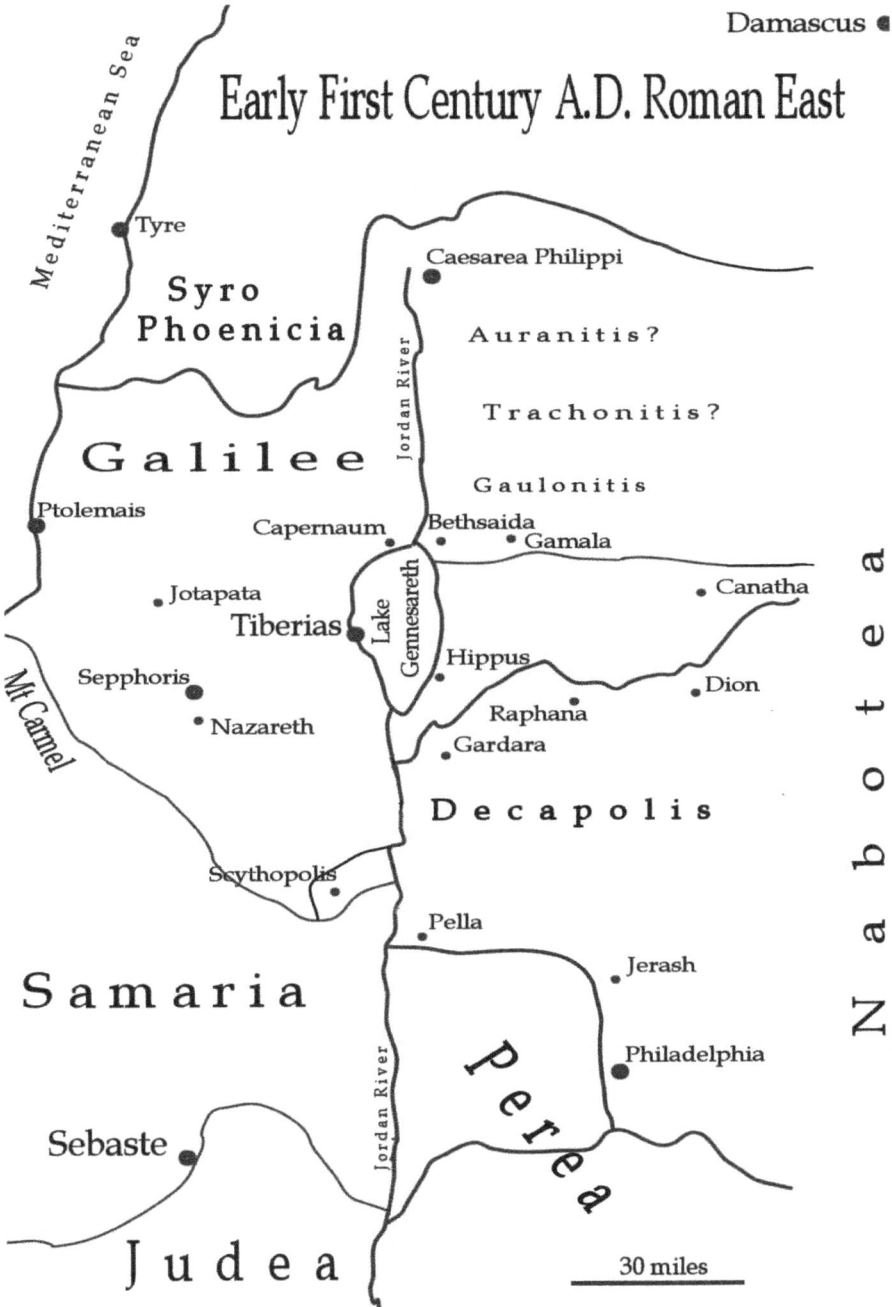

Mediterranean Sea

Damascus

Tyre

Syro Phoenicia

Caesarea Philippi

Auranitis?

Jordan River

Trachonitis?

Galilee

Gaulonitis

Ptolemais

Capernaum

Bethsaida

Gamala

Nabotea

Jotapata

Canatha

Tiberias

Lake Gennesareth

Hippus

Sepphoris

Dion

Mt Carmel

Nazareth

Raphana

Gardara

Decapolis

Scythopolis

Pella

Samaria

Jerash

Jordan River

Perea

Philadelphia

Sebaste

Judea

30 miles

Mediterranean Sea

• Caesarea

Samaria

Jordan River

• Pella

Decapolis

Jerash
•

Sebaste
•

Jabbok R.

Philadelphia
•

Jericho
•

Bethany-by-the-Jordan
•

Jerusalem
•

Qumran
Herodium
•

Bethlehem
•

Madaba
•

Ashkelon
•

J u d e a

Idumea

Lake Asphaltitis

P e r e a

Macherus
•

Arnon R.

Masada
•

Nabotea

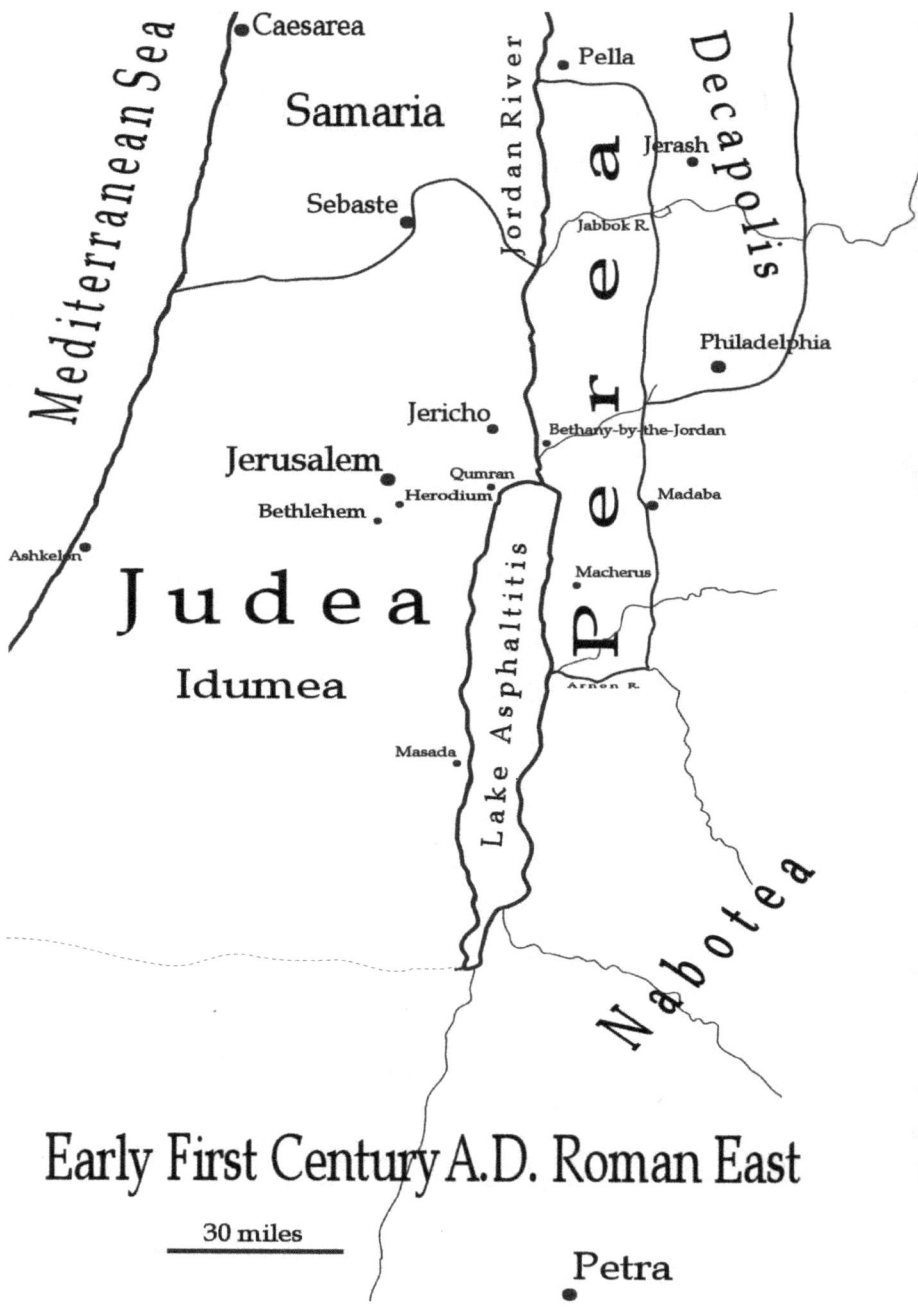

Early First Century A.D. Roman East

30 miles

Petra
•

The Roman Empire
Mid-First Century A.D.

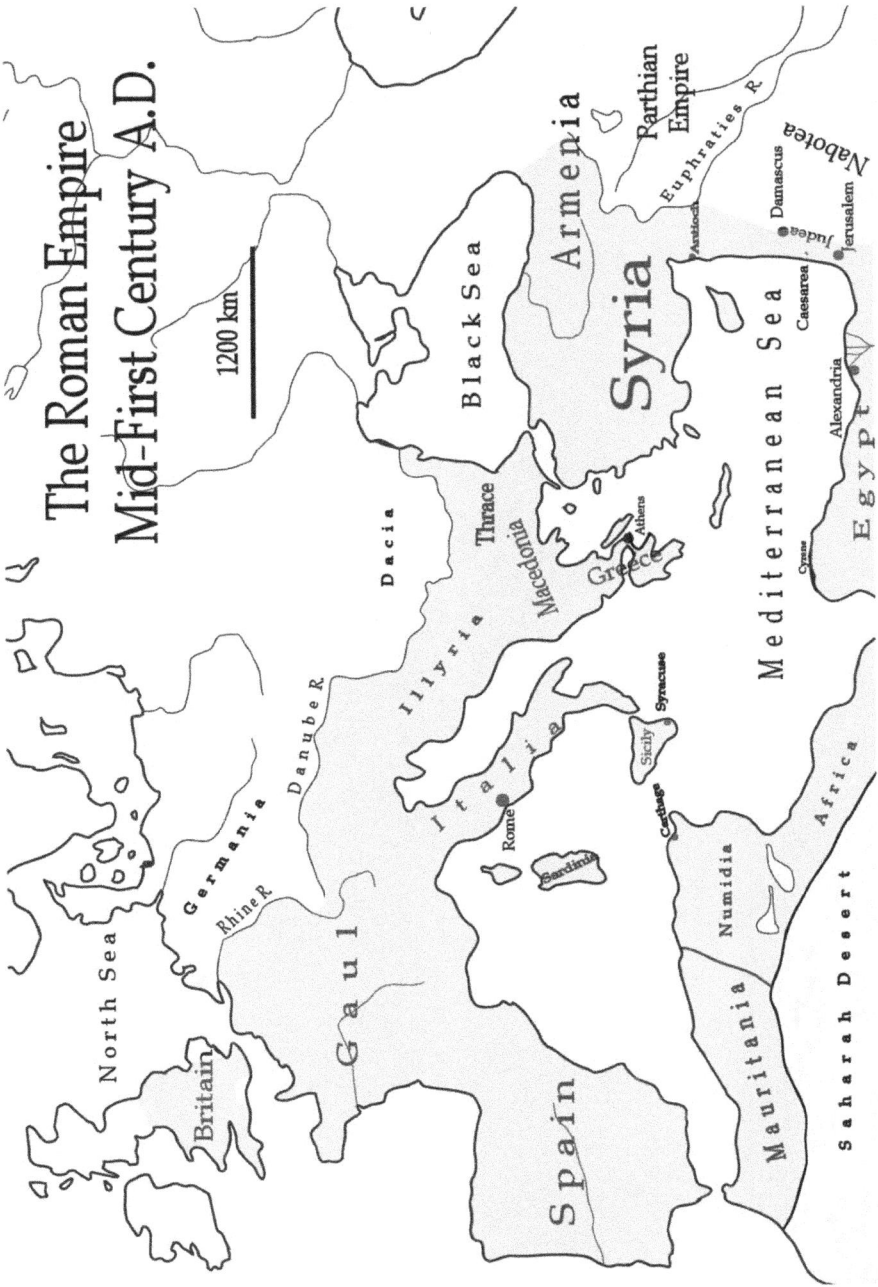

1200 km

North Sea

Britain

Germania

Rhine R.

Gaul

Danube R.

Dacia

Spain

Italia

Illyria

Rome

Sardinia

Macedonia

Thrace

Black Sea

Armenia

Syria

Athens

Greece

Carthage

Sicily

Syracuse

Numidia

Mauritania

Africa

Saharah Desert

Mediterranean Sea

Crete

Alexandria

Egypt

Caesarea

Antioch

Damascus

Jerusalem

Judea

Nabotea

Euphrates R.

Parthian Empire

xix

Asia Minor

Macedonia

Galatia

Achaia

Greece

Ionian
Sea

Crete

Mediterranean Sea

Africa

250 miles

Pisidian
Antioch

Iconium
Lystra

Derbe

Perga

Attalia

Pamphylia

Seleucia

Antioch

Syria

Salamis

Cyprus

Syria
Phoenicia

Nazareth

Samaria

Paphos

Jerusalem

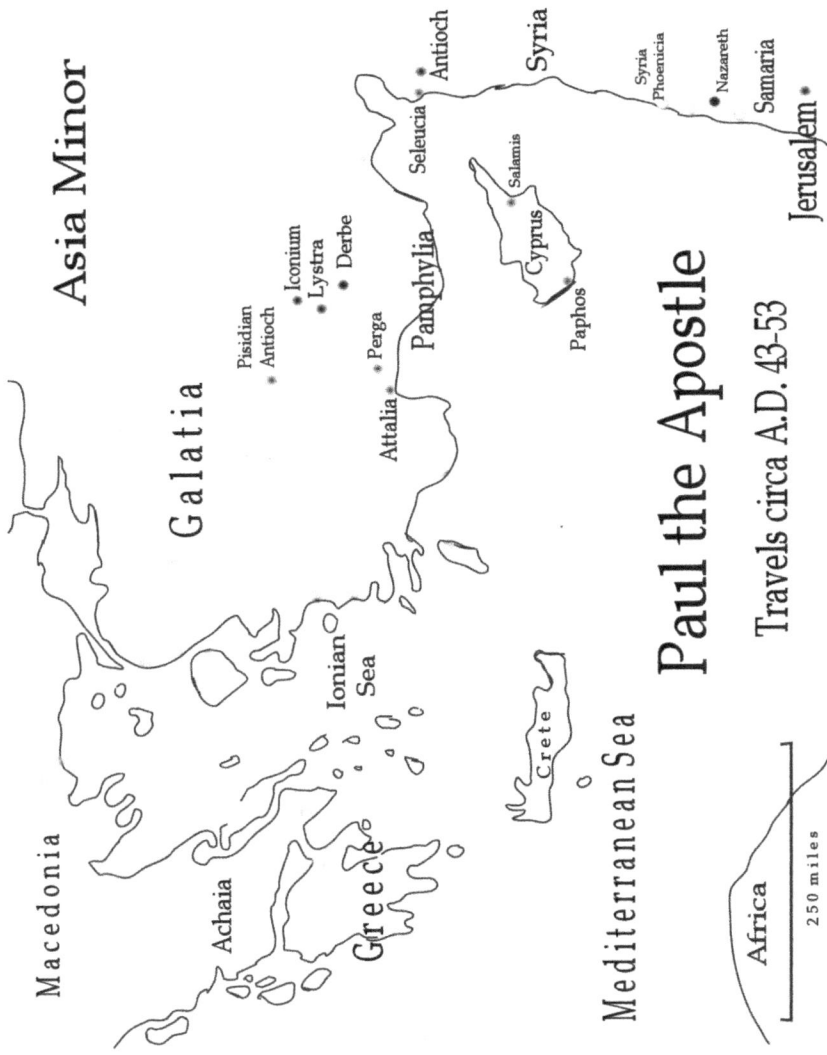

Paul the Apostle

Travels circa A.D. 43-53

Asia Minor

- Ancyra

Galatia

- Bithynia

Phyrgia

- Iconium
- Lystra
- Derbe

- Tarsus

- Antioch

Syria

- Tyre

- Nazareth
- Caesarea

Jerusalem •

Cyprus

- Thyatire

Mysia
Troas

- Ephesus

Rhodes

Samothrace

Macedonia

- Philippi
Neapolis
- Amphipolis
- Apollonia
Thessalonica
- Berea

Achaia

Athens

Greece

- Corinth
Cenchrea

Crete

Mediterranean Sea

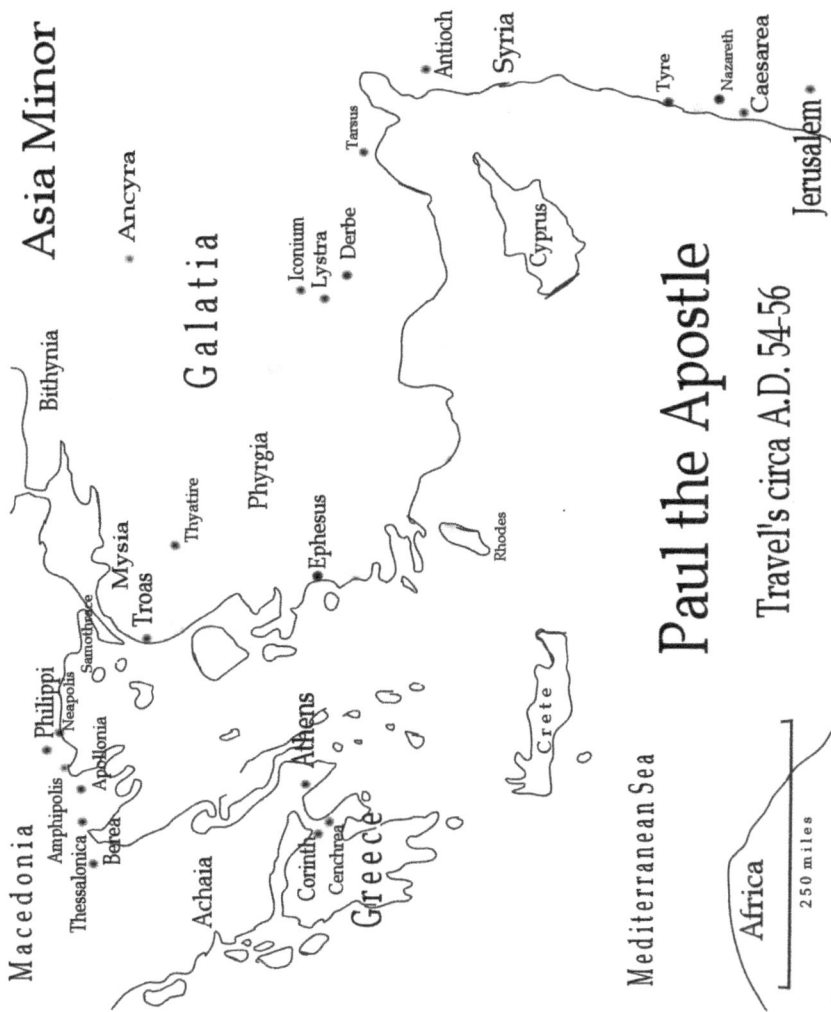

Paul the Apostle

Travel's circa A.D. 54-56

Africa

250 miles

Asia Minor

Macedonia

Philippi

Amphipolis
Apollonia
Thessalonica
Berea

Achaia

Troas
Assos

Mitylene
Chios

Samos
Ephesus
Miletus

Cos

Corinth
Cenchrea

Greece

Galatia

Phyrgia

Pisidian
Antioch

Iconium
Lystra
Derbe

Lycia

Patara

Rhodes

Crete

Mediterranean Sea

Tarsus

Antioch

Syria

Cyprus

Tyre
Ptolemais
Nazareth
Caesarea

Jerusalem

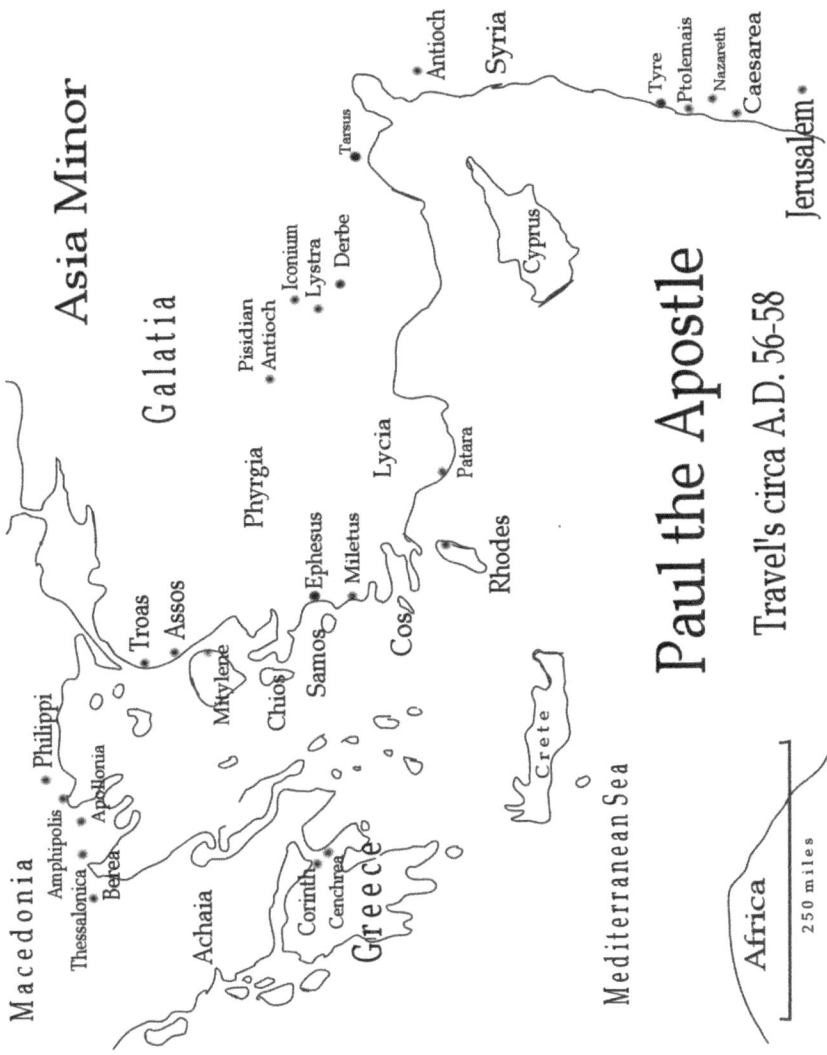

Paul the Apostle

Travel's circa A.D. 56-58

Africa

250 miles

Chapter 1   Ancient Jerusalem

a city... of great magnificence, and of mighty fame among all mankind.
(Wars VII 1:1)

Jerusalem was an ancient city even in Jesus' time. In fact, for as long as humans inhabited the Middle East the site of Jerusalem has been occupied. And for good reason–Jerusalem boasts an easily defended position on a mountain ridge, as well as having its own constantly flowing Artesian spring. Neanderthals have been found in northern Israel, and these humanoids could well have been Jerusalem's first inhabitants–pushing back the site's settled past some 36,000 years. Imagine, in that prehistoric era, Cro-Magnons battling the Neanderthals for control of the mountain ridge!

Over the recorded history of the past 3,000 years, Jerusalem has been destroyed dozens of time by invading armies and then rebuilt. In the ancient sections of modern-day Jerusalem, the city structures rest on rocky debris from those previous conquests. In some areas, the rubble layer is over 120 feet deep.

The Gihon Source

The Gihon Spring has a fascinating history. The original site was on the eastern bank of the lower city, but the flow was ingeniously diverted to within the city walls in 701 B.C. by means of a hastily-constructed tunnel. Then, King Hezekiah was preparing to defend the city against the advancing Assyrian army. He devised the tunnel strategy to protect Jerusalem's water supply — keeping it out of enemy hands. The tunnel was completed in only a few months with the original surface spring outside the city walls being buried. The resulting communal "fountain" was called Siloam. Recently rediscovered, this public well was referenced in the New Testament (Jn 9:7; Lk 13:4), as well as in Josephus' *Wars of the Jews*.

> ..Siloam; for that is the name of a fountain which hath sweet water in it, and this in great plenty also. (*Wars* V 4:1)

Even in dry years, the Gihon kept flowing unlike most other springs in the area. Today, the Gihon still supplies the water needs for about 20,000 people. The rediscovered ancient diversion tunnel is now a popular tourist attraction.

Artesian water flow is determined by not only ground geology but also by the amount of rainfall in the aquifer recharge zone. Core samples from the sediment layers on the bottom of Lake Asphaltitis suggest rainfall was far more plentiful in ancient times. From the written sources, too, it can be surmised that in Jesus' day the region had a period where rainfall could be expected. In most years, this would be enough to fill the cisterns and last the population until the next rainy season. Most of the cisterns of the area were cut into sheer bedrock and sealed with a waterproof plaster. Many of these cisterns are still extant. Some have their ancient plaster intact and still hold water.

Why did the weather change from ancient to modern times? Experts have speculated, based on prevailing wind patterns, that the Sahara desert in northern Africa plays a key role. The greater the desert area, the less rain falls in the Middle East. The hypothesis is that the Sahara desert was substantially smaller in ancient times. Over-cultivation and poor farming practices in North Africa in order to meet the food demands of the Roman Empire caused the desert to grow. More rainfall would have made Judea, Samaria, and Galilee far more productive and "green" than they are today.

Josephus' following description of ancient Samaria likely holds true for much of southern neighbor Judea as well:

They are not naturally watered by many rivers, but derive their chief moisture from rain-water, of which they have no want; and for those rivers which they have, all their waters are exceeding sweet: by reason also of the excellent grass they have, their cattle yield more milk than do those in other places; and, what is the greatest sign of excellency and of abundance, they each of them are very full of people. (*Wars* III 3:4)

Geology

The geologic mountain ridge formation upon which Jerusalem is built originally was made up of several smaller, but higher, ridges. Over thousands of years the inhabitants physically leveled the tops of these ridges, filling up the small valleys between them with the excavated rubble. This facilitated expansion and growth of the city.

Shaped like a narrow inverted triangle, Jerusalem's major defensive features are deep chasms that angle obliquely to the south on the city's east and west sides, eventually merging to a rough apex. The resulting single canyon then snakes to the southeast for several miles before meeting the briny and inhospitable Lake Asphaltitis. These natural chasms provided a formidable defensive barrier on two of Jerusalem's three sides. All successful invasions of Jerusalem throughout recorded history were mounted from the hills to the north. For this reason, the northern approach to Jerusalem in ancient times was protected by as many as three walls, while a single wall sufficed to protect the rest of the city.

Ancient Landmarks

The drama of Jesus' final Passover was played out 100 generations ago. What did Jerusalem look like then? Where were the temples, palaces, residences, and markets located? Where was Jesus imprisoned, and where did the Jewish Sanhedrin meet to decide his fate? Where was Golgotha, the place of Jesus' crucifixion, and the tomb in which he was laid?

Fortunately, Jewish historian Flavius Josephus gives us enough information in his writings to answer some of these questions.

Josephus was born in Jerusalem in A.D. 37—only a year after Jesus' crucifixion. He grew up knowing much the same city that Jesus did, and describes it in rough detail in his writings. A few of these ancient structures remain in part today and have been identified. These are Golgotha, the Second Temple, and the residential area of the High Priesthood. The location of others will have to be deduced through clues found in Josephus.

Golgotha

Golgotha was the rock outcropping upon which Jesus and two criminals were crucified. Then, the site was outside the walls of Jerusalem and overlooked an abandoned rock quarry whose cliffs were used for Jewish tombs. After his crucifixion, Jesus was placed in one of those nearby tombs. Most ancient landmarks within Jerusalem have long since been destroyed and their location is conjecture. The Church of the Holy Sepulcher, however, probably does mark the site of Golgotha. Archaeological investigations through the centuries have largely confirmed that the Church of the Holy Sepulcher was built over a filled-in chasm. First century A.D. Jewish tombs have been found in the ancient cliff faces when excavated. The location of Golgotha provides us with an excellent starting point when reconstructing the upper city of Jesus' Jerusalem.

The Church of the Holy Sepulcher was originally built by Roman Emperor Constantine in A.D. 325, when the empire adopted Christianity as the official state religion. Not much is left of the rock formation of Golgotha itself. In A.D. 1009, the soldiers of Arab Fatimid Caliph Hakim hacked away at whatever previous souvenir hunters had left of it, until just a small remnant remained. Jesus' tomb was similarly desecrated. Over the years the top and sides of it were cut away.

Under Jewish law, the dead could not be interred within the limits of any city, much less the holy city of Jerusalem. For that reason, the cemetery wherein Jesus was laid would have naturally been outside the city walls, as was Golgotha. The Gospel of John supports this.

...for the place where Jesus was crucified was nigh to the city..(Jn 19:20)

Matthew states that Golgotha was near a road or passage that many people would use.

And they that passed by railed on him, wagging their heads, (Mt 27:39)

In those days, the dead would be entombed for a year. After a year the bones would be removed and placed in an ossuary box and placed in a special tomb—possibly above-ground—with other ossuary boxes of long-dead relatives. The larger original tomb could then be used by another. Assuming that the Jewish cemetery had existed for centuries, it would have been the northern limit of whatever expansion plans Herod the Great had for the upper city.

While the Gospels strongly suggest that Golgotha was outside of Jerusalem's ancient city walls, the Church of the Holy Sepulcher is located well within the present old city walls. But the present old city walls are themselves of relatively recent construction. They were built by a powerful Arab sultan named Sulliman the Magnificent in the 16th century A.D., who at that time ruled Jerusalem.

The Second Temple

Another important fixed point that remains from ancient Jerusalem is the rectangular base of the Second Temple. Massive block walls defined the foundations of the famous Temple, reconstructed by Herod the Great's engineers over a 10 year period starting in 20 B.C. The perimeter is about 2500 yards in total length and the area of the Temple Mount is roughly 35 acres. The rock base and stone foundations of the tower of Antonia, built out of the north wall of the Temple, are still able to be identified. The construction and physical layout of the ancient Second Temple will be extensively dealt with in the next chapter.

House of Kathros

A third but lesser archaeological clue in Jerusalem is of a more recent discovery. Close to the Temple Mount are the burnt-out remains of a residence that dates to A.D. 70, when the Romans destroyed Jerusalem. A wealthy family of the High Priesthood class apparently inhabited the house. The structure is called the "Burned House" or the "House of Kathros" and is located approximately 200 yards to the west of the Second Temple. "Kathros" was chiseled into a stone found in the ruins, and from the Babylonian Talmud the name has been identified as an important pre-revolt Jewish priest and is the presumed owner of the house.

These three existing landmarks–the Church of the Holy Sepulcher, the perimeter of the Second Temple, and the house of Kathros–will be used along with the writings of Flavius Josephus to reconstruct the Jerusalem that Jesus knew.

The Walls of Jerusalem

Josephus described the defensive walls of Jerusalem in both of his major works, *Antiquities* and *Wars*.

> The city of Jerusalem was fortified with three walls, on such parts as were not encompassed with unpassable valleys; for in such places it had but one wall.. (*Wars* V 4:1)

A single ancient wall surrounded Jerusalem, to include both the upper and lower cities, with a total perimeter of about three miles. Parts of this wall likely dated from the times of David and Solomon 1,000 years previously. Because the northern aspect of Jerusalem was the most vulnerable to attack, the Asamoneans built a reinforcing second wall centuries later to enclose the tower of Antonia and the north wall of the Temple. This double-walled defensive northern barrier would have been in existence when Jesus was alive (page 19).

Eight years after Jesus had been crucified, in A.D. 36 King Agrippa I built a third wall outside of the other two and extended it over to the east to enclose the entirety of the eastern Second Temple. Later, in A.D. 70 during the siege of Jerusalem, Titus built a fourth wall five miles in length enclosing the entire city in order to prevent the escape of any Jews (page 29), using the already-conquered Asamonean wall as its northern section.

Herod the Great rebuilt much of the first and most-ancient wall after re-conquering the city in 37 B.C. He heightened and reinforced it, and inter-spaced 60 guard towers every 300 feet along its entire length. In roughly 26 B.C., Herod constructed a sprawling palace complex immediately to the south of north wall, enclosing it with 40-foot high walls on the remaining three sides. The palace grounds took up an estimated 15 acres with three opulent residential towers built into the first north wall.

In the following section of *Antiquities*, pay particular attention to the construction of the first north wall and especially to a key tower called "Hippicus"–one of three arising within Herod's palace complex.

The city of Jerusalem was fortified with three walls, on such parts as were not encompassed with unpassable valleys; for in such places it had but one wall. The city was built upon two hills, which are opposite to one another, and have a valley to divide them asunder; at which valley the corresponding rows of houses on both hills end. Of these hills, that which contains the upper city is much higher, and in length more direct. Accordingly, it was called the "Citadel," by king David; he was the father of that Solomon who built this temple at the first; but it is by us called the "Upper Market–place." But the other hill, which was called "Acra," and sustains the lower city, is of the shape of a moon when she is horned; over against this there was a third hill, but naturally lower than Acra, and parted formerly from the other by a broad valley. However, in those times when the Asamoneans reigned, they filled up that valley with earth, and had a mind to join the city to the temple. They then took off part of the height of Acra, and reduced it to be of less elevation than it was before, that the temple might be superior to it. Now the Valley of the Cheesemongers, as it was called, and was that which we told you before distinguished the hill of the upper city from that of the lower, extended as far as Siloam; for that is the name of a fountain which hath sweet water in it, and this in great plenty also. But on the outsides, these hills are surrounded by deep valleys, and by reason of the precipices to them belonging on both sides they are every where unpassable.

Now, of these three walls, the old one was hard to be taken, both by reason of the valleys, and of that hill on which it was built, and which was above them. But besides that great advantage, as to the place where they were situated, it was also built very strong; because David and Solomon, and the following kings, were very zealous about this work. Now that wall began on the north, at the tower called "Hippicus," and extended as far as the "Xistus," a place so called, and then, joining to the council-house, ended at the west cloister of the temple. But if we go the other way westward, it began at the same place, and extended through a place called "Bethso," to the gate of the Essens; and after that it went southward, having its bending above the fountain Siloam, where it also bends again towards the east at Solomon's pool, and reaches as far as a certain place which they called "Ophlas," where it was joined to the eastern cloister of the temple. The second wall took its beginning from that gate which they called "Gennath," which belonged to the first wall; it only encompassed the northern quarter of the city, and reached as far as the tower Antonia. The beginning of the third wall was at the tower Hippicus, whence it reached as far as the north quarter of the city, and the tower Psephinus, and then was so far extended till it came over against the monuments of Helena, which Helena was queen of Adiabene, the daughter of Izates; it then extended further to a great length, and passed by the sepulchral caverns of the kings, and bent again at the tower of the corner, at the monument which is called the "Monument of the Fuller," and joined to the old wall at the valley called the "Valley of Cedron." It was Agrippa who encompassed the parts added to the old city with this wall, which had been all naked before; for as the city grew more populous, it gradually crept beyond its old limits, and those parts of it that stood northward of the temple, and joined that hill to the city, made it considerably larger, and occasioned that hill, which is in number the fourth, and is called "Bezetha," to be inhabited also. It lies over against the tower Antonia, but is divided from it by a deep valley, which was dug on purpose, and that in order to hinder the foundations of the tower of Antonia from joining to this hill, and thereby affording an opportunity for getting to it with ease, and hindering the security that arose from its superior elevation; for which reason also that depth of the ditch made the elevation of the towers more remarkable. This new-built part of the city was called "Bezetha," in our language, which, if interpreted in the Grecian language, may be called "the New City." Since, therefore, its inhabitants stood in need of a covering, the father of the present king, and of the same name with him, Agrippa, began that wall we spoke of; but he left off building it when he had only laid the foundations, out of the fear he was in of Claudius Caesar, lest he should suspect that so strong a wall was built in order to make some innovation in public affairs; for the city could no way have been taken if that wall had been finished in the manner it was begun; as its parts were connected together by stones twenty cubits long, and ten cubits broad, which could never have been either easily undermined by any iron tools, or shaken by any engines. The wall was, however, ten cubits wide, and it would probably have had a height greater than that, had not his zeal who began it been hindered from exerting itself. After this, it was erected with great diligence by the Jews, as high as twenty cubits, above which it had battlements of two cubits, and turrets of three cubits altitude, insomuch that the entire altitude extended as far as twenty–five cubits. (*Wars* V 4:1–2)

Hippicus and the First North Wall

Can these ancient walls be sited in modern Jerusalem? Josephus begins his description of the oldest of the north walls at the tower of Hippicus, the westernmost of the three towers of Herod's palace. The first ancient wall then extended east from Hippicus to include the tower of Mariamne and Phasaelus. Then past the palace grounds, the wall continued to the east to the major northern entrance to Jerusalem, the Gennath gate.

Past the Gennath gate was a structure called Xystus, which was located at the base of the western wall of the Second Temple. The Xystus was apparently contiguous with a structure termed the "council house" and also a another structure where the archives were kept. The first north wall actually abutted the walls of tower of Antonia, which jutted out from the Second Temple. The western wall of the Temple would have dwarfed the defensive north wall at 135 feet, the ancient wall only being only 40 feet high.

To complete the picture, at the Temple's northwest corner would have been located one of the four square towers of the castle of Antonia. This corner tower was 200 feet high from the Jerusalem ground proper. The tallest of Antonia's four towers–and the tallest aspect in Jerusalem at perhaps 240 feet–would have been the southeast tower, located an estimated 300 feet east along the Temple's north wall and built out from it.

Extending west from the tower of Hippicus, the first ancient wall traveled south of an area called Bethso for an unspecified distance, ending at the gate of the Essens (Essenes). Golgotha was likely located in this area of Bethso. The gate of the Essenes opened to the north–or to the northwest–with the end of the first north wall marked by a square guard tower.

After turning south at the guard tower, the western portion of the first wall ran for several furlongs to the fountain of Siloam and the pools of Solomon in the lower city. The first wall then turned to the east for a short distance and then turned northwards, forming an rough apex and enclosing the southern-most expanse of the lower city. The eastern portion of the first wall was built on the rim of the chasm of the Kidron Valley. Eventually, the wall joined up with the Second Temple at an area known as Ophlas. Sixty towers, each 30 feet high, were constructed on this 40-foot high wall as it circuited Jerusalem for a distance of over three miles — one tower every 100 yards.

> Now the towers that were upon it were twenty cubits in breadth, and twenty cubits in height; they were square and solid, as was the wall itself, wherein the niceness of the joints, and the beauty of the stones, were no way inferior to those of the holy house itself. Above this solid altitude of the towers, which was twenty cubits, there were rooms of great magnificence, and over them upper rooms, and cisterns to receive rain–water. They were many in number, and the steps by which you ascended up to them were every one broad: of these towers then the third wall had ninety, and the spaces between them were each two hundred cubits; but in the middle wall were forty towers, and the old wall was parted into sixty, while the whole compass of the city was thirty–three furlongs. (*Wars* V 4:3)

The Second North Wall

The Asamonean-built second wall was constructed to enclose land north and east of the Gennath Gate extending over to the rim of the Kidron Valley. This would encompass land north of the great Temple and the tower of Antonia. The exact phrase in Josephus describing its limits, however, is "reached as far as the tower Antonia." That suggests that eastward progression of the second wall stopped at the tower of Antonia. However, it is clear from Josephus' writings (*Wars* V 8:2), that the second wall had to be breached in order to get to the tower of Antonia. This logically means that the second wall had to surround Antonia completely, and likely extended parallel to the north wall of the Temple to the canyon's edge to the east. At the very least, the second wall turned to the south and abutted the Temple's north wall at some point past the castle of Antonia. This middle wall had 40 towers built on it, in the same fashion as the first wall.

..in the middle wall were forty towers, (*Wars* V 4:3)

How far out from the tower of Antonia did the second wall extend? During the A.D. 70 siege of Jerusalem by General Titus, Josephus documents that Jewish defenders standing on the top of the tower of Antonia and the Temple's north wall could sling darts (small spears) far enough to reach the Roman soldiers working to destroy the second wall.

He then presently began his attacks, upon which the Jews divided themselves into several bodies, and courageously defended that wall; while John and his faction did it from the tower of Antonia, and from the northern cloister of the temple, and fought the Romans before the monuments of king Alexander; (*Wars* V 7:3)

The ramparts of the Temple north wall were 135 feet high. The two northernmost corner towers from Antonia reached a height of about 170 feet, and extended out from the Temple's north wall for perhaps 200 feet. How close would the second wall have been to this section of Antonia for the Jewish soldiers to be minimally effective in their dart-throwing from a height of 135 feet? A reasonable estimate might be 400 feet.

In Jesus' day, this area enclosed a bustling marketplace with two- and three-story buildings fronting narrow angled streets, as the nearby Gennath Gate served as the major road that led northwest to Damascus and Caesarea.

Now Caesar took this wall there on the fifth day after he had taken the first; and when the Jews had fled from him, he entered into it with a thousand armed men, and those of his choice troops, and this at a place where were the merchants of wool, the braziers, and the market for cloth, and where the narrow streets led obliquely to the wall. (*Wars* V 8:1)

Herod's Palace

Herod's palace provided a stronghold should the city collapse in violence–just as the Second Temple and the tower of Antonia could also serve as last-ditch defensive "keeps." Along with three towers and two Royal apartments, Herod's palace 15-acre grounds contained beautiful natural gardens, canals, fountains, and exotic birds. Herod the Great built his Jerusalem palace during the years 26-24 B.C., after he had been affirmed in power by Augustus and married Mariamne II.

(Herod).. also built himself a palace in the Upper city, containing two very large and most beautiful apartments; to which the holy house itself could not be compared [in largeness]. The one apartment he named Caesareum, and the other Agrippium, from his [two great] friends. (Wars I 21:1)

The Herodian apartments were square and 100 feet on a side, with likely a second story added on as well. Most Royal apartments or towers of the time had their own rooftop cisterns, and garden terraces.

Of the three palace towers built into the first north wall, the sturdiest and most westerly was Hippicus–named after Herod's great friend. It was a square tower, almost 120 feet high, and 40 feet on a side. The other two towers were called Mariamne, named after his Royal wife, and Phasaelus, named after his brother. The tower of Phasaelus was over 135 feet high and shaped like the lighthouse at Alexandria with a square base that was 60 feet on a side. Mariamne tower was 75 feet tall, with a square base of 30 feet on a side.

These (three towers) were for largeness, beauty, and strength beyond all that were in the habitable earth; for besides the magnanimity of his nature, and his magnificence towards the city on other occasions, he built these after such an extraordinary manner, to gratify his own private affections, and dedicated these towers to the memory of those three persons who had been the dearest to him, and from whom he named them. They were his brother, his friend, and his wife. This wife he had slain, out of his love [and jealousy], as we have already related; the other two he lost in war, as they were courageously fighting. Hippicus, so named from his friend, was square; its length and breadth were each twenty-five cubits, and its height thirty, and it had no vacuity in it. Over this solid building, which was composed of great stones united together, there was a reservoir twenty cubits deep, over which there was a house of two stories, whose height was twenty-five cubits, and divided into several parts; over which were battlements of two cubits, and turrets all round of three cubits high, insomuch that the entire height added together amounted to fourscore cubits. The second tower, which he named from his brother Phasaelus, had its breadth and its height equal, each of them forty cubits; over which was its solid height of forty cubits; over which a cloister went round about, whose height was ten cubits, and it was covered from enemies by breast-works and bulwarks. There was also built over that cloister another tower, parted into magnificent rooms, and a place for bathing; so that this tower wanted nothing that might make it appear to be a royal palace. It was also adorned with battlements and turrets, more than was the foregoing, and the entire altitude was about ninety cubits; the appearance of it resembled the tower of Pharus, which exhibited a fire to such as sailed to Alexandria, but was much larger than it in compass. This was now converted to a house, wherein Simon exercised his tyrannical authority. The third tower was Mariamne, for that was his queen's name; it was solid as high as twenty cubits; its breadth and its length were twenty cubits, and were equal to each other; its upper buildings were more magnificent, and had greater variety, than the other towers had; for the king thought it most proper for him to adorn that which was denominated from his wife, better than those denominated from men, as those were built stronger than this that bore his wife's name. The entire height of this tower was fifty cubits.

Now as these towers were so very tall, they appeared much taller by the place on which they stood; for that very old wall wherein they were was built on a high hill, and was itself a kind of elevation that was still thirty cubits taller; over which were the towers situated, and thereby were made much higher to appearance. The largeness also of the stones was wonderful; for they were not made of common small stones, nor of such large ones only as men could carry, but they were of white marble, cut out of the rock; each stone was twenty cubits in length, and ten in breadth, and five in depth. They were so exactly united to one another, that each tower looked like one entire rock of stone, so growing naturally, and afterward cut by the hand of the artificers into their present shape and corners; so little, or not at all, did their joints or connexion appear. low as these towers were themselves on the north side of the wall, the king had a palace inwardly thereto adjoined, which exceeds all my ability to describe it; for it was so very curious as to want no cost nor skill in its construction, but was entirely walled about to the height of thirty cubits, and was adorned with towers at equal distances, and with large bed-chambers, that would contain beds for a hundred guests a-piece, in which the variety of the stones is not to be expressed; for a large quantity of those that were rare of that kind was collected together. Their roofs were also wonderful, both for the length of the beams, and the splendor of their ornaments. The number of the rooms was also very great, and the variety of the figures that were about them was prodigious; their furniture was complete, and the greatest part of the vessels that were put in them was of silver and gold. There were besides many porticoes, one beyond another, round about, and in each of those porticoes curious pillars; yet were all the courts that were exposed to the air every where green. There were, moreover, several groves of trees, and long walks through them, with deep canals, and cisterns, that in several parts were filled with brazen statues, through which the water ran out. There were withal many dove-courts of tame pigeons about the canals. But indeed it is not possible to give a complete description of these palaces; and the very remembrance of them is a torment to one, as putting one in mind what vastly rich buildings that fire which was kindled by the robbers hath consumed; for these were not burnt by the Romans, but by these internal plotters, as we have already related, in the beginning of their rebellion. That fire began at the tower of Antonia, and went on to the palaces, and consumed the upper parts of the three towers themselves. (Wars V 4:3-4)

How do we determine that Herod's palace grounds took up 15 acres? When General Titus was organizing his plan of attack on Jerusalem, and before his breaching of the outer wall of Jerusalem (the third wall), Josephus describes the placement of his legions.

But as for Titus himself, he was but about two furlongs distant from the wall, at that part of it where was the corner and over against that tower which was called Psephinus, at which tower the compass of the wall belonging to the north bended, and extended itself over against the west; but the other part of the army fortified itself at the tower called

Hippicus, and was distant, in like manner, by two furlongs from the city. (Wars V 3:5)

Hippicus was two furlongs south of the tower of Psephinus, and also "two furlongs from the city." It can be reasonably inferred that "two furlongs" distant from Hippicus referred to the beginning of the residential area of the upper city, immediately to the south of the wall of Herod's palace. Assuming a modern furlong value of 220 yards (a debatable assumption) and assuming that the palace grounds were square and symmetric in true Roman style, nearly 15 acres in total area is not unreasonable.

In A.D. 70, General Titus was so impressed by Herod's three towers, despite them being partially burned out, that he ordered them spared when he methodically leveled the city.

Herod's Palace Today?

Archaeologists place Herod's palace complex where the Citadel is located today, just south of the Jaffe Gate in the old city of Jerusalem. This conclusion must be questioned, as the Citadel is far to the west of the Second Temple and even west of the Church of the Holy Sepulcher.

The origins of the Citadel are unknown, but the fact that a few stone blocks in the base had typical Herodian facings (a beveled border) has been enough to sway many experts that the Citadel — with its unmistakable Crusader architectural elements — was originally built upon the remnants of one of Herod's palace structures.

Josephus, however, suggests that the palace grounds were located more to the east toward the center of the present-day old city, and far from the Citadel, as he describes an event that happened during the Jewish Revolt in A.D. 69.

That fire began at the tower of Antonia, and went on to the palaces, and consumed the upper parts of the three towers themselves. (Wars V 4:4)

The circumstances were this: Two zealot factions were in-fighting on the Second Temple's outer courtyard, setting fire to the tower of Antonia cloisters in the process. The fire soon got out of control, with some of the flaming material from Antonia falling on the wooden ramparts of the old north wall 100 feet below. From there, the fire spread along the wall ramparts west to the palace of Herod and burned the top sections of all three towers.

If today's Citadel marks the Herod palace complex, the fire would have had to have marched unimpeded along the ramparts for nearly a half mile–700 yards–before reaching the easternmost of the palace structures. In contrast, placing the palace east of the Church of the Holy Sepulcher–the assumed site of Golgotha–would mean that the closest palace tower to the Temple would have been less than 200 feet away. Simon of Gerasa, the military leader of the Jews at that time, lived in the tower of Phasaelus, which would have been the tower first reached by the fire. Undoubtedly, he and his men would have worked hard to stop the fire's spread before it reached Phasaelus. The fact that they were unsuccessful suggests that the tower was far closer to 200 feet from the Temple than 700 yards.

The following passage also indicated that the palace with its three towers was relatively close to the tower of Antonia.

> There was also a peculiar fortress belonging to the upper city, which was Herod's palace; but for the hill Bezetha, it was divided from the tower Antonia, as we have already told you; (*Wars* V 5:8)

In this passage, Herod's palace was "divided" from the tower of Antonia. This suggests that the two fortresses were far closer than a half mile away. Josephus writes that the first north wall of Jerusalem bridged the hilly, rocky terrain and linked both Herod's palace and the tower of Antonia. Remember, too, that Bezetha was enclosed by the second and third walls of Jerusalem and was outside of the first wall and east of the main north wall gate of Gennath.

Josephus in *Antiquities* provides additional information suggesting that the palace was located close to the Temple.

Now in the western quarters of the enclosure of the temple there were four gates; the first led to the king's palace, and went to a passage over the intermediate valley; two more led to the suburbs of the city; and the last led to the other city, where the road descended down into the valley by a great number of steps, and thence up again by the ascent for the city lay over against the temple in the manner of a theater, and was encompassed with a deep valley along the entire south quarter; but the fourth front of the temple, which was southward, had indeed itself gates in its middle, as also it had the royal cloisters, (*Antiq* XV 11:5)

Four gates out of the western Temple wall are described. One gate "led" directly to Herod's palace. These Second Temple gates were built through the columned cloisters of the outer courtyard which were constructed on top of the main Temple wall. The base wall itself rose to a height of 95 feet. The northernmost passage was linked to a bridge over an "intermediate" valley, which then led to the king's palace. This provided a private access to the Temple for Herod the Great and his guests.

In order to fit with the location of the Citadel as being Herod's palace, this private pathway would have been over a half-mile long! Also, it would have to be 95 feet high at the Temple end and at least 40 feet high at the palace wall end. A structure of this elevation, mass, and length for such a limited purpose would make little sense.

But, one might ask, how can the Herodian blocks–seen in sections of the Citadel–be explained away? And then why was the Citadel, an ancient structure in itself, built where it was? As with so many questions, the answer lies in Josephus' accounts of Titus' destruction of Jerusalem. As will be seen later in the chapter, not only do the actions of Titus explain the origin and purpose of the current Citadel, but also account for the modern location of the "old" walls of Jerusalem and the obliteration of the site of Golgotha and the tomb of Jesus.

The Asamonean Palace

Josephus describes another palace in Jerusalem–one even more ancient than Herod's. This had been built by the Asamonean

Royal kings before the Romans arrived. Even though the Asamoneans had been out of power for decades as a ruling family, some had married into the Herodian line and still had position and wealth. Their descendants occupied this "secondary" Royal palace throughout the period of the Roman occupation.

The Asamonean palace can be located in the upper city from clues in Josephus. Many of the families living in this exclusive neighborhood were either wealthy and privileged, or of the High Priesthood class. In the construction of houses in this neighborhood, "vaults" underground were made, probably to house water cisterns as well to provide naturally cool rooms for the storage of perishable goods. Josephus also hints at a defensive tunnel system. In the conflict between the different Jewish factions within Jerusalem in the years A.D. 69-70, sections of the upper city that housed families thought to be sympathetic to Rome–largely those of the High Priesthood class–were destroyed. The House of Kathros was likely one of those burned in this action.

> The others then set fire to the house of Ananias the high priest, and to the palaces of Agrippa and Bernice;....And when they had thus burnt down the nerves of the city, they fell upon their enemies; at which time some of the men of power, and of the high priests, went into the vaults under ground, and concealed themselves, while others fled with the king's soldiers to the upper palace, and shut the gates immediately; among whom were Ananias the high priest, and the ambassadors that had been sent to Agrippa. (*Wars* II 17:6)

Josephus refers to King Agrippa II and Queen Bernice, Agrippa's sister, in the above passage. Their "palaces" refer to the old Asamonean palace complex. When these structures were burned, the people — including ex-High Priest Ananias — fled for safety to the walled palace of Herod to the north.

Jerusalem

present day

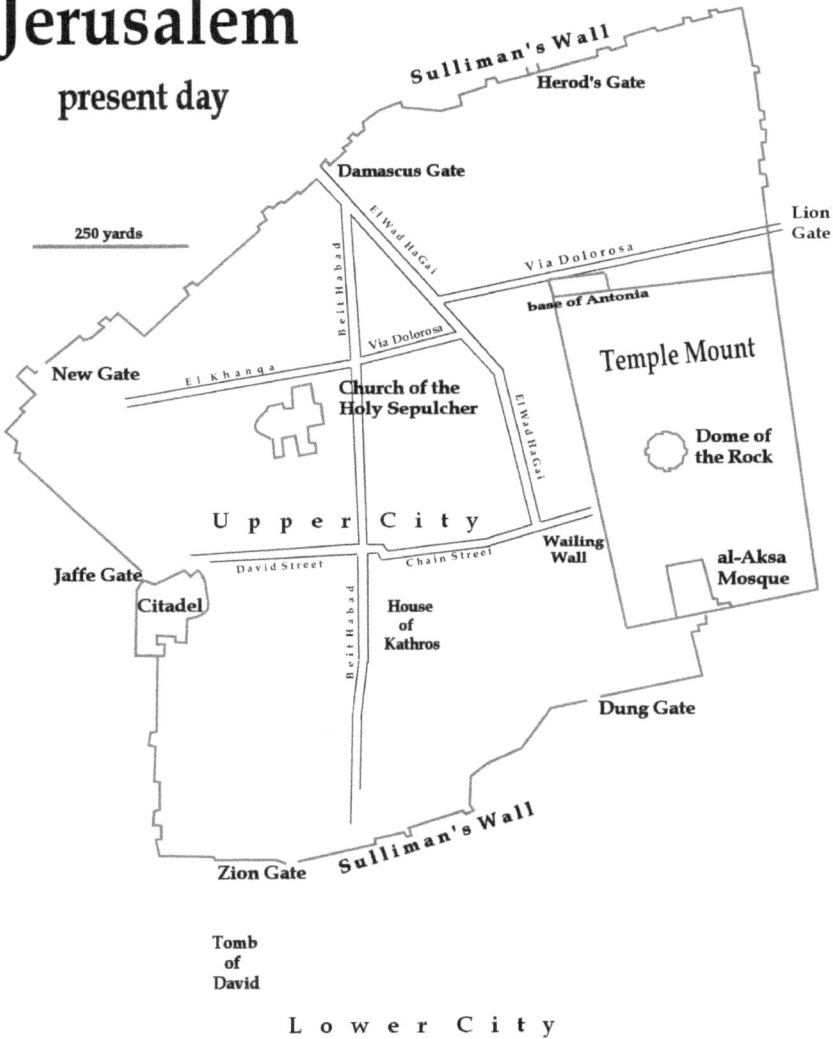

Sulliman's Wall

Herod's Gate

Damascus Gate

Lion Gate

250 yards

El Wad HaGai

Via Dolorosa

Beit Habad

base of Antonia

New Gate

El Khanqa

Via Dolorosa

Temple Mount

Church of the Holy Sepulcher

El Wad HaGai

Dome of the Rock

U p p e r   C i t y

David Street

Chain Street

Wailing Wall

al-Aksa Mosque

Jaffe Gate

Citadel

Beit Habad

House of Kathros

Dung Gate

Sulliman's Wall

Zion Gate

Tomb of David

L o w e r   C i t y

Old City of Jerusalem. The northeast portion of Sulliman's wall roughly follows the ancient wall of Agrippa, the northwest and western segments track the ancient wall of Titus. The Citadel likely lies outside of the ancient western wall of the upper city of Jerusalem.

But on the next day, which was the fifteenth of the month Lous, [Ab,] they made an assault upon Antonia, and besieged the garrison which was in it two days, and then took the garrison, and slew them, and set the citadel on fire; after which they marched to the palace, whither the king's soldiers were fled, and parted themselves into four bodies, and made an attack upon the walls. (*Wars* II 17:7)

The next day, the tower of Antonia was attacked and burned, while many of the "loyalist" guards retreated to the walled "upper palace," or the palace of Herod. As has been determined, Herod's palace was quite close to Antonia and had a special access bridge connecting the walled palace grounds to a western gate of the Second Temple.

These excerpts from *Wars* affirm that the palace of Agrippa–or the old Asamonean palace–was separate from Herod's palace ("upper palace"). Also, the Asamonean palace was apparently close enough to the luxurious houses of the High Priest Ananias and his family to be burned in the same action.

From another passage, in *Antiquities*, Agrippa's palace (the Asamonean palace) can be approximately located.

About the same time king Agrippa built himself a very large dining-room in the royal palace at Jerusalem, near to the portico. Now this palace had been erected of old by the children of Asamoneus. and was situate upon an elevation, and afforded a most delightful prospect to those that had a mind to take a view of the city, which prospect was desired by the king; and there he could lie down, and eat, and thence observe what was done in the temple.. (*Antiq* XX 8:11)

As the Asamoneans also served as the High Priests of the Temple, it would make sense that their palace and private residences would be close to it. Josephus tells us that the palace of Agrippa was "near the portico" of the Temple which refers to the either the Royal Portico on the south side of the Temple, or, more likely, the cloisters on top of the Temple's western wall.

A better set of clues comes from *Wars*. In A.D. 66, a desperate King Agrippa II addressed an angry crowd in Jerusalem, pleading with them not to revolt against the Romans.

Jerusalem
A.D. 36

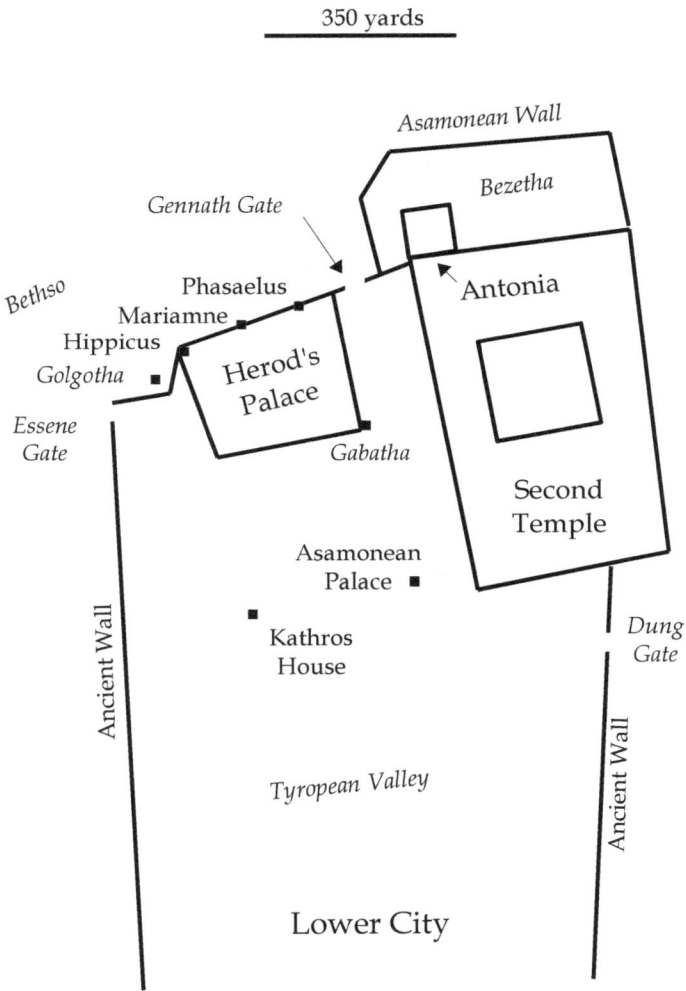

350 yards

Asamonean Wall

Bezetha

Gennath Gate

Bethso

Phasaelus
Mariamne
Hippicus
Golgotha

Antonia

Herod's Palace

Essene Gate

Gabatha

Second Temple

Asamonean Palace

Kathros House

Dung Gate

Ancient Wall

Tyropean Valley

Ancient Wall

Lower City

Jerusalem at the Time of Jesus' Crucifixion. Note the site of Golgotha, Hippicus tower, and the Gabbatha. The Asamonean wall comes off the ancient wall and partially encloses Bezetha. The Tyropean Valley divides the upper and lower cities.

He (Agrippa) therefore called the multitude together into a large gallery, and placed his sister Bernice in the house of the Asamoneans, that she might be seen by them, (which house was over the gallery, at the passage to the upper city, where the bridge joined the temple to the gallery,) and spake to them as follows: (*Wars* II 16:3)

The supporting remnants of this bridge can now be seen on the southern part of the western wall, just south of the "wailing" wall. The structure is called Robinson's Arch and is composed of outcroppings of stone that presumably supported the arch underpinnings of the elevated walkway to the Temple entrance.

From Josephus, it is known that the southernmost gate on the Temple's western wall exited onto a staircase that led to the lower city. But here Josephus states that the Asamonean palace was near a similar Temple passage to the upper city–one of two such arcuated structures in southern portion of the western wall. These two passageways likely shared the same first arch as they descended from the Temple before splitting off to their own separate destinations.

It is easy to visualize the Asamonean palace being near one of those bridges, built across the shallow valley and the road that ran along the base of the Temple's western wall. This access structure would have been hundreds of feet south of the passage that led to Herod's palace. The hill opposite the Temple's west wall, upon which the Asamonean palace was built, had to have been high enough to allow a three-story structure built upon it a view over the top of the western wall cloisters to the inner Sanctuary and the elevated sacrificial altar (*Antiq* XX 8:11). From Agrippa's portico across from the Temple, the bronze altar could apparently be seen from over the top of the cedar-roofed cloister.

The Third North Wall

King Agrippa I in the years A.D. 41-44 constructed a third north wall. It encompassed a huge area north of the second wall–crossing the Kidron Valley to the base of the Mount of Olives. Agrippa also built his own showpiece tower at the wall's northwest corner, named Psephinus.

Jerusalem
A.D. 70

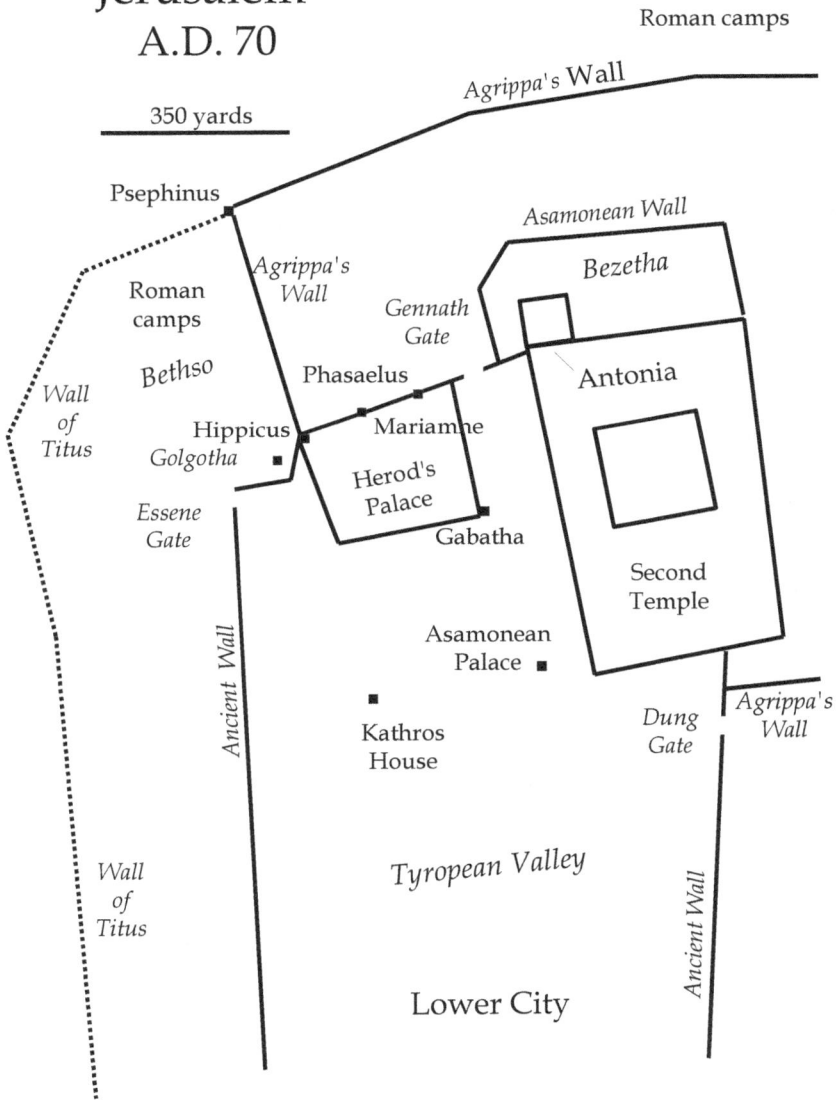

Roman camps

Agrippa's Wall

350 yards

Psephinus

Asamonean Wall

Agrippa's
Wall

Bezetha

Roman
camps

Gennath
Gate

Bethso

Phasaelus

Antonia

Wall
of
Titus

Hippicus
Golgotha

Mariamne

Herod's
Palace

Essene
Gate

Gabatha

Second
Temple

Asamonean
Palace

Ancient Wall

Dung
Gate

Agrippa's
Wall

Kathros
House

Tyropean Valley

Wall
of
Titus

Ancient Wall

Lower City

Jerusalem During the Siege of Titus. Agrippa's wall is now present, built to the north of Hippicus to avoid the Jewish cemetery and the rough terrain of the old stone quarry of Bethso. Titus built a strong, high wall that enclosed the entire city to a total length of approximately five miles.

> Now the third wall was all of it wonderful; yet was the tower Psephinus elevated above it at the north-west corner, and there Titus pitched his own tent; for being seventy cubits high it both afforded a prospect of Arabia at sun-rising, as well as it did of the utmost limits of the Hebrew possessions at the sea westward. Moreover, it was an octagon, and over against it was the tower Hipplicus, and hard by two others were erected by king Herod, in the old wall. (*Wars* V 4:3)

The third north wall ran due north from the tower of Hippicus for two furlongs–450 yards–until reaching the tower of Psephinus. Psephinus was octagonal in shape and faced with brilliant white marble. From the tower's roof at a height of 105 feet, the mountains of Nabotea could be seen to the east, and the Mediterranean Sea to the west.

From Psephinus tower, Agrippa's wall then ran eastward, sweeping all the way across the Kidron Valley. Then it turned south and paralleled the Kidron for approximately the length of the Temple, but not including the the sepulchers of the kings, which still can be seen to this day. Agrippa's wall then turned east, crossing back over the Kidron Valley, and abutted the first wall south of the Second Temple.

One of the purposes of this third wall was to enclose fully the fourth "hill" of the upper city, called Bezetha, which was located directly north of the tower of Antonia. This hill had already partially been enclosed by the second wall built by the Asamoneans. The third wall of Agrippa was 15-feet thick and at times rose to a height of 40 feet.

> The wall was, however, ten cubits wide, and it would probably have had a height greater than that, had not his zeal who began it been hindered from exerting itself. After this, it was erected with great diligence by the Jews, as high as twenty cubits, above which it had battlements of two cubits, and turrets of three cubits altitude, insomuch that the entire altitude extended as far as twenty-five cubits. (*Wars* V 4:1-2)

This third wall had 30-foot high towers erected upon it which were spaced 300 feet apart.

> of these towers then the third wall had ninety, and the spaces between them were each two hundred cubits; (*Wars* V 4:3)

Tacitus reports that the top of this wall appeared level, but the wall itself was built to varying heights along its base to accommodate the undulating ground. In the background, the Second Temple was built on a small mountain, as was the Herod palace complex built on an adjoining mountain–connected by the first wall. The third wall to the north of them had to compensate for similarly uneven terrain.

> ..a series of towers dominated the scene, 105 feet high where the rising ground helped, and 135 or 120 feet high on the lower contours. These presented an impressive appearance, and to the distant observer seemed to be on a level. There were further walls inside around the palace, and a conspicuous landmark was the lofty castle of Antonia, so named by Herod in honour of Mark Antony. (Tacitus *Histories* V:11)

Josephus states that some of the base blocks for the third wall were 30 feet long, with proportionate measures of both width and thickness. Agrippa I had designs to encompass the entire city with the formidable structure, but was ordered to stop by Emperor Claudius — who suspected Agrippa's motives. As it was, this northern defensive wall of Agrippa combined with the enclosing first wall reinforced by Herod the Great made the entire defensive perimeter of Jerusalem faced by Titus' Roman legions about four miles in length.

> As for the walls of Jerusalem, that were adjoining to the new city [Bezetha], he (Agrippa) repaired them at the expense of the public, and built them wider in breadth, and higher in altitude; and he had made them too strong for all human power to demolish, unless Marcus, the then president of Syria, had by letter informed Claudius Caesar of what he was doing. And when Claudius had some suspicion of attempts for innovation, he sent to Agrippa to leave off the building of those walls presently. So he obeyed, as not thinking it proper to contradict Claudius. (*Antiq* XIX 7:2)

The Legacy of Titus

The Jewish revolt was an action of such scope and consequence that the final five chapters of this work are devoted to it. It will briefly be discussed here because Jerusalem was permanently transformed topographically as a direct result of it.

One of Vespasian's first acts when he became emperor in late A.D. 69 was to order his 31-year-old son Titus to complete the Jewish campaign that Vespasian had started two years previously. While Nero had given Vespasian three legions plus auxiliaries with which to quell the Jewish revolt, Titus was given the equivalent of nine legions.

Titus faced formidable physical obstacles in Jerusalem in addition to the strength and zeal of hundreds of thousands of entrenched and desperate Jewish warriors. The terrain was in many ways the city's best defense. Its northern three walls combined with natural chasms on the other two sides would make Jerusalem a difficult conquest, indeed!

> Titus Caesar, seeing that the position forbad an assault or any of the more rapid operations of war, determined to proceed by earthworks and covered approaches. (*Histories* 5:13)

Titus was taking no chances. Early on he used the strength and numbers of the Roman army in terraforming the rough country surrounding the northern aspect of Jerusalem. Most of the naturally rocky and hilly areas were either chiseled flat or filled in to make a relatively even and workable military surface. Titus also filled in with rubble the northern portion of the Kidron Valley, which was to the northeast of the great Temple. Upon that broad expanse, Titus placed his main army camp.

Site of the Crucifixion

A popular modern belief is that the site of Golgotha became enclosed within the Jerusalem city proper when King Agrippa I constructed this third wall. Clearly, however, this is not supported by Josephus.

Assuming that the Church of the Holy Sepulcher marks the true Golgotha and that Herod's palace is far more centrally located than is generally accepted, the Jewish cemetery (the old quarry) would be placed in the area called Bethso.

Why did Josephus start his description of the first and most ancient north wall at the tower of Hippicus? Probably for two reasons. Hippicus was the westernmost of the three towers of the palace and Agrippa's third wall started off to the north at that point. More importantly, Hippicus probably marked where the old wall angled to the south in order to avoid the ancient stone quarry of Bethso. Then past the quarry, the first north wall straightened out for a distance before reaching the gate of the Essenes.

So the Jewish cemetery located in the old quarry in Bethso proved to be a barrier to King Agrippa I just as it was 30 years later to Titus. Agrippa decided to avoid it completely and begin his third wall at Hippicus and run it to the north.

Titus decided to fill Bethso in.

Bethso was an area that provided a natural barrier to attacking the first north wall. Also, it could provide a haven for Jews to hide in after they escaped from the city. Escaped Jews could smuggle out gold and valuables and foment more problems in other parts of Judea and the Jewish East. Titus also wanted as many prisoners for slaves as possible.

So Titus used the brutish force of the Roman soldiers to his advantage. He ordered Bethso filled in with rock and debris. The Jewish cemetery was obliterated along with the ancient open pit quarry. The area that surrounded what was left of Golgotha was flattened to serve as a base for Roman bulwarks, war engines, and as a camp for Roman troops.

But Titus, intending to pitch his camp nearer to the city than Scopus, placed as many of his choice horsemen and footmen as he thought sufficient opposite to the Jews, to prevent their sallying out upon them, while he gave orders for the whole army to level the distance, as far as the wall of the city. So they threw down all the hedges and walls which the inhabitants had made about their gardens and groves of trees, and cut down all the fruit trees that lay between them and the wall of the city, and filled up all the hollow places and the chasms, and demolished the rocky precipices with iron instruments; and thereby made all the place level from Scopus to Herod's monuments, which adjoined to the pool called the Serpent's Pool. (*Wars* V 3:2)

And now when the space between the Romans and the wall had been leveled, which was done in four days, and as he was desirous to bring the baggage of the army, with the rest of the multitude that followed him, safely to the camp, he set the strongest part of his army over against that wall which lay on the north quarter of the city, and over against the western part of it, and made his army seven deep, with the foot-men placed before them, and the horsemen behind them, each of the last in three ranks, whilst the archers stood in the midst in seven ranks. And now as the Jews were prohibited, by so great a body of men, from making sallies upon the Romans, both the beasts that bare the burdens, and belonged to the three legions, and the rest of the multitude, marched on without any fear. (*Wars* V 3:5)

Tacitus also supports the writings of Josephus by reporting that Titus spent much time on mounting "earthworks" around the walls of Jerusalem.

This, then, was the city and nation which Titus faced. Since a headlong assault and the element of surprise were ruled out by the lie of the ground, he proposed to employ earthworks and mantlets. Each legion had its allotted task, and there was a lull in the fighting while they pushed on with the construction of every conceivable device for storming Cities, whether invented long ago or due to the ingenuity of modern times. (Tacitus *Histories* V:13)

The works that belonged to the four legions were erected on the west side of the city, over against the royal palace; (*Wars* VI 8:1)

So the site of Golgotha was transformed by Titus and the Jewish cemetery and ancient quarry was buried forever. In time, the Roman containment wall built by Titus would become the "official" western wall of Jerusalem and so the site of Golgotha would become enclosed within Jerusalem proper.

Very possibly, the template for much of Jerusalem's present old city walls could have been the five-mile long enclosing structure that Titus had built in A.D. 70.

Titus began the wall from the camp of the Assyrians, where his own camp was pitched, and drew it down to the lower parts of Cenopolis; thence it went along the valley of Cedron, to the Mount of Olives; it then bent towards the south, and encompassed the mountain as far as the rock called Peristereon, and that other hill which lies next it, and is over the valley which reaches to Siloam; whence it bended again to the west, and went down to the valley of the Fountain, beyond which it went up again at the monument of Ananus the high priest, and encompassing that mountain where Pompey had formerly pitched his camp, it returned back to the north side of the city, and was carried on as far as a certain village called "The House of the Erebinthi;" after which it encompassed Herod's monument, and there, on the east, was joined to Titus's own camp, where it began. (*Wars* V 12:2)

What Titus Spared

Intentionally destroyed by General Titus in the aftermath were most of the the defensive walls, the Second Temple, and parts of Herod's palace–as well as many other buildings and homes of substance. In fact, what is important is not what he destroyed, but what he chose to save.

Titus was impressed enough by the towers of Herod's palace, even in their burned state, to preserve them. He also spared a portion of the western city wall.

Now as soon as the army had no more people to slay or to plunder, because there remained none to be the objects of their fury, (for they would not have spared any, had there remained any other work to be done,) Caesar gave orders that they should now demolish the entire city and temple, but should leave as many of the towers standing as were of the greatest eminency; that is, Phasaelus, and Hippicus, and Mariamne; and so much of the wall as enclosed the city on the west side. This wall was spared, in order to afford a camp for such as were to lie in garrison, as were the towers also spared, in order to demonstrate to posterity what kind of city it was, and how well fortified, which the Roman valor had subdued; but for all the rest of the wall, it was so thoroughly laid even with the ground by those that dug it up to the foundation, that there was left nothing to make those that came thither believe it had ever been inhabited. This was the end which Jerusalem came to by the madness of those that were for innovations; a city otherwise of great magnificence, and of mighty fame among all mankind. (*Wars* VII 1:1)

Note that there is a clear distinction here between the western wall of Jerusalem and the three towers of the Herod palace complex. It is possible that Titus spared a portion of the Jerusalem upper city western wall with a specific purpose in mind. Using the parallel portion of his own western wall 100 yards further out and constructing two enclosing walls on the north and south ends, a strong, walled military camp could be formed. The Citadel could well have first been the Roman military camp headquarters and constructed largely out of scavenged Herodian blocks–which were plentiful and of good quality.

The Passover of A.D. 36

All of the significant events of Jesus' crucifixion took place in the upper city of Jerusalem, where the wealthy and upper class lived. In the upper city was the lofty Second Temple as well as Herod's palace, and a large and exclusive residential neighborhood. Many of the especially wealthy families had their own walled compounds in which to live. Located, too, in the upper city was a major north gate of Jerusalem, the Gennath. There, travelers and merchant caravans from Caesarea and Damascus would enter Jerusalem. The area north of the tower Antonia (Bezetha) and along the north-south road that ran along the base of the Temple's west wall would have been devoted to trade and commerce, with shops offering a myriad of goods and services.

The upper city was separated from the lower by the Tyropean Valley, or the valley of the cheese mongers. Many of the common people coming to Jerusalem for the purposes of worship would enter through a lesser gate in the eastern wall close to the Tyropean Valley. This was called the Dung Gate, and was located just to the south of the Temple. Leading down into the Kidron Valley, this would have been the approach used by Jesus, his Disciples, and the people of Bethany, when coming to Jerusalem and the Second Temple.

With this rough layout of ancient Jerusalem in mind, we will now take a closer look at Herod's magnificent Second Temple, as described by Josephus, and other ancient sources in light of the archaeological evidence present today.

Chapter 2   The Second Temple

And now Herod, in the eighteenth year of his reign.. undertook a very great work, that is, to build of himself the temple of God, and make it larger in compass, and to raise it to a most magnificent altitude, as esteeming it to be the most glorious of all his actions, as it really was, to bring it to perfection; and that this would be sufficient for an everlasting memorial of him..(*Antiq* XV 11:1)

The God of the ancient Jews was thought to exist in an unseen form that needed sheltering, or at least required a dedicated place in which to dwell. The Ark of the Covenant served that purpose in the times of Moses as the tribal Jews wandered through the desert, and also during the early era of the great Jewish kings. When the Jews fought for the promised land, the Ark was brought out onto the battlefield to inspire the warriors.

Nearly 1,000 years before the times of Jesus, the Hebrew tribes triumphed over the Philistines and the Canaanites and established their kingdom. In the capital city of Jerusalem, King Solomon constructed a religious temple to God upon a small mountain just to the north of the city. Solomon only partially walled in the mountain and its top was leveled sufficiently to allow for the construction of a temple and sacrificial alter. The Ark was kept in a special room in the temple and served as the focal point of Jewish worship. The Ark, however, disappeared during the conquest of Jerusalem by the Babylonians in 586 B.C.

In the following centuries, the Temple Sanctuary replaced the function of the Ark and served as the house of God. Interestingly, the Samaritans, an offshoot branch of Temple-based Judaism, came to believe that the Ark was buried on the top of their holy mountain, Gerizzim. All attempts throughout history to find the Ark, buried on Gerizzim or anywhere, have been unsuccessful.

Herod the Great

Over the opposition of the High Priesthood, Herod the Great undertook a massive rebuilding of the Jerusalem Temple in 20 B.C. At that time Emperor Augustus himself was in the midst of many ambitious construction projects in Rome and throughout the empire. Herod wanted to emulate Augustus and so recruited Roman architects and engineers to the East for his own projects. They were many, ambitious, and varied — the Jerusalem Temple being only one of them. According to Josephus, Herod built a Temple complex on a similar scale for the Samaritan Jews in the city of Sebaste.

Herod also greatly expanded the marginal port city of Strato's Tower on the Mediterranean seacoast. Renamed Caesarea in honor of Augustus, Herod built within it an amphitheater, a circus, and a Royal palace by the sea. Herod also constructed a massive quay and breakwater for the harbor and two aqueducts that brought in fresh water from sources miles away. When completed in 10 B.C., Caesarea became the center of Roman culture and commerce in the East, and its harbor became a marvel of the ancient world.

The impressive temple of Apollo on the island of Rhodes was constructed by Herod the Great as well. Rhodes was a major port and considered the gateway to the East. Herod also constructed a colonnaded thoroughfare through the heart of Antioch on the coast of Asia which was then referred to as Herod's Way. Antioch was the seat of Roman power in the East.

Josephus suggests that Herod the Great brought the Jewish East to near-bankruptcy with his incessant and ego-driven projects (*Antiq* XVII 11:2). But as long as the Jews were a productive people, Herod could get as much money as he needed through taxes, extortion, and even murder. Additionally, by the time of the rebuilding of the Temple, Herod had long since given up trying to win the affections of his Jewish subjects. His goal was to impress the Romans in power–who kept him in power–and to insure his own fame throughout the ages.

By 10 B.C., the walls and foundations of the Jerusalem Temple had been complete as well as the main portion of the Sanctuary building. But it would be decades before the Temple complex in its entirety was finished. Josephus suggests that thousands of workmen were still working on the Temple complex 60 years later in the time of King Agrippa II. After Herod's renovation, it was called the Second Temple, or Herod's Temple, and this was the Temple that Jesus knew and preached in. In A.D. 70, however, the Roman army under General Titus would destroy it, so it lasted for about 80 years in total and in finished form for about 20 years.

Construction of the Second Temple

The most comprehensive description of the Second Temple comes from Flavius Josephus. Josephus was born and raised in Jerusalem and trained as a priest in the Second Temple, so he is by far our most veracious authority.

The Temple complex was built on top of a small mountain plateau in the northeastern section of Jerusalem which was the site of the old temple. Foundation walls were erected around the mountain in the shape of an asymmetric rectangle to the height of the plateau, about 95 feet. Originally, all of the ashlar blocks making up the wall were the same size–37 feet long, 12 feet high and 18 feet in depth. These would have weighed over 100 tons apiece. How they were moved into place is still a matter of conjecture. They were "bound" together with lead and iron for added strength. The spaces between the angled slope of the mountain and the straight walls were filled in with stone and rubble which was then tightly packed. A flat rectangular surface of about 35 acres was thus created 95 feet above ground level on the western side, with the Kidron Valley plunging down on the east. This area was tiled over, with a 15-acre walled inner set of courtyards built in its center, as will be described.

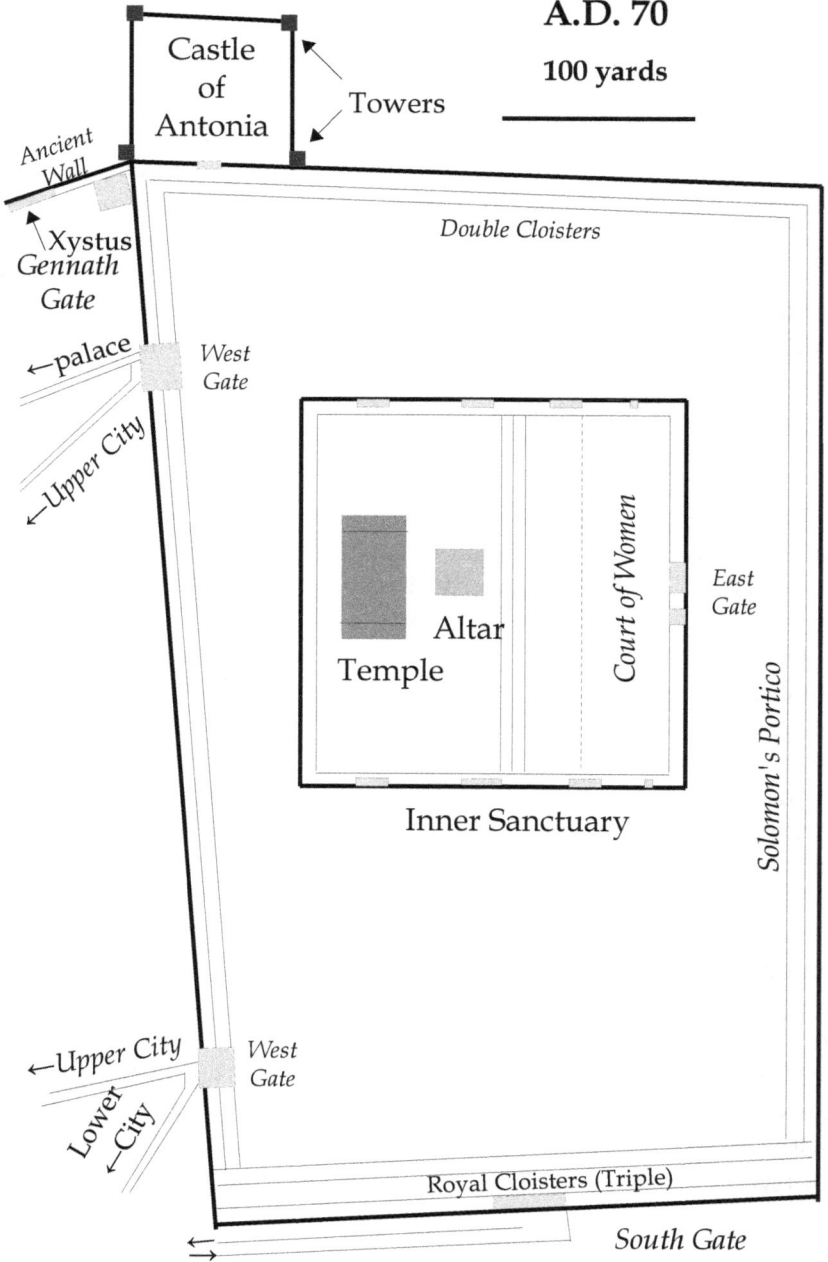

Second Temple
A.D. 70

100 yards

Castle of Antonia

Towers

Ancient Wall

Xystus

Gennath Gate

←palace

←Upper City

West Gate

Double Cloisters

Court of Women

Temple

Altar

East Gate

Inner Sanctuary

Solomon's Portico

←Upper City

West Gate

Lower City→

Royal Cloisters (Triple)

South Gate

36 Fires of Rome

Porticos, or cloisters, were built along the tops of these four outer walls, several steps up from the main courtyard. On three sides the cloisters were double and supported by three rows of 40-foot columns placed 50 feet apart. The outer row of the columns was blocked in forming a solid face which made the total height of the outer wall approximately 135 feet. The roof of the cloisters was constructed using large wooden beams overladen with cedar planking. The roofs also formed the base for ramparts used by the Temple guards and Roman soldiers for surveillance and crowd control.

On the south side of the Temple a triple cloister was created called Royal portico which ran its 1000 foot length. Four rows of columns supported three separate roofs–the middle roof several yards higher than the adjoining two. Both outer porticos were 30 feet in width, with the middle portico being 45 feet wide. The major public entrance to the Second Temple was on the south side, hence the triple cloisters were needed to shelter the numerous merchants and their goods.

Half of the 35-acre area of the Second Temple plateau was taken up with three inner courtyards, called the inner Sanctuary, that was set off from the outer courtyard by 60-foot walls and accessed through several large gates. It is in the easternmost of these inner courtyards that the Temple itself was constructed.

Out of the north wall of the Second Temple jutted a military-style fortress with four square corner guard towers. This was called the castle, or tower, of Antonia — named after Herod the Great's patron, Marc Antony. The castle had originally been built by the Asamonean King Hyrcanus I 100 years before and then later rebuilt by Herod.

The Foundations

The following passages from *Wars* were written eight years after General Titus ordered the Temple's destruction. Note that an ancient cubit was approximately 18 inches with a probable error in the translation of the length of the furlong. Wall heights indicated by Josephus for the Temple are well off modern estimates, but Josephus writes that much of the lower portions were intentionally buried to make the ground level as equal as possible on all four sides of the Temple.

> Now this temple, as I have already said, was built upon a strong hill. At first the plain at the top was hardly sufficient for the holy house and the altar, for the ground about it was very uneven, and like a precipice; but when king Solomon, who was the person that built the temple, had built a wall to it on its east side, there was then added one cloister founded on a bank cast up for it, and on the other parts the holy house stood naked. But in future ages the people added new banks, and the hill became a larger plain. They then broke down the wall on the north side, and took in as much as sufficed afterward for the compass of the entire temple. And when they had built walls on three sides of the temple round about, from the bottom of the hill, and had performed a work that was greater than could be hoped for, (in which work long ages were spent by them, as well as all their sacred treasures were exhausted which were still replenished by those tributes which were sent to God from the whole habitable earth,) they then encompassed their upper courts with cloisters, as well as they [afterward] did the lowest [court of the] temple. The lowest part of this was erected to the height of three hundred cubits, and in some places more; yet did not the entire depth of the foundations appear, for they brought earth, and filled up the valleys, as being desirous to make them on a level with the narrow streets of the city; wherein they made use of stones of forty cubits in magnitude; for the great plenty of money they then had, and the liberality of the people, made this attempt of theirs to succeed to an incredible degree; and what could not be so much as hoped for as ever to be accomplished, was, by perseverance and length of time, brought to perfection. (*Wars* V 5:1)

Josephus in *Antiquities* also describes the Temple foundations.

> Now the temple was built of stones that were white and strong, and each of their length was twenty-five cubits, their height was eight, and their breadth about twelve; and the whole structure, as also the structure of the royal cloister, was on each side much lower, but the middle was much higher, till they were visible to those that dwelt in the country for a great many furlongs, but chiefly to such as lived over against them, and those that approached to them...He (Herod) also encompassed the entire temple with very large cloisters, contriving them to be in a due proportion thereto; and he laid out larger sums of money upon them than had been done before him, till it seemed that no one else had so greatly adorned the temple as he had done. There was a large wall to both the cloisters which wall was itself the most prodigious work that

was ever heard of by man. The hill was a rocky ascent, that declined by degrees towards the east parts of the city, till it came to an elevated level. This hill it was which Solomon, who was the first of our kings, by Divine revelation, encompassed with a wall; it was of excellent workmanship upwards, and round the top of it. He also built a wall below, beginning at the bottom which was encompassed by a deep valley; and at the south side he laid rocks together, and bound them one to another with lead, and included some of the inner parts, till it proceeded to a great height, and till both the largeness of the square edifice and its altitude were immense, and till the vastness of the stones in the front were plainly visible on the outside, yet so that the inward parts were fastened together with iron, and preserved the joints immovable for all future times. When this work [for the foundation] was done in this manner, and joined together as part of the hill itself to the very top of it, he wrought it all into one outward surface, and filled up the hollow places which were about the wall, and made it a level on the external upper surface, and a smooth level also. This hill was walled all round, and in compass four furlongs, [the distance of] each angle containing in length a furlong:..(*Antiq* XV 11:3)

The outer, or first, courtyard with its spectacular porticos are described.

Now for the works that were above these foundations, these were not unworthy of such foundations; for all the cloisters were double, and the pillars to them belonging were twenty-five cubits in height, and supported the cloisters. These pillars were of one entire stone each of them, and that stone was white marble; and the roofs were adorned with cedar, curiously graven. The natural magnificence, and excellent polish, and the harmony of the joints in these cloisters, afforded a prospect that was very remarkable; nor was it on the outside adorned with any work of the painter or engraver. The cloisters [of the outmost court] were in breadth thirty cubits, while the entire compass of it was by measure six furlongs, including the tower of Antonia; those entire courts that were exposed to the air were laid with stones of all sorts. (*Wars* V 5:1,2)

Note that in the previous quote from *Antiq* XV 11:3, Josephus wrote that the total perimeter of the Temple walls was four furlongs, but in the following excerpt from *Wars* V 5:2, the total length of the cloisters that were built on top of those outer walls was six furlongs! Both measurements are erroneous, as the length base perimeter as measured today is roughly 11 furlongs, or 2500 yards.

The Royal cloisters on the south side of the outer, or first, courtyard Josephus pays special attention to.

> ...the royal cloisters, with three walks, ...reached in length from the east valley unto that on the west, for it was impossible it should reach any farther: and this cloister deserves to be mentioned better than any other under the sun; for while the valley was very deep, and its bottom could not be seen, if you looked from above into the depth, this further vastly high elevation of the cloister stood upon that height, insomuch that if any one looked down from the top of the battlements, or down both those altitudes, he would be giddy, while his sight could not reach to such an immense depth. This cloister had pillars that stood in four rows one over against the other all along, for the fourth row was interwoven into the wall which [also was built of stone]; and the thickness of each pillar was such, that three men might, with their arms extended, fathom it round, and join their hands again, while its length was twenty-seven feet, with a double spiral at its basis; and the number of all the pillars [in that court] was a hundred and sixty-two. Their chapiters were made with sculptures after the Corinthian order, and caused an amazement [to the spectators], by reason of the grandeur of the whole. These four rows of pillars included three intervals for walking in the middle of this cloister; two of which walks were made parallel to each other, and were contrived after the same manner; the breadth of each of them was thirty feet, the length was a furlong, and the height fifty feet; but the breadth of the middle part of the cloister was one and a half of the other, and the height was double, for it was much higher than those on each side; but the roofs were adorned with deep sculptures in wood, representing many sorts of figures. The middle was much higher than the rest, and the wall of the front was adorned with beams, resting upon pillars, that were interwoven into it, and that front was all of polished stone, insomuch that its fineness, to such as had not seen it, was incredible, and to such as had seen it, was greatly amazing. Thus was the first enclosure. (*Antiq* XV 11:5)

Philo, from Alexandria in Egypt, was also personally familiar with the Second Temple in Jerusalem. A contemporary of Jesus, Philo describes it well, although not with the detail of Josephus (Philo *Special Laws* 71).

To access the elevated Temple complex from Jerusalem, broad stone stairways were built out of the west and south walls. There were multiple gates to the Temple, leading down into various parts of Jerusalem.

Now in the western quarters of the enclosure of the temple there were four gates; the first led to the king's palace, and went to a passage over the intermediate valley; two more led to the suburbs of the city; and the last led to the other city, where the road descended down into the valley by a great number of steps, and thence up again by the ascent for the city lay over against the temple in the manner of a theater, and was encompassed with a deep valley along the entire south quarter; but the fourth front of the temple which was southward, had indeed itself gates in its middle, as also it had the royal cloisters, (*Antiq* VX 11:5)

Tower of Antonia

The tower of Antonio is next described by Josephus. From it, the actual the height of the Temple wall can be determined.

Now as to the tower of Antonia, it was situated at the corner of two cloisters of the court of the temple; of that on the west, and that on the north; it was erected upon a rock of fifty cubits in height, and was on a great precipice; it was the work of king Herod, wherein he demonstrated his natural magnanimity. In the first place, the rock itself was covered over with smooth pieces of stone, from its foundation, both for ornament, and that any one who would either try to get up or to go down it might not be able to hold his feet upon it. Next to this, and before you come to the edifice of the tower itself, there was a wall three cubits high; but within that wall all the space of the tower of Antonia itself was built upon, to the height of forty cubits. (*Wars* V 5:8)

From the ground, the top of the main wall of the tower of Antonia would be equal to the rock base and the height of the tower wall itself–90 cubits, or 135 feet. This height probably was carried over to the temple itself, with the tops of the cloisters being 135 feet as well.

Now on the north side [of the temple] was built a citadel, whose walls were square, and strong, and of extraordinary firmness. This citadel was built by the kings of the Asamonean race, who were also high priests before Herod, and they called it the Tower, in which were reposited the vestments of the high priest which the high priest only put on at the time when he was to offer sacrifice... But for the tower itself, when Herod the king of the Jews had fortified it more firmly than before, in order to secure and guard the temple, he gratified Antonius, who was his friend, and the Roman ruler, and then gave it the name of the Tower of Antonia. (*Antiq* XV 11:4)

According to Josephus, the tower, or castle, of Antonia had four separate square towers at its corners. Antonia's towers were high enough to be used by the Romans for surveillance over the entire city.

> And as the entire structure resembled that of a tower, it contained also four other distinct towers at its four corners; whereof the others were but fifty cubits high; whereas that which lay upon the southeast corner was seventy cubits high, that from thence the whole temple might be viewed; (*Wars* V 5:8)

Were the heights of these towers measured from the ramparts of the wall of Antonia which roughly corresponded to the ramparts of the walls of the Second Temple, or from the floor of Antonia? Josephus is not clear on this, but from his other writings it will be assumed that the towers were measured from the ramparts of the walls. This would make three of the square corner towers 75 feet above the ramparts, and 200 feet above the base ground. The fourth square tower, on the southeast corner of Antonia, and likely built into the Temple's north wall, was 150 feet above the floor of the outer courtyard, or 105 feet or so above the ramparts. From the base ground, this tower would be approximately 240 feet high, the highest aspect in Jerusalem and just above the roof of the Temple Sanctuary building in the walled inner courtyards.

Within the castle of Antonia was a secret "king's" tunnel that led south to the main Sanctuary building in the inner courtyard.

> There was also an occult passage built for the king; it led from Antonia to the inner temple, at its eastern gate; over which he also erected for himself a tower, that he might have the opportunity of a subterraneous ascent to the temple, in order to guard against any sedition which might be made by the people against their kings.(*Antiq* XV 11:7)

To get to the first court from Antonia, steps downward had to be navigated. The entrance was narrow, probably not more than 10 feet wide. This proved to be a difficult bottleneck for the attacking Romans in A.D. 70 when they were trying to storm the Temple courtyard proper from Antonia.

The Inner Courtyards

The walled inner courtyards were located in the center of the Temple complex, and perhaps 15 acres in total area. The enclosing block walls were five feet high, and on top of these thick walls were columned cloisters of a similar construction to the outer walls. A double row of 50-foot tall columns supported the cedar roofs of these single porticos for the entire perimeter of the inner courtyards, save the gates. The outer row of columns was blocked in to show a solid face. The total height of the inner courtyard wall was then 60 feet. The inner walled complex served as the "keep" of Jerusalem in the case of a siege. Imagine how disheartened attackers would have been to discover these 60 foot inner walls after just having breached the 135 foot outer walls!

The inner courtyards were only for purified Jews on pain of death, and there were warnings saying as much placed on each outer column of the portico in either Greek or Latin. There were separate entrances for Jewish women properly purified–except for those women having their "courses" who were not even allowed in the outer courtyard.

There were several entrances to the inner courtyard that were controlled by strong gates and flanked by guard houses. The most famous and largest was set into the middle of the eastern wall and was made of bronze and ornately decorated with gold grape vines. Women had their own lesser entrances, one on each of the north, south, and east walls.

The 15-acre inner courtyard was divided up into three separate "courts" each with its own purpose, as Josephus describes.

> Now, then, all such as ever saw the construction of our temple, of what nature it was, know well enough how the purity of it was never to be profaned; for it had four several courts encompassed with cloisters round about, every one of which had by our law a peculiar degree of

separation from the rest. Into the first court every body was allowed to go, even foreigners, and none but women, during their courses, were prohibited to pass through it; all the Jews went into the second court, as well as their wives, when they were free from all uncleanness; into the third court went in the Jewish men, when they were clean and purified; into the fourth went the priests, having on their sacerdotal garments; but for the most sacred place, none went in but the high priests, clothed in their peculiar garments. (*Apion* II 8)

When you go through these [first] cloisters, unto the second [court of the] temple, there was a partition made of stone all round, whose height was three cubits: its construction was very elegant; upon it stood pillars, at equal distances from one another, declaring the law of purity, some in Greek, and some in Roman letters, that "no foreigner should go within that sanctuary" for that second [court of the] temple was called "the Sanctuary," and was ascended to by fourteen steps from the first court. This court was four-square, and had a wall about it peculiar to itself; the height of its buildings, although it were on the outside forty cubits, was hidden by the steps, and on the inside that height was but twenty-five cubits; for it being built over against a higher part of the hill with steps, it was no further to be entirely discerned within, being covered by the hill itself. Beyond these thirteen steps there was the distance of ten cubits; this was all plain; whence there were other steps, each of five cubits a-piece, that led to the gates which gates on the north and south sides were eight, on each of those sides four, and of necessity two on the east. For since there was a partition built for the women on that side, as the proper place wherein they were to worship, there was a necessity for a second gate for them: this gate was cut out of its wall, over against the first gate. There was also on the other sides one southern and one northern gate, through which was a passage into the court of the women; for as to the other gates, the women were not allowed to pass through them; nor when they went through their own gate could they go beyond their own wall. This place was allotted to the women of our own country, and of other countries, provided they were of the same nation, and that equally. The western part of this court had no gate at all, but the wall was built entire on that side. But then the cloisters which were betwixt the gates extended from the wall inward, before the chambers; for they were supported by very fine and large pillars. These cloisters were single, and, excepting their magnitude, were no way inferior to those of the lower court..(*Wars* V 5:2)

..but within this wall, and on the very top of all, there ran another wall of stone also, having, on the east quarter, a double cloister, of the same length with the wall; in the midst of which was the temple itself. This cloister looked to the gates of the temple; and it had been adorned by many kings in former times; and round about the entire temple were fixed the spoils taken from barbarous nations; all these had been dedicated to the temple by Herod, with the addition of those he had taken from the Arabians. (*Antiq* XV 11:3)

In the midst of which, and not far from it (the first court), was the second, to be gone up to by a few steps: this was encompassed by a stone wall for a partition, with an inscription which forbade any foreigner to go in under pain of death. Now this inner enclosure had on its southern and northern quarters three gates [equally] distant one from another; but on the east quarter, towards the sun-rising, there was one large gate, through which such as were pure came in, together with their wives; but the temple further inward in that gate was not allowed to the women; but still more inward was there a third [court of the] temple, where into it was not lawful for any but the priests alone to enter. The temple itself was within this; and before that temple was the altar, upon which we offer our sacrifices and burnt-offerings to God. Into none of these three did king Herod enter, for he was forbidden, because he was not a priest. However, he took care of the cloisters and the outer enclosures, and these he built in eight years. (*Antiq* XV 11:5)

The second court comprised the eastern section of the 15-acre inner Temple complex. Here only Jewish men and women could go. The western section contained the third and fourth courts. The third court was only for purified Jewish males. As Jewish men were allowed to stand at the altar with their sacrifices, the altar itself was likely between the third and the fourth courts. The fourth court contained the Sanctuary building, and here only the priests could enter. The Temple and altar were surrounded by a low wall, and the entire fourth court separated from the third by a double cloister running north-south.

The Sanctuary Building

The front of the Sanctuary building faced the east and the rising sun, and was accessed by 12 steps. The gold-faced main center structure was 150 feet wide, 150 feet high, and 100 feet deep. It was flanked by two lower "shoulder" structures on the south and north sides that winged out 30 feet apiece, giving the Temple building a width of 210 feet in total. The Temple's flat cedar roof was covered with spikes to discourage birds from perching upon it. The height of the roof of the Sanctuary building was only a little more than the highest tower of the castle of Antonia 600 feet away to the north and beyond the 60 foot walls of the inner courtyards.

The entryway of the Temple was without a door or curtain. It was 37 feet wide and close to 100 feet tall. Immediately inside was an open area for the priests. On the back wall of this entrance hall, perhaps 50 feet away, was a massive gold-plated set of double doors that led to the inner chambers and the "God" room of the Temple. The doors to these holy chambers were 80 feet tall and 25 feet wide. These golden doors were kept covered by massive and colorful embroidered curtains covered with mystical symbols and figures. Over the golden doors and along the walls were large decorative grape vines also made of gold. Behind these doors was not only the most-holy room, but also the Corban–the holy money–along with piles of precious spices, jewels, and other valuable items.

On the north and south sides of the open entrance area were the two three-story wings previously described, filled with rooms and offices that were likely used for various practical and administrative purposes.

In front of the Sanctuary building on the east, and in front of the entrance steps but behind the double cloister separating the fourth and third courtyards was the sacrificial alter. This sat on a structure that was 25 feet high and accessed by means of steep steps. The alter itself was bronze and 75 feet on a side, with metallic horn-like formations at each corner. The total area of it was almost 6,000 square feet! Multiple sacrifices could be made at once with 25 supplicants for each sacrifice, so there had to be a substantial stone base around all four sides to accommodate them. Plus, there were fires underneath the altar that were kept going all year long.

According to Josephus, millions would come here to sacrifice over the course of a Passover with many hundreds of thousands coming for the other festivals–both major and minor. A minor festival, Xylophory, was dedicated solely to the replenishment of the wood for the altar's fire (*Wars* II 17:6).

As to the holy house itself which was placed in the midst [of the inmost court], that most sacred part of the temple, it was ascended to by twelve steps; and in front its height and its breadth were equal, and each a hundred cubits, though it was behind forty cubits narrower; for on its front it had what may be styled shoulders on each side, that passed twenty cubits further. Its first gate was seventy cubits high, and twenty-five cubits broad; but this gate had no doors; for it represented the universal visibility of heaven, and that it cannot be excluded from any place. Its front was covered with gold all over, and through it the first part of the house, that was more inward, did all of it appear; which, as it was very large, so did all the parts about the more inward gate appear to shine to those that saw them; but then, as the entire house was divided into two parts within, it was only the first part of it that was open to our view. Its height extended all along to ninety cubits in height, and its length was fifty cubits, and its breadth twenty. But that gate which was at this end of the first part of the house was, as we have already observed, all over covered with gold, as was its whole wall about it; it had also golden vines above it, from which clusters of grapes hung as tall as a man's height. But then this house, as it was divided into two parts, the inner part was lower than the appearance of the outer, and had golden doors of fifty-five cubits altitude, and sixteen in breadth; but before these doors there was a veil of equal largeness with the doors. It was a Babylonian curtain, embroidered with blue, and fine linen, and scarlet, and purple, and of a contexture that was truly wonderful. Nor was this mixture of colors without its mystical interpretation, but was a kind of image of the universe; for by the scarlet there seemed to be enigmatically signified fire, by the fine flax the earth, by the blue the air, and by the purple the sea; two of them having their colors the foundation of this resemblance; but the fine flax and the purple have their own origin for that foundation, the earth producing the one, and the sea the other. This curtain had also embroidered upon it all that was mystical in the heavens, excepting that of the [twelve] signs, representing living creatures.

Now the outward face of the temple in its front wanted nothing that was likely to surprise either men's minds or their eyes; for it was covered all over with plates of gold of great weight, and, at the first rising of the sun, reflected back a very fiery splendor, and made those who forced themselves to look upon it to turn their eyes away, just as they would have done at the sun's own rays. But this temple appeared to strangers, when they were coming to it at a distance, like a mountain covered with snow; for as to those parts of it that were not gilt, they were exceeding white. On its top it had spikes with sharp points, to prevent any pollution of it by birds sitting upon it. Of its stones, some of them were forty-five cubits in length, five in height, and six in breadth. Before this temple stood the altar, fifteen cubits high, and equal both in length and breadth; each of which dimensions was fifty cubits. The figure it was built in was a square, and it had corners like horns; and the passage up to it was by an insensible acclivity. It was formed without any iron tool, nor did any such iron tool so much as touch it at any time. There was also a wall of partition, about a cubit in height, made of fine stones, and so as to be grateful to the sight; this encompassed the holy house and the altar, and kept the people that were on the outside off from the priests. Moreover, those that had the gonorrhea and the leprosy were excluded out of the city entirely; women also, when their courses were upon them, were shut out of the temple; nor when they were free from that impurity, were they allowed to go beyond the limit before-mentioned; men also, that were not thoroughly pure, were prohibited to come into the inner [court of the] temple; nay, the priests themselves that were not pure were prohibited to come into it also. (*Wars* V 5:4,6)

Now the doors of the holy house were seventy cubits high, and twenty cubits broad; they were all plated over with gold, and almost of solid gold itself, and there were no fewer than twenty men required to shut them every day; nor was it lawful ever to leave them open.. (*Apion* II 10)

Philo also describes the Temple building and the most-holy room.

(72) And in the centre was the temple itself, beautiful beyond all possible description, as one may conjecture from what is now seen around on the outside; for what is innermost is invisible to every human creature except the high priest alone, and even he is enjoined only to enter that holy place once in each year. Everything then is invisible. For he carries in a brasier full of coals and frankincense; and then, when a great smoke proceeds from it, as is natural, and when everything all around is enveloped in it, then the sight of men is clouded, and checked, and prevented from penetrating in, being wholly unable to pierce the cloud. (Philo *Special Laws* 72)

Through the great curtains and golden doors and inside the most Holy room were golden objects that symbolized those used by the Jews in the exodus. These included two large menorahs, a golden ceremonial table, golden vessels, and ceremonial garments.

When any persons entered into the temple, its floor received them. This part of the temple therefore was in height sixty cubits, and its length the same; whereas its breadth was but twenty cubits: but still that sixty cubits in length was divided again, and the first part of it was cut off at forty cubits, and had in it three things that were very wonderful and famous among all mankind, the candlestick, the table [of shew-bread], and the altar of incense. Now the seven lamps signified the seven planets; for so many there were springing out of the candlestick. Now the twelve loaves that were upon the table signified the circle of the zodiac and the year; but the altar of incense, by its thirteen kinds of sweet-smelling spices with which the sea replenished it, signified that God is the possessor of all things that are both in the uninhabitable and habitable parts of the earth, and that they are all to be dedicated to his use. But the inmost part of the temple of all was of twenty cubits. This was also separated from the outer part by a veil. In this there was nothing at all. It was inaccessible and inviolable, and not to be seen by any; and was called the Holy of Holies. Now, about the sides of the lower part of the temple, there were little houses, with passages out of one into another; there were a great many of them, and they were of three stories high; there were also entrances on each side into them from the gate of the temple. But the superior part of the temple had no such little houses any further, because the temple was there narrower, and forty cubits higher, and of a smaller body than the lower parts of it. Thus we collect that the whole height, including the sixty cubits from the floor, amounted to a hundred cubits. (*Wars* V 5:5)

Only the Temple High Priest was pure enough to enter this "God" chamber, and only after a rigorous preparatory process. The High Priest wore a special ceremonial dress on this occasion as well. This occurred only once a year, during the Passover.

Before the Priest entered the chamber, the room itself had to be purified–enshrouded in a fog of holy smoke (hence the origin of the popular expression) generated by the burning and smoldering of spices and frankincense in brass pots. Other details of the ceremony have been lost through time, although Philo describes the robes and headdress of the High Priest used in the ceremony (Philo *Special Laws* 82-98).

Now there is so great caution used about these offices of religion, that the priests are appointed to go into the temple but at certain hours; for in the morning, at the opening of the inner temple, those that are to officiate receive the sacrifices, as they do again at noon, till the doors are shut. Lastly, it is not so much as lawful to carry any vessel into the holy house; nor is there any thing therein, but the altar [of incense], the table [of shew-bread], the censer, and the candlestick which are all written in the law; for there is nothing further there, nor are there any mysteries performed that may not be spoken of; nor is there any feasting within the place. For what I have now said is publicly known, and supported by the testimony of the whole people, and their operations are very manifest; for although there be four courses of the priests, and every one of them have above five thousand men in them, yet do they officiate on certain days only; and when those days are over, other priests succeed in the performance of their sacrifices, and assemble together at mid-day, and receive the keys of the temple, and the vessels by tale, without any thing relating to food or drink being carried into the temple; nay, we are not allowed to offer such things at the altar, excepting what is prepared for the sacrifices. (*Apion* II 8)

But for those that were taken in the temple of Jerusalem, they made the greatest figure of them all; that is, the golden table, of the weight of many talents; the candlestick also, that was made of gold, though its construction were now changed from that which we made use of; for its middle shaft was fixed upon a basis, and the small branches were produced out of it to a great length, having the likeness of a trident in their position, and had every one a socket made of brass for a lamp at the tops of them. These lamps were in number seven, and represented the dignity of the number seven among the Jews; and the last of all the spoils, was carried the Law of the Jews. (*Wars* VII 5:5)

Completion

The Second Temple was completed decades after the crucifixion of Jesus and during the era of Agrippa II. At one time, according to Josephus as many as 18,000 men were employed working on the Temple under Agrippa II's supervision. But as we have cautioned, Josephus' number might be reduced by a factor of ten.

And now it was that the temple was finished. So when the people saw that the workmen were unemployed, who were above eighteen thousand and that they, receiving no wages, were in want because they had earned their bread by their labors about the temple; and while they were unwilling to keep by them the treasures that were there deposited, out of fear of [their being carried away by] the Romans; and while they had a regard to the making provision for the workmen; they had a mind to expend these treasures upon them; for if any one of them did but labor for a single hour, he received his pay immediately; so they persuaded him to rebuild the eastern cloisters. These cloisters belonged to the outer court, and were situated in a deep valley, and had walls that reached four hundred cubits [in length], and were built of square and very white stones, the length of each of which stones was twenty cubits, and their height six cubits. This was the work of king Solomon, who first of all built the entire temple. But king Agrippa, who had the care of the temple committed to him by Claudius Caesar, considering that it is easy to demolish any building, but hard to build it up again, and that it was particularly hard to do it to these cloisters which would require a considerable time, and great sums of money, he denied the petitioners their request about that matter; but he did not obstruct them when they desired the city might be paved with white stone. (*Antiq* XX 9:7)

Note that the eastern cloisters refer to Solomon's portico, the area of the outer courtyard where Jesus liked to hold forth.

The Second Temple Today

The walls of the Temple Mount have been rebuilt but not to the heights or standards of the original Herodian design. The columned cloisters are completely gone. Most of the upper wall blocks seen today came from broken portions of the original Temple blocks which were reset by later builders. The floor of the Temple Mount, however, is roughly at the same level of the outer courtyard of 2,000 years ago.

The lower blocks of the wall appear to be original. At the southwest corner of the Temple Mount, south of the famous Wailing Wall in the Jewish Quarter, excavations confirm this. These large blocks with unmistakable Herodian facings stack up only to a height of around 30 or 40 feet. Smaller blocks make up the rest of the wall–to a height of about 100 feet.   The lower blocks remained undisturbed probably because they were covered up by a mountain of rubble thrown down during the destruction of the Temple in A.D. 70. It can be presumed at the now-excavated southeast corner of the Temple, that the debris pile from the fallen upper blocks would have been about 40 feet– reaching a height that just covered the remnants of "Robinson's" arch. The arch likely supported one of the great staircases on the western side.

The Temple in A.D. 36

In the times of Jesus, the outer courtyard of the Temple was truly a public religious forum. The High Priesthood was surprisingly tolerant to other religions and philosophies in the outer courtyards, given their later actions against the Christians. Jesus was a known troublemaker and yet was allowed to preach there in the months leading up to his crucifixion. Even after the crucifixion, the Nazarenes were not banned from the outer courtyard. Those who underwent purification were even allowed into the walled inner Sanctuary as well.

Most mornings Jesus would hold forth with his Disciples and interested spectators and pilgrims on Solomon's portico. During that time of the day the roof of the double cloisters would have protected Jesus from the heat and glare of the sun. If Jesus was bold enough he might have held his sessions directly across from the ornate bronze-and-gilded east gate of the walled inner Sanctuary.

Chapter 3   The Crucifixion: Betrayal by Judas

Then Judas, who betrayed him, when he saw that he was condemned, repented himself, (Mt 27:3)

The Jerusalem Passover was one of the great celebrations in ancient times. Taking place every year in the springtime after the harvest and lasting for a week, the Jewish holy city saw its population increase dramatically. Josephus reports that as many as three million people swelled Jerusalem and its environs for the festival. Even dividing that number by 10 to account for the Josephus "factor," 300,000 people is a huge number for a city of 50,000. Many of these pilgrims and travelers were forced to stay in neighboring towns, or in makeshift campgrounds that had been prepared in the surrounding rolling pastureland, tree orchards, and freshly harvested fields.

The celebration centered around the Second Temple–the most holy of the Jewish holy places and the masterwork of Herod the Great. Styled after the Greek Acropolis, the gold-faced central inner Sanctuary building would appear to float over the white-walled Temple plateau and the rest of Jerusalem to the approaching pilgrims from afar.

West of the great Temple were residential neighborhoods where the wealthy and powerful of Jerusalem lived, as well as the 15-acre walled palace of Herod the Great—marked by a tall trio of square cloistered towers.

The great Temple was bordered on the east by the Kidron Valley, through which a brook flowed during most of the year. On the other side of the brook was the Mount of Olives, a small mountain where the Garden of Gethsemane was located. To the north of the Second Temple, there was a second wall, built by the Asamoneans, that guarded the upper city. North of the Asamonean wall were orchards and pastureland. To the south, across the Tyropean Valley, was the old city of Jerusalem. This was where most of Jerusalem's citizens lived and worked.

In contrast to the relatively stately upper city, the lower city was jammed with a ramshackle collection of shoulder-to-shoulder, three-story rock and mud plaster buildings–most sharing common walls and with outside ladders to access the upper levels. The streets were numerous, narrow, and meandering.

Huge numbers of people came to Jerusalem for the Passover, and commerce was every bit as important as religious ceremonies, personal introspection, and affirmation of faith. The regular markets in Jerusalem would be jammed with vendors, exhibitors, and shoppers. Additional temporary marketplaces would be set up wherever there was room — in the alleyways, outside all of the city gates, and along the major roads leading to Jerusalem. Individual vendors would prowl the major streets pushing their carts and noisily hawking wares as hundreds of thousands of people browsed, traded, and socialized from sunup to sundown–Jew and non-Jew alike. Old friends became reacquainted, new friends or business contacts were made, and news and rumors and gossip from all over the world were shared and disseminated during the week-long festival.

The appeal of the Passover was not limited to Jews alone–far from it. People of all classes, cultures, and religions came to Jerusalem to congregate and mingle–including Roman officials of high rank as well as many wealthy non-Jew travelers from throughout the Roman Empire and beyond. They would come to socialize, yes, but to also pay their respects to the Jewish God and to see the wondrous Temple where this god "lived." During the Passover, the palace of Herod, and the older Asamonean Royal house, were filled with important people and their attendants. For the non-religious, rounds of parties were likely held–albeit quietly–almost every night of the celebration.

Congregation of Zealots

Also present at these festivals, inevitably, were the seditious, the malcontents, and the religious zealots–people who took the opportunity of celebration to spread their message of revolt and revolution. Resentment was high against the Romans and especially among those Jews who did not participate in the Roman-facilitated economic boom that had been going on for decades. This resentment was also directed toward the powerful Jewish High Priesthood and the family of Herod the Great, who were viewed by many Jews as Roman collaborators.

Fully aware of this potential for violence, the Roman soldiers and Temple guards were ever-vigilant in watching for signs of trouble and quick to act if they saw any. On the lofty ramparts of the great Temple or high in the towers of Antonia, the soldiers and guards would scan the crowds ceaselessly. Antonia was a military storehouse, but it also held sleeping quarters and mess facilities for the soldiers. There were also temporary prisons set up to handle those arrested for petty crimes and seditious activities.

With the stage set and the major characters in place, it is now time to look more closely at the Gospel narratives. In this chapter, the betrayer Judas is detailed, as well as the last supper and the subsequent arrest of Jesus.

The Betrayal in Mark

The Book of Mark states that Judas betrayed Jesus two days before the last supper which took place on the evening of the second day of the feast. At that time, an unexpected bounty had been placed on the head of Jesus by High Priest Joseph Caiaphas. That was a rare thing for the High Priesthood to do, and if Jesus stayed in Judea, his arrest would be a certainty.

When Jesus and his Disciples were at the house of Simon the Leper in Bethany, all sitting "at meat," an unidentified woman came up to Jesus and anointed his head with expensive ointment of "pure nard" worth about "three hundred shillings." Some of the Disciples objected to the waste of the expensive substance.

> 14:3 And while he was in Bethany in the house of Simon the leper, as he sat at meat, there came a woman having an alabaster cruse of ointment of pure nard very costly; *and* she brake the cruse, and poured it over his head. 14:4 But there were some that had indignation among themselves, *saying*, To what purpose hath this waste of the ointment been made? 14:5 For this ointment might have been sold for above three hundred shillings, and given to the poor. And they murmured against her. 14:6 But Jesus said, Let her alone; why trouble ye her? she hath wrought a good work on me. 14:7 For ye have the poor always with you, and whensoever ye will ye can do them good: but me ye have not always. 14:8 She hath done what she could; she hath anointed my body beforehand for the burying. 14:9 And verily I say unto you, Wheresoever the gospel shall be preached throughout the whole world, that also which this woman hath done shall be spoken of for a memorial of her. (Mk)

This story is an indication that Jesus himself had a shaven head–as did many ascetics of the day. Pouring oil into long and flowing locks would be a messy business, indeed! At any rate, soon afterward this episode, Judas left Simon the leper's house for the purpose of betraying Jesus to the chief priests.

> 14:10 And Judas Iscariot, he that was one of the twelve, went away unto the chief priests, that he might deliver him unto them. 14:11 And they, when they heard it, were glad, and promised to give him money. And he sought how he might conveniently deliver him *unto them*. (Mk)

Two days later, at the last supper as described in the Book of Mark, Judas Iscariot is presumably present in the guest-chamber for the meal and breaks bread with Jesus and the other Disciples.

> 14:18 And as they sat and were eating, Jesus said, Verily I say unto you, One of you shall betray me, *even* he that eateth with me. 14:19 They began to be sorrowful, and to say unto him one by one, Is it I? 14:20 And he said unto them, *It is* one of the twelve, he that dippeth with me in the dish. (Mk)

Interestingly, Jesus states that a Disciple "shall" betray him as if that act was to come, but Judas had already betrayed Jesus to the chief priests.

Judas next shows up late that night in the Garden of Gethsemane with the arresting mob.

> 14:43And straightway, while he yet spake, cometh Judas, one of the twelve, and with him a multitude with swords and staves, from the chief priests and the scribes and the elders. 14:44Now he that betrayed him had given them a token, saying, Whomsoever I shall kiss, that is he; take him, and lead him away safely. 14:45And when he was come, straightway he came to him, and saith, Rabbi; and kissed him. 14:46And they laid hands on him, and took him. (Mk)

The Betrayal in Matthew

In the Book of Matthew, much the same story is told about the anointing woman and the alabaster oil. It was then that Judas left to see the chief priests. Was Judas stung simply by Jesus' rebuke to him about the use of the expensive oil? What savage revenge if that was the case!

> 26:14Then one of the twelve, who was called Judas Iscariot, went unto the chief priests, 26:15and said, What are ye willing to give me, and I will deliver him unto you? And they weighed unto him thirty pieces of silver. 26:16And from that time he sought opportunity to deliver him *unto them.* (Mt)

Later during the last supper, Judas is identified as the betrayer. That Judas leaves the room of the last supper early to betray Jesus is not established, as was the case in Mark.

> 26:20Now when even was come, he was sitting at meat with the twelve disciples; 26:21and as they were eating, he said, Verily I say unto you, that one of you shall betray me. 26:22And they were exceeding sorrowful, and began to say unto him every one, Is it I, Lord? 26:23And he answered and said, He that dipped his hand with me in the dish, the same shall

betray me. $^{26:24}$The Son of man goeth, even as it is written of him: but woe unto that man through whom the Son of man is betrayed! good were it for that man if he had not been born. $^{26:25}$And Judas, who betrayed him, answered and said, Is it I, Rabbi? He saith unto him, Thou hast said. (Mt)

Like the Book of Mark, Judas comes with the arresting mob to the Garden of Gethsemane.

$^{26:47}$And while he yet spake, lo, Judas, one of the twelve, came, and with him a great multitude with swords and staves, from the chief priest and elders of the people. $^{26:48}$Now he that betrayed him gave them a sign, saying, Whomsoever I shall kiss, that is he: take him. $^{26:49}$And straightway he came to Jesus, and said, Hail, Rabbi; and kissed him. $^{26:50}$And Jesus said unto him, Friend, *do* that for which thou art come. Then they came and laid hands on Jesus, and took him. (Mt)

The Book of Matthew also relates what happened to Judas after the betrayal.

$^{27:3}$Then Judas, who betrayed him, when he saw that he was condemned, repented himself, and brought back the thirty pieces of silver to the chief priests and elders, $^{27:4}$saying, I have sinned in that I betrayed innocent blood. But they said, What is that to us? see thou *to it*. $^{27:5}$And he cast down the pieces of silver into the sanctuary, and departed; and he went away and hanged himself. $^{27:6}$And the chief priests took the pieces of silver, and said, It is not lawful to put them into the treasury, since it is the price of blood. $^{27:7}$And they took counsel, and bought with them the potter's field, to bury strangers in. $^{27:8}$Wherefore that field was called, the field of blood, unto this day. $^{27:9}$Then was fulfilled that which was spoken through Jeremiah the prophet, saying, And they took the thirty pieces of silver, the price of him that was priced, whom *certain* of the children of Israel did price; $^{27:10}$and they gave them for the potter's field, as the Lord appointed me. (Mt)

The "field of blood" has a different meaning in Acts, as will be seen.

The Betrayal in Luke

In the Book of Luke, more is learned about the activities of Jesus in the time immediately leading up to the Passover of A.D. 36 than is found in either the Books of Mark or Matthew.

> [21:37]And every day he was teaching in the temple; and every night he went out, and lodged in the mount that is called Olivet. [21:38]And all the people came early in the morning to him in the temple, to hear him. (Lk)

Note that the raising of Lazarus from the dead is not mentioned in Luke, nor is it in Mark and Matthew. The name "Olivet" is likely a mistranslation of "Olives." The area on the Mount of Olives where Jesus "lodged" was probably the Garden of Gethsemane–where Jesus would later be arrested.

But not mentioned in Luke is the meal held before the Passover at Simon the Leper's house, where Jesus was anointed with expensive oil. But Judas does make plans to betray Jesus at about the same time when the Passover was "nigh."

> .[22:1]Now the feast of unleavened bread drew nighwhich is called the Passover. [22:2]And the chief priests and the scribes sought how they might put him to death; for they feared the people. [22:3]And Satan entered into Judas who was called Iscariot, being of the number of the twelve. [22:4]And he went away, and communed with the chief priests and captains, how he might deliver him unto them. [22:5]And they were glad, and covenanted to give him money. [22:6]And he consented, and sought opportunity to deliver him unto them in the absence of the multitude. (Lk)

At this last supper there is no mention of Judas or Jesus' knowledge of his imminent betrayal. But during the arrest sequence at Gethsemane, Judas is there.

> [22:47]While he yet spake, behold, a multitude, and he that was called Judas, one of the twelve, went before them; and he drew near unto Jesus to kiss him. [22:48]But Jesus said unto him, Judas, betrayest thou the Son of man with a kiss? (Lk)

Luke tells us nothing about the fate of Judas, though in Acts of the Apostles, authored by the same man (the physician Luke of Macedonia), Judas' fate is detailed.

The Betrayal in John

In the Book of John, still more is learned about the final year of Jesus leading up to the Passover of A.D. 36. As the feast of the Tabernacles in October of A.D. 35 approaches, Jesus is in Galilee and intentionally staying away from Jerusalem and Judea, fearing that he might be killed by the Jews.

While in a synagogue in Capernaum with his Disciples, Jesus teaches them the communion ceremony which many followers objected to, leaving his Ministry. More importantly for our immediate purposes, Jesus comments on one of his 12 Disciples who was to betray him.

> [6:70]Jesus answered them, Did not I choose you the twelve, and one of you is a devil? [6:71]Now he spake of Judas *the son* of Simon Iscariot, for he it was that should betray him, *being* one of the twelve. (Jn)

Jesus is later talked into returning to Judea by his "brethren," which could refer to either his real brothers or to his Disciples.

> [7:1]And after these things Jesus walked in Galilee: for he would not walk in Judaea, because the Jews sought to kill him. [7:2]Now the feast of the Jews, the feast of tabernacles, was at hand. [7:3]His brethren therefore said unto him, Depart hence, and go into Judaea, that thy disciples also may behold thy works which thou doest. [7:4]For no man doeth anything in secret, and himself seeketh to be known openly. If thou doest these things, manifest thyself to the world. (Jn)

It can be speculated that the political uncertainty in the region was caused partially by the recent defeat of Herod Antipas' army by King Aretas IV of Nabotea. With this debacle, the unavoidable perception was that Rome was losing its grip on the Jewish East. Another factor was the return of the Tetrarch Herod Antipas to Galilee in shame. Less than a year before, Antipas had executed

John the Baptist, Jesus' cousin. Would he seek out and kill Jesus as well?

These considerations were likely major factors in Jesus' returning to Judea for the feast of the Tabernacles in A.D. 35. Even so, Jesus had to return in secret. There was still potential danger to Jesus not only from the High Priesthood, but also some of the common people who were supporters of the Temple priests — heretics were to be stoned, after all.

When Jesus finally arrived in Judea in October, he began to preach almost daily in the outer courtyard of the Second Temple. This was curious, because it has been established that Jesus knew that many of the Judean Jews were bent on killing him. What had changed to make Jesus so bold?

Jesus might have gotten unofficial word from the High Priesthood or the Sanhedrin-through Nicodemus, perhaps-that if his preachings were non-inflammatory he would not be bothered. Remember that by late A.D. 35, Jesus' Ministry might have been in existence for as long as seven years. In that time, Jesus had gained many "secret" disciples in Jerusalem — with the powerful Nicodemus being one of them. The High Priesthood likely had a practical side as well. Recognizing the political uncertainty that existed, the priesthood had no desire to provoke the people by arresting the popular Jesus-unless they had to.

However, despite this apparent truce with the High Priesthood, in the two-month period between the feast of the Tabernacles in October and the feast of the Dedication in December, John documents that Jesus was in danger of being stoned on two separate occasions.

8:57The Jews therefore said unto him, Thou art not yet fifty years old, and hast thou seen Abraham? 8:58Jesus said unto them, Verily, verily, I say unto you, Before Abraham was born, I am. 8:59They took up stones therefore to cast at him: but Jesus hid himself, and went out of the temple. (Jn)

^{10:29}My Father, who hath given *them* unto me, is greater than all; and no one is able to snatch *them* out of the Father's hand. ^{10:30}I and the Father are one. ^{10:31}The Jews took up stones again to stone him. (Jn)

Jesus also gave the High Priesthood some potent ammunition to use against him. Mere weeks before the Passover of A.D. 36, Jesus raised Lazarus from the dead–at the same time also raising the ire of Caiaphas, the High Priest.

^{11:46}But some of them went away to the Pharisees, and told them the things which Jesus had done. ^{11:47}The chief priests therefore and the Pharisees gathered a council, and said, What do we? for this man doeth many signs. ^{11:48}If we let him thus alone, all men will believe on him: and the Romans will come and take away both our place and our nation. ^{11:49}But a certain one of them, Caiaphas, being high priest that year, said unto them, Ye know nothing at all, ^{11:50}nor do ye take account that it is expedient for you that one man should die for the people, and that the whole nation perish not. ^{11:51}Now this he said not of himself: but, being high priest that year, he prophesied that Jesus should die for the nation; ^{11:52}and not for the nation only, but that he might also gather together into one the children of God that are scattered abroad. ^{11:53}So from that day forth they took counsel that they might put him to death. ^{11:54}Jesus therefore walked no more openly among the Jews, but departed thence into the country near to the wilderness, into a city called Ephraim; and there he tarried with the disciples. ^{11:55}Now the passover of the Jews was at hand: and many went up to Jerusalem out of the country before the passover, to purify themselves. ^{11:56}They sought therefore for Jesus, and spake one with another, as they stood in the temple, What think ye? That he will not come to the feast? ^{11:57}Now the chief priests and the Pharisees had given commandment, that, if any man knew where he was, he should show it, that they might take him. (Jn)

Note that Caiaphas was concerned that if the people were swayed over to Jesus that "the Romans will come and take away both our place and our nation." Was the raising of Lazarus the true breaking point for Caiaphas, or was it the impending and unexpected visit of Vitellius to Jerusalem for the Passover?

The Book of John then moves to the six days before Passover of A.D. 36. Here, at supper, Jesus had his feet anointed with precious nard (not his head, as was related in the Books of Mark and Matthew). Also, the woman anointer is identified as Mary, the sister of Martha, who was also the sister of Lazarus–whom Jesus had raised from the dead a short time before. The place of the supper may well have been at Simon the Leper's house, but John only states that the meal was served by Martha with no mention of Simon or a specific location in Bethany. Judas Iscariot protests the use of the expensive ointment but does not leave immediately to betray Jesus.

The people of the region gathering for the Passover soon learn that Jesus is in Bethany. They crowd into the town not only to see Jesus, but Lazarus as well. The day after the anointing, the crowd persuades Jesus to ride a young ass. They accolade him with shouts and wave palm branches. When word of this incident got back to the priests in Jerusalem they were alarmed at Jesus' popularity and "the chief priests took counsel that they might put Lazarus also to death" as well as Jesus (Jn 12:10).

> The Pharisees therefore said among themselves, Behold how ye prevail nothing: lo, the world is gone after him. (Jn 12:19)

The Book of John then moves on to the so-called "last supper." John gives few details as to its location and its arrangement is not as mysterious or dramatic as the Synoptic Gospels relate. At the last supper in the Book of John, Judas betrays Jesus.

> 13:2And during supper, the devil having already put into the heart of Judas Iscariot, Simon's *son*, to betray him, 13:3*Jesus*, knowing that the Father had given all the things into his hands, and that he came forth from God, and goeth unto God, 13:4riseth from supper, and layeth aside his garments; and he took a towel, and girded himself. (Jn)

As the supper progresses, Jesus predicts that one of the Disciples will betray him and he is pressed to reveal who it is.

> 13:26Jesus therefore answereth, He it is, for whom I shall dip the sop, and give it him. So when he had dipped the sop, he taketh and giveth it to Judas, *the son* of Simon Iscariot. 13:27And after the sop, then entered

Satan into him. Jesus therefore saith unto him, What thou doest, do quickly. $^{13:28}$Now no man at the table knew for what intent he spake this unto him. $^{13:29}$For some thought, because Judas had the bag, that Jesus said unto him, Buy what things we have need of for the feast; or, that he should give something to the poor. $^{13:30}$He then having received the sop went out straightway: and it was night. $^{13:31}$When therefore he was gone out, Jesus saith, Now is the Son of man glorified, and God is glorified in him; $^{13:32}$and God shall glorify him in himself, and straightway shall he glorify him. (Jn 13: 26-32)

As with the other Gospels, in the Book of John, Judas leads the mob to where Jesus is resting.

$^{18:2}$Now Judas also, who betrayed him, knew the place: for Jesus oft-times resorted thither with his disciples. $^{18:3}$Judas then, having received the band *of soldiers*, and officers from the chief priests and the Pharisees, cometh thither with lanterns and torches and weapons. $^{18:4}$Jesus therefore, knowing all the things that were coming upon him, went forth, and saith unto them, Whom seek ye? $^{18:5}$They answered him, Jesus of Nazareth. Jesus saith unto them, I am *he*. And Judas also, who betrayed him, was standing with them. (Jn 18:2-5)

The Betrayal in Acts

In Acts, after the ascension of Jesus the now-11 Disciples decided that they needed to choose a disciple to replace Judas, in order to keep their number at 12. The fate of Judas is then told.

$^{1:16}$Brethren, it was needful that the Scripture should be fulfilledwhich the Holy Spirit spake before by the mouth of David concerning Judas, who was guide to them that took Jesus. $^{1:17}$For he was numbered among us, and received his portion in this ministry. $^{1:18}$(Now this man obtained a field with the reward of his iniquity; and falling headlong, he burst asunder in the midst, and all his bowels gushed out. $^{1:19}$And it became known to all the dwellers at Jerusalem; insomuch that in their language that field was called Akeldama, that is, The field of blood.) (Acts)

In the Book of Matthew, the "field of blood" was a cemetery that the priests bought with Judas' money after Judas hanged himself. In Acts, "field of blood" refers not to a cemetery, but the field that Judas bought with the money. Judas' death was unusually violent. Was it an accident, or was he murdered?!

The Last Supper and Communion

The final meal of Jesus, the famous "last supper," took place at the start of the second day of the feast of the Unleavened Bread which was shortly after sunset on the 16th of Nisan in A.D. 36. According to Josephus the Paschal meal would take place on the 14th of Nisan with the seven days of the feast of the Unleavened Bread starting the next day. So the first day of the feast would start on the evening of the 15th day of Nisan and the second day on the 16th day. While the Book of John gives few physical details of the location of the gathering, the Synoptic Gospels do.

In the Book of Mark, the place of the last supper was wrapped in apparent mystery.

> 14:13 And he sendeth two of his disciples, and saith unto them, Go into the city, and there shall meet you a man bearing a pitcher of water: follow him; 14:14 and wheresoever he shall enter in, say to the master of the house, The Teacher saith, Where is my guest-chamber, where I shall eat the passover with my disciples? 14:15 And he will himself show you a large upper room furnished *and* ready: and there make ready for us. (Mk)

Jesus later came to the "guest-chamber" with the other Disciples. During the meal, Jesus stated that one of the Disciples present will betray him, but he doesn't name him. Jesus then revealed that this will be his last meal, and he introduced the communion ceremony.

> 14:22 And as they were eating, he took bread, and when he had blessed, he brake it, and gave to them, and said, Take ye: this is my body. 14:23 And he took a cup, and when he had given thanks, he gave to them:

and they all drank of it. [14:24]And he said unto them, This is my blood of the covenant which is poured out for many. (Mk)

After singing a hymn, Jesus led his Disciples out of the guest-chamber into the dark city, on through the city gates, and across the Kidron Valley to the Mount of Olives.

In the Book of Matthew, much the same story is related as in the Book of Mark, except that Judas is identified as the betrayer (Mt 26:17-30).

In the Book of Luke, the two Disciples whom Jesus sends to help prepare the chamber for the last supper are identified as Peter and John (likely the son of Zebedee) (Lk 22:8). During the supper the ceremony of communion is introduced, and Jesus states that one of the Disciples who is breaking bread with them will betray him.

[22:19]And he took bread, and when he had given thanks, he brake it, and gave to them, saying, This is my body which is given for you: this do in remembrance of me. [22:20]And the cup in like manner after supper, saying, This cup is the new covenant in my blood, *even* that which is poured out for you. [22:21]But behold, the hand of him that betrayeth me is with me on the table. (Lk)

The Disciples want to know who the betrayer will be. Getting no answer from Jesus the conversation then turns to who among them is the "greatest" Disciple (Lk 22:24). Jesus chided the Disciples, even going so far as to tell Simon Peter that "Satan asked to have you, that he might sift you as wheat" (Lk 22:31). Upon Peter's protest, Jesus said "I tell thee, Peter, the cock shall not crow this day, until thou shalt thrice deny that thou knowest me" (Lk 22:34). Jesus then led his Disciples out of house, out of Jerusalem, and on to the Mount of Olives. Peter's denial did, in fact, occur later on in the early pre-dawn hours as Jesus predicted.

In the Book of John, it is not clear where the site of the last supper is. We assume it is in Jerusalem because after it Jesus leads the Disciples across the Kidron Valley and into a garden area — presumably Gethsemane on the Mount of Olives.

Immediately before the last supper in the Book of John, Jesus washes the feet of the Disciples. Some of the Disciples protest this action. Jesus answers:

> [13:13]Ye call me, Teacher, and, Lord: and ye say well; for so I am. [13:14]If I then, the Lord and the Teacher, have washed your feet, ye also ought to wash one another's feet. [13:15]For I have given you an example, that ye also should do as I have done to you. [13:16]Verily, verily, I say unto you, a servant is not greater than his lord; neither one that is sent greater than he that sent him. (Jn)

During the course of the meal, Jesus talks a considerable amount. In fact, in the Book of John, Jesus' pontifications take up four chapters of John's 21 total chapters. During this discourse, Jesus identifies Judas as the betrayer. Soon after, Judas leaves the supper chamber to seek out the chief priests.

While the Synoptic Gospels describe the communion ceremony as first occurring during this last supper, in the Book of John this is not the case. Indeed, in John, the communion did not take place at all. The ceremony had been introduced six months earlier. At that time, Jesus was in Galilee and was soon to leave for the Jerusalem feast of the Tabernacles of A.D. 35.

> [6:48]I am the bread of life. [6:49]Your fathers ate the manna in the wilderness, and they died. [6:50]This is the bread which cometh down out of heaven, that a man may eat thereof, and not die. [6:51]I am the living bread which came down out of heaven: if any man eat of this bread, he shall live for ever: yea and the bread which I will give is my flesh, for the life of the world. [6:52]The Jews therefore strove one with another, saying, How can this man give us his flesh to eat? [6:53]Jesus therefore said unto them, Verily, verily, I say unto you, Except ye eat the flesh of the Son of man and drink his blood, ye have not life in yourselves. [6:54]He that eateth my flesh and drinketh my blood hath eternal life: and I will raise him up at the last day. [6:55]For my flesh is meat indeed, and my blood is drink indeed. [6:56]He that eateth my flesh and drinketh my blood abideth in me, and I in him. (Jn)

The shock of this ceremony with its suggestion of cannibalism caused many disciples to abandon Jesus' Ministry that very day.

^{6:66}Upon this many of his disciples went back, and walked no more with him. (Jn 6:66)

As shall be seen, this negative perception of the communion ceremony–deserved or not–would later cause huge problems for the early Christians.

All of the Gospels considered, it can be concluded that the house of the last supper was probably owned by a wealthy "secret" disciple of Jesus–one who also knew and had connections with Caiaphas and the High Priesthood. That a measure of secrecy was necessary indicates that house of the last supper was located in the upper city — perhaps close to the residential compounds of Ananus and Caiaphas.

To the Garden

After the supper, Jesus leads his Disciples out of the house, through the streets of Jerusalem, through the Dung Gate, and down into the Kidron Valley. For months, Jesus had been preaching in the outer courtyard of the Second Temple. Usually, this would occur in the relative cool of the morning. Jesus would then retreat across the Kidron Brook to the Garden of Gethsemane in the late afternoon for meditation and prayer. Sometimes, Jesus would spend the night in the gardens instead of walking back to Bethany. Likely, Jesus was becoming so popular that people would constantly seek him out for his healing powers and his words of wisdom. In Gethsemane, Jesus could find peace and solitude and his Disciples could serve as guards. After Jesus' "last" supper, he decided to sleep in Gethsemane.

Bethany was on the other side of the Mount of Olives and "fifteen furlongs" (Jn 11:18) away from Jerusalem. This is about a two-mile distance which involved navigating a steep descent from Jerusalem into the Kidron Valley and an equally steep ascent up the side of the Mount of Olives. The trek would then either continue to the east and over the mountain ridge to Bethany, or follow a more level path though longer path around the south face of the mountain. For the hardy people of those times neither route was particularly formidable.

For the Passover, Bethany and the surrounding area would have been packed with pilgrims. Perhaps many of them had placed themselves near the road to Bethany just to get a glimpse of Jesus. How many sick and ill people were hoping to touch Jesus and so be cured of their afflictions? Jesus knew that if he appeared in Bethany–even after dark–he would precipitate pandemonium. Also, by then the warrant from the High Priest had gone out for Jesus' arrest. Far better for Jesus to stay in the country than to risk a confrontation with potential bounty hunters.

The Dung Gate of the ancient wall of Jerusalem was located to the south of the great Temple with the main road from it meandering down into the Kidron Valley. Then, crossing the brook, the road switch-backed up the steep slope of Mount of Olives. At some point, or perhaps at several points, a road or path would peel off north into the agricultural areas of the mountain–largely tree orchards, hillside pastures, and terraced plots of tilled earth. This was presumably where the Garden of Gethsemane was located. After the last supper and the city of Jerusalem, Jesus and his Disciples went first unto the Mount of Olives, and then to Gethsemane (Mk 26:30; 26:36; Mt 26:30; 26:36).

The Roman legions under General Titus in A.D. 70 obliterated the northern portion of the Kidron Valley years later. They had filled it in with rocks and debris–as the army had done to many other rough and militarily inconvenient features around the northern approaches to Jerusalem. The accepted current placement of the Garden of Gethsemane on the Mount of Olives is south of where Titus had one of his camps, but it is possible that the true site lies more north and buried under tons of Roman-placed rubble.

The Passover was a celebration carefully timed by the High Priesthood to follow the growing season. This was so the "first fruits" day of the Passover would prove to be a bountiful one. An added benefit was that after the fresh harvest, the owners of the tree groves and other agricultural areas or pasture lands would then open their properties to pilgrim campers. It was customary that these landowners would not charge for the campsites. This was their way of giving thanks to God for a prosperous year and to insure a prosperous upcoming year. Jesus and the Disciples had gone to this area in Gethsemane many times before, so perhaps Jesus had an arrangement with the landowner. At any rate, on the way to their campsite, Jesus and his Disciples would have passed thousands of other people sleeping by fading campfires in makeshift settlements close to the road.

Arrest and Interrogation

In the Garden of Gethsemane, Jesus could not sleep, anticipating his arrest. He prayed off by himself while his Disciples slept nearby. Jesus was discovering, to his dismay, that he was not as strong-willed as he thought. As the Bible documents, Jesus was fearful of what was to come (Lk 22:44; Mk 14:38). If Jesus was an Essene, he knew he had a quite a tradition to uphold. In similar situations, the Essenes were known to endure severe torture to the point of death without compromise. Would Jesus be able to do the same?!

The armed mob eventually came in the night with Judas leading them. Jesus was identified by the light of the campfire. After a brief show of force by the Disciples–which Jesus repudiated–Jesus was arrested and bound. With most of his Disciples fleeing, Jesus was brought back by the mob into the upper city of Jerusalem, likely over the same route he and his Disciples had taken away Jerusalem just hours before.

Jesus, now a prisoner, was led through the gates of Jerusalem and up into the wealthy residential area of the upper city where most in the High Priesthood had their homes. This neighborhood was probably very close to the house where Jesus had just held his last supper and communion. The most luxurious of the three-story dwellings would have been in walled-off compounds composed of several houses. Access would be through guarded gates with many having garden-like courtyards in the center.

In one of the largest of these compounds, Ananus, the elder former High Priest, had his house and was waiting to talk to Jesus–having been alerted hours before to Jesus' likely arrest. Brought inside through the courtyard and still bound, Jesus was questioned by Ananus (Jn 18:13).

High Priest Joseph Caiaphas would have had a house within the same walled compound. Both Caiaphas and Ananus were important, wealthy men. Their families would have lived close to each other — not only because they were related but for purposes of safety and convenience. The family of Ananus had dominated Jerusalem for so long that likely Ananus had built within the complex a meeting place for the Sanhedrin. Indeed, Caiaphas' courtyard was where Peter found himself after following Jesus after his arrest at Gethsemane.

> 26:57 And they that had taken Jesus led him away to *the house of* Caiaphas the high priest, where the scribes and the elders were gathered together. 26:58 But Peter followed him afar off, unto the court of the high priest, and entered in, and sat with the officers, to see the end. (Mt)

> And Peter had followed him afar off, even within, into the court of the high priest; and he was sitting with the officers, and warming himself in the light *of the fire*. (Mk 14:54)

It was here, during the hours spent waiting for news of Jesus' fate, that the Disciple Peter denied knowing Jesus to several people who thought Peter looked and dressed like a Galilean. A roughly-dressed Galilean in the heart of the courtyard of the High Priest Caiaphas would have been an unusual sight.

> 18:12 So the band and the chief captain, and the officers of the Jews, seized Jesus and bound him, 18:13 and led him to Annas first; for he was father in law to Caiaphas, who was high priest that year. (Jn)

Ananus interrogated Jesus first. Jesus' responses were guarded and unenlightening. Ananus was disappointed. Jesus was certainly no Messiah, but on the other hand Ananus found no reason to believe that Jesus was a zealot troublemaker either, as Caiaphas was so certain of.

During the questioning of Jesus by Ananus, which is found only in the Book of John, a guard strikes Jesus across the mouth when his answers are thought to be haughty and disrespectful.

> 18:19The high priest therefore asked Jesus of his disciples, and of his teaching. 18:20Jesus answered him, I have spoken openly to the world; I ever taught in synagogues, and in the temple, where all the Jews come together; and in secret spake I nothing. 18:21Why askest thou me? Ask them that have heard *me*, what I spake unto them: behold, these know the things which I said. 18:22And when he had said this, one of the officers standing by struck Jesus with his hand, saying, Answerest thou the high priest so? 18:23Jesus answered him, If I have spoken evil, bear witness of the evil: but if well, why smitest thou me? 18:24Annas therefore sent him bound unto Caiaphas the high priest. (Jn)

Ananus, finished with his questioning of Jesus, then ordered the guards to take Jesus to a nearby basement cell, possibly an empty cistern or storage vault. Ananus then retired for the evening. He was not interested in the trial. The disposition of Jesus was now in the hands of Caiaphas.

Trial by Sanhedrin?

Several hours later enough of the Sanhedrin had gathered in the Caiaphas compound for the trial to commence. The Gospels are not consistent on when the trial occurred–whether at night or early the next morning–, or whether it occurred at all. It should be noted that Jerusalem Sanhedrin is not directly referred to in any of the Gospels; instead, the word "council" is used. As has been speculated, the council could well have been an executive committee of the Sanhedrin whose purpose was to deal with emergency Passover situations like this one. Certainly, the entire 70-member Sanhedrin would be difficult and unwieldy to assemble on such short notice.

The Book of Mark gives a succinct summary of Jesus' time spent before the High Priesthood and this religious council.

14:55Now the chief priests and the whole council sought witness against Jesus to put him to death; and found it not. 14:56For many bare false witness against him, and their witness agreed not together. 14:57And there stood up certain, and bare false witness against him, saying, 14:58We heard him say, I will destroy this temple that is made with hands, and in three days I will build another made without hands. 14:59And not even so did their witness agree together. (Mk)

According to the Book of Mark, this was quite a production. The reference to "whole council" suggests that, indeed, the entire 70-member Sanhedrin was present. During the course of it High Priest Joseph Caiaphas provided the council with false witnesses in his zeal to convict Jesus. Eager to please the powerful Caiaphas, there were probably many volunteers willing to perjure themselves. But the Sanhedrin would not have appreciated the witnesses' obvious false testimony–did Caiaphas really have so little respect for them?! In the end, the bound Jesus did not present an imposing or threatening figure, so the council declined to convict him.

And straightway in the morning the chief priests with the elders and scribes, and the whole council, held a consultation, and bound Jesus, and carried him away, and delivered him up to Pilate. (Mk 15:1)

The Book of Matthew agrees with the account in Mark.

26:59Now the chief priests and the whole council sought false witness against Jesus, that they might put him to death; 26:60and they found it not, though many false witnesses came. But afterward came two, 26:61and said, This man said, I am able to destroy the temple of God, and to build it in three days. (Mt)

According to the Book of Matthew, Jesus was physically abused during the examination with the High Priest present.

26:67Then did they spit in his face and buffet him: and some smote him with the palms of their hands, 26:68saying, Prophesy unto us, thou Christ: who is he that struck thee? (Mt)

As in the Book of Mark, the assembled council made a decision when morning came.

27:1Now when morning was come, all the chief priests and the elders of the people took counsel against Jesus to put him to death: 27:2and they bound him, and led him away, and delivered him up to Pilate the governor. (Mt)

The Sanhedrin of Jerusalem had the authority to order stoned to death anyone who claimed divine status, as Jesus had been accused. But the council declined to do so. Was the Sanhedrin fearful of ordering the mob to kill Jesus? Did they think the mob would instead turn against them? Was this the trap that Jesus had laid for them? Better to send Jesus on to Pilate for the actual execution!

The Book of Luke describes an abbreviated "assembly of the elders" that took place early in the morning after Jesus had been roughly handled by his captors. Again, there is no reference to the formal Sanhedrin.

22:63And the men that held *Jesus* mocked him, and beat him. 22:64And they blindfolded him, and asked him, saying, Prophesy: who is he that struck thee? 22:65And many other things spake they against him, reviling him. 22:66And as soon as it was day, the assembly of the elders of the people was gathered together, both chief priests and scribes; and they led him away into their council, saying, 22:67If thou art the Christ, tell us. But he said unto them, If I tell you, ye will not believe: 22:68and if I ask *you*, ye will not answer. 22:69But from henceforth shall the Son of man be seated at the right hand of the power of God. 22:70And they all said, Art thou then the Son of God? And he said unto them, Ye say that I am. 22:71And they said, What further need have we of witness? for we ourselves have heard from his own mouth. (Lk)

And the whole company of them rose up, and brought him before Pilate. (Lk 23:1)

The Book of John is the most veracious source on several issues concerning Jesus, but in it neither the Sanhedrin nor any formal religious council is mentioned. Jesus is, however, questioned at different times by both Ananus and Caiaphas. At daybreak, Jesus is then brought before Pilate. Significantly, the author of John–perhaps John the Evangelist–might have been a member of the High Priesthood himself. If the Sanhedrin was involved at all, John the Evangelist would have surely known about it. So it can be very reasonably argued that Ananus and Caiaphas wanted to avoid a trial by Sanhedrin–knowing that on the council Jesus had his supporters. The quickest and surest way to Jesus' death was through Pilate.

The Secret Disciples

The Book of John tells us that many of Jerusalem's "rulers" were secret believers in Jesus.

> Nevertheless even of the rulers many believed on him; but because of the Pharisees they did not confess it, lest they should be put out of the synagogue: (Jn 12:42)

Jewish life in Jerusalem revolved around religion and by extension the Second Temple. Being "put out" of the synagogue would mean a slow but certain spiritual death to any devout Jew.

Nicodemus was a member of the Sanhedrin in A.D. 36. Surely, at least he would have been a voice against Jesus' execution if there was a formal trial.

> 3:1Now there was a man of the Pharisees, named Nicodemus, a ruler of the Jews: 3:2the same came unto him by night, and said to him, Rabbi, we know that thou art a teacher come from God; for no one can do these signs that thou doest, except God be with him (Jn)

That the Sanhedrin of A.D. 36 was composed of sober, reasonable individuals unlikely to convict Jesus is also suggested by a story in Acts. The Disciples Peter and John only months after Jesus' crucifixion were arrested for preaching and healing in the Second Temple courtyard. Gamaliel spoke in their defense.

Gamaliel was a powerful member of the Sanhedrin at the time. He was a Pharisee as well as a doctor of Jewish law. The

Sanhedrin's examination of Peter and John occurred very soon after the Pentecost of A.D. 36 and the "miracle of the tongues"which emboldened all of the Nazarenes.

> .[5:35]And he (Gamaliel) said unto them...[5:38]And now I say unto you, Refrain from these men, and let them alone: for if this counsel or this work be of men, it will be overthrown: [5:39]but if it is of God, ye will not be able to overthrow them; lest haply ye be found even to be fighting against God (Acts)

So Caiaphas had several reasons to avoid a trial of Jesus before the Sanhedrin. For one, Jesus' conviction would not have been a foregone conclusion. Caiaphas likely knew that some of the Sanhedrin members were secret supporters of Jesus, and that his case against Jesus was a weak one. And even if the Sanhedrin were to convict Jesus, would the public respond to a call by the Sanhedrin for a stoning? A riot against the High Priesthood could easily be the result — given the many Galileans present for the Passover.

More importantly, Caiaphas also knew that if he opened up a Sanhedrin trial process for Jesus, delays might occur. Would the Sanhedrin demand additional witnesses and evidence against Jesus? The more time Jesus spent in a Sanhedrin jail the more likely it would be that the masses would rebel — realizing that their prophet Jesus was in chains. And the powerful Syrian President Lucius Vitellius was due to arrive very soon. He had to find Jerusalem a peaceful city!

Because of these considerations, a good case can be made that no formal Sanhedrin trial of Jesus ever took place — even on an executive committee level.

Chapter 4   The Crucifixion: Pilate's Decision

When Jesus therefore had received the vinegar, he said, It is finished:
and he bowed his head and gave up his spirit. (Jn 19:30)

When the Jerusalem council declined to sentence Jesus to a public
stoning, High Priest Joseph Caiaphas had no choice. He sent
Jesus the few hundred yards away to Judean Prefect Pontius
Pilate, who was staying in Herod's palace for the Passover.
Caiaphas changed the charge against Jesus from religious
sedition to civil sedition–crimes against Caesar! This brought
Jesus under Pilate's jurisdiction and bypassed Jewish law.

Witnesses were prepared to testify that Jesus claimed to be the
"king" of the Jews. This was political sedition of the highest
order and, if convicted, crucifixion by the Romans would be
mandatory.

Pilate was still in the shadow of the executed conspirator
General Lucius Sejanus—he needed the backing of the High
Priesthood now more than ever. Syrian President Lucius Vitellius
was perhaps very close to arriving in Jerusalem from Caesarea.
His trip had not been publicized, but word was now getting out
amongst the population. Vitellius was obviously making an
appearance to ease the fears of the Jews over Antipas' recent
defeat by the Arabs. There was a chance that he might remove
Pontius Pilate as prefect as well.

Antipas was currently in Jerusalem and would have no kind
words for Vitellius concerning Pilate. Trouble and unrest in
Jerusalem when Vitellius arrived was the last thing Pilate—and

Caiaphas — wanted. Important, too, was the fact that Pilate had become wealthy off graft from Temple operations. In exchange, Caiaphas expected Pilate to do his bidding and ask few questions. So, after giving explicit instructions to his chief priests, a confident Caiaphas either went off to bed after what had been a very long night, or left to attend to his morning Temple duties as High Priest.

Place of Judgment

The palace built by Herod the Great was located just to the north of the upper city residential neighborhood of the High Priesthood and west of the Second Temple. Herod's palace was 15 acres in area and surrounded by a 40-foot wall with turreted guard towers spaced every 200 feet. There, Pilate, his wife, and his personal escort of Roman soldiers were staying. Herod Antipas, the tetrarch of Galilee, was also staying at the palace in one of the three towers along with his wife Herodias and probably Herodias' daughter Salome. Vitellius was almost certainly going to stay in one of the remaining luxury towers when he arrived.

Two areas are prominently mentioned in the New Testament regarding Jesus' Roman "trial." One was the Praetorium which was an armory-type structure. Used for military purposes and also serving as a soldier barracks and prison, this is where the Gospels say Jesus was interrogated and scourged by Pilate. Also mentioned is the Gabbatha which was an open place where the Gospels say Pilate set down his judgment seat to hear the charges against Jesus.

According to both the Books of John and Mark, Jesus was first brought to the Praetorium for examination by Pilate. The chief priests, after explaining Jesus' alleged crimes to Pilate, stayed outside the palace walls.

[18:28]They lead Jesus therefore from Caiaphas into the Praetorium: and it was early; and they themselves entered not into the Praetorium, that they might not be defiled, but might eat the passover. [18:29]Pilate

therefore went out unto them and saith, What accusation bring ye against this man? (Jn 18:28-29)
And the soldiers led him away within the court which is the Praetorium; and they call together the whole band. (Mk 15:16)

When Pilate therefore heard these words, he brought Jesus out and sat down on the judgment-seat at a place called The Pavement, but in Hebrew, Gabbatha. (Jn 19:13)

From the passages, it can be concluded that Pilate had his quarters very close to the Praetorium. Every province of the empire important enough to merit an administrative prefect or governor had its own Praetorium. The fact that some of the chief priests did not enter the Praetorium is consistent with the Praetorium being a part of Herod's palace complex. The palace of Herod was considered by the Jews to be unclean. In diplomatic terms, it was considered a part of Rome.

In order to speak to the chief priests who had brought Jesus, Pilate consented to leave the palace grounds so the priests could be kept pure. The priests and Temple guards with the bound Jesus waited at the Gabbatha, a public area which we can now assume to be just outside the main palace gate. This gate was probably located at the southeast corner of the palace walls, close to the Temple and the adjoining commercial area. After hearing the charges, Pilate ordered Jesus brought inside.

Pilate went out again and saith unto them, Behold, I bring him out to you, that ye may know that I find no crime in him Jesus therefore came out, wearing the crown of thorns and the purple garment. (Jn 19:4-5).

Pilate went back inside the gates of Herod's palace to talk with Jesus, and then returned outside to the chief priests, who were waiting at the Gabbatha, on at least two separate occasions. When a trial was finally thought necessary, Pilate's judgment chair was brought out and set up in the Gabbatha.

The following selection from *Wars* is the strongest evidence that Pilate's interrogation and trial of Jesus took place in or near Herod's palace.

> Now at this time Florus took up his quarters at the palace; and on the next day he had his tribunal set before it and sat upon it, when the high priests and the men of power and those of the greatest eminence in the city, came all before that tribunal; (*Wars* II 14:8)

Procurator Flores served from A.D. 64-66. From the above excerpt, Flores had his own separate quarters in Herod's palace. It is a safe assumption that Pilate, when his job required him to stay in Jerusalem, lived there as well.

Also in this passage, the tribunal chair (judgment seat) was "set before" the palace for Flores to use. Was this area the Gabbatha? The Gabbatha was a public area but convenient to where both Flores and Pilate lived when they were in Jerusalem (though the governors lived in Caesarea most of the time). The Gabbatha was outside of the the unholy area of the palace, but for security reasons would logically be situated near the weapons and soldiers of the Praetorium should there be trouble.

The Tower of Antonia

Tradition has it that the Praetorium was a part of the tower of Antonia and the Gabbatha was just outside of it, but this popular assumption is not supported by the ancient sources. Nowhere is it documented that Antonia was unclean to purified Jews as the Praetorium is stated to be. On the contrary, a special cloister linked Antonia with the outer courtyard of the Second Temple. In fact, the mystical ceremonial garb of the High Priest was even sequestered by the Romans under lock and key in the tower of Antonia.

Would Pilate have lived at Antonia instead of Herod's palace when he was in Jerusalem? Certainly, the castle had room enough, but Pilate would have stayed in the vastly more sumptuous Herod's palace–especially for the duration of the Passover. Just the noise alone from the hundreds of thousands of pilgrims in the Temple's outer courtyard would have been a determining factor. Would Pilate–or any high Roman official–want to live close to such a ruckus? Apart from the noise, during the times of sacrifice, the acrid smoke from the altar fires would been very strong. During the major festivals, Antonia would be a very unpleasant place to stay.

Antonia was built out of the north wall of the Temple and was designed for the use of the soldiers and Temple guards, as well as a storehouse for supplies needed in times of war. The ancient literature does not suggest that trials were held within Antonia. Plus, by all the evidence, Antonia could only be accessed from the Second Temple courtyard.

The Tribunal Chair

Roman justice in the provinces had to be necessarily expeditious and mobile. Wherever the Roman prefect–or procurator–decided to hold a trial, his tribunal chair (or judgment seat) was set up and the trial commenced. The chair was the symbol of Roman power and authority.

In an incident years earlier, Pilate held a trial of sorts for Jewish petitioners in Caesarea. In that circumstance, the Jews objected to the effigies that Pilate had ordered placed in Jerusalem. Pilate then placed his tribunal chair in an "open place" of the city of Caesarea. An "open place" to Josephus likely meant some sort of public plaza where many people had room to congregate and could legally do so.

> while he (Pilate) came and sat upon his judgment-seat which seat was so prepared in the open place of the city (*Antiq* XVIII 3:1)

Pilate always kept this chair near him–no matter to where he traveled. Wherever the chair was "prepared" (assembled?) defined the place of judgment and not the other way around. This made perfect sense in a society where travel was difficult. Most times, it was far easier for the magistrate (or tetrarch or prefect) to travel to where the crime occurred in order to hold the trial, than to have all the witnesses and interested parties travel to where the magistrate happened to be. Additionally, before the trial the magistrate or prefect could do his own investigation as much as he cared to. This Roman provincial justice system had evolved over centuries, and it worked well.

A major part of Herod the Great's duties as king–as with any king–was to settle disputes. He built his palace partially with that in mind. Certainly Herod, the epitome of the paranoid king, mainly constructed his palace to serve as a stronghold and a place able to withstand a lengthy siege. But a strong secondary consideration would have been the administration of law. Within the palace walls would have been an area set aside for trials and perhaps even a place for the punishment of the guilty. This building would have been in the "business" end of the palace grounds and probably what the Gospels called the Praetorium. The Praetorium "complex" would have also held the elite soldiers' quarters, military training and exercise areas and storehouses for weapons and other articles of war. Perhaps early in Herod the Great's reign, the Jews protested that the ground inside of his palace was Romanized and not holy. In order to be accommodating–which he was upon occasion early on–Herod would have moved the Jewish trials a short distance outside the walls to the Gabbatha.

Another point to consider: would Herod the Great have bothered to walk all the way to the tower of Antonia to judge the accused? Not likely, even though he had constructed a private elevated walkway that led from the ramparts of the palace wall to a dedicated Second Temple gate. In fact, due to his unpopularity with the people — especially at the end of his reign — Herod the Great probably avoided the Second Temple as much as possible. Pilate, no friend of the Jews, would have felt the same way.

Pilate in Mark

Sent from Caiaphas in the early morning, Pilate obligingly saw Jesus. Any request from the High Priest was to be taken seriously and addressed promptly–even one so early in the day. Pilate wanted no trouble this Passover–Vitellius would be arriving at any time (as we have postulated).

The Book of Mark quotes Pilate extensively during the day of Jesus' execution. Was there an eyewitness later interviewed by Mark who provided the details? Remember, according to Christian legend, Mark (John Mark) was a disciple of Peter the Apostle, who was the prime source for Mark's Gospel. Peter was in the courtyard of Caiaphas at night when Jesus was first held prisoner. It would have been logical for him to have followed Jesus to Herod's palace for the interrogations – standing outside the gates as events unfolded. Perhaps the gathered crowd got first-hand reports from accommodating Roman soldiers as to the verbal exchange between Pilate and Jesus in the Praetorium.

At any rate, outside of the palace gates in the early morning with Jesus standing in front of him, Pilate would have quickly determined that Jesus was no threat. Jesus was in his late forties and tired from having had no sleep. He would have been viewed by Pilate as a singularly unimpressive warrior-zealot Messiah– and certainly no king of the Jews. And where were the followers of the "king" who posed such a threat to Rome?!

> For he (Pilate) perceived that for envy the chief priests had delivered him up.(Mk 15:10)

It was a custom, however, for the Romans to release a prisoner each Passover as a token of goodwill toward the Jews. To test the resolve of the chief priests, and perhaps to irritate them, Pilate proposed to designate Jesus as this fortunate prisoner. Otherwise, Pilate said, he had no choice but to release Barabbas.

Barabbas was a notorious murderer, probably the worst in the palace prison. Given Pilate's twisted sense of humor, Barabbas had likely targeted only wealthy Jews in his crimes – as many criminal zealots did. The justification was that their Jewish victims had gained their wealth through collaboration with the Romans–which was true in many cases. But the danger and threat of a freed Barabbas did not matter to the chief priests; they had been instructed by Caiaphas in no uncertain terms that Jesus had to be executed.

15:15And Pilate, wishing to content the multitude, released unto them Barabbas and delivered Jesus, when he had scourged him, to be crucified. 15:16And the soldiers led him away within the court which is the Praetorium; and they call together the whole band. 15:17And they clothe him with purple and platting a crown of thorns, they put it on him; 15:18and they began to salute him, Hail, King of the Jews! 15:19And they smote his head with a reed and spat upon him and bowing their knees worshipped him. 15:20And when they had mocked him, they took off from him the purple and put on him his garments. And they lead him out to crucify him. (Mk)

For a capital crime, both Caiaphas and Pilate acted extraordinarily quickly against Jesus, even though Pilate feigned reluctance. This makes sense during the Passover of A.D. 36, when neither man wanted to stir up the mob–a mob that might rally to Jesus' rescue if given the chance. Considering that Lucius Vitellius, the supreme Roman commander in the East, was due to arrive in Jerusalem at any time, the haste of both men makes added sense.

Pilate must have been especially perturbed and irritated over Jesus' arriving at the palace gates. The act would have been incredibly inconsiderate of Caiaphas, unless Pilate had been forewarned by Caiaphas and a plan had been agreed to.

Pilate in Matthew

The Book of Matthew gives us a degree of detail during Jesus' Roman trial that almost suggests embellishment. After questioning Jesus, Pilate doubts Jesus is guilty of anything but the chief priests insist upon execution. Pilate offers them a choice between releasing a "notable" prisoner called Barabbas, or Jesus. The assembled crowd chooses Jesus.

27:24So when Pilate saw that he prevailed nothing, but rather that a tumult was arising, he took water and washed his hands before the multitude, saying, I am innocent of the blood of this righteous man; see ye to it. 27:25And all the people answered and said, His blood be on us and on our children. 27:26Then released he unto them Barabbas; but Jesus he scourged and delivered to be crucified. (Mt)

All this occurs while Pilate is on his judgment seat, presumably outside the palace walls in the Gabbatha. After Pilate's verdict, Jesus is taken into the palace grounds.

[27:27]Then the soldiers of the governor took Jesus into the Praetorium and gathered unto him the whole band. [27:28]And they stripped him and put on him a scarlet robe. [27:29]And they platted a crown of thorns and put it upon his head and a reed in his right hand; and they kneeled down before him and mocked him, saying, Hail, King of the Jews! [27:30]And they spat upon him and took the reed and smote him on the head. [27:31]And when they had mocked him, they took off from him the robe and put on him his garments and led him away to crucify him. (Mt)

Jesus was then led to Golgotha with Simon of Cyrene compelled to carry Jesus' cross (Mt 27:32). Cyrene, formerly a north African Greek colony, was a Roman province.

Pilate and Antipas in Luke

In the Book of Luke, before his final judgment Pilate turned Jesus over to the Galilean Tetrarch Herod Antipas. This is the only Gospel that documents Antipas being in Jerusalem for the Passover of A.D. 36.

And when he (Pilate) knew that he (Jesus) was of Herod's jurisdiction, he sent him unto Herod, who himself also was at Jerusalem in these days. (Lk)

Admittedly, in the Book of Acts, Peter the Apostle states that Herod Antipas was at the Passover of A.D. 36 along with Pilate and involved in the judging of Jesus. But this is not really an independent corroboration, as both books were written by the same person.

[4:27]for of a truth in this city against thy holy Servant Jesus, whom thou didst anoint, both Herod and Pontius Pilate, with the Gentiles and the peoples of Israel, were gathered together, [4:28]to do whatsoever thy hand and thy council foreordained to come to pass. (Acts)

Pilate's sending of the prisoner Jesus to Herod Antipas was actually a brilliant move by the beleaguered prefect. Just as Caiaphas sent Jesus to Pilate, so Pilate would turn over Jesus to Antipas. But this act of Pilate's was not without some justification. Jesus was a Galilean Jew, after all, so it would be logical to have him judged by the Galilean Tetrarch Herod Antipas. If Herod was agreeable to see Jesus and assume the disposition of him, Pilate would get out of a thorny situation with relative ease.

Herod Antipas and his entourage were probably staying only a short distance away in one of the towers of Herod's palace. Pilate had the option of staying in any of the three opulent high-rise residences; all were spacious, had panoramic vistas of the surrounding city and country, and had roof-top gardens among many other amenities. Pilate himself probably stayed in one of the two apartments closer to the Praetorium and the palace's main gates. The three towers were most likely reserved for important guests, such as Roman officials used to luxury and who might need the protection afforded by the soldiers and the palace walls. Many of the elite Roman and Galilean soldiers likely camped out on the expansive palace grounds.

On the morning of the day of Preparation, after a brief examination, Pontius Pilate sent Jesus across the palace grounds to Antipas' quarters. Jesus would have been accompanied by several Roman soldiers as well as several of the chief priests who were forced to break purity.

Pontius Pilate and Herod Antipas were hardly friends, though they were civil enough to each other as their positions required. Antipas was probably being reclusive in his palace tower this Passover, awaiting with anticipation the arrival of Lucius Vitellius from Antioch. Antipas was well aware that the common people hated him even more so than usual, and he would have avoided public areas as much as possible. Thousands of Galilean soldiers had been killed in Antipas' ill-conceived military adventure into Nabotea only six months before. Antipas, in fact, was likely only in Jerusalem on the command of Vitellius.

Otherwise, he would have been sulking in his lakeside city of Tiberias.

Antipas also had reason be cool towards Pilate. Only a few years before, Pilate had punished those who rioted in Jerusalem over Pilate's aqueduct project; many of those slain were from Galilee. While more freshwater to Jerusalem would have been a benefit to all, to finance it Pilate allegedly wanted to use the holy Corban money that was stored up in the Sanctuary building of the Second Temple. The Jews protested and there were riots in the city over it. In the Book of Luke, Peter the Apostle talks of an instance, possibly related to the aqueduct affair, where Galilean blood was shed in Jerusalem on the orders of Pilate.

> [13:1]Now there were some present at that very season who told him of the Galilaeans, whose blood Pilate had mingled with their sacrifices.(Lk)

Antipas would not have been pleased that his subjects would have been so abused.

So Pilate's deference to Antipas over Jesus' disposition served a double purpose. Antipas–ostensibly Jewish himself–would be able to play a role in the trial of one of his own Jewish Galilean subjects. Additionally, through the gesture, Pilate would give a signal to Antipas that he respected and trusted his judgment as a fellow ruler. Perhaps, too, Pilate was told of Jesus' reputation as a prophet and healer. Herod Antipas had a well-known fascination with astrology and fortunetelling, and Pilate might have suspected that Antipas would appreciate a meeting with Jesus simply for that reason alone.

To Pilate, it was a perfect solution to a tough problem. No matter what the outcome with Antipas, Pilate would gain. In the best case scenario, Antipas would remove Jesus to Tiberias in Galilee for a more formal trial. If, on the other hand, Antipas immediately determined Jesus to be guilty of a capital offense, Pilate would have Jesus crucified. Even if Antipas sent Jesus back to Pilate without an opinion, the tetrarch could not later say that he had not been involved. In that case, Antipas couldn't avoid sharing some of the responsibility for any repercussions that might come from Pilate's ultimate decision of this "king" of the Jews.

Interlude: Questioning by Antipas

On that day of Preparation, Antipas was in a generally good mood; perhaps he had heard that Vitellius would be arriving that day. The Roman General Vitellius was to be Antipas' avenging Angel against King Aretas IV–it had been so ordered by Emperor Tiberius, after all! As Pilate had anticipated, Antipas was pleasantly surprised when Jesus showed up in the garden of his sumptuous tower complex, accompanied by several Roman soldiers and chief priests. Antipas had heard of Jesus and was delighted to be able to finally see and talk with him. Jesus had a growing reputation as a miracle worker in Galilee.

> 23:8Now when Herod saw Jesus, he was exceeding glad: for he was of a long time desirous to see him, because he had heard concerning him; and he hoped to see some miracle done by him. 23:9And he questioned him in many words; but he answered him nothing. 23:10And the chief priests and the scribes stood, vehemently accusing him. 23:11And Herod with his soldiers set him at nought and mocked him and arraying him in gorgeous apparel sent him back to Pilate. 23:12And Herod and Pilate became friends with each other that very day: for before they were at enmity between themselves. (Lk 23:8-12)

Both Herodias and Salome were probably with Herod Antipas in Jerusalem for the festival. The Passover was the most important social event of the year, as well as being the most important religious event. Also, it was very possible that Herodias' brother Aristobulos would be accompanying Vitellius to Jerusalem. Possibly, too, Cypros, the wife of Herodias' brother Herod Agrippa, was staying at the tower with her three children.

Herodias was probably more restrained about the situation, thinking that nothing good could come from it, especially if she knew that Jesus was the cousin of John the Baptist. Herodias was still suffering from the well-deserved perception that she had caused the prophet's death. Was she avoiding the Jerusalem crowds as well for that reason?

Antipas was totally in love with the younger Herodias and probably did nothing of consequence without her by his side. Was Herodias with Antipas when Jesus was brought to him? Salome was perhaps also present and looked on with bored disinterest as Jesus was roughly escorted into the tower entrance hall. Cypros could also have been there.

As the Roman guards watched, Antipas and perhaps Herodias, asked Jesus questions. Jesus' responses were uniformly unremarkable and monotonic, as they had been when questioned by Ananus hours earlier and later in front of Pontius Pilate. The chief priests were appropriately respectful toward the tetrarch, but they made sure that the witnesses–if they were present–told their stories of Jesus' seditious statements and alleged revolutionary plans against Rome and Caesar.

Despite the show, Antipas, too, was unimpressed with Jesus.. Disappointed, he soon ran out of questions to ask. Now what? Antipas saw no advantage in getting further involved and decided that the Galilean would be sent back to Pilate without judgment.

But Antipas also recognized the symbolic meaning in Pilate's sending of Jesus over to him. It was a peace offering and not to be taken lightly. Before returning Jesus to Pilate, however, Antipas had his soldiers clothe Jesus in one of his own expensive Royal purple robes and paraded about the grounds as if in a Royal procession. Were Herodias and Salome amused at this? Was it done to amuse the three young children of Cypros? At any rate, sfter tiring of making sport of Jesus, Antipas sent him back to Pilate, still clothed in purple.

The other three Gospels also have the Roman soldiers dressing Jesus in Royal robes in order to mock him, with the suggestion that the action was on the soldiers' own initiative. But the Book of Luke indicates that Jesus was mistreated and humiliated on the orders of Herod Antipas. In this instance, Luke makes more sense. What would Roman soldiers–or Pilate–be doing with Royal finery so close at hand? In fact, this might be the strongest indication that Luke was quite correct in his story of Herod Antipas' role on Jesus' last day.

Pilate in John

The Book of John details many interesting events about the final day of Jesus. It is from information provided in John that the Praetorium and Gabbatha can be located. Pilate had several conversations with the chief priests sent by Caiaphas that John documents. This necessitated Pilate to walk through the palace gates several times, since the priests could not enter unholy ground. The words from Pilate are detailed and succinct, and the exchange between Pilate and Jesus has a raw and terse power.

> [18:28]They lead Jesus therefore from Caiaphas into the Praetorium: and it was early; and they themselves entered not into the Praetorium, that they might not be defiled, but might eat the passover. [18:29]Pilate therefore went out unto them and saith, What accusation bring ye against this man? [18:30]They answered and said unto him, If this man were not an evildoer, we should not have delivered him up unto thee. [18:31]Pilate therefore said unto them, Take him yourselves and judge him according to your law. The Jews said unto him, It is not lawful for us to put any man to death: [18:32]that the word of Jesus might be fulfilledwhich he spake, signifying by what manner of death he should die. [18:33]Pilate therefore entered again into the Praetorium and called Jesus and said unto him, Art thou the King of the Jews? [18:34]Jesus answered, Sayest thou this of thyself, or did others tell it thee concerning me? [18:35]Pilate answered, Am I a Jew? Thine own nation and the chief priests delivered thee unto me: what hast thou done? [18:36]Jesus answered, My kingdom is not of this world: if my kingdom were of this world, then would my servants fight, that I should not be delivered to the Jews: but now is my kingdom not from hence. [18:37]Pilate therefore said unto him, Art thou a king then? Jesus answered, Thou sayest that I am a king. To this end have I been born and to this end am I come into the world, that I should bear witness unto the truth. Every one that is of the truth heareth my voice. [18:38]Pilate saith unto him, What is truth? And when he had said this, he went out again unto the Jews and saith unto them, I find no crime in him. (Jn 18:28-38)

According to John, Pilate declared three times to the gathered crowd that he found no crime in Jesus. Each time, he was shouted down. Pilate then allowed Jesus to be scourged and mocked by his soldiers, as if that alone would satisfy the crowd.

> [19:1]Then Pilate therefore took Jesus and scourged him. [19:2]And the soldiers platted a crown of thorns and put it on his head and arrayed him in a purple garment; [19:3]and they came unto him and said, Hail, King of the Jews! and they struck him with their hands. (Jn 9:1-3)

Pilate proposed to release Jesus after this severe punishment, but according to the Book of John, the chief priests and the gathered crowd would have none of it. The prefect then ordered his tribunal chair brought outside the palace walls and set up on the Gabbatha.

> [19:12]Upon this Pilate sought to release him: but the Jews cried out, saying, If thou release this man, thou art not Caesar's friend: every one that maketh himself a king speaketh against Caesar. [19:13]When Pilate therefore heard these words, he brought Jesus out and sat down on the judgment-seat at a place called The Pavement, but in Hebrew, Gabbatha. [19:14]Now it was the Preparation of the passover: it was about the sixth hour. And he saith unto the Jews, Behold, your King! [19:15]They therefore cried out, Away with *him*, away with *him*, crucify him! Pilate saith unto them, Shall I crucify your King? The chief priests answered, We have no king but Caesar. [19:16]Then therefore he delivered him unto them to be crucified. (Jn 19:12-16)

According to John, when it appeared that Pilate had finally decided to release Jesus, the crowd, accused the prefect of not being Caesar's "friend." Pilate knew that his job was in jeopardy, so any suggestion that he wasn't loyal to Tiberius had to be taken seriously, even if it meant the execution of an innocent man. Pilate also probably saw few supporters of Jesus in the Gabbatha. Indeed, the Disciple Peter might have been the only one there. The rest of the disciples were either praying in the Temple courtyard or hiding in Bethany in fear for their lives.

Pilate then sentenced Jesus to crucifixion.

Crucifixion

That Pilate crucified Jesus immediately that day suggests that Pilate's initial reticence to convict Jesus was exaggerated, a show put on for the amusement of his soldiers, or completely fabricated. Pilate was fully aware that it was the day of Preparation. At the ninth hour–three o'clock in the afternoon–all those set up on the cross would have to be killed and taken down.

According to John, Jesus was set up at the sixth hour.

> [19:14]Now it was the Preparation of the passover: it was about the sixth hour. And he saith unto the Jews, Behold, your King! [19:15]They therefore cried out, Away with *him*, away with *him*, crucify him! Pilate saith unto them, Shall I crucify your King? The chief priests answered, We have no king but Caesar. (Jn 19:14-15)

In fact, it was likely that Jesus was on the cross far closer to two hours than three.

Crucifixion was a common punishment for civil sedition in the Roman Empire. Some of the men so executed had been known to survive for many days on the cross which further served the purpose of Rome. The crucified were to serve as warnings to others–the longer they stayed "up" the better. For this reason, it would have made more sense for Pilate to hold Jesus in a cell and crucify him on the first day of the week–after the Sabbath day–when the condemned could die slowly over several days and be in the public eye.

The site of Golgotha today is within Church of the Holy Sepulcher. As has been postulated, in ancient times Golgotha would have been located just outside of the first north wall between the tower of Hippicus and the gate of the Essenes. Golgotha was a site that saw many crucifixions, so it was placed close to the 40-foot wall in order to be hidden from view from the palace towers–an important consideration if Romans were staying in one or more of them.

The Gospels themselves give few clues as to the location of Golgotha.

And they bring him unto the place Golgothawhich is, being interpreted, The place of a skull.(Mk 15:22)

Matthew gives us a similar description (Mt 27:33), likely drawn from the same source, as is the case with Luke (Lk 23:33). Even John, the lone non-Synoptic Gospel, gives little more information other than the site was "nigh" (close) to the city.

[19:17]They took Jesus therefore: and he went out, bearing the cross for himself, unto the place called The place of a skullwhich is called in Hebrew, Golgotha: [19:18]where they crucified him and with him two others, on either side one and Jesus in the midst. [19:19]And Pilate wrote a title also and put it on the cross. And there was written, JESUS OF NAZARETH, THE KING OF THE JEWS. [19:20]This title therefore read many of the Jews, for the place where Jesus was crucified was nigh to the city; and it was written in Hebrew and in Latin and in Greek. (Jn 19:17-20)

In Acts, another intriguing possibility is suggested for the crucifixion site. Simon Peter is quoted:

The God of our fathers raised up Jesus, whom ye slew, hanging him on a tree. (Acts 5:30)

Jesus dying on a tree and not a cross would contradict all four Gospels. If a tree were involved, that would move the site of crucifixion from the barren stone quarry to an area north of the upper city, where the agricultural hills began. In one respect, it would fit better, since the groves would be closer to the main northwestern road that linked Jerusalem to Caesarea and Damascus. The Romans liked to place their crucified close to well-traveled roads! But with the weight of all four Gospels against Acts in this instance, the conclusion must be made that the word "tree" in Acts represents an early error in translation.

Therefore, without much additional help from the Gospels, the traditional site of Golgotha–the Church of the Holy Sepulcher– will be considered authentic. And the evidence is strong; careful investigations have found first century A.D. Jewish burial tombs under the Church. Eusebius, the Bishop of the Church of

Caesarea, reports that in A.D. 135, after Hadrian's crushing of the second Jewish revolt, a temple to Venus was constructed over the site of Golgotha.

> Hadrian built a huge rectangular platform over this quarry, concealing the holy cave beneath this massive mound. (Eus Onomastikon)

Hadrian then placed a statue of Venus over the site of Golgotha and a statue of Jupiter over the site of Jesus' tomb a dozen yards to the east.

In A.D. 325, Eusebius accompanied Roman Emperor Constantine on a trip to Jerusalem. There, the site of Golgotha was excavated, making Constantine one of the first Christian archaeologists. Under the Roman debris, evidence of a tomb was found. Constantine then ordered that the dome of the Sepulcher be built which, although renovated many times later, stands roughly where it did in early Christian times. Recent excavations have confirmed much of what Eusebius claims.

The Path of Crucifixion

That Jesus was forced to carry his own cross suggests that the location of Golgotha was not far from the Praetorium where presumably the supply of wooden crosses was kept. From our reconstruction of the upper city of Jerusalem, Jesus would have had to carry his cross for perhaps 900 yards from the gates of Herod's palace to the lip of the cemetery, or two-thirds of a mile.

An outside road likely ran along the base of the first wall from the gate of the Essenes in the west to the Gennath gate in the east, coming close to Golgotha in its course.

> And they that passed by railed on him, wagging their heads and saying, Ha! Thou that destroyest the temple and buildest it in three days, (Mk 15:29)

Golgotha itself was a prominent rock outcropping just west of the road. The formation was so distinctive that it was given its own name. In the ancient past, Golgotha perhaps started out as an anomalous rock deposit of granite buried within the softer, more desirable malakey, a soft white marble. Over the centuries, the marble was quarried out and Golgotha became exposed.

To the northwest from Golgotha would have been the steep chasms of the stone quarry marked with Jewish tombs dotting its craggy walls. At intervals, narrow paths would peel off from the road at the base of the wall and switchback down into the depths of the old quarry. When Jesus walked on that road with the Roman soldiers on the way to meet his destiny, the cemetery was probably a colorful place. Many of the tombs would have been decorated with brightly colored remembrance flowers for the Passover.

On that day of Preparation in A.D. 36, Jesus and two other condemned men were put up on crosses set into the rock and crucified. From the north, Golgotha could probably be seen easily by travelers on the heavily trafficked road that connected Jerusalem with Damascus and Caesarea. The road ran to the northwest and would have connected with the smaller road that led to Golgotha and past it. This road to Caesarea would have continued along the north rim of the old stone quarry, with Golgotha seen about a quarter mile away south on the other side.

Only a handful people saw the crucifixion. Most of the Jews lived in the lower city and almost no one lived near the Jewish cemetery. Even though it was the second day of the Passover feast and hundreds of thousands would be massing in the Temple barely a half mile away, the vast majority of those people would have accessed the great Temple and the upper city of Jerusalem from its eastern or southern approaches.

The western half of the upper city, in fact, was virtually closed off to most of the common people. The palace of Herod was walled and heavily guarded, and likewise the rich and wealthy of the upper city, who lived to the immediate south of the palace, discouraged casual pedestrians. Most of these people lived in their own walled-off luxurious enclaves. Private guards were ever-present and strangers walking in that area would be closely monitored. Roman soldiers were a constant presence as well as they patrolled outside of the palace of Herod.

Few of Jesus' followers were present to see the execution, since most were afraid of being arrested and suffering a fate similar to Jesus'. Only one disciple, the author of the Book of John, was there. The other Disciples in Jerusalem were aware of what was happening, but the swiftness of Jesus' trial and execution had taken them all by surprise. Many chose to retreat to the Second Temple to Jesus' favorite spot by Solomon's portico. There, while Jesus was dying, these simple men from Galilee desperately prayed for God to intervene and save their rabbi.

But many did see the crucifixion of Jesus. Some were pilgrims who had set up campsites in the orchards and pastured north of the road to Caesarea. Most, however, were travelers on that road. To the southeast, they could see the Second Temple complex looming in the distant background and the rising smoke from the sacrificial altar wafting in the sky. In the foreground of the Temple wall, the triple towers of Herod's palace could be seen, enclosed by the 40-foot tall defensive first wall of Jerusalem with turreted guard towers every 300 feet.

Impressive scenery, to be sure, but the eyes of the travelers were also likely drawn more to the south and across the stone quarry to the base of the first wall, where the large rock of Golgotha could be seen 400 yards away. Twin hollowings on the rock ledge beneath Golgotha–perhaps caves–made it look like a human skull. What an eerie sight it must have been to see the trio of condemned men dying on crosses set on the top of the skull-shaped formation. Did the Romans purposefully choose that site for their executions with that chilling effect in mind?!

Death on the Cross

For Jesus, no divine intervention came that day. After almost three hours of agony, he died at the ninth hour–three o'clock in the afternoon. It was the day of Preparation, the day before the Sabbath. If Jesus had not died by the ninth hour, he would have been killed by one of the Roman soldiers and then removed from the cross.

Despite being already dead, Jesus still received a sword thrust in his side from a Roman soldier. The two men who had been crucified on either side of Jesus were still living. They were quickly dispatched, and then all three were taken down from their crosses.

Joseph of Arimathea then appears in the Book of John. Arimathea, as it is used in John, would seem to be a town, but there is no record of it exiting in any ancient sources. It is possible that an early copy of John was mistranslated, with the proper appellation being Joseph bar Matthias (Joseph, son of Matthias). At any rate, this Joseph was a secret Disciple of Jesus, apparently one of many. Nicodemus was one also.

> 19:38 And after these things Joseph of Arimathaea, being a disciple of Jesus, but secretly for fear of the Jews, asked of Pilate that he might take away the body of Jesus: and Pilate gave *him* leave. He came therefore and took away his body. 19:39 And there came also Nicodemus, he who at the first came to him by night, bringing a mixture of myrrh and aloes, about a hundred pounds. 19:40 So they took the body of Jesus and bound it in linen cloths with the spices, as the custom of the Jews is to bury. (Jn)

The body of Jesus was hastily prepared for interment by Joseph, Nicodemus, and their servants. He was then laid to rest in a nearby tomb, not far away from Golgotha itself. More thorough preparation of Jesus' body would have to wait until the Sabbath day ended in 24 hours.

But sometime during that period the body was removed from the tomb. Mary Magdalene came to the site as early as she dared–minutes after sunset on the day following the Sabbath day. But she found Jesus' tomb empty.

> Now on the first *day* of the week cometh Mary Magdalene early, while it was yet dark, unto the tomb and seeth the stone taken away from the tomb. (Jn 20:1)

The news quickly spread through the Nazarene community. While some feared that the body of Jesus had been stolen by robbers, many were just as sure that he had risen from the dead.

After all, Jesus himself had raised Lazarus from the dead only a few weeks before.

High Priest Joseph Caiaphas was disturbed that the body was missing when he learned of it. But, as the days passed, no public protest or outcry of any significance was precipitated by Jesus' crucifixion. The Passover, for the hundreds of thousands of pilgrims in Jerusalem, proceeded peacefully and without disruption–just as Caiaphas and Pilate desired.

Chapter 5   Interlude: Vitellius Arrives

Besides which.. (Vitellius) also deprived Joseph, who was also called Caiaphas, of the high priesthood and appointed Jonathan the son of Ananus, the former high priest, to succeed him. After which, he took his journey back to Antioch. (*Antiq* XVIII 4:3)

High Priest Joseph Caiaphas knew that when Syrian President Lucius Vitellius arrived, Jerusalem had to be as tranquil and peaceful as possible. Accordingly, the arrest, trial and execution of Jesus was carried out expeditiously. By all indications, Jesus' crucifixion took place before most of the Jews in Jerusalem were even aware of his arrest. Given this urgency displayed by both Caiaphas and Pilate,   Vitellius was probably very close to Jerusalem when Jesus was executed–perhaps only hours away. When Vitellius and his soldiers passed through the Gennath Gate of Jerusalem, was Jesus still on the cross?!

Showing his contempt for the Jews, Pilate maneuvered the chief priests into agreeing to a release of Barabbas, the most dangerous criminal held in the jail. Barabbas was notorious for preying upon wealthy Jewish citizens. Now, he was a free man. Who would his next victim be? Pontius Pilate had probably planned on crucifying Barabbas and the two other Jewish criminals after the Passover.

While the Gospels portray Pilate as being a reluctant executioner, in reality he had far more to lose than Caiaphas if General Lucius Vitellius was witness to zealot violence. As will be seen, the Gospels were written in times when the Jerusalem High Priesthood was unrelenting in their persecution of the

Christians. During those times as well the Roman Judean prefects and procurators were somewhat protective and sympathetic to the plight of the Christians. Because of this, Pilate's image might have benefited whereas Caiaphas' did not.

Lucius Vitellius

When Jesus was arrested and later crucified, was the powerful Vitellius and his soldiers already in Jerusalem? It can be reasonably assumed that they were not. If Vitellius was already in Jerusalem, then why wasn't he included in the "trial" of Jesus orchestrated by Pilate? Pilate was quick enough to send Jesus off to Herod Antipas for examination when he sensed the chief priests were up to something, why not to Vitellius as well? Technically, Vitellius was Pilate's immediate supervisor and the next highest authority of appeal in capital cases like this one. In fact, the Syrian president was the senior Roman official for the entire eastern Roman Empire and the immediate superior to the Tetrarch Herod Antipas as well. If Vitellius had arrived sooner, it might have been Vitellius rendering judgment and not Pilate.

Admittedly, in all four Gospel records there is no mention of Lucius Vitellius, even though in some there is great detail about Jesus' arrest and crucifixion. This is interesting, as the expectation of Vitellius' imminent arrival is our hypothesized driving force behind Jesus' execution. Without Vitellius' visit, Jesus would probably not have been executed–at least not at the Passover of A.D. 36.

But for all the salient events in Jesus' crucifixion story that are in the Gospels, Vitellius played no overt role. And the principals involved had little reason to bring up Vitellius' name.

Aristobulos

Aristobulos, the brother of Herodias and Herod Agrippa (later King Agrippa I), was likely a part of Vitellius' entourage as they traveled from Antioch to Jerusalem. But neither the Gospels nor

Josephus mentions Aristobulos' presence in Jerusalem for the Passover of A.D. 36. Is it reasonable to assume that he was there?

Aristobulos had occupied a high magisterial position within the previous Syrian administration of Pomponius Flaccus, who had died suddenly in late A.D. 34. It is very possible that Emperor Tiberius was grooming Aristobulos to take over Herod Philip's old kingdom which he was holding under the temporary control of Syria. Tiberius could have given Philip's kingdom to Herod Antipas when Philip died in early A.D. 34, but Antipas himself had no heir, nor was he likely to have one. Tiberius might have thought it better to wait and award the kingdom to the most deserving and capable of the next generation of Herods. If this were the case, Aristobulos would have been a strong candidate.

After Flaccus died, no evidence suggests that Vitellius replaced Aristobulos when Vitellius assumed control of Syria in early A.D. 35. Aristobulos, for his part, had every reason to want to remain in the Syrian government. After the banishment of his brother Herod Agrippa from Syria almost a year earlier, Aristobulos was the most politically important Jew in Antioch. Aristobulos was also well aware that Herod Philip's former kingdom at some point would need be assigned by Tiberius. Without a doubt, Aristobulos had ambitions to gain control of the tetrarchy and become a king, as was the ambition of his brother Herod Agrippa (and a third brother, who was simply called "Herod"). Of course, Herod Antipas and Herodias coveted the old kingdom of Philip as well, and how many other descendants of Herod the Great of the second and third generations had similar hopes, however faint? But by impressing Vitellius and serving him well, Aristobulos knew he would have a powerful ally when it came time for Tiberius to make a final award of the prize territory.

General Lucius Vitellius, for his part, was new to the East and was not Tiberius' first or even second choice for the difficult job. He would have naturally relied on Aristobulos for his family connections to the Herods and Asamonean Jews and Aristobulos' expertise on Jewish affairs. Aristobulos and Vitellius probably knew each other well from the Royal court of Rome earlier in

Tiberius' reign. As the conflict developed between Antipas and King Aretas, Aristobulos would have become especially indispensable. In fact, it may well have been Aristobulos who suggested to Vitellius that he travel to Jerusalem for the Passover, knowing the symbolic importance the Jews placed on the celebration, as well as the value of military reconnaissance in that difficult area of the Jewish East. For these reasons, it is a safe assumption that Aristobulos, the brother of Herodias, accompanied Vitellius in his trip to Jerusalem for the Passover of A.D. 36.

Vitellius' Trip to Jerusalem

The final leg of the trip would have begun in Caesarea–the jewel city of the eastern Mediterranean that had been improved and expanded to a great degree by Herod the Great 40 years before. Vitellius and his men likely arrived by quadrareme. In those days, two large quadraremes with four rows of oars on each side could easily hold 300 men between them. It is hard to imagine Vitellius traveling with less than a cohort of Roman soldiers–perhaps 500 in all. Add to this another 100 people in personal attendance to Vitellius and his staff, the Roman mini-flotilla was composed of either three large quadraremes or four smaller ones.

From Caesarea, the trip overland to Jerusalem would take at most three days. Aristobulos would have also advised Vitellius to avoid arriving during the Sabbath day if at all possible. The sanctity of the holy day would be sorely disrupted by the dusty arrival of hundreds of tired and hungry Roman soldiers. Vitellius would have approached the upper city of Jerusalem on a well-traveled road that in its final approach to the Gennath Gate would skirt the north rim of the old stone quarry.

As Vitellius' military procession emerged from the Judean hills and approached the city, in the distance first seen might have been the white-faced western aspect of the top of the Temple Sanctuary building and the equally-tall southeast tower of the castle of Antonia to the north of it. Soon the other towers of

Antonia could be seen and the cloisters of the inner courtyards of the Second Temple and then the cloisters of the outer courtyard. Then, the 135-foot white-blocked west wall of the Temple plateau would be visible, stretching for over 700 yards in the north-south direction. Next, in front of the wall, the turreted tops of the three towers of Herod's palace would come into view. As Vitellius and his men came closer, the 40-foot-high north wall of Jerusalem could be seen, enclosing Herod's palace and the rest of the upper city.

These masterworks of Herod the Great were impressive to be sure, but, perhaps for a brief moment, Vitellius' attention might have been focused on a disturbing scene not 400 yards away from where he was riding. At the base of this old north wall, along the far rocky ledge of the quarry, ran a narrow road.

If Vitellius, Aristobulos and their entourage arrived in Jerusalem in the early afternoon on that fateful day of Preparation, did they happen to see three men hanging on crosses that were set into the stone of an oddly-shaped outcropping that looked like a skull? What a disturbing picture that would have been to them–several Roman soldiers standing guard and a handful of mourners watching the condemned from a safe distance away.

It was certainly not unusual to see the crucified outside of any Roman provincial city, especially one with such a long and violent history of sedition as Jerusalem. But perhaps from reports received in Caesarea just days ago, Vitellius was under the impression that this Passover was going to be a peaceful one. Vitellius' curiosity might have been aroused at what he saw. If this was an indication of the violence that was to come, he would have wanted to have been better prepared, perhaps. And could Vitellius read the sign "King of the Jews," written in Latin, Greek and Hebrew, that was placed over the cross of the condemned man in the middle? Probably not, but, as Vitellius passed by the distant scene and took it all in, he might have made a mental note to discuss what he saw with Pilate.

Vitellius Celebrates

Vitellius would have entered into the city through the Gennath Gate which was in the oldest wall of the upper city of Jerusalem, between the Second Temple and the eastern wall of Herod's palace. Pontius Pilate, his staff and attendants would have been there to welcome Vitellius personally, alerted by the advance horsemen of Vitellius' personal guard. Perhaps Pilate met him on horseback outside the Gennath gate as a show of respect, but, of course, it had been a busy day.

The common people who used the gate would have been ushered out of the way as the Roman contingent approached. Herod Antipas would have been among the VIPs present to greet Vitellius as well, along with his wife Herodias. For Herodias, it might have been years since she had last seen her brother Aristobulos. Herodias also might have known Vitellius personally from her days in the Roman Royal court. The crowd would have cheered Vitellius–Pilate would have made sure to arrange it so.

After the welcoming, in the hours of remaining daylight, Vitellius and his staff would have been escorted into their quarters within Herod's palace. Vitellius and his personal attendants would stay in the tower of Phasaelus, perhaps, with one of the main palace buildings holding the rest of the Syrian delegation. Most of Vitellius' soldiers would have been directed to an area within the expansive palace grounds, where they could pitch their tents.

At sundown, the mighty horn sounded from atop the Temple and echoed throughout Jerusalem: the Sabbath day was beginning! Most Jews were now in their homes or in restful place where the holy day could be observed in quiet prayer. By this time, Jesus had been already taken down from the cross by the Roman soldiers and claimed by Joseph of Arimathea and Nicodemus. Jesus' body had then been carried to a nearby tomb in the old quarry by these secret disciples and prepared.

Most likely on that evening, as the followers of Jesus mourned in the same Jerusalem house where the previous evening they had supped with Jesus, Vitellius held informal discussions with both Pilate and Antipas concerning the threat of Aretas and the Naboteans.

In the days following the Sabbath, Vitellius would have met Joseph Caiaphas and Ananus, and he certainly would have been given a tour of the Temple complex and the tower of Antonia. Both Antipas and Pontius Pilate would have been at the side of the powerful Vitellius as much as possible.

While touring the Temple, Vitellius announced his reduction of the tax on Temple offerings. This would have been enthusiastically received by the priest hierarchy–a popular move! At some point, too, Vitellius announced that Rome had decided to let the Temple priests regain possession of the holy vestments, ritual garments that the High Priest used in festival ceremonies. For almost 100 years, these vestments had been locked up the tower of Antonia under Roman guard and taken out and used only once yearly for the Passover (*Antiq* XVIII 4:3). The change would have again been huge news to the priesthood. Rome was giving them more trust and autonomy! Caiaphas especially would have been pleased that he would be the first High Priest in a century to care for these sacred robes–garments that held great and mystical significance for the Jews.

During the feasts, parties, military inspections, and tours in the days that followed, Vitellius would have had ample time for more formalized discussions with Pilate, Antipas, their attendant generals, and military experts. The Syrian president probably also sent spies and agents east into the countryside to assess the true situation of the Naboteans and the intent of Aretas IV. Vitellius would have soon realized–if he did not already–that there could be no peaceful settlement between Aretas and Antipas. Vitellius himself certainly traveled at least to the top of the Mont of Olives, scouting out the terrain himself. And he assured Antipas that when things were more settled with the Parthians, he would return with his army.

Antipas would have been greatly pleased. Antipas also probably volunteered some of his own forces to help Vitellius resolve the situation with Artabanus to the north. He would have tried hard to convince Vitellius of an alliance between between King Artabanus of Parthia and King Aretas of Nabotea, Antipas' nemesis — which may well have been the case.

Herodias

Herodias was in her element during this Passover, arranging social gatherings as well as attending those put on by others. She had a joyous reunion with her cousin Cypros and her three children. If they were not staying at the tower of Mariamne at the palace, then she would have made sure that they had the best suites in the old Asamonean palace across from the Second Temple.

The relationship between Pilate and Antipas had improved, due to the Galilean prisoner Pilate had consulted Antipas on. Herodias might also have worked closely with Pilate's wife on a few of the social events, even though Pilate's wife was a generation older than she was. Herodias would have also fawned over Vitellius, who was roughly her age and whom she might have known from her previous life in Rome. How many other officials in Vitellius' entourage came from Rome and also knew Herodias — and Cypros? It was proving to be a grand Passover for Herodias, and it made her momentarily forget her hated status among the Jews.

Herodias was especially happy to see her brother Aristobulos, who was a chief aide to Vitellius and his resident expert on Jewish affairs. In fact, her brother was, in many ways, more powerful than her own husband Herod Antipas.

Vitellius and Pilate

Through the rounds of parties, special meetings, and sightseeing, Vitellius made it a point to question Herod Antipas about Pilate on several occasions. Was Antipas willing to stand by what he had written to Tiberius? Did Pilate deserve to remain in power? Was Pilate popular with the Romans in Caesarea and would they oppose his removal? Vitellius might have been surprised at Antipas' support for Pilate which was in contrast to what Tiberius had led Vitellius to expect. Puzzled, Vitellius might have pressed the tetrarch, bringing up many past actions that Pilate had been criticized for–details of which were on record in Rome. Antipas perhaps shrugged them all off and admitted with a smile that his most recent accusations against Pilate had arisen out of the bitterness of defeat. Antipas might have even suggested that Pilate would prove to be useful in the upcoming war against Aretas. Vitellius, for his part, had no choice but to accept this and was perhaps relieved that he didn't have to remove Pilate after all. If Antipas was satisfied with Pilate, then Vitellius would be as well. Pilate would remain in power–for now, at least.

Taking our speculations a bit further, perhaps during one of the feasts held in Vitellius' honor, the Syrian president mentioned to Pilate the three criminals he had seen hanging on crosses outside the city wall when he first arrived. And if Vitellius had arrived too late to see them in person, certainly he had heard about the crucifixions from others. What, Vitellius inquired of Pilate, was the nature of their crimes?

Vitellius had the power of review over all of Pilate's judgments, so the question was a legitimate one. Pilate knew that his answer must be measured. Taking a few seconds to gather his thoughts, Pilate then told Vitellius that two of the condemned men justly deserved their fate and discussed their particular crimes. Then, referring to the third man, the one on the middle cross–with the sign proclaiming him to be the king of the Jews–Pilate might have shrugged his shoulders and told Vitellius about his dilemma with Caiaphas and the chief priests. The priests thought the man was a false Messiah, a zealot, and a revolutionary. They had demanded that he execute him for the sake of peace during the Passover, and he had reluctantly done so. As for the sign, Pilate simply said that witnesses had testified that this man Jesus claimed to be a king, and so the sign was made.

Vitellius, not satisfied, might have pressed Pilate further; was this man truly a threat to Rome–a murderer or a robber, perhaps?

Was he the leader of a gang of criminals? Had their been violent outbreaks in recent weeks? In response, Pilate would have had to be truthful and said not as far as he could determine, but that the priests had claimed that this man had challenged Tiberius' authority on several occasions. Pilate would have added quickly that Jesus clearly had not been a real threat, but what was he to do? In defense of his actions, Pilate might have told Vitellius that he had even appealed to Herod Antipas for help in jurisdiction, but the tetrarch offered no reprieve for the Galilean. So, in order to placate the priests, Pilate had had the man crucified.

It is likely that Vitellius would have expressed his strong disapproval to Pilate, as Tiberius would have done if he were there. The Roman Empire should serve a higher purpose than be used as an executioner, Vitellius might have said with some anger. The Jewish High Priesthood using the power of Caesar for religious revenge? Rome was too great to involve herself in such petty, religious squabbles. After this postulated discussion, Vitellius would have lost a measure of whatever respect he had for Pilate; surely a Roman prefect should have the backbone to stand up to local religious authorities!

Vitellius, Caiaphas, and Ananus

Vitellius would have talked to several other people to verify what Pilate had told him. He would have discussed his options with Aristobulos and his other advisers. Then, after much consideration, Vitellius decided to send a message to the arrogant Jerusalem priesthood as well as to Pilate. Vitellius decided to remove Caiaphas as High Priest. Not wanting to interfere with the running of the admittedly impressive Passover celebration, Vitellius delayed this announcement until after the Passover was over and he was ready to leave.

Caiaphas, who thought things were going well with the Syrian president, would have been stunned at the unexpected news–a cruel blow to a vain and proud man. Caiaphas had been entrenched as High Priest for more than 10 years now (and possibly as many as 18). The entire community of Jerusalem priests–many thousands of them–would also have been shocked by the news.

After the announcement, Vitellius likely asked Ananus, as the most senior and respected of the former High Priests, for a recommendation to replace Caiaphas. Ananus, himself caught unawares, would have asked for time to consider the question. He had several sons, all of whom coveted the exalted position. Vitellius agreed to approve whomever Ananus chose and appointed Ananus as temporary High Priest.

It is tempting to speculate that when Vitellius publicly announced the replacement of Caiaphas, he looked with significance over at Pilate. By removing Caiaphas as High Priest, Vitellius was also putting Pilate on notice. Vitellius could have removed Pilate just as easily and for the same reason. Both Caiaphas and Pilate had been in their respective positions for about 10 years.

Ananus' Role?

A slightly different scenario can also be hypothesized. Without question, Ananus would have had long and detailed talks with Vitellius about the political situation in the Jewish lands during his visit. At the meetings, large bribes would have been offered to Vitellius by Ananus — and accepted. Can it be supposed that Ananus himself was behind Vitellius' dismissal of Caiaphas as High Priest?

Remember that, according to the Synoptic Gospels, the Sanhedrin did not support Caiaphas at the trial of Jesus. This trial had been very inconvenient for them, and Caiaphas clearly presented false witnesses–insulting to the Sanhedrin in and of itself. If Caiaphas had skipped the Sanhedrin entirely in his pursuit of Jesus' execution, as the Book of John suggests, that might have concerned the Sanhedrin even more. The majority of the Sanhedrin members, made up of the most powerful and wealthy men in Judea, would have been outraged at this display of arrogance on Caiaphas' part. Most of the Sanhedrin probably thought that, in the Jesus affair, Caiaphas was demonstrating an instability and paranoia that was unbecoming of a High Priest. Did members of the Sanhedrin later present their concerns to Ananus? And did Ananus act upon them by suggesting to Vitellius that it was time for a change? Vitellius would have taken little convincing to remove Caiaphas, given what he had seen and had been told.

Legacy of a Passover

At the Passover of A.D. 36, Vitellius rocked the Temple establishment and the Jewish world. It can be very reasonably concluded that the immediate cause of Vitellius' dismissal of Caiaphas was his zeal in pursuing the elimination of an accused false prophet, Jesus of Nazareth. In successfully forcing an initially reluctant Pilate to execute Jesus, Caiaphas had. in fact, sealed his own fate with Rome. And Pontius Pilate, as a result of his complicity, moved ever closer to outright dismissal.

For the High Priesthood, another problem was developing. Jesus' body had disappeared from his tomb. The followers of this Nazarene were saying that he had risen from the dead. These Galileans were now preaching that a resurrected Jesus would soon lead legions of Angels and smite the wicked in Jerusalem as God's kingdom on earth was being established.

It was all nonsense, of course, but Ananus and others of the High Priesthood had the feeling that this cult would be more difficult to stamp out than most. Ananus was perhaps realizing that Caiaphas had been a fool to go after the harmless Galilean so aggressively, just as Herod Antipas had made a grave error in executing Jesus' cousin, John the Baptist, a year earlier. Gamaliel the Pharisee had been right: Jesus had now become a martyr around whom the seditious were rallying.

Chapter 6   Mysteries of the Passover

Nevertheless even of the rulers many believed on (Jesus); but because of the Pharisees they did not confess *it*, lest they should be put out of the synagogue: (Jn 12:42)

Jesus had many followers who lived in Jerusalem but chose not to be a main part of his Ministry or espouse their beliefs publicly. These "secret" disciples were mainly wealthy and important citizens of Jerusalem who could ill-afford to be associated with the zealots, Galileans, and John the Baptist devotees who were the usual sorts attracted to Jesus' Ministry. Who specifically were these disciples and what role could they have played in Jesus' final Passover?

The stories of the disciples after Jesus crucifixion and resurrection are continued in Acts of the Apostles (Acts), written by Luke of Macedon. In Acts, the original 12 Disciples and other certain early Christian evangelists are then referred to as "Apostles." The careful reader has already noted that the word "disciple" is only capitalized when it refers to one or more of the original 12 devotees of Jesus.

The Book of Luke documents that Jesus appointed 70 more men to serve as "advance" teams during his postulated eight-year ministry. They would be sent out in groups of two to towns Jesus planned on visiting. Their job was to publicize the upcoming arrival of Jesus, thus ensuring adequate and enthusiastic crowds. These disciples would also physically prepare the site for the gatherings and arrange for a safe and comfortable place for Jesus and his Disciples to stay.

> Now after these things the Lord appointed seventy others and sent them two and two before his face into every city and place, whither he himself was about to come. (Lk 10:1)

After a time, the most steadfast of these advance men were probably accepted into the inner circle that included Jesus' 12 original Disciples. Many of these disciples were staying in and around Bethany for the approaching Passover of A.D. 36. At that time, Jesus was preaching almost daily in the great Temple, and he had a lesser need for his disciples to promote and manage vast crowds–they were already in the Second Temple courtyards.

During Jesus' 40 days on earth after his resurrection, all those who saw him and subsequently converted to his teachings were also referred to as disciples. By the time of Jesus' ascension, hundreds of men could legitimately use that appellation. But apart from these known followers of Jesus, others kept their faith a secret for varying reasons.

Nicodemus and Joseph of Arimathea

The Book of John reveals two of these secret disciples: Nicodemus and Josephus of Arimathea. Nicodemus was a Pharisee and a member of the Sanhedrin and Joseph was a counselor, a specialist in Roman and Jewish law.

> And after these things Joseph of Arimathaea, being a disciple of Jesus, but secretly for fear of the Jews, (Jn 19:38)

> Now there was a man of the Pharisees, named Nicodemus, a ruler of the Jews: (Jn 3:1)

Nicodemus plays a key role in the Book of John. He is first seen after Jesus challenges the moneychangers in Jesus' first visit to the Second Temple after starting his Ministry. Nicodemus became aware of the incident, possibly even witnessing it, and sought Jesus out to ask him questions. Jesus responded in a long and poetic passage (Jn 3:1-21). Nicodemus and Joseph of Arimathea were also key people in the preparation of the crucified body of Jesus (Jn 19:38-42). If any characters mentioned in the New Testament played a role in the disappearance of Jesus' body, it would have been those two.

Who else in the Gospels might have been part of the secret following of Jesus? Following the chronology of the Passover of A.D. 36 as it develops in the Gospels, several other mystery individuals associated with Jesus add to the enigma of his final days on earth.

The Greeks

In the Book of John, just before the Passover of A.D. 36, "certain Greeks" sought out Jesus.

> [12:20]Now there were certain Greeks among those that went up to worship at the feast: [12:21]these therefore came to Philip, who was of Bethsaida of Galilee and asked him, saying, Sir, we would see Jesus. (Jn)

Were these Greeks part of a greater brotherhood that Jesus was also a part of, perhaps the Pythagoreans? Or were these men ascetics of no particular affiliation, as John the Baptist had been? Did they meet Jesus during one of his sojourns in Tyre or upon Mount Carmel? According to the Book of John, the Greeks were in Jerusalem during the Passover of A.D. 36 for a specific purpose that involved Jesus.

A hint as to the nature of the relationship between Jesus and the Greeks might be derived from an earlier chapter in the Book of John. During the feast of the Tabernacles in A.D. 35, Jesus spent many mornings in the Second Temple courtyard preaching. To the assembled crowds, Jesus spoke symbolically that he would be going to a place where he could not be found. The people listening to him thought he was referring to departing physically from Judea.

7:33Jesus therefore said, Yet a little while am I with you and I go unto him that sent me. 7:34Ye shall seek me and shall not find me: and where I am, ye cannot come. 7:35The Jews therefore said among themselves, Whither will this man go that we shall not find him? will he go unto the Dispersion among the Greeks and teach the Greeks?

This suggests that Jesus, at an earlier point in his Ministry, had indeed traveled and taught among the Greeks. The Mount Carmel area was reasonably close to Nazareth and Galilee, and it was famous for serving as the base for several eclectic bands of ascetics, including the Pythagoreans. Possibly, the "dispersion" was a reference to the Decapolis, the loose collection of cities in the eastern Galilee that were dominated by Syrian Greeks. Previous, Jesus had been living in and around the Decapolis area for almost a year as he kept his distance from Tetrarch Herod Antipas.

With this additional passage, a possible link is provided between Jesus and those Greeks who visited him for the Passover of A.D. 36. Jesus may also have referred to certain Greeks in his preachings and parables–stories that were not recorded in any of the four Gospels.

When Jesus was told that there were Greek visitors at the Second Temple looking for him, his response, while typically cryptic, was suggestive of some plan afoot that the Greeks were to play a part in.

12:23And Jesus answereth them, saying, The hour is come, that the Son of man should be glorified. 12:24Verily, verily, I say unto you, Except a grain of wheat fall into the earth and die, it abideth by itself alone; but if it die, it beareth much fruit. 12:25He that loveth his life loseth it; and he that hateth his life in this world shall keep it unto life eternal. 12:26If any man serve me, let him follow me; and where I am, there shall also my servant be: if any man serve me, him will the Father honor. 12:27Now is my soul troubled; and what shall I say? Father, save me from this hour. But for this cause came I unto this hour. (Jn)

Unfortunately, the Book of John gives us little more information about the Greeks.

Disciples of the Last Supper

In the hours preceding the last supper on the first day of the feast of the unleavened bread, Jesus arranged to have two of his Disciples meet a man at a particular fountain in Jerusalem. He would be carrying a distinctive water jug and the Disciples were to follow him. The Disciples carried out Jesus' orders and the man led them to a chamber-house that would serve as the place of the last supper. The three Synoptic Gospels describe much the same event.

> [14:13] And he sendeth two of his disciples and saith unto them, Go into the city and there shall meet you a man bearing a pitcher of water: follow him; [14:14] and wheresoever he shall enter in, say to the master of the house, The Teacher saith, Where is my guest-chamber, where I shall eat the passover with my disciples? (Mk)

The man carrying the water jug and the "master of the house" where the last supper was held could both have been a part of Jesus' secret circle of disciples in Jerusalem. In fact, it would make sense that they had to be. By then, a warrant had been issued for Jesus' arrest by the High Priest. Who else would risk their property and life so Jesus could put on a feast for his Disciples?

How many others in this secret group were there? Jesus had been fearful of preaching in Judea for more than a year, ever since the arrest of John the Baptist. Early in Jesus' Ministry, it had become clear that a certain faction of the Jews would like nothing better than to kill him (Jn 5:18).

It has been postulated that the defeat of Herod Antipas in the early fall of A.D. 35 was the catalyst for the return of Jesus to Jerusalem. Did the defeat cause a shift within the ranks of the Sanhedrin–was Jesus was now welcomed by the Sanhedrin instead of feared? As the Book of John relates, a few high ranking officials believed in Jesus but probably not enough to sway the entire group (Jn 7:30). In Antipas' military defeat, did Jesus see the beginning of the fulfillment of his own apocalyptic visions? Is this why he dared to return to Judea and preach under the very noses of the High Priesthood? Or did he decide to return to Judea and Jerusalem simply because Herod Antipas was returning to Galilee, and Jesus was still in fear of him?!

From the time of his arrival in Judea for the feast of the Tabernacles in A.D. 35, Jesus spent considerable time preaching in the Second Temple. What happened to the Jews who sought to kill him? For some reason, they apparently were not a major concern for Jesus; perhaps they were held in check by others. Was Jesus somehow protected by his powerful "secret" disciples–over and above the overt physical protection afforded him by his strong Galilean Disciple/bodyguards? Did secret disciples of the Sanhedrin guarantee Jesus' personal safety? And, if so, was this the reason that Joseph Caiaphas dispensed with a religious trial against Jesus, as the Book of John suggests?

Two Mystery Disciples

The Book of John describes two disciples who play an important role in Jesus' final Passover. One is simply referred to as the disciple whom Jesus "loved." The other disciple is referred to as one "who was known unto the High Priest" (Jn 18:16). Were these disciples a part of the original 12? Why would the author of the Book of John not tell us their names? He obviously knew who they were.

It is generally accepted that the disciple whom Jesus "loved" was the author of the Book of John himself, using the third person in order to disguise his identity. What of the secret disciple who knew Caiaphas? The author of the Book of John might have wanted to keep that Disciple anonymous to protect him or his relatives from retribution from the High Priesthood even decades after Jesus' crucifixion.

The Disciple Who Knew Caiaphas

The Book of John first mentions this disciple after Jesus' arrest of in the Garden of Gethsemane. It is assumed that this disciple could only have been with Jesus in the garden if he had also been with Jesus at the last supper, held only hours earlier. According to the Book of John, he followed Jesus and the mob after Jesus' arrest by the chief priests as the Nazarene was led back into Jerusalem. Somewhat surprisingly, this disciple was then allowed entrance into the very house of Caiaphas! If the disciple didn't know Caiaphas personally, he was at least on good terms with Caiaphas' household staff.

The disciple also arranged to have the Disciple Peter allowed into Caiaphas' courtyard. It was a cold early morning and Peter could then warm himself beside the fire. This unknown disciple possessed no small measure of influence. Caiaphas was one of the most powerful and wealthy men in the Jewish East. It is very unlikely that any of the 12 original Disciples–poor Galilean fishermen for the most part–would have Jerusalem connections even remotely close to that level.

In order to determine who this disciple was, clues might be found in the Gospel accounts of the last supper. Was the meal attended by only the 12 original Disciples, or were others disciples present? According to the Book of Mark, earlier in the day Jesus had sent two Disciples to help with the preparation of the last supper.

14:16 And the disciples went forth and came into the city and found as he had said unto them: and they made ready the passover. 14:17 And when it was evening he cometh with the twelve. (Mk)

Interpreting Mark literally, this indicates that two disciples who attended the last supper were not part of the original 12, for a total of 15 people, including Jesus.

In the Book of Matthew, however, the number of Disciples at the last supper is stated clearly:

Now when even (evening) was come, he was sitting at meat with the twelve disciples.(Mt 26:20)

But does this passage in Matthew mean that there were only 12 men in total present (apart from Jesus), or that the 12 Disciples were among those who attended? In the Book of Luke, a specific number of attendees is not given.

> 22:14 And when the hour was come, he sat down and the apostles with him. (Lk)

In the Book of John, as in Luke, no exact number of disciples is given.

After the supper, Jesus retreated with his disciples to the Garden of Gethsemane. It is probable that the disciple who knew Caiaphas was at the last supper with Jesus, but it is also possible that that particular disciple met Jesus at the Garden of Gethsemane. Jesus had used that spot as a retreat before. Possibly, the disciple who knew Caiaphas actually joined up with Judas and the mob from Jerusalem and traveled with them as they sought out Jesus by torchlight.

At Gethsemane, Jesus was arrested. Most of the disciples scattered. Many sought refuge in Bethany not far away. But the disciple who knew Caiaphas followed the bound Jesus as he was led back into Jerusalem. The Disciple Peter followed the arresting mob as well. After passing across the Kidron Valley and entering the gates of Jerusalem, the mob along with its followers arrived at the exclusive upper city neighborhood of the High Priesthood. Peter must have been astounded when he saw one of his fellow disciples freely enter Caiaphas' well-guarded, walled compound. Peter himself dared not even approach the gates!

But the disciple knew that Peter was outside the compound, shivering in the cold and darkness. Using his influence, he arranged to get Peter admitted into courtyard. There, Peter could await the fate of Jesus and warm himself by the fire. After tending to Peter, the disciple then re-entered the High Priest's house and disappeared into historical oblivion; the Book of John never mentions him again.

What did this disciple of Jesus do and see inside the house of Caiaphas? He might have been an eyewitness to the interrogation of Jesus himself, perhaps even speaking on Jesus' behalf. Did he witness a meeting of the full Sanhedrin? Or were the gathered judges merely chief priests hastily assembled at Caiaphas' bidding? Was there a religious trial at all?

> 18:15And Simon Peter followed Jesus and *so did* another disciple. Now that disciple was known unto the high priest and entered in with Jesus into the court of the high priest; 18:16but Peter was standing at the door without. So the other disciple, who was known unto the high priest, went out and spake unto her that kept the door and brought in Peter. (Jn)

The author of John chooses not tell us this disciple's name, though he certainly knew it. We can infer that this disciple was a wealthy and powerful man; who else would be so familiar and trusted by Caiaphas' staff? It then follows that this disciple would not have been a part of the original 12. Could this secret disciple have been the same man who was the "master" of the house where Jesus and his followers had just eaten supper and undergone their first communion ceremony? At the very least, this wealthy disciple might have been responsible for procuring the room for the celebration.

The Book of Mark details a nameless "young man" who ran off without his linen after struggling with the arresting mob at Gethsemane. This young man was not identified as a Disciple, however, and apparently, according to Mark, did not accompany Peter in following the arresting mob to Caiaphas' gated compound in the upper city.

> 14:51And a certain young man followed with him, having a linen cloth cast about him, over *his* naked *body*: and they lay hold on him; 14:52but he left the linen cloth and fled naked. (Mk 14:51-52)

It is possible, however, that the Books of John and Mark are talking about the same person. That Mark doesn't refer to him as a disciple indicates at the very least that the young man wasn't one of the original 12 Disciples. Perhaps in the Book of John, a more liberal interpretation of the word "disciple" was used.

The Disciple Whom Jesus Loved

The Book of John refers several times to another mystery disciple who is simply called the "one that Jesus loved." This disciple is first referred to during the last supper when he was reclining on Jesus' chest. Previously, it was postulated from the Book of Mark that there were 15 people at Jesus' last supper: Jesus, the 12 Disciples, and two extra ones. Was this the second of the two from Mark, with the first being the disciple who knew Caiaphas?

> 13:22The disciples looked one on another, doubting of whom he spake. 13:23There was at the table reclining in Jesus' bosom one of his disciples, whom Jesus loved. 13:24Simon Peter therefore beckoneth to him and saith unto him, Tell *us* who it is of whom he speaketh. 13:25He leaning back, as he was, on Jesus' breast saith unto him, Lord, who is it? 13:26Jesus therefore answereth, He it is, for whom I shall dip the sop and give it him. So when he had dipped the sop, he taketh and giveth it to Judas, *the son* of Simon Iscariot. (Jn)

This disciple is next found at or near Golgotha when Jesus was crucified. He is the only disciple to have had the courage to witness Jesus' death. In the Book of John, Jesus' mother, Mary, is also with this disciple at Golgotha, along with several other women who followed the Ministry.

> 19:26When Jesus therefore saw his mother and the disciple standing by whom he loved, he saith unto his mother, Woman, behold thy son! 19:27Then saith he to the disciple, Behold, thy mother! And from that hour the disciple took her unto his own *home*. (Jn)

The Book of John lends credence to Jesus' affection for this disciple by telling us that, while on the cross, Jesus entrusted his mother's care to him. Perhaps Jesus knew that this disciple was a relative of Caiaphas'. Who better to insure his mother's safety? The passage also speaks of this disciple taking Jesus' mother into his own home. Does this provide us with a link to the "master" who provided the large upper room for the last supper? The disciples and the female followers of Jesus stayed in that same place for months after Jesus' crucifixion.

There is another possible reference to this disciple at the crucifixion scene. The Book of John reports that, after Jesus was presumed dead, his side was pierced by a Roman spear before he was taken down from the cross.

> And he that hath seen hath borne witness and his witness is true: and he knoweth that he saith true, that ye also may believe.(Jn 19:35)

Is the author of the Book of John telling us in this passage that he was a witness to the crucifixion? Possibly so. But we know of only one male disciple who was at Golgotha that day–the disciple whom Jesus loved. Was the author of the book of John that disciple?

This "beloved" disciple is referenced again soon after the crucifixion. It occurred on the first day of the week, just after the Sabbath day. Then, Mary Magdalene went out to the tomb to tend to the body of Jesus, but she found his tomb empty.

> .20:2She runneth therefore and cometh to Simon Peter and to the other disciple whom Jesus loved and saith unto them, They have taken away the Lord out of the tomb and we know not where they have laid him. 20:3Peter therefore went forth and the other disciple and they went toward the tomb. 20:4And they ran both together: and the other disciple outran Peter and came first to the tomb; 20:5and stooping and looking in, he seeth the linen cloths lying; yet entered he not in. 20:6Simon Peter therefore also cometh, following him and entered into the tomb; and he beholdeth the linen cloths lying, 20:7and the napkin, that was upon his head, not lying with the linen cloths, but rolled up in a place by itself. 20:8Then entered in therefore the other disciple also, who came first to the tomb and he saw and believed. (Jn 20:2-8)

The disciple who Jesus loved was with the Disciple Peter when the tomb was found empty.

The final reference to this mystery disciple in the Book of John comes at an undefined length of time later. Several of the disciples have returned to Galilee and are out on a boat fishing.

Jesus appears on the shore about 300 feet away; he calls out to the men and asks them if they have caught any fish. The disciples, not recognizing Jesus, reply that they had caught nothing. Jesus then calls out and instructs them to cast their nets on the other side of the boat. Puzzled, but with nothing to lose, the disciples do so and their nets quickly overflow with fish. Amazed, they look more closely at the man on the shore.

> That disciple therefore whom Jesus loved saith unto Peter, It is the Lord. (Jn 21:7)

This can be interpreted another way, but for now, it is assumed that the mystery disciple–the "beloved" disciple–is in the boat with Peter. This is an important clue. The author of the Book of John writes that two unnamed "other" disciples are in the boat, along with a number of known disciples.

> There was together Simon Peter and Thomas called Didymus and Nathanael of Cana in Galilee and the *sons* of Zebedee and two other of his disciples. (Jn 21:2)

John, the son of Zebedee?

Arguments have been made that the author of the Book of John was one of the sons of Zebedee. Two sons are mentioned in the Bible: John and James. James will be executed by King Agrippa I in late A.D. 41, five years after the crucifixion. Did John meet a similar fate? If so, it is not recorded. Remember, the earliest estimated time for the writing of the Book of John is A.D. 85– more than 40 years after the death of James. Also, if John, the author of the Gospel, was in fact John, the son of Zebedee, then why in the fishing episode late in his book were the "sons of Zebedee" specifically referenced? If John did not want to be identified, calling himself only the "disciple that Jesus loved", then why identify the sons of Zebedee (himself being one of them) at all? John could have easily identified his brother James and then have written that three other Disciples, instead of two, were in the boat.

Who was John?

In the beginning of Acts, the author, Luke of Macedon, lists the original Disciples of Jesus. There are 11 of them now, as it is shortly after the crucifixion and Judas Iscariot is not counted.

> Then returned they unto Jerusalem from the mount called Olivet which is nigh unto Jerusalem, a Sabbath day's journey off. And when they were come in, they went up into the upper chamber, where they were abiding; both Peter and John and James and Andrew, Philip and Thomas, Bartholomew and Matthew, James *the son* of Alphaeus and Simon the Zealot and Judas *the son* of James. (Acts 1:12)

The Book of Luke also names the 12 Disciples. Of course, Luke of Macedon is also the author of that Gospel.

> 6:13 And when it was day, he called his disciples; and he chose from them twelve, whom also he named apostles: 6:14 Simon, whom he also named Peter and Andrew his brother and James and John and Philip and Bartholomew, 6:15 and Matthew and Thomas and James *the son* of Alphaeus and Simon who was called the Zealot, 6:16 and Judas *the son* of James and Judas Iscariot, who became a traitor; (Lk 6:13-16)

Melding this list in with the list given by the author of the Book of John, it can be determined who could have been the disciple whom Jesus loved, assuming that he was one of the original 12. Given that the sons of Zebedee were James and John, the Disciple whom Jesus loved could have been either Simon the Zealot, Judas the son of James, James the son of Alphaeus, Matthew, Bartholomew, Philip, or Andrew.

Well and good, but remember that the secret followers of Jesus could also be termed disciples, as well as those appointed in ancillary positions to help with the operation of the Ministry as is reported in the Book of Luke. Supporting evidence indicates that in the Book of Mark at least two extra disciples were at the last supper who could not have been part of the original 12.

John as the Mystery Disciple?

There is, however, another avenue open in the identification of the two mystery disciples. There is no reason why the disciple who knew Caiaphas and the disciple whom Jesus "loved"–both found in the Book of John–could not be one and the same person. This disciple could have also been the young man who lost his linen during the fracas of Jesus' arrest, as described in the Book of Mark. Three mystery figures all rolled up in one individual–a neat solution! Decades later and after many other adventures with his fellow Christians, this disciple settles down to write his Gospel, the Book of John, in the Greek-Asian city of Ephesus and becomes known as John the Evangelist.

To speculate even further, could this John originally have been from an honored and wealthy Jerusalem family with strong ties to the High Priesthood, perhaps from the extended family of Ananus himself? Furthermore, could the last supper have been held in John's house, located in the High Priesthood residential district of the upper city of Jerusalem?

If so, then a fourth mystery figure is now identified: the "master" of the house of the last supper is the future John the Evangelist. After Jesus' crucifixion, the disciples and the women of the Ministry were welcomed back in the house of the last supper. The early Christians (Nazarenes) would stay in that house for months afterward as they prayed and waited for Jesus' return.

Years before, a younger John, training for the priesthood, would have been fascinated with the ministry of John the Baptist, just as he would later become drawn to the Ministry of Jesus. Young John would have made every effort to meet John the Baptist and probably did. This would account for the lengthy quote from John the Baptist in the Book of John, the only Gospel that quotes John the Baptist directly. Nicodemus, also interested in John's ministry and later with Jesus', would have naturally become acquainted with this younger John within the close-knit community of the Jerusalem power elite. This would also account for the section in the Book of John where Nicodemus questioned

Jesus after an earlier Passover when Jesus came into prominence by challenging the moneychangers (Jn 3:1-21). The detail of passage is now understandable: John was actually present to hear the exchange between Nicodemus and Jesus firsthand!

John the Evangelist

Early church historian Eusebius agrees that the author of the Book of John was one of Jesus' disciples and an eyewitness to many of the events described in his book. Eusebius relies on the historical record provided by earlier church historians (Clement, Irenaeus and Hegesippus) who also identified John as the disciple whom Jesus "loved." What we know of John the Evangelist comes from these three early Church historians. Each source, unfortunately, is of dubious reliability.

John supposedly left Jerusalem and Judea after Jesus' crucifixion, eventually settling in the liberal seacoast Syrian city of Ephesus. There, he became a leader in the Christian Church that Paul the Apostle had helped found. Ephesus was located east across the Ionian Sea some 300 miles from Athens. It was considered an open-minded city for the times, being somewhat tolerant of different religious practices. The Greek temple of Artemis was the town's centerpiece and masterwork. The building was three times the size of the Greek Parthenon in Athens and considered a wonder of the ancient world. A cottage industry had grown up around this temple serving the pilgrims who traveled there in order to worship Artemis, or tourists who simply wanted to marvel at the amazing structure. In the eclectic and open atmosphere encouraged by this diverse population, the Christian Church flourished.

But this happy state of affairs changed when Vespasian's youngest son Domitian came to power in A.D. 81. Emperor Titus, Flavius Josephus' old friend and patron, had died of a fever after less than two years in power. Domitian then ruled the empire for the next 15 years until his murder in A.D. 96. In late A.D. 85, Emperor Domitian appointed himself Censor Perpetuus (Censor for Life) with special authority over conduct and morals for the peoples of the empire. Bad news for the Christians! At that time, Domitian apparently exiled John the Evangelist, although no independent record specifically supports that date. Eusebius does tell us that in the 15th and last year of Domitian's reign, many Christians of no mean importance were exiled to Pontia. Executions of Christians were also ordered.

Some sources hold that John was exiled shortly after finishing his Gospel. In truth, John might have hastily written his Gospel after learning of his banishment to Patmos, thinking that once there he would face a quick execution. But a death on the exile island was not to be his fate. During his years on Patmos, John also wrote the Book of Revelation, although that was a disputed work even in Eusebius' time (Eusebius *History* 3:19).

Fortunately for John the Evangelist and the other exiled Christians, all of Domitian's banishments were lifted by the Roman Senate shortly after Domitian's murder in A.D. 96 (Eusebius *History* III:18). John the Evangelist then returned to Ephesus.

> John returned to Ephesus, where he lived a long life and died sometime during the reign of Trajan, A.D. 98-117. (Eusebius *History* III:20)

> Then, again, the Church in Ephesus, founded by Paul and having John remaining among them permanently until the times of Trajan, is a true witness of the tradition of the apostles. (Irenaeus Book III-II:4)

Eusebius states that John decided to produce his own Gospel in order to fill a void that then existed. The three Synoptic Gospels concentrated only on the last year of Jesus' Ministry–from the death of John the Baptist to Jesus' own crucifixion in Jerusalem. In his work, John attempted to fill in earlier events in Jesus' Ministry as best he could from his own memories.

This postulated history of John the Evangelist answers many questions. Being a "renegade" member of the Jerusalem priesthood as a secret disciple of Jesus, the much-younger John used a pseudonym when he became a disciple for the Nazarene. Even decades later, when writing his Gospel about those times John still did not reveal his true name, referring to himself as the disciple who knew the High Priest or the disciple whom Jesus loved.

That John the Evangelist was a former Jewish priest is suggested in an ancient letter of Polycrates, who was the Bishop of Ephesus circa A.D. 190. He writes the missive to the Church of Rome and in it John the Evangelist is mentioned.

> And there is John, who leant back on the Lord's breast and who became a priest wearing the mitre.. (Eusebius *History* 5:24)

A mitre is a ceremonial flat-topped headdress worn by members of the Jewish High Priesthood.

Apparently, though a Christian, John continued in his duties as a Temple priest for some time after the crucifixion. James, the brother of Jesus, as a leader of the Christian Church in Jerusalem, also followed Judaic law and ritual as much as possible. Both men probably irritated the "true" priests of the Temple for their pretensions. James was eventually executed by the Sanhedrin.

For this reason, John eventually left the Temple priesthood entirely. It is easy to see John following the other disciples as they retreated to Galilee years afterward–he had few other options. As a part of his rough, new life, John perhaps even learned to cast the nets with his Galilean friends. Later, how many other places did John wander in and preach before settling permanently in Ephesus to work within the Church? Assuming that John was perhaps 18 years of age during Jesus' last Passover in A.D. 36, John lived well into his nineties, as Eusebius tells us that John died during the reign of Trajan.

Taking a step back, however, are too many roles given to John the Evangelist in pursuit of a neat solution to all the mystery figures found in the New Testament? One major problem remains: why, at the end of the Book of John, is the disciple whom Jesus loved is considered deserving of death? This is even more curious if one considers that the Book of John might have been written by that very disciple. However, unless there is a discovery of the first magnitude in early Christians manuscripts, that mystery will remain unsolved.

Resurrection

Finally, the mystery of Jesus' missing body after his crucifixion must be addressed. The several "documented" appearances of Jesus after his execution, discussed in the next chapter, become more believable, especially to the non-Christian, if Jesus survived the crucifixion. Had Jesus been revived and carried off to a place where he could fully recover from his ordeal? As we have just seen, the Book of John conveniently provides a whole cadre of secret disciples in and around Jerusalem–some very wealthy and powerful–who could have facilitated such an action. In fact, Pilate's suspicion that Jesus survived the cross might explain his unusual enthusiasm in moving against a Samaritan prophet–an action that would cost Pilate his position.

Chapter 7 After the Crucifixion: A.D. 36

And Jesus came to them and spake unto them, saying, All authority hath
been given unto me in heaven and on earth. Go ye therefore and make
disciples of all the nations, baptizing them into the name of the Father
and of the Son and of the Holy Spirit: teaching them to observe all things
whatsoever I commanded you: and lo, I am with you always, even unto
the end of the world. (Mt 28:18-20)

Events of great consequence occurred during the rest of the year
following Jesus' crucifixion,   including 40-day resurrection of
Jesus, the stoning of Stephen, and the epiphany of Saul of Tarsus
on the road to Damascus.

The Passover of A.D. 36, as described by Josephus, was a
peaceful one. In the weeks leading up to the following Pentecost
festival, the Jerusalem High Priesthood was tolerant of Nazarene
activity. Judean Prefect Pontius Pilate, perhaps under orders
from General Lucius Vitellius, might have made it clear to the
High Priesthood that the Galileans were not to be harassed. In
the removal of Caiaphas from his long-held office as High Priest,
the Syrian president was sending two clear messages. To the
High Priesthood, Vitellius was demonstrating that Rome held the
ultimate power in the Jewish East, God or no God. To Pilate, he
was saying that he could be removed just as easily as Caiaphas
had been. The Jerusalem Sanhedrin — that had declined to convict
Jesus of religious sedition (according to the three Synoptic
Gospels) — might also have come down hard on Ananus and
Caiaphas for their high-handed actions in the Jesus affair.

For the Nazarenes, the resurrection of Jesus was a most significant event. After the body disappeared, Jesus was reported as being being seen on several occasions in and around Jerusalem. This served to further convince Jesus' followers of his divine origins, if they were not totally convinced of it already. Hundreds of believers were also added to the ranks of the Nazarenes because of Jesus' reappearances.

Resurrection in Matthew

In the Book of Matthew, the resurrection of Jesus takes up chapter 28 and is only three paragraphs long.

> 28:1Now late on the sabbath day, as it began to dawn toward the first *day* of the week, came Mary Magdalene and the other Mary to see the sepulchre. 28:2And behold, there was a great earthquake; for an angel of the Lord descended from heaven and came and rolled away the stone and sat upon it. 28:3His appearance was as lightning and his raiment white as snow: 28:4and for fear of him the watchers did quake and became as dead men. 28:5And the angel answered and said unto the women, Fear not ye; for I know that ye seek Jesus, who hath been crucified. 28:6He is not here; for he is risen, even as he said. Come, see the place where the Lord lay. 28:7And go quickly and tell his disciples, He is risen from the dead; and lo, he goeth before you into Galilee; there shall ye see him: lo, I have told you. 28:8And they departed quickly from the tomb with fear and great joy and ran to bring his disciples word. 28:9And behold, Jesus met them, saying, All hail. And they came and took hold of his feet and worshipped him. 28:10Then saith Jesus unto them, Fear not: go tell my brethren that they depart into Galilee and there shall they see me.
>
> 28:11Now while they were going, behold, some of the guard came into the city and told unto the chief priests all the things that were come to pass. 28:12And when they were assembled with the elders and had taken counsel, they gave much money unto the soldiers, 28:13saying, Say ye, His disciples came by night and stole him away while we slept. 28:14And if this come to the governor's ears, we will persuade him and rid you of care. 28:15So they took the money and did as they were taught: and this saying was spread abroad among the Jews and *continueth* until this day. (Mt)

To summarize, Mary Magdalene went to the tomb of Jesus on the morning after the Sabbath day, only to find a brilliant Angel there and the guards struck dumb by the Angel's presence. The Angel told Mary Magdalene that Jesus had risen from the dead, and that Jesus would go to Galilee where the Disciples could see him. Mary Magdalene left the tomb and told the Disciples what she had seen and heard. Subsequently, Jesus appeared to the Disciples in Jerusalem, also telling them to go to Galilee where he would meet them again.

The tomb guards who witnessed the appearance of the Angel told the chief priests what had happened. The priests were concerned and they paid the guards to spread the story that the body of Jesus had been stolen by his Disciples.

In the Garden of Gethsemane on the eve of his crucifixion, Jesus in fact had promised to meet his Disciples again in Galilee, after he had been risen up from the dead.

> $^{26:32}$But after I am raised up, I will go before you into Galilee.(Mt)

The 11 Disciples did then travel to Galilee after the crucifixion, where they saw Jesus.

> $^{28:16}$But the eleven disciples went into Galilee, unto the mountain where Jesus had appointed them. $^{28:17}$And when they saw him, they worshipped *him*; but some doubted. $^{28:18}$And Jesus came to them and spake unto them, saying, All authority hath been given unto me in heaven and on earth.(Mt)

The Book of Matthew ends with Jesus, in Galilee, instructing his Disciples to spread the word.

Resurrection in Mark

The Book of Mark is much like Matthew regarding the resurrection story.

> $^{16:1}$And when the sabbath was past, Mary Magdalene and Mary the *mother* of James and Salome, bought spices, that they might come and

anoint him. $^{16:2}$And very early on the first day of the week, they come to the tomb when the sun was risen. $^{16:3}$And they were saying among themselves, Who shall roll us away the stone from the door of the tomb? $^{16:4}$and looking up, they see that the stone is rolled back: for it was exceeding great. $^{16:5}$And entering into the tomb, they saw a young man sitting on the right side, arrayed in a white robe; and they were amazed. $^{16:6}$And he saith unto them, Be not amazed: ye seek Jesus, the Nazarene, who hath been crucified: he is risen; he is not here: behold, the place where they laid him! $^{16:7}$But go, tell his disciples and Peter, He goeth before you into Galilee: there shall ye see him, as he said unto you. $^{16:8}$And they went out and fled from the tomb; for trembling and astonishment had come upon them: and they said nothing to any one; for they were afraid.

Mary Magdalene and two other women, on the day after the Sabbath, went to the tomb of Jesus with the intent to prepare Jesus' body further for interment. As they walked to the cemetery they were wondering how they would roll away the large stone that they knew secured the tomb. But upon arrival they found that the stone had already been moved aside. To their surprise, the tomb was empty save for an Angel! The Angel told them that Jesus had risen from the dead and that he would be found in Galilee.

$^{16:9}$Now when he was risen early on the first day of the week, he appeared first to Mary Magdalene, from whom he had cast out seven demons. $^{16:10}$She went and told them that had been with him, as they mourned and wept. $^{16:11}$And they, when they heard that he was alive and had been seen of her, disbelieved. $^{16:12}$And after these things he was manifested in another form unto two of them, as they walked, on their way into the country. $^{16:13}$And they went away and told it unto the rest: neither believed they them. $^{16:14}$And afterward he was manifested unto the eleven themselves as they sat at meat; and he upbraided them with their unbelief and hardness of heart, because they believed not them that had seen him after he was risen. $^{16:15}$And he said unto them, Go ye into all the world and preach the gospel to the whole creation. $^{16:16}$He that believeth and is baptized shall be saved; but he that disbelieveth shall be condemned. $^{16:17}$And these signs shall accompany them that believe: in my name shall they cast out demons; they shall speak with new tongues; $^{16:18}$they shall take up serpents and if they drink any deadly thing, it shall in no wise hurt them; they shall lay hands on the sick and they shall recover. 16:19So then the Lord Jesus, after he had spoken unto them, was received up into heaven and sat down at the right hand of God. 16:20And they went forth and preached everywhere, the Lord working with them and confirming the word by the signs that followed. Amen.

Jesus manifested himself to Mary Magdalene soon afterward, but the Book of Mark is not clear on the timing of it. Jesus then was seen by two other people as they walked in the countryside. Later, Jesus appeared to all 11 Disciples as they sat at a meal and related the powers that each would receive if they believed in him and spread his message.

Resurrection in Luke

In the Book of Luke, the resurrected Jesus instructs the disciples to remain in Jerusalem to await the receiving of "power." Mary Magdalene and several other women went to Jesus' tomb on the first day after the Sabbath. There, they found the tomb empty save for two Angels who told them that Jesus has risen from the dead. The women returned to their Christian enclave to tell Peter, who then went to the Tomb to see for himself. No Angels were there to talk to Peter, and so he returned to where the Disciples were gathered. Later that day, two of the disciples, Cleopas and Simon, were on the road to Emmaus, a village about eight miles from Jerusalem (Lk 24:13). A stranger fell in with them as they walked, and they all talked about what had happened to Jesus. The two then invited the stranger to eat with them and he agreed. After breaking bread, the two disciples recognize Jesus, and then Jesus vanished!

Subsequently, Cleopas and Simon traveled to Jerusalem, where they told the 11 Disciples there what had happened. As they related their experience, Jesus appeared to the entire assemblage— out of thin air!

24:37But they were terrified and affrighted and supposed that they beheld a spirit. 24:38And he said unto them, Why are ye troubled? and wherefore do questionings arise in your heart? 24:39See my hands and my feet, that it is I myself: handle me and see; for a spirit hath not flesh and bones, as ye behold me having. [24:40]And when he had said this, he showed them his hands and his feet. (Lk)

Jesus spoke to them at the meal and then he led them to a place near Bethany. There, he instructed them to remain in Jerusalem until he showed them a sign.

[24:47]and that repentance and remission of sins should be preached in his name unto all the nations, beginning from Jerusalem. [24:48]Ye are witnesses of these things. [24:49]And behold, I send forth the promise of my Father upon you: but tarry ye in the city, until ye be clothed with power from on high. (Lk)

Jesus was then carried up into heaven in some fashion that is not detailed. The meaning of being "clothed with power from on high" likely refers to the miracle of the tongues which was to occur a few days later, as described in Acts. It should be remembered that both Luke and Acts were written by the same man, Luke of Macedon.

Resurrection in John

In the Book of John, Mary Magdalene discovered the empty tomb on the first day after the Sabbath and told Peter. He rushed out to confirm it, accompanied by Mary Magdalene and Jesus' beloved disciple, who is suspected to be John the Evangelist. Seeing the tomb empty, Peter then left the cemetery in order to tell the other disciples in Jerusalem. The beloved disciple left the cemetery with him. Mary Magdalene stayed at the tomb weeping, and then Jesus appeared to her.

[20:1]Now on the first *day* of the week cometh Mary Magdalene early, while it was yet dark, unto the tomb and seeth the stone taken away from the tomb. [20:2]She runneth therefore and cometh to Simon Peter and to the other disciple whom Jesus loved and saith unto them, They have taken away the Lord out of the tomb and we know not where they have laid him. [20:3]Peter therefore went forth and the other disciple and they went toward the tomb. [20:4]And they ran both together: and the other disciple outran Peter and came first to the tomb; ^{20:5}and stooping and looking in, he seeth the linen cloths lying; yet entered he not in. ^{20:6}Simon Peter therefore also cometh, following him and entered into the tomb; and he beholdeth the linen cloths lying, ^{20:7}and the napkin, that was upon his head, not lying with the linen cloths, but rolled up in a place by itself. ^{20:8}Then entered in therefore the other disciple also, who came first to the tomb and he saw and believed. ^{20:9}For as yet they knew not the scripture, that he must rise from the dead. ^{20:10}So the disciples went away again unto their own home. ^{20:11}But Mary was standing without at the tomb weeping: so, as she wept, she stooped and looked into the tomb; ^{20:12}and she beholdeth two angels in white sitting, one at the head and one at the feet, where the body of Jesus had lain. ^{20:13}And they say unto her, Woman, why weepest thou? She saith unto them, Because they have taken away my Lord and I know not where they have laid him. ^{20:14}When she had thus said, she turned herself back and beholdeth Jesus standing and knew not that it was Jesus. ^{20:15}Jesus saith unto her, Woman, why weepest thou? whom seekest thou? She, supposing him to be the gardener, saith unto him, Sir, if thou hast borne him hence, tell me where thou hast laid him and I will take him away. ^{20:16}Jesus saith unto her, Mary. She turneth herself and saith unto him in Hebrew, Rabboni; which is to say, Teacher. ^{20:17}Jesus saith to her, Touch me not; for I am not yet ascended unto the Father: but go unto my brethren and say to them, I ascend unto my Father and your Father and my God and your God. (Jn)

Mary Magdalene left the tomb to tell the disciples. Later that day, Jesus became visible to all the disciples in Jerusalem at a place where "the doors were shut... for fear of the Jews" (Jn 20:19). Jesus also appeared to the disciples eight days later, when he showed his wounds to "doubting" Thomas (Jn 20:26-29).

^{20:18}Mary Magdalene cometh and telleth the disciples, I have seen the Lord; and *that* he had said these things unto her. ^{20:19}When therefore it was evening, on that day, the first *day* of the week and when the doors were shut where the disciples were, for fear of the Jews, Jesus came and stood in the midst and saith unto them, Peace *be* unto you. ^{20:20}And when he had said this, he showed unto them his hands and his side. The disciples therefore were glad, when they saw the Lord. ^{20:21}Jesus therefore said to them again, Peace *be* unto you: as the Father hath sent me, even so send I you. ^{20:22}And when he had said this, he breathed on

them and saith unto them, Receive ye the Holy Spirit: $^{20:23}$whose soever sins ye forgive, they are forgiven unto them; whose soever *sins* ye retain, they are retained. $^{20:24}$But Thomas, one of the twelve, called Didymus, was not with them when Jesus came. $^{20:25}$The other disciples therefore said unto him, We have seen the Lord. But he said unto them, Except I shall see in his hands the print of the nails and put my hand into his side, I will not believe. $^{20:26}$And after eight days again his disciples were within and Thomas with them. Jesus cometh, the doors being shut and stood in the midst and said, Peace *be* unto you. $^{20:27}$Then saith he to Thomas, Reach hither thy finger and see my hands; and reach *hither* thy hand and put it into my side: and be not faithless, but believing. $^{20:28}$Thomas answered and said unto him, My Lord and my God. $^{20:29}$Jesus saith unto him, Because thou hast seen me, thou hast believed: blessed *are* they that have not seen and *yet* have believed. $^{20:30}$Many other signs therefore did Jesus in the presence of the disciples which are not written in this book: $^{20:31}$but these are written, that ye may believe that Jesus is the Christ, the Son of God; and that believing ye may have life in his name. (Jn)

The third and last appearance of Jesus in the Book of John takes up the entire 21st chapter. In that section, an undetermined amount of time had passed after the crucifixion. Several of the disciples were   fishing on Lake Gennesareth in Galilee when Jesus appeared to them on the shore.

$^{21:1}$After these things Jesus manifested himself again to the disciples at the sea of Tiberias; and he manifested *himself* on this wise. $^{21:2}$There was together Simon Peter and Thomas called Didymus and Nathanael of Cana in Galilee and the *sons* of Zebedee and two other of his disciples. $^{21:3}$Simon Peter saith unto them, I go a fishing. They say unto him, We also come with thee. They went forth and entered into the boat; and that night they took nothing. $^{21:4}$But when day was now breaking, Jesus stood on the beach: yet the disciples knew not that it was Jesus. $^{21:5}$Jesus therefore saith unto them, Children, have ye aught to eat? They answered him, No. $^{21:6}$And he said unto them, Cast the net on the right side of the boat and ye shall find. They cast therefore and now they were not able to draw it for the multitude of fishes. $^{21:7}$That disciple therefore whom Jesus loved saith unto Peter, It is the Lord. So when Simon Peter heard that it was the Lord, he girt his coat about him (for he was naked) and cast himself into the sea. $^{21:8}$But the other disciples came in the little boat (for they were not far from the land, but about two hundred cubits off), dragging the net *full* of fishes. $^{21:9}$So when they got out upon the land, they see a fire of coals there and fish laid thereon and bread. $^{21:10}$Jesus saith unto them, Bring of the fish which ye have now taken. $^{21:11}$Simon Peter therefore went up and drew the net to land, full of great fishes, a hundred and fifty and three: and for all there were so many, the net was not rent. $^{21:12}$Jesus saith unto them, Come *and* break your fast. And none of the disciples durst inquire of him, Who art thou? knowing that it was the Lord. $^{21:13}$Jesus cometh and taketh the bread and giveth them and the fish likewise. $^{21:14}$This is now the third time that Jesus was manifested to the disciples, after that he was risen from the dead. $^{21:15}$So when they had broken their fast, Jesus saith to Simon Peter, Simon, *son* of John, lovest thou me more than these? He saith unto him, Yea, Lord; thou knowest that I love thee. He saith unto him, Feed my lambs. $^{21:16}$He saith to him again a second time, Simon, *son* of John, lovest thou me? He saith unto him, Yea, Lord; thou knowest that I love thee. He saith unto him, Tend my sheep. $^{21:17}$He saith unto him the third time, Simon, *son* of John, lovest thou me? Peter was grieved because he said unto him the third time, Lovest thou me? And he said unto him, Lord, thou knowest all things; thou knowest that I love thee. Jesus saith unto him, Feed my sheep. $^{21:18}$Verily, verily, I say unto thee, When thou wast young, thou girdedst thyself and walkedst whither thou wouldest: but when thou shalt be old, thou shalt stretch forth thy hands and another shall gird thee and carry thee whither thou wouldest not. $^{21:19}$Now this he spake, signifying by what manner of death he should glorify God. And when he had spoken this, he saith unto him, Follow me. $^{21:20}$Peter, turning about, seeth the disciple whom Jesus loved following; who also leaned back on his breast at the supper and said, Lord, who is he that betrayeth thee? $^{21:21}$Peter therefore seeing him saith to Jesus, Lord and what shall this man do? $^{21:22}$Jesus saith unto him, If I will that he tarry till I come, what *is that* to thee? Follow thou me. $^{21:23}$This saying therefore went forth among the brethren, that that disciple should not die: yet Jesus said not unto him, that he should not die; but, If I will that he tarry till I come, what *is that* to thee? $^{21:24}$This is the disciple that beareth witness of these things and wrote these things: and we know that his witness is true. (Jn)

Acts of the Apostles

The Book of the Acts of the Apostles (Acts) is a continuation of the Book of Luke. Acts begins with the resurrected Jesus appearing to his disciples after the crucifixion. Jesus subsequently reappeared several times to his devotees in a 40-day period starting three days after his execution.

> [1:3]To whom he also showed himself alive after his passion by many proofs, appearing unto them by the space of forty days and speaking the things concerning the kingdom of God: (Lk)

Jesus was last seen on the Mount of Olives where he instructed his disciples to remain in Jerusalem and wait for "the promise of the Father" (Acts 1:4). The disciples then asked Jesus how long that would be.

> [1:7]And he said unto them, It is not for you to know times or seasons which the Father hath set within His own authority. [1:8]But ye shall receive power, when the Holy Spirit is come upon you: and ye shall be my witnesses both in Jerusalem and in all Judaea and Samaria and unto the uttermost part of the earth. [1:9]And when he had said these things, as they were looking, he was taken up; and a cloud received him out of their sight. (Acts 1:7-9)

This is consistent with the Book of Luke where the resurrected Jesus tells his disciples to remain in Jerusalem until they receive the "power." Acts is also the only Gospel where it is suggested–by two Angels–that Jesus will return on the Mount of Olives.

> [1:10]And while they were looking stedfastly into heaven as he went, behold, two men stood by them in white apparel; [1:11]who also said, Ye men of Galilee, why stand ye looking into heaven? this Jesus, who was received up from you into heaven shall so come in like manner as ye beheld him going into heaven. (Acts)

This promise was of great consequence to the Apostles. For this reason, many chose to stay in ever-dangerous Jerusalem rather than leaving and avoiding the animosity of the High Priesthood.

At the time of Jesus' last appearance, the disciples, Jesus' mother, Mary Magdalene and other devotees, were living in Jerusalem in a very large house in an upper-level chamber that could hold 120 people. As has been speculated, this could have been the house of John the Evangelist, a secret disciple of Jesus', the author of the Book of John, and the disciple whom Jesus "loved." But whoever the owner, he was a wealthy and an important man.

It is interesting that so close to the Pentecost and just weeks after Jesus' crucifixion, the disciples lived openly in the Jerusalem house. This was a significant change from the days immediately after the crucifixion, when the very location of the house was a secret.

> When therefore it was evening, on that day, the first *day* of the week and when the doors were shut where the disciples were, for fear of the Jews, Jesus came and stood in the midst and saith unto them, Peace *be* unto you. (Jn 20:19)

But now, a great many things had changed. Jesus, even though his body was missing, was still presumed dead by the High Priesthood and no longer a threat. The atmosphere was markedly more relaxed. Jesus' followers did not prove to be men of violence. The Second Temple priests realized that the Nazarenes were going to be more of a nuisance than anything else. Over time, it was expected that the religious fervor of these disciples would diminish as Jesus' memory faded.

Furthermore, the High Priest Joseph Caiaphas, the most vociferous opponent of Jesus and his followers, had been removed from that position by General Lucius Vitellius several weeks before. By acting against Caiaphas, Vitellius had given a message to the entire Second Temple High Priesthood that Rome would not tolerate the selective persecution of the Christians or any other sect.

In Acts, after Jesus had been taken up into heaven from the Mount of Olives, the disciples returned to their large Jerusalem apartment. There, they chose by lots a Galilean to replace the betrayer Judas, as the Disciples felt that the mystical number 12 had to be maintained. The lot fell upon Matthias (Acts 1:21-26). The Nazarenes continued to live in the same place and preached almost daily in the Second Temple.

The Tongues of Flame

The Pentecost is a major Jewish festival celebrated 50 days after the Passover (one day after a week of weeks). Jesus' ascension from the Mount of Olives occurred 40 days after first appearing to his disciples which was three days after his crucifixion, or five days after the Paschal meal of A.D. 36. So the day of the Pentecost would have been only four days after Jesus' ascension from the Mount of Olives. During his 40 days among them, Jesus had promised his disciples a baptism of sorts in the near future, but no one knew exactly when it would be.

> For John indeed baptized with water; but ye shall be baptized in the Holy Spirit not many days hence. (Acts 1:5)

On the morning of the Pentecost, the disciples were gathered in a room, possibly the large upper-floor apartment in the house of John the Evangelist, where many of them lived.

> 2:2 And suddenly there came from heaven a sound as of the rushing of a mighty wind and it filled all the house where they were sitting. 2:3 And there appeared unto them tongues parting asunder, like as of fire; and it sat upon each one of them. 2:4 And they were all filled with the Holy Spirit and began to speak with other tongues, as the Spirit gave them utterance. (Acts)

The loud noise attracted the attention of Jews who were staying nearby for the festival. Many of these Jews had originated from different parts of the eastern empire and were apparently unfamiliar with Aramaic, the common language of the local Jews — even though Aramaic was the major language of most of Parthia as well as Nabotea and the Jewish East.

At any rate, the disciples found, to their amazement, that they had mastery over several languages. Inspired, they began to evangelize to these Jews in the Jews' own native tongues. On that day, 3,000 were converted to Christianity (Acts 2:1-41).

The "miracle" of the tongues was a hallmark event. If any of the disciples had lingering doubts about Jesus' divinity, this clearly supernatural event put those doubts to rest. From that day forward, many of the disciples abandoned their previous lives completely and began to live communally – adopting an Essenic lifestyle as they preached to the public.

> 2:44 And all that believed were together and had all things common; 2:45 and they sold their possessions and goods and parted them to all, according as any man had need. 2:46 And day by day, continuing stedfastly with one accord in the temple and breaking bread at home, they took their food with gladness and singleness of heart (Acts)

Many of these evangelizing disciples now are referred to as "Apostles" in Acts. The Nazarene movement gained momentum as these men devoted all their time to preaching the word of Jesus. Christian believers began to donate voluntarily in order to support the activities of these men, just as devout Jews were expected to tithe to the Second Temple.

> 4:33 And with great power gave the apostles their witness of the resurrection of the Lord Jesus: and great grace was upon them all. 4:34 For neither was there among them any that lacked: for as many as were possessors of lands or houses sold them and brought the prices of the things that were sold, 4:35 and laid them at the apostles' feet: and distribution was made unto each, according as any one had need. (Acts)

Eusebius quantifies the number of these early apostles as being in the hundreds (Eusebius *History* I-12). He bases this on a lost work of Clement, *Outlines*. Included in this number are the original 12 Disciples, the 70 disciples appointed by Jesus late in the course of his ministry (Lk 10:1) and 500 "brethren" who joined the Church later. All of these latter apostles claimed to have seen Jesus in some form or fashion in the 40-day period after the resurrection.

Of the original Disciples, Simon Peter and James and John the sons of Zebedee, were the lions of the early Nazarene movement. John the Evangelist, a secret disciple who played a role in Jesus' final Passover, also figured prominently, as did James the Just, the brother of Jesus. Interestingly, James the Just is not mentioned in any of the Gospels. According to Clement (from Eusebius), Peter and the brothers Zebedee deferred to Jesus' brother James when it came to designating the first leader of the Christian Church in Jerusalem. James, of course, was only the half-brother of Jesus.

Somewhat incongruous to Acts' depiction of the first year of the Apostles is the entire 21st chapter of the Book of John. In that narration several of the disciples–Peter among them–encountered Jesus when they were fishing on the Gennesareth in Galilee. This happening is certainly consistent with both the Books of Mark and Matthew, where the resurrected Jesus said that he expected to meet the disciples in Galilee. But the disciples could well have been taking a respite from Jerusalem in Galilee, visiting family and friends. In Luke and Acts, written by the same man, the disciples are instructed to wait in Jerusalem until they receive the "power" and then to preach the word in all countries.

Conflict with the High Priesthood

After the miracle of the tongues in late June of A.D. 36, Acts documents two incidents where the Nazarenes clashed with the High Priesthood. In chapters three and four of Acts, the story is told of Peter healing a cripple at the Jerusalem Second Temple gate called "Beautiful." John, presumably one of the sons of Zebedee, was with Peter. After the healing, huge crowds gathered and extolled both Disciples. The priests were alarmed and had them arrested.

> $^{4:1}$And as they spake unto the people, the priests and the captain of the temple and the Sadducees came upon them, $^{4:2}$being sore troubled because they taught the people and proclaimed in Jesus the resurrection from the dead. $^{4:3}$And they laid hands on them and put them in ward unto the morrow: for it was now eventide. (Acts)

The next morning, the two were brought before the High Priesthood.

and Annas the high priest *was there* and Caiaphas and John and Alexander and as many as were of the kindred of the high priest (Acts 4:6)

Significantly, the ex-High Priest Caiaphas was apparently silent as the punishment for the Nazarenes was being considered. In the end, Peter and John were simply released.

And they, when they had further threatened them, let them go, finding nothing how they might punish them, because of the people; for all men glorified God for that which was done. (Acts 4:21)

Only a few months before, Caiaphas had been seething in his desire to execute Jesus, but then he had been the High Priest of the Temple. In this passage, however, Simon Ananus was called "High Priest" and not Caiaphas.

Josephus documents that Jonathan was the new High Priest that eventually succeeded Caiaphas, but Ananus still played a large role. The High Priest Jonathan displayed a level of tolerance for the followers of Jesus for a time. However, it is doubtful whether this sprang from a sense of true contrition, or fear of retribution from Vitellius. Though Vitellius had left Judea for Syria months before, it was no secret that Vitellius would return at some point to wage war with Nabotea–as soon as Roman affairs were settled with the Parthian Empire.

In the fifth chapter of Acts a second incident is described. Despite admonitions from the elder Ananus, Peter continued to evangelize in the Second Temple. Almost every day, Peter and his fellow disciples could be seen in their usual spot at Solomon's portico on the Temple's east cloister. As they preached and healed the sick, the popularity of the Galileans grew.

5:16And there also came together the multitudes from the cities round about Jerusalem, bring sick folk and them that were vexed with unclean spirits: and they were healed every one. 5:17But the high priest rose up and all they that were with him (which is the sect of the Sadducees) and they were filled with jealousy, 5:18and laid hands on the apostles and put them in public ward. (Acts)

The High Priest Jonathan noted that the huge crowds were being drawn to the Nazarenes. Additionally, Jonathan might have suspected that Peter was using trickery to dupe the masses.

> [5:17]But the high priest rose up and all they that were with him (which is the sect of the Sadducees) and they were filled with jealousy, [5:18]and laid hands on the apostles and put them in public ward.

Peter was arrested and imprisoned, probably in the tower of Antonia. Before a trial could be held, however, an Angel appeared and released Peter from his cell (Acts 5:17-24). The Angel told Peter not to flee, but to continue to preach in the courtyard of the Second Temple. And that was where Peter was found the next day by the guards, who were astounded at his escape from prison.

Peter was then brought before the Sanhedrin. The religious council considered executing Peter for his trickery, along with a few other of the Nazarenes. But in a practical assessment of the real problem, Gamaliel, a learned Jewish scholar of the law and a Sanhedrin member, advocated tolerance towards the Christians.

> [5:38]And now I say unto you, Refrain from these men and let them alone: for if this counsel or this work be of men, it will be overthrown: [5:39]but if it is of God, ye will not be able to overthrow them; lest haply ye be found even to be fighting against God. [5:40]And to him they agreed: and when they had called the apostles unto them, they beat them and charged them not to speak in the name of Jesus and let them go. (Acts 5:38-40)

At that time, Gamaliel had a student named Saul of Tarsus, who would soon achieve fame as one of Christianity's greatest scourges. Like Ananus, Gamaliel headed up his own powerful Jerusalem family. He would have a son, Jesus, who would become High Priest in A.D. 64., just before the Jewish revolt.

Gamaliel's opinion temporarily carried the day in the resolution of Peter's trial. After due consideration by the Sanhedrin, the Disciple was set free, although not before he received a sound thrashing and was warned against further preaching in the Temple.

Stephen and the Seven

As the first year after Jesus' crucifixion progressed, the success of the early Nazarenes in recruiting converts meant that the time-demands on the disciples was overwhelming. To alleviate this, seven special "Apostles" were chosen to help with the work in Jerusalem. The exact original purpose of the seven is not clear from reading Acts. Were these men meant to be evangelists — or housekeepers?!

> $^{6:1}$Now in these days, when the number of the disciples was multiplying, there arose a murmuring of the Grecian Jews against the Hebrews, because their widows were neglected in the daily ministration. $^{6:2}$And the twelve called the multitude of the disciples unto them and said, It is not fit that we should forsake the word of God and serve tables. $^{6:3}$Look ye out therefore, brethren, from among you seven men of good report, full of the Spirit and of wisdom, whom we may appoint over this business. (Acts)

The number seven held a mystical significance for the early Christians, thus its choice. Stephen was among them. Perhaps these seven were to be stewards for the communal house where most of the disciples lived. There, they would take care of all the mundane necessities of life for the semi-ascetic Apostles so their time could be devoted to preaching.

> And the saying pleased the whole multitude: and they chose Stephen, a man full of faith and of the Holy Spirit and Philip and Prochorus and Nicanor and Timon and Parmenas and Nicolaus a proselyte of Antioch; (Acts 6:5)

Whatever was the original purpose in their "ordination," at least Stephen and Philip soon became powerful evangelists in their own right. Stephen apparently became a miracle-worker.

> And the word of God increased; and the number of the disciples multiplied in Jerusalem exceedingly; and a great company of the priests were obedient to the faith. And Stephen, full of grace and power, wrought great wonders and signs among the people (Acts 6:7-8)

However, within months — if not weeks — of his initiation, Stephen would be stoned to death for his preaching and harsh words spoken to High Priest Jonathan. Subsequently, with the increasingly dangerous climate in Jerusalem, Philip would leave Judea for Samaria. There, Philip would preaching the word and later become famous for converting the first non-Jew to Christianity. As will be seen, Philip would also become great friends with Paul the Apostle. Before converting, Paul was known as Saul of Tarsus and a Jewish priest. Saul played a leading role in stoning of Stephen, who had also been Philip's friend.

Chronology of the Apostles: An Overview

In placing events in the Acts of the Apostles in context, two dates are especially key: the crucifixion year of Jesus and the date when Paul the Apostle (the former Saul) was imprisoned in Caesarea by Procurator Antonius Felix. The former has been determined to be the spring of A.D. 36. The latter date is generally accepted to be the summer of A.D. 58.

Bracketed by these two dates, the New Testament gives enough solid information to accurately place other important Christian events. The documented travels of Paul the Apostle are central to this, as well as information found Paul's Letters. The reasons will be coming in future chapters, but the following assumptions are presented now to put things in context.

Stephen the Apostle was stoned in late summer of A.D. 36., and Saul of Tarsus had his epiphany on the road to Damascus perhaps two or three months later. Changing his name to Paul and starting to evangelize, Paul returned to Jerusalem from Damascus in A.D. 39 and again 14 years later in A.D. 53. At that time, Paul attended a Christian "summit" meeting in Jerusalem dealing with the Christian conversion of Gentiles. Paul's final return to Jerusalem was for the Pentecost of A.D. 58, where he was arrested, taken to Caesarea, and subsequently imprisoned for two years.

Chapter 8   Saul and the Nazarenes

..beyond measure I persecuted the church of God (Gal 1:13)

Saul of Tarsus is one of the most famous figures in the history of Christianity. Later, as Paul the Apostle, he was an early advocate of an all-inclusive and catholic Christian Church when few other Jewish Church leaders were.   Incongruously, Saul of Tarsus started out his religious life as a priest of the Second Temple and a persecutor of the Nazarenes.

The Young Priest Saul

Saul of Tarsus had a boundless energy that bordered on the manic. As a Temple-trained Jewish priest, Saul was the early Christians' greatest scourge and was a ringleader in the stoning of Stephen the Apostle. But after a roadside epiphany, Saul spent the next 28 years evangelizing Christianity as the Apostle Paul and ended his life martyrdom.

Saul's family had originally moved from Tarsus in Cilicia to Jerusalem. Cilicia was a coastal country south of Syria which is now a part of Turkey. The city of Tarsus exists to this day. Saul's family were tent makers, including Saul himself.

> [18:2]And he found a certain Jew named Aquila, a man of Pontus by race, lately come from Italy, with his wife Priscilla, because Claudius had commanded all the Jews to depart from Rome: and he came unto them; [18:3]and because he was of the same trade, he abode with them and they wrought, for by their trade they were tentmakers. (Acts)

Jerusalem and Judea were very robust markets for tents. During the feast of the Tabernacles, the different Jewish tribes would pitch tents symbolically in the outer courtyard of the Temple to show their nomadic desert origins. For the Passover and other fesitvals, Jerusalem teemed with pilgrims and many stayed in tents outside the city walls and perhaps even in the outer courtyard of the Second Temple. Josephus confirms this when writing about the seditious Passover of 3 B.C. in Jerusalem.

> ..and sent the horsemen to prevent those that had their tents without the temple from assisting those that were within the temple (*Antiq* XVII 9:3)

Jerusalem was located on the fringe of the Judean desert close to Nabotea where nomadic tribesmen had a need for tents. The products that Saul's family produced were in great demand in Jerusalem, and it would be a logical place for them to migrate. By all indications, the family of Saul prospered in the holy city.

But the family might have moved to Jerusalem partially to advance the religious career of their son. That Saul showed an interest in religion early in life is assumed. In those days, one of the few ways for Jews to improve their station — apart from a good marriage and success in business — was through the priesthood. In Jerusalem, Saul would be solidly on the "fast track" to power within the Second Temple establishment. Perhaps his family hoped that Saul would even marry into the High Priesthood, as Joseph Caiaphas had.

> I am a Jew, born in Tarsus of Cilicia, but brought up in this city, at the feet of Gamaliel, instructed according to the strict manner of the law of our fathers, being zealous for God, even as ye all are this day: (Acts 22:3)

Rare among Jews in the priesthood, Saul was a natural-born citizen of the Rome Empire. His father was non-Jewish and likely of Greek origin. Perhaps Saul's grandfather had been a soldier in the Roman army and gained citizenship that way. Saul made it a point to let people know that he did not buy a citizenship, as wealthy Jews of that time would sometimes do; it came by birthright.

Paul's mother was Jewish and so Paul was a natural-born Jew as well. Did Paul enjoy the best of both worlds as a Roman citizen Jew, or the worst? As a Roman citizen Paul had rights and privileges that few other Jews did. For example, a Roman citizen could not be judged before a non-Roman court such as the Sanhedrin. Paul also could not be summarily beaten by a Roman soldier without an official Roman indictment. Paul escaped several dangerous situations in the course of his travels through the exercising of these rights. It is safe to assume that a Roman citizenship would be an asset within the Second Temple hierarchy but a negative with the common Jewish people — who generally hated the Romans.

Training for the Priesthood

Saul, in order to be accepted by the priests for training, had to be exceptionally bright and show an aptitude for writing and argument. Perhaps, too, Saul's family had to buy his enrollment into a religious school. It would have been a rigorous and competitive program. The young priests were expected to recite by rote the most important of the Old Testament passages, so Saul had to have a first-rate memory. Also as part of the training, long hours would have been spent in didactic with the various Jewish philosophers and Pharisees who ran their own schools out of the Second Temple.

Saul also would have been an expert in the Hebrew language which was the holy language of the Temple and Jerusalem. Likely Saul was trained in Latin as well, the language of the Roman occupiers and the economic language of the empire. Knowledge of Aramaic was a given. Saul probably already had a mastery of Greek from his years in Tarsus and his family heritage. Josephus indicates that Greek was not taught to the young Jewish priests.

An important step in the training of the Jewish priest was to be a scribe under the tutelage of the senior priests. Saul would have spent long hours making copies of various important Jewish documents such as supplemental Pharisaical laws to the Torah that had been set down over the generations, or perhaps family ancestries, or lists of High Priests. Josephus, writing in the first century A.D., states that the recorded history of the Jews went back over 2,000 years, so a significant body of Jewish writings needed to be replicated and preserved. Making copies of the holy Torah itself, however, was probably reserved for the most senior and accomplished of the Jewish priests–men adjudged to have the purest souls as well as the most perfectly honed calligraphic skills.

Jonathan and Christian Persecutions

The High Priest Jonathan, newly appointed after the Passover of A.D. 36, had no love for the Nazarenes. He would soon be challenging the sect even to the point of violence. One of the early Christian evangelists, Stephen, was stoned to death (Acts 7:59) by group of Jewish religious partisans who were encouraged to do so by Jonathan. In this, Jonathan himself was likely encouraged by his brother-in-law, Joseph Caiaphas.

In the weeks and months after Jesus' crucifixion, the priests were reasonably tolerant of Jesus' Disciples and followers. Vitellius' anger over Caiaphas' actions was clear and the High Priesthood had no choice but to respect that. The Jerusalem Christian sect itself was keeping a low profile in public places, as they were fearful of the Temple priesthood.

But late in June of A.D. 36, the "miracle of the tongues" occurred. The disciples received the "power" that Jesus had promised to give to them before his ascension. The faith of the Nazarenes was re-affirmed in a spectacular way. As Jesus instructed them to do, the early Christians began to recruit converts and proselytize with renewed energy.

The Apostles Peter and John, the son of Zebedee, and others would preach and effect cures of the afflicted — many times while on Solomon's portico in the Second Temple. Thousands would come to hear them, and many were healed and converted. Jonathan and the High Priesthood were alarmed at this sudden increase in Christian activity and realized that something had to be done.

Between the Passovers of A.D. 36 and A.D. 37 there was a great amount of fear in Jerusalem and the surrounding countryside. The Naboteans had unexpectedly defeated Herod Antipas less than a year and a half before in a battle 25 miles away from the city. It was a surety that General Lucius Vitellius would return with his legions and invade the Arab country in order to bring King Aretas to justice, for Tiberius Caesar had so commanded it. The exact time, however, was unknown. Even if the Romans eventually prevailed, it would mean violent times ahead. Vitellius, though he had won diplomatic successes in Armenia, like the Tetrarch Herod Antipas was unproven on the battlefield. Out of fear of another disaster, many Jews probably fled Jerusalem with their families to wait out the uncertainty in a distant city. An even greater number of Jews likely crowded into Jerusalem seeking safety from their small exposed towns in the immediate surrounding countryside. These people provided grist for the Christian evangelists, and many were converted away from traditional Judaism. This made the High Priesthood very angry.

Fears of the High Priesthood

The High Priesthood early on recognized the potential mass appeal of Christianity. The Jerusalem Nazarenes threatened not only the tenets of Judaism but also the successful operation of the huge business enterprise that the Second Temple had become. With a myriad of major and minor festivals, the Temple earned vast amounts of money from the Jewish pilgrims and tourists. This not only supported the High Priesthood, but also the economy of Jerusalem.

For centuries, all male Jews throughout the ancient world were required to travel to the Second Temple each year in order to tithe and to bring in the first fruits from recent harvests. At the Temple, agents of the High Priesthood sold sacrificial animals to religious pilgrims. After the sacrifice, the Temple would retain control of the valuable carcasses. The income from this and other fees from Temple-based activities was substantial. According to Josephus, this revenue would supported a priesthood that numbered more than 20,000 men.

> for although there be four courses of the priests and every one of them have above five thousand men in them, (Apion II:8).

Even if this is adjusted by a "Josephus factor" of a tenth, 2,000 men and their families would still be a significant portion of the estimated Jerusalem population of 50,000. Jerusalem's economic well-being depended on a prosperous Temple operation. Certainly, the powerful Jewish families who controlled the Temple–Ananus, Gamaliel, Boethus and others–would especially suffer if the Christian movement made significant inroads into their Jewish base.

Another concern was political. The Romans only supported the High Priesthood because they had confidence that the Temple-based theocracy controlled the hearts and minds of the Jewish people. If the Nazarenes grew in power, the Romans might well turn away from the High Priesthood and favor the Christians.

The Controversy of Communion

There was another factor that drove the High Priesthood's intolerance for the Nazarenes. Jesus in establishing the rituals of his Ministry had given the priests a sharp sword to use against him.

According to the Book of John, Jesus first introduced the communion ceremony during a Synagogue gathering in Capernaum. The time was the early summer in A.D. 35 and a few months after the execution of John the Baptist. Jesus earlier had celebrated the Passover in Galilee in semi-seclusion. At the Sabbath gathering, Jesus had unveiled the communion ritual when he had cryptically suggested that he was the Messiah — which caused quite a stir in itself.

The mystical ritual was meant to strengthen the spiritual link between Jesus and his followers, and it is a central ritual of Christianity to this day. But the overtones of cannibalism were obvious, and Jesus lost a considerable number of disciples because of his introduction of it.

> [6:53]Jesus therefore said unto them, Verily, verily, I say unto you, Except ye eat the flesh of the Son of man and drink his blood, ye have not life in yourselves. [6:54]He that eateth my flesh and drinketh my blood hath eternal life: and I will raise him up at the last day. [6:55]For my flesh is meat indeed and my blood is drink indeed. [6:56]He that eateth my flesh and drinketh my blood abideth in me and I in him. [6:57]As the living Father sent me and I live because of the Father; so he that eateth me, he also shall live because of me. [6:58]This is the bread which came down out of heaven: not as the fathers ate and died; he that eateth this bread shall live for ever. [6:59]These things said he in the synagogue, as he taught in Capernaum. [6:60]Many therefore of his disciples, when the heard *this*, said, This is a hard saying; who can hear it? [6:61]But Jesus knowing in himself that his disciples murmured at this, said unto them, Doth this cause you to stumble? [6:62]*What* then if ye should behold the Son of man ascending where he was before? [6:63]It is the spirit that giveth life; the flesh profiteth nothing: the words that I have spoken unto you are spirit, are are life. [6:64]But there are some of you that believe not. For Jesus knew from the beginning who they were that believed not and who it was that should betray him. [6:65]And he said, For this cause have I said unto you, that no man can come unto me, except it be given unto him of the Father. [6:66]Upon this many of his disciples went back and walked no more with him. (Jn)

While the early secular writings denigrated the Christians without being very specific, early Christian historian Justin Martyr specifically linked these negative opinions to the communion ceremony. Justin originally came from Samaria and wrote in the mid-second century A.D. Raised a Greek, Justin studied philosophy as a young man and later converted to Christianity.

> I myself found satisfaction in Plato's teachings and used to hear the Christians abused, but when I found them fearless in the face of death

and all that men think terrible, it dawned on me that they could not possibly be living in wickedness and self-indulgence. For how could a self-indulgent or licentious person who took pleasure in devouring human flesh greet death with a smile, as if he wanted to be deprived of the things he loved most? (Eusebius *History* 4:7 from Justin Martyr *Defense to Antoninus* I:29)

This negative perception of the communion ceremony ("devouring human flesh") was what most of the anti-Christian world used against the Nazarenes. When High Priest Jonathan initiated his campaign against the Christians in A.D. 36, the communion ceremony was the linchpin indictment. The missing body of Jesus certainly would have brought up ghoulish accusations against the Nazarenes by the High Priesthood.

Saul and the Christians

Saul never admitted to knowing Jesus, or to hearing him preach, or to interacting in any way with the early Christians before the stoning of Stephen. This is somewhat curious. As a novitiate Jewish Priest, Saul would have been scuttling about the Second Temple during the Passover of A.D. 36, helping out the priests in any number of ways. Remember, too, that in the weeks and months preceding the fateful Passover, Jesus was preaching in the outer courtyard of the Second Temple to ever-larger and larger crowds. How could Saul not have been aware of him?!

Saul would also have been physically very close to where the Sanhedrin trial of Jesus was held and to the Gabbatha where Pilate held his own trial of Jesus. Golgotha, the site of the crucifixion, was also not far away — although it lay to the west on the other side of the walled Herod palace complex. Despite this, Saul writes nothing about Jesus' arrest, trial, and crucifixion.

Perhaps, as is suggested in the Book of John, this indicates that the Sanhedrin never convened to judge Jesus of Nazareth. What of the crowds at the Gabbatha that assembled to urge Pilate to convict Jesus? Perhaps the crowd, if it existed at all, was a small one made up of High Priesthood partisans who were "in the know" about what Caiaphas wanted. Probably only a very few people knew about Jesus' arrest, much less his crucifixion, before it was over. Caiaphas wanted it that way–the fewer people who knew it the better and that included the lower-level priests. Plus, Caiaphas might have suspected that several Sanhedrin members were secret disciples of Jesus. They would never have stood for a conviction of the Galilean and would have protested vigorously.

Saul's resorting to physical violence against the Christians is another question. Interestingly, Saul himself boasts that his teacher was the peace-loving and practical Gamaliel.

> [1:13]For ye have heard of my manner of life in time past in the Jews' religion, how that beyond measure I persecuted the church of God and made havoc of it: [1:14]and I advanced in the Jews' religion beyond many of mine own age among my countrymen, being more exceedingly zealous for the traditions of my fathers. (Gal 1:13-14)

Modern western sensibilities makes it hard to accept the fact that a priest trainee would kill on the command of a religious superior. But that, apparently, was the case with Saul and his compatriots. In truth, religious zealotry to the point of taking a life was common in ancient times and not unknown even today.

How old was Saul at this time at the time of Stephen's martyrdom? In A.D. 36, Saul is still under the tutelage of High Priesthood, but he is also old enough to have the strength and inclination to physically confront the Nazarenes, who themselves were strong, working-class men — formidable opponents, indeed. With some confidence, it can be hypothesized that Saul at the time of the stoning of Stephen was in his late teens, giving him a birth year of about A.D. 20.

The Martyrdom of Stephen

Stephen had been proselytizing for only a few months, perhaps only weeks, before the confrontation between him and a group of devout Jews took place. His story is told in the sixth chapter of Acts. For this particular gathering of Jews, Stephen presented lucid and powerful arguments in support of the teachings of Jesus, criticizing the traditional Judaic establishment in the process. The Jews couldn't out-debate Stephen and so became frustrated and angry. Stephen's confidence and self-assurance was infuriating to them.

> 6:10And they were not able to withstand the wisdom and the Spirit by which he spake. 6:11Then they suborned men, who said, We have heard him speak blasphemous words against Moses and *against* God. 6:12And they stirred up the people and the elders and the scribes and came upon him and seized him and brought him into the council, 6:13and set up false witnesses, who said, This man ceaseth not to speak words against this holy place and the law: 6:14for we have heard him say, that this Jesus of Nazareth shall destroy this place and shall change the customs which Moses delivered unto us. 6:15And all that sat in the council, fastening their eyes on him, saw his face as it had been the face of an angel. (Acts)

Stephen was then examined by the new High Priest, Jonathan. After a lengthy espousal on the merits of Christianity by Stephen, Acts documents a particularly inflammatory statement that Stephen hurled at the Sanhedrin and the Temple High Priest.

> 7:51Ye stiffnecked and uncircumcised in heart and ears, ye do always resist the Holy Spirit: as your fathers did, so do ye. 7:52Which of the prophets did not your fathers persecute? and they killed them that showed before of the coming of the Righteous One; of whom ye have now become betrayers and murderers; 7:53ye who received the law as it was ordained by angels and kept it not. 7:54Now when they heard these things, they were cut to the heart and they gnashed on him with their teeth. (Acts)

The Jewish High Priest was considered to be a semi-divine. The remark, "uncircumcised heart," would have been a deadly insult. Stephen was comparing the heart of the High Priest with the male private part–and an uncircumcised one at that! Stephen also suggested that Ananus, the father of Jonathan, was a murderer. With this, Stephen's fate was sealed; his insults were unforgivable. Saul and others enthusiastically participated in his stoning.

and when the blood of Stephen thy witness was shed, I also was standing by and consenting and keeping the garments of them that slew him. (Acts 22:20)

Was Stephen's invective an example of the usual aggressive language of the evangelizing Christians, or was Stephen the exception? As will be seen, Paul the Apostle could be just as insulting–and with similar effect.

Saul's hostility didn't stop with just Stephen. Encouraged by the High Priesthood, Saul began to attack as many Christians as he could find.

> [8:1]And Saul was consenting unto his death. And there arose on that day a great persecution against the church which was in Jerusalem; and they were all scattered abroad throughout the regions of Judaea and Samaria, except the apostles. [8:2]And devout men buried Stephen and made great lamentation over him. [8:3]But Saul laid waste the church, entering into every house and dragging men and women committed them to prison. [8:4]They therefore that were scattered abroad, went about preaching the word. (Acts)

Why did Saul persecute the Christians with such zeal? Several reasons can be postulated. For all his years in training, Saul might have realized that intellectually he could not compete with the best of the young priesthood candidates. Persecuting the Christians could have been a way for Saul to stand out in front of the High Priesthood elders. Also, perhaps Saul had come to the realization that since his father had not been born a Jew, his potential for advancement within the Second Temple High Priesthood was limited. Saul needed something extra to recommend him for a high position. Or it could have been that Saul was simply trying to attract the attention of a young woman through his high-profile anti-Christian activities.

As for the Christians themselves, after the stoning of Stephen they realized that Jerusalem was no longer a safe place for them. Clearly, the High Priest was resorting to Caiaphas-like tactics to counter them. Many of the disciples then began to leave Jerusalem and proselytize in cities in Asia Minor, but only to Jews.

They therefore that were scattered abroad upon the tribulation that arose about Stephen travelled as far as Phoenicia and Cyprus and Antioch, speaking the word to none save only to Jews. (Acts 11:19)

Eusebius quotes from Origen, a third century A.D. Christian theologian and historian, on this planned dispersal that began in A.D. 36.

> Thomas, tradition tells us, was chosen for Parthia andrew for Scythia, John for Asia, where he remained until his death at Ephesus. Peter seems to have preached in Pontus, Galatia and Bithynia, Cappadocia and Asia to the Jews of the dispersion. Finally, he came to Rome, where he was crucified head-downwards at his own request What needs to be said of Paul, who from Jerusalem as far as Illyricum preached in all its fullness the gospel of Christ and was later martyred in Rome under Nero? (Eusebius *History* from *Origen* 3:1)

Philip in Samaria

Chapter eight of Acts details the evangelical adventures of Philip, who was one of the ordained seven along with the martyred Stephen (Acts 6:5). Philip soon left Jerusalem after Stephen's death for Samaria and other countries. While Acts states that the Christian disciples lived communally as they evangelized in the early years, this probably did not apply to Philip, as Philip had a wife and four daughters. This also suggests that the disciples (Apostles) were not required to take a vow of chastity, as the Essenes did. Partially to protect his family, Philip was among the first Christians to leave increasingly dangerous Jerusalem for foreign lands (Acts 21:8-9).

From Jerusalem, Philip traveled to neighboring Samaria. Even though the Samaritan population was also Jewish, they practiced their own variant form of Judaism. In consideration of this, Herod the Great had built the Samaritan Jews their own Temple in Sebaste supposedly on a par with the Second Temple in Jerusalem, although, given the extent and grandeur of the Second Temple, that is difficult to believe.

In Samaria at this time, Simon the Magician was a popular religious figure. Simon held sway over much of the population. As his name suggests, Simon's power came from practicing the occult arts.

> 8:9But there was a certain man, Simon by name, who beforetime in the city used sorcery and amazed the people of Samaria, giving out that himself was some great one: 8:10to whom they all gave heed, from the least to the greatest, saying, This man is that power of God which is called Great (Acts 8:9-10)

Simon observed the preaching of Philip and was impressed with Philip's ability to heal the sick and exorcise demons. In the hopes of gaining the same powers, Simon the Magician underwent Christian baptism. Apparently, Philip ascribed to the immersion ritual of John the Baptist and used it frequently. But unfortunately for Simon the Magician, after his baptism he found he had no more powers than before. Disappointed, Simon offered Philip a huge sum of money to buy his healing powers (Acts 8:1-25). Philip, of course, could not oblige.

Not long afterward, Simon left Samaria for Rome. Early Church Father Justin Martyr gives more information about this Samaritan sorcerer (whom Justin calls Simon the Magus) and gives a hint as to the time frame when all this occurred.

> There was a Samaritan, Simon, a native of the village called Gitto, who in the reign of Claudius Caesar and in your royal city of Rome, did mighty acts of magic, by virtue of the art of the devils operating in him. He was considered a god and as a god was honoured by you with a statue which statue was erected on the river Tiber, between the two bridges and bore this inscription, in the language of Rome.. "To Simon the holy God." And almost all the Samaritans and a few even of other nations, worship him and acknowledge him as the first god; and a woman, Helena, who went about with him at that time and had formerly been a prostitute, they say is the first idea generated by him. (Justin Martyr *Apology* I-26)

While having a statue in Rome sounds impressive enough, in fact, anyone with enough money could get one made and have it placed in an approved public area. In Simon's case, the statue was thoroughly Romanized as a pagan god, making it especially acceptable to the authorities.

Simon the Magician probably moved on to Rome years later after having fine-tuned his occult skills in Samaria and well after his encounter with Philip. While Simon's presence in Rome was not mentioned in Acts, Justin does affirm that Simon was in Rome sometime during the reign of Claudius (A.D. 41-54).

Later in the same chapter in Acts, the Apostles Peter and John also came to Samaria to proselytize and had great success. They, too, probably started to travel in the aftermath of the recent stoning of Stephen. In Samaria, the Apostle Peter also became familiar with Simon the Magician. Years later, Peter would move on to Rome. It is possible that one of Peter's motives in doing so was to counter the evil Simon, who apparently had established a strong base there and was corrupting potential Christian converts.

Philip, under a command from God, then went to Gaza, a country just to the north of the Egyptian Sinai on the eastern Mediterranean coast. Philip there met the chief eunuch of Queen Candide of Ethiopia and converted him to Christianity, the first non-Jew to profess the faith.

Philip the Apostle went on to Caesarea, where he settled down with his family and continued to proselytize. Was Jerusalem too dangerous a place during the tenures of High Priests Jonathan (A.D. 36) and Theophilis (A.D. 37-41) for Philip and his family? Perhaps so.

Epiphany of Saul

Many Christians fled Jerusalem in a controlled panic after the stoning of Stephen the Apostle and the increase in Temple-sanctioned persecutions. The Apostles who chose to stay were forced into a low-profile survival mode and practiced Jewish ritual in order to blend in. Unfortunately for Saul, he was finding fewer and fewer Christians to victimize. He had received a measure of fame and approbation for his role in Stephen's stoning and his subsequent persecutions of the Christians, and he had liked it. Later in A.D. 36 Saul had a proposal for the High Priest Jonathan.

> $^{9:1}$But Saul, yet breathing threatening and slaughter against the disciples of the Lord, went unto the high priest, $^{9:2}$and asked of him letters to Damascus unto the synagogues, that if he found any that were of the Way, whether men or women, he might bring them bound to Jerusalem. (Acts 9:1-2)

In A.D. 36, Damascus was under the rule of King Aretas IV of Nabotea. Its population was significantly Jewish, and the religious Jews there apparently complained to the Second Temple priests about the presence of the Christians. The "problem" Christians could well have been those newly-arrived from Jerusalem who sought a haven away from the violence of Saul and his like-minded friends. The Nazarenes in Damascus might have been disrupting Jewish services in the Synagogues, or perhaps harassing Jews in the open-air markets with their tireless evangelizing.

In Jerusalem, Saul presented a plan to Jonathan, the High Priest. Saul wanted to go to Damascus and arrest the most aggressive and egregious of the Christians. He would then bring them back to the Second Temple, presumably in chains, for examination and trial. Jonathan thought this was an excellent idea.

Letters of authority were given to Saul for that purpose by Jonathan in case the Arabic governor of Damascus objected. Remember, too, that at that time a Roman invasion of Nabotea was thought to be imminent. The papers gave Saul a level of "diplomatic" immunity should there arise problems of a political nature.

But while on the road to Damascus, Saul had a wondrous and life-changing vision of Jesus. The power of it caused him to go blind.

> .$^{9:3}$And as he journeyed, it came to pass that he drew nigh unto Damascus: and suddenly there shone round about him a light out of heaven: $^{9:4}$and he fell upon the earth and heard a voice saying unto him,

Saul, Saul, why persecutest thou me? $^{9:5}$And he said, Who art thou, Lord? And he *said*, I am Jesus whom thou persecutest: $^{9:6}$but rise and enter into the city and it shall be told thee what thou must do. $^{9:7}$And the men that journeyed with him stood speechless, hearing the voice, but beholding no man. $^{9:8}$And Saul arose from the earth; and when his eyes were opened, he saw nothing; and they led him by the hand and brought him into Damascus. $^{9:9}$And he was three days without sight and did neither eat nor drink. (Acts)

Years later, when on trial in front of Agrippa II, Saul (now Paul) related additional details of his epiphany.

$^{26:12}$Whereupon as I journeyed to Damascus with the authority and commission of the chief priests, $^{26:13}$at midday, O king, I saw on the way a light from heaven, above the brightness of the sun, shining round about me and them that journeyed with me. $^{26:14}$And when we were all fallen to the earth, I heard a voice saying unto me in the Hebrew language, Saul, Saul, why persecutest thou me? it is hard for thee to kick against the goad. (Acts)

According to Acts, this "spirit" of Jesus then appeared before a disciple named Ananias who lived in Damascus. The spirit told Ananias to leave his house and find the blinded Saul and minister to him. Ananias followed those instructions and indeed found Saul on the side of the road. He returned with Saul to Damascus and put him up in his house. Through the ministrations of Ananias and others, and the powerful and lasting effect of his vision of Jesus, Saul converted to Christianity. When Saul accepted the teachings of Jesus, his sight returned.

$^{9:18}$And straightway there fell from his eyes as it were scales and he received his sight; and he arose and was baptized; $^{9:19}$and he took food and was strengthened. And he was certain days with the disciples that were at Damascus. $^{9:20}$And straightway in the synagogues he proclaimed Jesus, that he is the Son of God. $^{9:21}$And all that heard him were amazed and said, Is not this he that in Jerusalem made havoc of them that called on this name? and he had come hither for this intent, that he might bring them bound before the chief priests. (Acts)

Saul proved to be no casual convert. All of Saul's capabilities and considerable energy were now focused on the promotion of Christianity instead of its destruction. As the eventful year of A.D. 36 ended, Saul was in Damascus and living the Christian evangelical life. He would not return to Jerusalem for three years.

> 1:16 ..straightway I conferred not with flesh and blood: 1:17neither went I up to Jerusalem to them that were apostles before me: but I went away into Arabia; and again I returned unto Damascus. 1:18Then after three years I went up to Jerusalem to visit Cephas and tarried with him fifteen days. 1:19But other of the apostles saw I none, save James the Lord's brother. (Gal)

As Saul's activities continued (Saul is hereafter referred to as Paul) and his reputation spread, the Jews' hostility against him increased. The Jerusalem High Priesthood was especially incensed for now Paul was more than just a Nazarene–he was a traitor! Their concern was understandable: if the most dedicated and vigorous of their Christian persecutors had succumbed to the power of Jesus, what did that portend for the rest of the Jews? Would all Second Temple ritual be totally forgotten and the High Priesthood hierarchy become useless and anachronistic as more and more Jews converted to Christianity?

Chapter 9　Rumors of War

> So Vitellius..ordered Pilate to go to Rome, to answer before the emperor to the accusations of the Jews. So Pilate, when he had tarried ten years in Judea, made haste..in obedience to the orders of Vitellius which he durst not contradict; (*Antiq* XVIII 4:2)

In late A.D. 36, the Nazarenes were in a state of uncertainty and disarray. The stoning of Stephen the Apostle marked the start of increased hostility and violence towards the Christians by the Jerusalem High Priesthood. At the same time, important political events were occurring in the Jewish East. Within a year of condemning Jesus to the cross, the Roman Prefect Pontius Pilate committed one of his boldest actions. As a direct result, Syrian President Lucius Vitellius removed Pilate from office in early A.D. 37.

The incident involved a charismatic religious leader of the Samaritans who was, apparently, much like Jesus of Nazareth.

> But the nation of the Samaritans did not escape without tumults. The man who excited them to it was one who thought lying a thing of little consequence and who contrived every thing so that the multitude might be pleased; so he bid them to get together upon Mount Gerizzim which is by them looked upon as the most holy of all mountains and assured them, that when they were come thither, he would show them those sacred vessels which were laid under that place, because Moses put them there So they came thither armed and thought the discourse of the man probable; and as they abode at a certain village which was called Tirathaba, they got the rest together to them and desired to go up the mountain in a great multitude together; but Pilate prevented their going up, by seizing upon file roads with a great band of horsemen and foot-

men, who fell upon those that were gotten together in the village; and when it came to an action, some of them they slew and others of them they put to flight and took a great many alive, the principal of which and also the most potent of those that fled away, Pilate ordered to be slain.

But when this tumult was appeased, the Samaritan senate sent an embassy to Vitellius, a man that had been consul and who was now president of Syria and accused Pilate of the murder of those that were killed; for that they did not go to Tirathaba in order to revolt from the Romans, but to escape the violence of Pilate. So Vitellius sent Marcellus, a friend of his, to take care of the affairs of Judea and ordered Pilate to go to Rome, to answer before the emperor to the accusations of the Jews. So Pilate, when he had tarried ten years in Judea, made haste to Rome and this in obedience to the orders of Vitellius which he durst not contradict; but before he could get to Rome Tiberius was dead. (*Antiq* XVIII 4:1-2)

Interestingly, Vitellius did not consult Tiberius before removing Pilate from office. This suggests that Tiberius and Vitellius had already discussed the problematic Pilate and the sort of actions that they would and would not tolerate from him.

The Samaritans

A history of animosity had long existed between Judea and Samaria. It began almost 200 years before with the Greek-Syrian King Antiochus. Antiochus, after conquering the Jewish lands in 163 B.C., outlawed the practice of Judaism. The penalty for defying the new law was death. Many Judeans did, in fact, ignore the new laws and suffered accordingly. The Samaritans, seeing the Judeans so suffer, quickly converted over to Greek ways and abandoned their Jewish heritage.

When the Samaritans saw the Jews under these sufferings, they no longer confessed that they were of their kindred, nor that the temple on Mount Gerizzim belonged to Almighty God. This was according to their nature, as we have already shown. And they now said that they were a colony of Medes and Persians; (Antiq XII 5:5)

The Samaritans went to far as to build a temple dedicated to the Roman god Jupiter on top of their most holy Mount Gerizzim.

As for the conquered Judeans, the great Temple in Jerusalem was converted into a gymnasium by the Greek-Syrians, where sports could be practiced in true Greek style.

(certain Judean Jews) also hid the circumcision of their genitals, that even when they were naked they might appear to be Greeks. Accordingly, they left off all the customs that belonged to their own country and imitated the practices of the other nations. (*Antiq* XII 5:1)

But enough Judeans opposed the changes to organize an insurrection. Judas Maccabeus and his brothers led the revolt. After two years they successfully defeated Antiochus and a new Jewish nation was born. The Samaritans were now perceived as traitors to the faith by the ruling Maccabeans and the Judean Jews who remained loyal to their faith. The Samaritans suffered from Judean animosity ever since.

The Samaritans practiced their own variant form of Judaism and eschewed the great Temple in Jerusalem and its system of tithes and sacrifices. In fact, the ancient Samaritans had their own temple in Sebaste which had been rebuilt by Herod the Great and was detailed in writings of Josephus (*Antiq* XV 8:5). The Samaritans believed that the Ark of the Covenant and other lost treasures from the ancient Temple of Jerusalem–Solomon's Temple–were buried on the top of Mount Gerizzim in Samaria. Also on Gerizzim, according to Samaritan belief the Messiah would return someday to establish his kingdom.

Pilate Attacking the Samaritans

In late A.D. 36 Pilate found himself faced with another potentially violent religious leader. This time, the leader was not a Galilean but a Samaritan. Like Jesus, however, this Samaritan prophet was promising his followers a sort of salvation; in this case the promise involved the uncovering of the sacred First Temple vessels that supposedly lay buried on top of Mount Gerizzim. Josephus asserts that this Samaritan leader was a liar and a charlatan. Pilate was of the same opinion.

The Samaritan's thousands of followers gathered at the town of Tirathaba in Samaria. They were armed and were presumed dangerous by Pilate. Why else would they carry weapons?! Pilate decided this did not fit the picture of a peaceful, religious quest — he was convinced that rebellion, not salvation, was the actual intent of the mob. His Roman troops lay in wait and ambushed the Samaritans on their way to Gerizzim. Many were slain in the one-sided battle, and Pilate later executed all of the captured leaders.

After the slaughter, the Samaritan Senate wrote to Syrian President Lucius Vitellius in protest. In the letter, it was explained that the Samaritans needed the weapons to protect them from Pilate. This suggests that Pilate had clashed before with members of the sect.

Motives of Pilate

How large a role did Jesus and the Nazarenes play in Pilate's aggressive stance against the Samaritans in late A.D. 36? After the crucifixion, Jesus' body went missing. Pilate believed, as did the High Priesthood, that either the Nazarenes themselves stole it or that Jesus survived the crucifixion.

Pilate was fully aware that Jesus had spent only about three hours on the cross before he died which was an unusually short amount of time. When Joseph of Arimathea requested the body of Jesus, Pilate had trusted his centurion that Jesus was, in fact, dead. But with subsequent reports of Jesus' "resurrection" and now the sudden emergence of this mysterious Samaritan leader, Pilate might have made a logical connection: Jesus was that Samaritan leader. Pilate was certainly aware that the High Priesthood had driven many Christians into Samaria after the stoning of Stephen. Were these displaced Nazarenes at the heart of this rebel army?

To be sure, the Jerusalem Priesthood would have little love for any Messiah-like figure who threatened their authority- Samaritan, Galilean, or otherwise. The Second Temple High Priesthood would likely have encouraged Pilate to think that this

Samaritan was the "crucified" Jesus to insure the destruction of the rogue movement.

Pilate's Removal

When Emperor Tiberius appointed Lucius Vitellius as president of Syria in A.D. 35, he likely authorized the former Senate consul to remove Pilate if necessary. Undoubtedly, the Royal archives had many reports on file of Pilate's cruelty and outrageous behavior. The recent action against the group of religious Samaritans by Pilate drew an angry response from the Samaritan Senate. They petitioned Vitellius to investigate. Vitellius did so and determined that Pilate's actions were unjustified in the extreme. He removed Pilate from office and sent him to Tiberius for trial. Fortunately for the disgraced Pilate, while he was en route sailing to Italia to meet his fate, Tiberius died in Misenum.

What was the ultimate fate of Pilate? Did Emperor Caius care enough to carry on Tiberius' planned "trial?" Pilate was a wealthy man after all his years profiting from graft and corruption in the East. Evidence of this was found recently in Caesarea. A fragment of a marble engraving–a dedication motif for the opulent amphitheater–was discovered with Pilate's name on it. This suggests that Pilate, partially at his own expense, had built, or had rebuilt, the impressive public structure. This would have been no small financial undertaking.

The arrested Pilate in early A.D. 37 was traveling to Rome under an armed escort, but probably not in physical chains. He had been accused of a crime but not convicted, and he was a Roman citizen, after all. After learning that Tiberius had died, perhaps Pilate bought his way out of a difficult situation and subsequently retired, along with his wife, to some pleasant part of the empire.

Eusebius, however, suggests a different fate.

It is worthy of note that, as the records show, in the reign of Gaius (Caius), whose times I am describing, Pilate himself, the Governor of our

Saviour's day, was involved in such calamities that he was forced to become his own executioner and to punish himself with his own hand: divine justice, it seems, was not slow to overtake him. The facts are recorded by the Greeks who have chronicled the Olympiads together with the events occurring in each. (Eusebius *History* 2:7)

The Greek histories that Eusebius refers to are lost. As will be seen in future chapters, Emperor Caius, the young successor to Tiberius, did force the removal and execution of several powerful Roman administrators, but that was to be later in his reign. Early on, Caius, under the artful guidance of General Sertorius Macro, was on his best behavior and very popular with the Roman people. It was unlikely that Caius, in his first months of power, would have ordered the execution of any high-level official — much less a former prefect. And if Pilate did meet his end the way Eusebius asserts, then Jewish historian Philo Judaeus would have written about it, but he does not. Additionally, since Pilate's supposed fate was similar to the suicide of Judas Iscariot, Jesus' betrayer, suspicions must be raised as to its veracity.

Vitellius at the Euphrates

After the Passover of A.D. 36, Herod Antipas was confident of gaining revenge upon King Aretas IV of Nabotea. Aretas had brutally defeated Antipas' army in battle less than a year earlier. Vitellius had discussed Nabotea at length with Antipas, Pilate, and their generals at the festival. A rough battle plan had already been drawn up. The instrument of Antipas' revenge would be the Roman army, with Vitellius at the command. Vitellius had promised to bring down from Syria as many as three full legions for that purpose.

Vitellius had planned that first trip to Jerusalem already knowing that a summit meeting of sorts had been prearranged with the Parthian nobles for the upcoming summer. The meeting would occur by the Euphrates River, the boundary between the Roman and Parthian Empires. Did Vitellius expect King Artabanus himself to be there? Vitellius had told Herod Antipas in Jerusalem about the meeting with Parthia and the probability of a peaceful settlement.

Antipas was overjoyed at the news and could not be kept away from it. Antipas was eager to ingratiate himself to Vitellius in any way possible. Herod Antipas likely volunteered to bring his reorganized army–such as remained!–north to the Euphrates should it be needed. And, as will be seen, if Antipas knew about the reconciliation between Tiberius and his nephew Herod Agrippa in Capri, he would be especially motivated to gain revenge against Aretas and raise his stature in the eyes of the emperor.

In the matter of Vitellius' "summit" meetings with the Parthians, the historians Tacitus and Josephus have differing versions.

> When Tiberius had heard of these things, he desired to have a league of friendship made between him and Artabanus; and when, upon this invitation, he received the proposal kindly, Artabanus and Vitellius went to Euphrates and as a bridge was laid over the river, they each of them came with their guards about them and met one another on the midst of the bridge. And when they had agreed upon the terms of peace Herod, the tetrarch erected a rich tent on the midst of the passage and made them a feast there. (*Antiq* XVIII 4:5)

While Josephus states that Artabanus was present at the Euphrates summit meeting of A.D. 36, Tacitus does not agree.

> Vitellius, as soon as Artabanus had fled and his people were inclined to have a new king, urged Tiridates to seize the advantage thus offered and then led the main strength of the legions and the allies to the banks of the Euphrates. While they were sacrificing, the one, after Roman custom, offering a swine, a ram and a bull; the other, a horse which he had duly prepared as a propitiation to the river-god, they were informed by the neighbouring inhabitants that the Euphrates, without any violent rains, was of itself rising to an immense height and that the white foam was curling into circles like a diadem, an omen of a prosperous passage. Some explained it with more subtlety, of a successful commencement to the enterprise which, however, would not be lasting, on the ground, that though a confident trust might be placed in prognostics given in the earth or in the heavens, the fluctuating character of rivers exhibited omens which vanished the same moment. A bridge of boats having been constructed and the army having crossed, the first to enter the camp was

Ornospades, with several thousand cavalry. Formerly an exile, he had rendered conspicuous aid to Tiberius in the completion of the Dalmatic war and had for this been rewarded with Roman citizenship. (*Annuls* 6:37)

In this instance, Josephus is likely in error. Probably only a few of the major Parthian nobles surrendered their armies to Tiridates at the Euphrates in the summer of A.D. 36. Artabanus himself, perhaps unknown to Vitellius, at the time was busily raising another army in the heart of Parthia with the intention of reestablishing himself as king.

Suetonius documents a conference between Vitellius and King Artabanus at the Euphrates in both in his sections on Caius and Aulus Vitellius.

Lucius attained the consulate and then was made governor of Syria, where with supreme diplomacy having not only induced Artabanus, king of the Parthians, to hold a conference with him, but even to do obeisance to the standards of the legion. (Sue *Vitellius* 2:4)

Artabanus, for example, king of the Parthians, who was always outspoken in his hatred and contempt for Tiberius, voluntarily sought Caligula's friendship and came to a conference with the consular governor; then crossing the Euphrates, he paid homage to the Roman eagles and standards and to the statues of the Caesars._(Sue *Caligula* 14:3)

These passages from Suetonius suggest that there were two successive meetings between the Romans and the Parthians at the Euphrates, one in A.D. 36 and one in A.D. 38. Only at the second, when Tiberius was dead and Caius was emperor, did King Artabanus attend. At the first meeting, in the early summer of A.D. 36., the Roman-sponsored King Tiridates received enough support from the Parthian nobles and warlords to make Lucius Vitellius confident of peace in Armenia. This meant that Vitellius could proceed with the war plans he had tentatively made against King Aretas of Nabotea. Tiberius was very much alive in A.D. 36 and, if Suetonius is to be believed, King

Artabanus of Parthia passionately hated Tiberius. He would not have considered a treaty with Rome for any reason.

At a second meeting in the summer of A.D. 38, Vitellius might have finally met Artabanus personally and hammered out a definitive peace agreement between the two empires. At that meeting, Artabanus actually gave hostages to Rome in order to seal the treaty. In fact, Artabanus might have been very relieved when Tiberius died–it provided him with a face-saving way to justify peace with Rome. The fact that Caius did not pursue war with Aretas might have also been a factor in Artabanus' change in attitude towards Rome. Artabanus also had been a great supporter of Germanicus, and Caius was Germanicus' son.

Artabanus' ambitions in Armenia and Syria had been met with complete disaster and had even temporarily cost him his throne. Now, with Tiberius dead, Artabanus could claim that his quarrel had been only with Tiberius and not with the Roman people. He now espoused only the highest regard for the new Emperor Caius. So a peace between the two empires was established with Artabanus preserving a measure of dignity. A triumph for Vitellius!

It is interesting to note that Tacitus doesn't mention Herod Antipas as being present at the Euphrates meeting of A.D. 36. According to Josephus, however, Herod Antipas was not only there, but he put on a great feast for the participants. Antipas took this opportunity to ingratiate himself to Vitellius and also make sure that the Syrian president didn't forget the the command of Tiberius to avenge Antipas' recent defeat.

But Vitellius probably did not like being rushed into war and was undoubtedly irked not only by Antipas' presence, but also by Tiberius' order for Aretas' execution in the first place. Vitellius probably considered a war with Nabotea to be pointless and foolhardy. But by early A.D. 37, Vitellius would reluctantly decide that the time was right to confront Aretas in Nabotea.

Second trip to Judea

In early A.D. 37, despite the fact that a rejuvenated King Artabanus was on the loose and still somewhat of a threat, Vitellius led two Roman legions into Judea with the intent to invade Nabotea. Despite Artabanus' saber-rattling, the country of Armenia was secure and the western sections of Parthia were firmly controlled by Tiridates. Two more Roman legions were left in Syria should Tiridates need them. Possibly, one or more of Rome's mobile legions were now stationed in Antioch as well.

So for the second year in a row, Vitellius made a springtime trip to Judea. However, the journey in A.D. 37 was far from a relaxed reconnaissance mission. A grim Vitellius was preparing for all-out war with Arabia. He could only hope for a speedy capture and beheading of Aretas IV which were the specific orders of Emperor Tiberius.

Vitellius knew that there would be no guarantee of success in the mountainous and harsh country of Nabotea. The strength of the Roman army was on the open plains and not at all in the mountains. Herod Antipas joined Vitellius somewhere along the route to southern Perea with his own refurbished and re-conscripted army. More of his troops awaited in southern Perea, encamped close to the fortress of Macherus. Aristobulos, Herodias' brother, probably also accompanied Vitellius as an important adviser.

The principal men in several major Jewish cities along the way protested against the Roman army marching through their countries. To address the concerns of these principal men, Vitellius obligingly directed his army to take a more circuitous route to southern Perea and avoid the lush central highlands of Judea and Samaria.

At some point in the movement of troops through the Jewish lands, Vitellius heard the complaint of the Samaritan Sanhedrin about Pilate's atrocities. Vitellius, when he reached Judea, likely summoned Pilate so the man could give an account of himself. Hearing both sides, Vitellius decided to remove Pilate as prefect of Judea and Samaria. In his place, Vitellius appointed a staff member named Marcellus to oversee the important prefecture.

This personnel change gave Vitellius further reason to be in Jerusalem for the Passover of A.D. 37. Pilate had been removed only a few weeks before the start of the festival. Because the festival was known for turning violent with little warning, Vitellius would make sure that he and his personal army escort of several hundred men were there along with new Prefect Marcellus. Vitellius probably also remembered with fondness the pleasant time he had there the previous year. Jerusalem would be a restful stop before the arduous and unpredictable campaign in Nabotea—which Vitellius was not looking forward to.

Agrippa in Chains

The ensuing year after the crucifixion of Jesus was a tumultuous one for Herod Agrippa, the future King Agrippa I and the brother of Herodias. Earlier, in A.D. 36, Herod Agrippa had taken a great risk and traveled from Alexandria in Egypt to Campania in Italy in order to petition for an audience with Emperor Tiberius. Previously in Rome, Tiberius had banned Agrippa from his Royal court, a disgrace that Agrippa had lived with for almost 15 years. Agrippa and his wife Cypros had recently spent almost four years traveling through the Jewish East, hoping to find a stable place in which to live and raise their family. For one reason or another, Agrippa had been hounded out of Judea, Tiberias, Antioch, and Anthedon.

But much to Agrippa's pleasant surprise, Tiberius quickly answered his letter and invited him for a visit on the island of Capri. It can be speculated that to arouse Tiberius' interest, Agrippa had promised him a strategic information about Syria or Armenia. For several years, that part of the empire had been unsettled and a thorn in Tiberius' side. Apparently, Agrippa's former banishment presented no obstacle to Tiberius when it came to the greater interests of the empire. Tiberius was well aware that Agrippa had just spent more than three years in the area and might have learned useful information. For his part,

Agrippa was at his patronizing best during the initial meeting on Capri, and Tiberius decided to lay the banishment aside. In the intervening 15 years since his banishment, Agrippa had likely matured greatly, much to Tiberius' approval.

So in the summer of A.D. 36, Agrippa had found his way back into the good graces of Tiberius, and he was living the good life on the beautiful island of Capri. The patrician Antonia, of the same generation as Tiberius and his sister-in-law through Drusus the Great, was a strong supporter of the children of Bernice and might have played a key role in Tiberius' unexpected warming toward Agrippa. To live there and be accepted back into the Royal salon was a phoenix-like recrudescence for the grandson of Herod the Great.

This reconciliation of Herod Agrippa with Emperor Tiberius occurred about the time of the Passover of A.D. 36. Of course, both men were oblivious to the events concerning Jesus in Jerusalem. Cypros, Agrippa's wife whom he had left in Alexandria, may, however, have found her way to Jerusalem with Agrippa's three children in time to celebrate the Passover with her cousin Herodias. Could Cypros have learned about Agrippa's success with Tiberius earlier and, in Jerusalem, could she have communicated this to her cousin Herodias and uncle Antipas?! That would not have been good news for the Royal couple. Agrippa would have few good things to say about Antipas, for Antipas banished him from his kingdom not two years before. And there was still the question of the final disposition of the late Herod Philip's kingdom. Agrippa was now a serious contender to obtain the prize, along with Antipas.

For all his character flaws, Agrippa was a very learned and erudite man, and Emperor Tiberius himself had been a life-long student of Philosophy. The emperor was impressed enough to appoint Agrippa as the tutor for his grandson, Tiberius Gemellus. This young Tiberius was the odds-on favorite to inherit the empire. Agrippa also became the boon companion of Caius, Tiberius' nephew, who was also a potential, though less probable, successor to the throne. Caius was the 24-year-old son of the iconic Germanicus.

But it was this close association with the young Caius that caused Agrippa's second fall from the good graces of the all-powerful Tiberius. One day, Agrippa made a casual remark to Caius to the effect that Tiberius should hurry up and die so Caius could become emperor. A servant overheard this and remembered it.

Josephus then relates a long story in *Antiquities* about the situation and how Agrippa's ill-advised remark got back to Tiberius. When Tiberius learned of it, it was October A.D. 36 and close to the fifth anniversary of the conspiracy of Sejanus. For that reason, Tiberius might have been especially sensitive to any suggestion of treason in those he allowed to be close to him. Agrippa's words brought back Tiberius' old distaste for the Jewish prince. Agrippa was horrified when he realized he was to be arrested and imprisoned!

> upon which Agrippa betook himself to make supplication for himself, putting him in mind of his son, with whom he was brought up and of Tiberius [his grandson] whom he had educated; but all to no purpose; for they led him about bound even in his purple garments. (*Antiq* XX 6:6)

Herodias' brother stayed imprisoned and chained to a Roman soldier for six months, until the death of Tiberius in March A.D. 37.

Chapter 10   Emperor Caius

(Caius).. was a man who masked a savage temper under an artful guise of self-restraint..Hence the fame of a clever remark from the orator Passienus, that "there never was a better slave or a worse master." (*Annuls* 6:20)

Emperor Tiberius Caesar was 77 years old when Jesus was crucified in A.D. 36. Tiberius would die less than a year later on the 17th of March, A.D. 37—nearly 80 years to the day after Julius Caesar's infamous assassination in a crowded Roman Forum in 44 B.C. In contrast to Caesar's death in the crowded Roman Forum, Tiberius died in a quiet Misenum country estate. But like Caesar, Tiberius was murdered.

Misenum was located on the north seacoast of the deep-blue Sorrentum Sea, scores of miles away from the island of Capri, where Tiberius had spent the last 10 years of his life. Below the cliffs of Misenum, a protected bay harbored the western fleet of the Roman Empire. There, likely hundreds of warships, transport vessels, and support ships were at anchor. On the rocky shore were extensive and vast fleet support facilities and shipyards.

As the Ides of March in A.D. 37 passed, Tiberius was drifting in and out of consciousness with increasing frequency. The loyal General Sertorius Macro was there to watch over Tiberius' final hours. Macro had been catapulted to power seven years previously with his efficient arrangement of the arrest and the "spontaneous" mob execution of the traitor General Lucius Sejanus. But now Macro–who was a strong supporter of the young Caius for succession–was getting tired of Tiberius' stubborn refusal to die, and so he ordered the aged emperor smothered to death (*Annuls* 6:50). In a cruel but perhaps deserved twist of fate, Marco himself would die by the new-Emperor Caius' order within the year.

Only days before, Tiberius had finally named his successor. Two candidates were in the running–his nephew Caius and his grandson Tiberius Gemellus. Tiberius favored his blood grandson, but Gemellus was seven years younger than Caius and too young to rule on his own. Tiberius knew that Caius, at 24 years of age, possessed a keen and perceptive mind. Perhaps more importantly, Caius was the son of the popular Germanicus. A skilled and practiced orator as well, Caius was a clear favorite with the Roman people and would be accepted by them and the aristocracy.

In contrast to these practical considerations, the historian Philo Judaeus writes that on several occasions Tiberius was close to executing Caius for character flaws–flaws that in an emperor Tiberius fully realized could be disastrous for Rome. Tiberius also saw that Caius was more than capable of murdering his grandson Tiberius Gemellus if he gained any measure of power.

> And, as some person say, if Tiberius had lived a short time longer, Gaius would have been made away with, as he began to be looked upon by him with unalterable suspicion and the genuine grandson of Tiberius would have been named the future emperor and the inheritor of his paternal kingdom. (Philo *Embassy* IV 24)

Why did Tiberius then give Caius a share of the throne? Sertorius Macro could have been the reason. General Macro was a powerful defender of Caius, and he personally guaranteed Tiberius that young Tiberius Gemellus would remain safe if Caius gained a portion of the Imperial power. Marco himself was encouraged in the support and advancement of Caius by his own wife, who, unbeknownst to Macro, had been Caius' paramour (Philo *Embassy* VI 38).

But Tiberius favored his blood grandson and decided shortly before he died to name him his heir. He told Gemellus' tutor to make sure that Gemellus was in attendance to him in the morning so Tiberius could work out the details and formalize succession. The next morning, Tiberius told his servant to bring in whoever was waiting for him in his antechamber. Tiberius was expecting Gemellus, but Caius was ushered in—Gemellus was still eating breakfast.

Tiberius, a superstitious man, saw this as a sign that the gods wanted Caius to rule, and so Caius was named co-ruler in his will(*Antiq* XVIII 6:9). Tiberius died four days later. Tiberius Gemellus, though co-emperor, was young and largely ignored by the Praetorians and the Senate.

Emperor Caius

Suetonius paints an unflattering picture of Caius at the time of his Royal ascension at 24 years of age.

> He (Caius) was very tall and extremely pale, with an unshapely body, but very thin neck and legs._His eyes and temples were hollow, his forehead broad and grim, his hair thin and entirely gone on the top of his head, though his body was hairy. Because of this to look upon him from a higher place as he passed by, or for any reason whatever to mention a goat, was treated as a capital offence. While his face was naturally forbidding and ugly, he purposely made it even more savage, practising all kinds of terrible and fearsome expressions before a mirror...He was sound neither of body nor mind. (Sue *Caius* 50)

Suetonius displays bias in this; what, indeed, would a "grim" forehead even look like?!

But being the son of Germanicus counted for a lot with the Roman people. They hoped that Caius possessed the same noble character and far-reaching vision that his father demonstrated. Caius was also two generations younger than Tiberius. His youthful spirit would fit in well with what the Romans wanted in a leader at that time. Rome was prosperous and peaceful. It was a new age! It didn't take very many gratuitous acts on Caius' part before he was embraced as emperor by the Roman people. Over time, Tiberius Gemellus became little more than an inconvenient Royal footnote. Caius would arrange to have him killed a year later.

Philo paints an idyllic picture of the Roman Empire at the time of Caius' ascension to power.

> ..accordingly now there was nothing else to be seen in any city, but altars and victims and sacrifices and men clothed in white garments and crowned with garlands and wearing cheerful countenances and displaying their joy by the brightness of their looks and festivals and assemblies and musical contests and horse-races and revels and feasts lasting the whole night long, with the music of the flute and of the lyre and rejoicings and holidays and truces and every kind of pleasure addressed to every one of the senses. On this occasion the rich were not better off than the poor, nor the men of high rank than the lowly, nor the creditors than the debtors, nor the masters than the slaves, since the occasion gave equal privileges and communities to all men, so that the age of Saturn which is so celebrated by the poets was no longer looked upon as a fiction and a fable...on account of the universal prosperity and happiness which reigned every where and the absence of all grief and fear and the daily and nightly exhibitions of joy and festivity throughout every house and throughout the whole people which lasted continually without any interruption during the first seven months of his reign.
> (Philo *Embassy* II:12-13)

Emperors Augustus and Tiberius had together constructed a splendid administrative machine for running the Roman Empire. The military bureaucracy not only functioned efficiently and profitably, but it was largely impervious to rebellion and even deliberate sabotage–even sabotage caused by an emperor.

Caius had few real challenges to deal with during his reign. This lack of purpose helped facilitate his descent into delusion and madness. In time, Caius came to believe himself to be a god– a belief encouraged by the servile flatterers of the Royal court. The German-dominated Imperial guard enjoyed their elite status and protected Emperor Caius with a savage and unquestioning intensity. Even the most irrational of Caius' orders were carried out expeditiously and to the letter. All of Caius' enemies–real or imagined–were either banished or killed.

Despite this, the Roman Empire itself thrived even while Caius debauched and murdered his way through the last half of his near four-year reign.

> Gaius, after the death of Tiberius Caesar, assuming the sovereignty of the whole world in a condition free from all sedition and regulated by and obedient to admirable laws and adapted to unanimity and harmony in all its parts, east and west, south and north; the barbarian nations being in harmony with the Greeks and the Greeks with the barbarians and the soldiers with the body of private citizens and the citizens with the military; so that they all partook of and enjoyed one common universal peace-could fail to marvel at and be amazed at his extraordinary and unspeakable good fortune, (Philo *Embassy* II-8)

The Iconic Germanicus

It was no accident that Germanicus' son Caius was acclaimed emperor after the death of Tiberius. Nor was it surprising that four years later, Germanicus' stuttering brother Claudius also gained the supreme power. Germanicus' grandson Nero was to become emperor as well—the last in the line of the Caesars to rule.

For over 30 years, the aura of Germanicus–perhaps more than the aura of Julius Caesar or Augustus Caesar–held sway over the Roman people.

> (Germanicus).. was indeed a young man of unaspiring temper and of wonderful kindliness, contrasting strongly with the proud and mysterious reserve that marked the conversation and the features of Tiberius. (*Annuls* 1.33)

> Germanicus possessed all the highest qualities of body and mind, to a degree never equalled by anyone; a handsome persona unequalled valour, surpassing ability in the oratory and learning of Greece and Rome, unexampled kindliness and a remarkable desire and capacity for winning men's regard and inspiring their affection. (Sue Caius 3)

Augustus had forced Tiberius to adopt Germanicus as his son with the hope that he would succeed Tiberius eventually. But that was never to happen.

Drusus, Germanicus' father, had been Tiberius' younger brother and had previously himself attained demigod status among the Romans. Drusus died after a fall from a horse in 9 B.C., but not after gaining much fame and success battling the Germanic tribes.

Many Romans felt that if Drusus had ruled, he would have returned Rome to a Republican form of government. Drusus, apparently, had qualities that bordered on the Olympian. Emperor Augustus was so taken by Drusus that he was compelled to write a book about him as the perfect Roman to serve as a guide for young boys. Unfortunately, the book is now lost.

Drusus was commonly referred to posthumously and by later historians as Drusus the Great. Drusus' son Germanicus took up the mantle of his father–by all accounts with humility–and seemed to be destined to rule.

One of Augustus' last acts was to appoint Germanicus commander of the eight northern legions in A.D. 14. These legions initially rebelled against Tiberius' later ascension. The soldiers wanted their commander Germanicus to take control of the empire. Germanicus put down the revolt of his own men swiftly. Those whom Germanicus didn't execute outright were forced to pledge allegiance to his uncle and now-emperor Tiberius. But Germanicus' success in turning back the mutiny against Tiberius did not assuage the new emperor's concerns.

> Tiberius.. rejoiced that the mutiny was crushed, but the fact that Germanicus had won the soldiers' favour by lavishing money and promptly granting the discharge, as well as his fame as a soldier, annoyed him. (*Annuls* 1.52)

Germanicus went on to forge great victories for the Roman legions in Germany. In A.D. 17, Germanicus earned a tribunal from Tiberius for his successful campaigns. That same year, Tiberius appointed him senate consul and sent him in harm's way on a delicate mission to the East. At the time, Armenia was in a state of rebellion against Rome and was making overtures to the Parthian Empire for an alliance.

In time, Germanicus successfully settled the affairs of the East, taming King Artabanus of Parthia and installing King Artaxias on the throne of Armenia. As a result, his reputation in Rome was perhaps higher than Tiberius'. However, on a side trip into Egypt, Germanicus contracted a severe malady–some say he was poisoned–and died shortly after he returned to Antioch in late A.D. 19.

The death of the popular Germanicus stunned the empire and even former foe King Artabanus of Parthia was said to have suspended his hunting and feasting in honor of Germanicus (Sue *Caius* 5). In his panegyric, Germanicus was likened to Alexander the Great.

> Some there were who, as they thought of his beauty, his age and the manner of his death, the vicinity too of the country where he died, likened his end to that of Alexander the Great. Both had a graceful person and were of noble birth; neither had much exceeded thirty years of age and both fell by the treachery of their own people in strange lands. But Germanicus was gracious to his friends, temperate in his pleasures, the husband of one wife, with only legitimate children. He was too no less a warrior, though rashness he had none and, though after having cowed Germany by his many victories, he was hindered from crushing it into subjection. Had he had the sole control of affairs, had he possessed the power and title of a king, he would have attained military glory as much more easily as he had excelled Alexander in clemency, in self-restraint and in all other virtues. (*Annuls* 2:73)

It was suspected by many that either Tiberius or Tiberius' mother Livia was behind it–both of whom wanted Drusus, Tiberius' true son, to succeed to power. Drusus was younger than his brother Germanicus (his cousin by blood) and had not enjoyed the military success that Germanicus had achieved early in Tiberius' reign. But nothing was ever proved against Tiberius or his mother Livia–or Sejanus–to suggest that that any of them had a hand in Germanicus' death.

As the years passed after his death, the exploits and character of Germanicus quickly became the stuff of legends, and he assumed a god-like stature in the minds of the Roman people.

Agrippina the Elder

Caius was born in A.D. 12 to Germanicus and his wife Julia Agrippina (Agrippina the Elder). Agrippina was the granddaughter of the divine Augustus himself. Young Caius accompanied his father Germanicus on his assignments to Germany and then on to Armenia. His mother Agrippina was also with them, along with her surviving eight other children. As a toddler raised in a Roman army camp, Caius was given the affectionate nickname of "Caligula," an appellation referencing a type of army boot that young Caius wore (*Annuls* 1.41).

Julia Agrippina was a strong-willed, passionate woman. Caius was her youngest son. Already famous, Agrippina made an iconic name for herself through her energy and unbridled Roman patriotism. Agrippina aided her husband and the Romans as much as possible during the rebellion of the Germany-based legions early in Tiberius' reign. Agrippina enthusiastically played the role of the strong and prescient Roman warrior-wife. That over-the-top persona, however, would ultimately prove to be her downfall.

> A woman of heroic spirit, she assumed during those days the duties of a general and distributed clothes or medicine among the soldiers, as they were destitute or wounded. According to Caius Plinius, the historian of the German wars, she stood at the extremity of the bridge and bestowed praise and thanks on the returning legions. This made a deep impression on the mind of Tiberius. "Such zeal," he thought, "could not be guileless; it was not against a foreign foe that she was thus courting the soldiers. Generals had nothing left them when a woman went among the companies, attended the standards, ventured on bribery, as though it showed but slight ambition to parade her son in a common soldier's uniform and wish him to be called Caesar Caligula. Agrippina had now more power with the armies than officers, than generals. A woman had quelled a mutiny which the sovereign's name could not check." (*Annuls* 1.69)

After Germanicus died in the East in A.D. 19 under suspicious circumstances, Agrippina and her children accompanied Germanicus' ashes on a purposefully slow voyage from Antioch to Rome. Huge crowds gathered at every port along the way and great respect and accolades were given the dead Germanicus. This show of emotion by the mourning population only served to intensify Agrippina's unshakable belief that only she and her children possessed the true spirit of Augustus and deserved to rule the empire.

> But Agrippina, who could not endure equality and loved to domineer, was with her masculine aspirations far removed from the frailties of women. (*Annuls* 6:25)

Agrippina subsequently proved to be a constant thorn in the side of Tiberius. Undoubtedly, Agrippina the Elder suspected Tiberius of being complicit in Germanicus' death. As Tiberius' unforgiving and stone-fisted rule became more apparent to the Roman people, the popularity of the dead Germanicus grew. Agrippina was aware of this and encouraged it. Her sense of entitlement and destiny likewise was strengthened. Finally, Tiberius grew tired of her airs and demands. Through a Royal edict, Agrippina was banished from Rome in A.D. 29, along with Nero, the eldest of her sons. Another son, Drusus, followed them into exile a year later.

Caius, however, the youngest son, was given over to the care of Tiberius' mother, Livia, the wife of the late Augustus, along with Caius' sisters. Tiberius may have seen some potential in the young man–qualities that Caius' brothers did not seem to possess. But most likely Livia, horrified at her son Tiberius' actions, simply put her foot down!

Caius lived with Tiberius' mother Livia and enjoyed her protection until Livia's death later in the year. At the age of 17, Caius delivered Livia's panegyric (*Annuls* 5:1) with no small amount of eloquence. Afterward, Caius lived with his grandmother Antonia, the widow of Drusus the Great, until both were summoned by Tiberius to live in Capri in A.D. 31.

Life with Tiberius

Tiberius had made a fortunate decision in inviting Antonia to Capri. It was not long afterward that Antonia became aware of the Sejanus conspiracy and opened Tiberius' eyes to it. Caius also benefited from the move to Capri. Over time, he learned the finer points of governance from the crafty Tiberius.

> For though he (Caius) was of an excitable temper, he had thoroughly learnt the falsehoods of hypocrisy under the loving care of his grandfather. (*Annuls* 6:45)

Caius demonstrated a keen and perceptive mind. This likely impressed Emperor Tiberius as he considered his successor.

> ..for he (Gaius) was very acute at comprehending a man's inmost designs and feelings from his outward appearance and expression of countenance, (Philo Embassy XXXV 263)

In A.D. 33, Caius' brother Drusus died of starvation, with his mother Agrippina the Elder suffering a similar fate months later– both while exiled on the island of Pandataria. By that time, Nero, Caius' other older brother in exile, had already died. Tiberius celebrated Agrippina's death certainly, as he had shed no tears for Drusus or Nero. He ordered the bodies of Agrippina and Drusus burned and the ashes and bones hidden (Dio 58-23).

Caius' survival perhaps is more a testament to the protective powers of Livia and Antonia than anything else. The women also probably encouraged Caius to study hard, learn languages, and practice his rhetoric and oratory skills, for they knew what Tiberius thought important in a leader.

> As regards liberal studies, he gave little attention to literature but a great deal to oratory and he was as ready of speech and eloquent as you please, especially if he had occasion to make a charge against anyone. For when he was angry, he had an abundant flow of words and thoughts and his voice and delivery were such that for very excitement he could not stand still and he was clearly heard by those at a distance. (Sue *Caius* 53)

Early Reign

For the first few months of Caius' reign, the Roman world rejoiced. If Germanicus could not be emperor, then at least his son would rule. And, according to Philo at least, Tiberius had left Caius a stable and prosperous world. Josephus suggests that for two years, even after his bout with encephalitis, Caius was an admirable leader.

> Now Caius managed public affairs with great magnanimity during the first and second year of his reign and behaved himself with such moderation, that he gained the good-will of the Romans themselves and of his other subjects. But, in process of time, he went beyond the bounds of human nature in his conceit of himself and by reason of the vastness of his dominions made himself a god and took upon himself to act in all things to the reproach of the Deity itself. (*Antiq* XVIII 7:2)

Initially, Caius, worked hard to further endear himself to the Roman people, probably much of the time following the advice of the wise Sertorius Macro. Caius removed from banishment all those who had been so condemned by Tiberius, regardless of the crime. Money was given to every Roman soldier as a bonus. Caius paid off previous promises of monies by Tiberius to various people. Republican writings that had been banned by Tiberius for being seditious were returned to open publication.

Caius also traveled to island of Pandataria, where his mother, Agrippina, and brothers had been exiled and had died years before. With great ceremony, Caius gathered up their burnt bones and returned them to Rome. The charred remains were then interred with honor in the tomb of Augustus. Caius also renamed the month of September after his late father Germanicus and had other honors awarded his deserving relatives that Tiberius had found reason to dishonor.

A Kingdom for Agrippa

When Tiberius died in March of A.D. 37, Herod Agrippa, the brother of Herodias and the grandson of Herod the Great, had been in prison for six months. Agrippa had uttered some remarks to Caius that had gotten back to Tiberius. The emperor had considered them treasonous and threw Agrippa in a political jail in Campania. Agrippa spent much of that time outdoors exposed to the elements and chained to a Roman soldier. Happily for Agrippa, Caius released him quickly when he became emperor. At the same time, Caius made Agrippa a king by awarding him the plum tetrarchy of Agrippa's late uncle. Herod Philip had died in early A.D. 34, but Tiberius declined to assign his tetrarchy to anyone, putting it in semi-limbo and under the temporary control of Syria.

The land was rich and productive. The Jordan River bordered it on the west and to the south was Lake Gennesareth and the Decapolis. The revenue from the fertile lands was substantial and since Philip's death three years before those monies had been set aside and were accumulating in a separate account. Emperor Caius gave this money to Agrippa as well (*Antiq* XVIII 6:10). Overnight, the formerly wretched prisoner became free, wealthy, and a king! Caius also presented Agrippa with a large gold chain whose weight was equal to the weight of the iron chains that Tiberius had bound him with.

Considering these extraordinary actions by Caius toward Agrippa, it can only be concluded that Agrippa had evidence that, if known to Tiberius, could have gotten Caius imprisoned or even executed. But the loyal Agrippa had chosen to go to prison and remain silent, leaving Caius safe in Capri and secure in the line of succession (*Antiq* XVIII 6:6).

Herod Agrippa now became known as King Agrippa and became one of Caius' most trusted advisers. In fact, Agrippa spent far more time in Rome with Caius than in his own eastern kingdom. Agrippa was 20 years older than Caius and likely assumed the role of father or older brother in the increasingly out-of-touch and unsettled psyche of young Caius. Was Agrippa a stabilizing influence on young Caius? As Dio documents, many people did not think so.

Judean Rulers
Tiberius-Caius-Claudius

Emperor	King-Prefect/ Procurator	High Priest
Tiberius A.D. 14-37	Pontius Pilate A.D. 26-37	Joseph Caiaphas A.D. 27-36
	Marcellus (Marullus) A.D. 37-41	Jonathan bar Ananus A.D. 36-37
Caius A.D. 37-41		Theophilis bar Ananus A.D. 37-41
Claudius A.D. 41-54	Agrippa I A.D. 41-44	Simon Cantheras A.D. 41-42
		Matthis bar Ananus A.D. 42-44
	Cuspius Fadus A.D. 44-46	Elioneus bar Cantheras A.D. 44-45
	Tiberius Alexander A.D. 46-48	Joseph bar Cantos A.D. 45-48
	Ventidias Cumanus A.D. 48-52	Ananias bar Nebedeu A.D. 48-?

And they were particularly troubled on ascertaining that King Agrippa and King Antiochus were with him, like two tyrant-trainers. (Dio 59:24)

Antiochus was the king of Commagene which was an eastern land that had been split off from Syria. Caius had made Antiochus a king there in late A.D. 38. Josephus tells us little more about him.

Vitellius in Jerusalem

At the time Caius was crowned emperor in March of A.D. 37, Syrian President Lucius Vitellius was in Jerusalem, unenthusiastically finalizing plans for a war against Nabotea. Vitellius had also just removed Pontius Pilate from his duties as prefect–never a pleasant task. Pilate had then been sent off under armed escort to Campania to face Tiberius while Vitellius appointed his staff aide Marcellus to temporarily oversee the administration of Judea and Samaria.

Then the news had reached Vitellius by special courier that Tiberius had died. Even though Tiberius' health had been failing for years, his death was still a shock. This was also sad news for Vitellius, because Tiberius had been his benefactor and a great friend. But was Vitellius also secretly relieved? The war with Nabotean King Aretas IV was apparently driven only by the personalities of Tiberius and Herod Antipas. Nabotea posed no real threat to Rome and, in fact, was ostensibly an ally.

As the days passed, the new Emperor Caius sent no message to Vitellius about continuing on with the war against the Arabs. After waiting a defensible amount of time, Vitellius decided to abort the campaign. That Caius was silent on the issue was good enough for him. Over Antipas' objections, Vitellius halted war preparations, abandoned Jerusalem and sent his soldiers back to their regular quarters in Syria (*Antiq* XVIII 5:3).

Vitellius by now had likely developed a personal distaste for Herod Antipas. The previous summer at the first Euphrates summit, Antipas had become gratingly patronizing to Vitellius. While Antipas hosted a splendid feast after the summit meeting,

Vitellius easily saw through all of Antipas' self-serving actions. Both Vitellius and Antipas knew that, after a pact with the Parthian nobles had been made, Vitellius, under strict orders from Tiberius, would be forced to war with Aretas.

Vitellius was especially irritated that Antipas, after the first Euphrates agreement was sealed, took it upon himself to write immediately back to Tiberius describing details of it; not only had Antipas stolen his thunder, but no doubt had inflated his own role in the accord. In reading the following passage, it should be noted that Josephus was probably in error when he reports that Artabanus personally was at the A.D. 36 Euphrates meeting.

> After which Vitellius went to Antioch and Artabanus to Babylon; but Herod [the tetrarch] being desirous to give Caesar the first information that they had obtained hostages, sent posts with letters, wherein he had accurately described all the particulars and had left nothing for the consular Vitellius to inform him of. But when Vitellius's letters were sent and Caesar had let him know that he was acquainted with the affairs already, because Herod had given him an account of them before, Vitellius was very much troubled at it; and supposing that he had been thereby a greater sufferer than he really was, he kept up a secret anger upon this occasion, till he could be revenged on him which he was after Caius had taken the government. (*Antiq* XVIII 4:5)

In April of A.D. 37, Vitellius left Herod Antipas in Jerusalem without attempting any further contact with Emperor Caius. The departure from Judea probably brought Vitellius no small measure of relief. He knew that the Nabotean invasion could have been a disaster, just as Antipas' battle with Aretas had been two years before. Vitellius also knew that his success in Armenia had come through diplomacy and the judicious use of mercenary armies. Vitellius' own skills as a field general had not been tested; in Nabotea they would be. Vitellius was also likely well familiar with Caius from his days living at Capri. The president of Syria concluded that there was only a very slight chance that Caius would order Vitellius back to Judea in order to subjugate Nabotea.

The Removal of Jonathan

Before Vitellius left Jerusalem for Antioch, he removed Jonathan as the High Priest of the Second Temple and appointed Theophilis in his place. Theophilis was yet another of Ananus' sons. The reason for Jonathan's removal is unknown, but likely Vitellius, a perceptive and canny man, was well aware of the Temple-endorsed actions against the Christians. It has been postulated that Vitellius removed Caiaphas a year earlier for forcing Pilate to execute Jesus. Vitellius had hoped that this would send a message to the High Priesthood that Rome was a tolerant empire, and that the Temple priesthood should be as well.

Jonathan, after assuming the High Priest's position, was probably was tolerant towards the Nazarenes for a time. But after the "miracle of the tongues," the Nazarenes ramped up their evangelistic activities—even preaching in the courtyard of the Second Temple. Jonathan and the High Priesthood felt they had to act definitively despite possible repercussions from Rome.

In the months before Vitellius' return to Jerusalem in the spring of A.D. 37, Stephen was stoned to death and Jonathan unleashed a pack of young priests and hooligans, led by Saul of Tarsus, to harass and physically assault the Christians in an attempt to drive them out of Jerusalem.

Vitellius likely saw through the rationalizations of Jonathan. Rome didn't support the power of the High Priesthood in order for them to persecute their own people. Vitellius wanted to emphasis–again!–that it was Rome that controlled the Second Temple and the High Priesthood. So Jonathan was removed as High Priest—and perhaps Ananus concurred.

Caius' Near-Death Illness

Emperor Caius had lived a very austere life on Capri with his great-uncle Tiberius. Now freed from the constraints imposed by him, Caius moved back to Rome, where he enjoyed all the pleasures and spectacle that Rome had to offer–which was considerable. According to Philo, Caius' rapid descent into avarice, lust, and gluttony precipitated an illness that almost killed the new emperor in late August of A.D. 37. Likely a larger factor was that Rome, and especially its water supply, was much more germ-ridden than was Capri's. Additionally, Caius, in his drunken revery, might not have been as hygienic as he should have been.

> But in the eighth month a severe disease attacked Gaius who had changed the manner of his living which was a little while before, while Tiberius was alive, very simple and on that account more wholesome than one of great sumptuousness and luxury; for he began to indulge in abundance of strong wine and eating of rich dishes and in the abundant license of insatiable desires and great insolence and in the unseasonable use of hot baths and emetics and then again in wine-bibbing and drunkenness and returning gluttony and in lust after boys and women and in everything else which tends to destroy both soul and body and all the bonds which unite and strengthen the two; for the rewards of temperance are health and strength and the wages of intemperance are weakness and disease which bring a man near to death. (Philo *Embassy* II:14)

Caius fell into a coma at the height of the illness and remained in that condition for a considerable length of time. Caius ultimately recovered from what appears to have been a form of encephalitis, but afterward he was never quite the same. If Caius suspected he was a god before his illness, now he was quite sure of it. Near the end of A.D. 37, Caius began the murderous and debauched behavior that would make him one of history's great monsters.

Only weeks after his recovery, Caius ordered the young Tiberius Gemellus to commit suicide. The grandson of Tiberius and the legal co-emperor of the empire did so with some difficulty (Philo *Embassy* IV:30). Caius then put to death his former father-in-law, Marcus Silanus, who was the most powerful man in the Roman Senate at the time. Silanus' crime was to speak to Caius with a measure of condescension.

In late A.D. 37 or early A.D. 38, General Sertorius Macro was also forced by Caius to commit suicide. Macro's crime was to all-too-frequently admonish the young emperor on his increasingly unkingly behavior. Caius had just appointed Macro as the prefect of Egypt in order to get him out of Rome, but then changed his mind. Caius forced Macro's wife, Ennia, who once had been his paramour, to commit suicide as well.

> For it is said that the wretched man (Macro) was compelled to kill himself with his own hand; and his wife, too, experienced the same misery, even though she indeed had at one time been believed to be on the most intimate terms of familiarity with Gaius; but they say that none of the allurements of love are stable and trustworthy because it is a passion which quickly breeds satiety. But after Macro and all his house had been sacrificed..(Philo *Embassy* VIII-IX :61-62)

> (Caius).. was blamed likewise for compelling Macro together with Ennia to take their own lives, remembering neither the affection of the latter nor the benefits of the former, who had, among other things, assisted him to win the throne for himself alone; nor did the fact that he had appointed Macro to govern Egypt have the slightest influence. (Dio 59:10)

Others who might have challenged Caius for power were also executed. It was likely at this time that Caius recalled Mithridates as king of Armenia and had him imprisoned, as well as imprisoning Alexander the alabarch, who was the brother of Philo Judaeus and a rich and powerful man in Alexandria, Egypt (*Antiq* XIX 5:1).

Later in the year of A.D. 38, anti-Jewish activities in Egypt promoted by Governor Flaccus Avillius gave Caius an excuse to banish him to a remote Ionian island; later Caius had him executed.

> And by this time the matter began to be widely talked about in consequence of the continual deaths of so many eminent men, so that now these things began to be spoken of in every mouth as intolerable infamy and wickedness; not indeed openly, from fear, but gently and under the breath, in whispers; (Philo *Embassy* X:66)

It is an early Christian legend that at this time Caius forced Pontius Pilate to commit suicide, although this is not documented by any Roman historian. If true, it would certainly fit the new persona of the recovered Caius.

Spendthrift Caius

Within a year of gaining the throne, Caius had squandered Tiberius' considerable fortune.

> (Caius).. built villas and country houses with utter disregard of expense, caring for nothing so much as to do what men said was impossible. So he built moles out into the deep and stormy sea, tunnelled rocks of hardest flint, built up plains to the height of mountains and razed mountains to the level of the plain; all with incredible dispatch, since the penalty for delay was death. To make a long story short, vast sums of money, including the 2,700,000,000 sesterces which Tiberius Caesar had amassed, were squandered by him in less than the revolution of a year. (Sue *Caius* 37)

If a modern value of 10 US dollars is assigned to a sesterce, Tiberius' fortune would have been well over 20 billion dollars. This is not an unreasonable amount given Tiberius' length of time as complete master of the Roman Empire and his inheritance of Augustus' fortune as well.

Agrippa to the East

During the first year of his reign, King Agrippa had remained in his palace in Rome and never visited the Jewish East. His kingdom was a pleasant enough place, but decidedly rustic and provincial. Rome was far more exciting.

But in early A.D. 38, Agrippa felt that a trip East was in order. Was Caius' violent and unpredictable behavior the reason (*Antiq* XVIII 6:11)? Did Agrippa fear that he might become Caius' next victim? Or had Caius' money simply run out and the Royal parties in Rome were becoming less interesting and Agrippa more bored? A factor might have been that Agrippa missed his family, as there is no report that his wife Cypros, then living in Jerusalem, ever visited him in Rome.

But Agrippa certainly realized by A.D. 38 that having Emperor Caius as a friend was like holding the proverbial tiger by the tail. Caius looked up to Agrippa as a father-figure — as well as a boon companion. But Caius' increasingly erratic behavior made it clear to Agrippa that, under the right circumstances, Caius would turn against him. And even at that early period in Caius' reign, assassination plots were probably being fomented against the emperor. That Agrippa traveled to the East in order to stay out of Caius' line of fire was likely a strong if not dominant factor in his decision.

Dissolute Ways

Early in Caius' reign, he spared no expense in extravagant and opulent feasts, entertainments and gladiatorial contests. The Royal court must have been an amazing place to be then!

> In reckless extravagance he (Caius) outdid the prodigals of all times in ingenuity, inventing a new sort of baths and unnatural varieties of food and feasts; for he would bathe in hot or cold perfumed oils, drink pearls of great price dissolved in vinegar and set before his guests loaves and meats of gold, declaring that a man ought either to be frugal or Caesar. (Sue *Caius* 37)

Soon, Caius had gone through Tiberius' fortune. To gain more funds, he then turned to murdering wealthy people. First, of course, Caius would force them into naming him their beneficiary!

Caius is perhaps most famous for his construction of a floating bridge between two promontories five kilometers apart near the bay of Sorrentum. This occurred in A.D. 39.

> (Caius).. did not consider it any great achievement to drive a chariot on dry land; on the other hand, he was eager to drive his chariot through the sea, as it were, by bridging the waters between Puteoli and Bauli. (The latter place lies directly across the bay from the city of Puteoli, at a distance of twenty-six stades.) Of the ships for a bridge some were brought together there from other stations, but others were built on the spot, since the number that could be assembled there in a brief space of time was insufficient, even though all the vessels possible were got

together—with the result that a very severe famine occurred in Italy and particularly in Rome. In building the bridge not merely a passageway was constructed, but also resting-places and lodging-room were built along its course and these had running water suitable for drinking. When all was ready, he put on the breastplate of Alexander (or so he claimed) and over it a purple silk chlamys, adorned with much gold and many precious stones from India; moreover he girt on a sword, too a shield and donned a garland of oak leaves. Then he offered sacrifice to Neptune and some other gods and to envy (in order, as he put it, that no jealousy should attend him) and entered the bridge from the end at Bauli, taking with him a multitude of armed horsemen and foot-soldiers; and he dashed fiercely into Puteoli as if he were in pursuit of an enemy. There he remained during the following day, as if resting from battle; then, wearing a gold-embroidered tunic, he returned in a chariot over the same bridge, being drawn by race-horses accustomed to win the most victories. A long train of what purported to be spoils followed him, including Darius, a member of the Arsacid family, who was one of the Parthians then living in Rome as hostages. His friends and associates in flowered robes followed in vehicles and then came the army and the rest of the throng, each man dressed according to his individual taste. (Dio 59:17)

Tacitus might have presented a milder and more accurate picture of the young emperor, but, unfortunately, the books of *Annuls* dealing with Caius and his reign have been lost.

The Sisters of Caius

Caius' immorality was legendary, to even include his own sisters. Early in his reign, Caius elevated the stature of his three sisters–and only surviving siblings–to goddess levels.

He (Caius) caused the names of his sisters to be included in all oaths: "And I will not hold myself and my children dearer than I do Gaius and his sisters"; as well as in the propositions of the consuls: " Favor and good fortune attend Gaius Caesar and his sisters." (Sue *Caius* XV)

Caius' older sister was Agrippina the Younger, who was born in A.D. 15. Agrippina was destined to become the mother of the future Emperor Nero and, in A.D. 49, became the wife of Claudius—a most fortunate occurrence for her. According to some sources, Agrippina was born with a double set of canine incisor teeth–a sure sign of being favored by the gods.

Caius' youngest sister was Julia Lavilla, born in A.D. 18. Drusilla, Caius' favorite, was born in A.D. 16. He was reputed to have had an incestuous relationship with her. When Drusilla died in late A.D. 38, Caius was crushed and mourned her death with all due ceremony and gave her great accolades and honors besides.

> All the honours that had been bestowed upon Livia were voted to her (Drusilla) and it was further decreed that she should be deified, that a golden effigy of her should be set up in the senate-house and that in the temple of Venus in the Forum a statue of her should be built for her, that she should have twenty priests, women as well as men; women, whenever they offered testimony, should swear by her name and on her birthday a festival equal of the Ludi Megalenses should be celebrated and the senate and the knights should be given a banquet. She accordingly now received the name Panthea and was declared worthy of divine honours in all the cities. (Dio 59:11)

> When she died, he appointed a season of public mourning, during which it was a capital offence to laugh, bathe, or dine in company with one's parents, wife, or children. (Sue *Caius* XXIV)

Caius was rumored to have incestuous relationships with all of his sisters. Julia and Agrippina he treated badly after the death of Drusilla, to the point of allegedly forcing them into prostitution.

> He (Caius) lived in habitual incest with all his sisters and at a large banquet he placed each of them in turn below him, while his wife reclined above. Of these he is believed to have violated Drusilla when he was still a minor and even to have been caught lying with her by his grandmother Antonia, at whose house they were brought up in company. Afterwards, when she was the wife of Lucius Cassius Longinus, an ex-consul, he took her from him and openly treated her as his lawful wife; and when ill, he made her heir to his property and the throne. . The rest of his sisters he did not love with so great affection, nor honor so highly, but often prostituted them to his favorites; so that he was the readier at the trial of Aemilius Lepidus to condemn them, as adulteresses and privy to the conspiracies against him; and he not only made public letters in the handwriting of all of them, procured by fraud and seduction, but also dedicated to Mars the Avenger, with an

explanatory inscription, three swords designed to take his life. (Sue *Caius* XXIV)

It was not long before Caius exiled Julia and Agrippina to the island of Pandataria for their perceived immorality(!). When their uncle Claudius became emperor in A.D. 41, one of Claudius' first acts was to return both his nieces from the dreaded island of exile.

Caius' Military Campaign

The Roman Empire had no credible outside threats during the reign of Emperor Caius–a fact that Caius himself even complained about.

> Indeed from the time that the Divine Augustus consolidated the power of the Caesars, the wars of the Roman people had been in remote places and had caused anxiety or brought honour to but one man. Under Tiberius and Caius men dreaded for the Commonwealth only the miseries of peace. (Tacitus *Histories* 1:89)

In the last full year of his reign, A.D. 40, Caius decided to mount an expedition to Germany, for no good reason other than allay his boredom.

> So without delay he assembled legions and auxiliaries from all quarters, holding levies everywhere with the utmost strictness and collecting provisions of every kind on an unheard of scale. Then he began his march and made it now so hurriedly and rapidly, that the praetorian cohorts were forced, contrary to all precedent, to lay their standards on the pack-animals and thus to follow him; again he was so lazy and luxurious that he was carried in a litter by eight bearers, requiring the inhabitants of the towns through which he passed to sweep the roads for him and sprinkle them to lay the dust. (Sue *Caius* 43)

During his "campaign," Caius freely murdered local citizens to gain additional funds for the expedition and otherwise looted the wealth of whatever country he happened to in. When Caius returned to Rome, a triumph of sorts was celebrated by the masses. While the mob welcomed any public holiday that came their way, it was clear that Caius was no conqueror!

It was perhaps this unhappy knowledge that led Caius to provoke the Jews of the East to the point of war. Did Caius intentionally want rebellion so he could prove to the Roman people that he was every bit the warrior that his father Germanicus had been?

Chapter 11   The Politics of the Jewish East

"..But let us go to Rome and let us spare no pains nor expenses, either of silver or gold, since they cannot be kept for any better use than for the obtaining of a kingdom." (*Antiq* XVIII 7:1)

The nearly four-year reign of Caius saw the dramatic downfall and banishment of the Tetrarch Herod Antipas and Queen Herodias. Furthermore, the president of Syria, Lucius Vitellius, came perilously close to being executed by the mercurial young emperor. But Herod Agrippa, Herodias' brother, prospered during Caius' tenure. He quickly rose to power as King Agrippa I with his own tetrarchy and played a key role in not only avoiding a Jewish revolt late in Caius' reign, but also in establishing Claudius Caesar on the throne after Caius' assassination in A.D. 41.

The Banishment of Herod Antipas

Herod Antipas was bitterly disappointed in Vitellius' decision to abandon the Nabotean campaign in early A.D. 37. The death of Emperor Tiberius was a tragedy for Antipas on another level as well. Over the decades, Tiberius had been a great and supportive friend. The new Emperor Caius, however, was an unknown quantity. Could Herod Antipas expect his support? Certainly, Antipas knew early on that Caius had no desire to send Roman legions into Nabotea. Would Caius set himself against Antipas on other important issues as well?

Three years previously, in A.D. 34, Emperor Tiberius had denied Herod Antipas the domain of his deceased brother. Philip's land` had been ruled by the Herod family for more than a century. Partially in an attempt to prove his military prowess and worth to Tiberius, Antipas had ordered his armies to war with King Aretas IV of Nabotea. In battle, his armies had been largely destroyed by the Arabs in a humiliating defeat.

So it was a dispirited tetrarch who returned to Galilee after the Jerusalem Passover celebration of A.D. 37. In the weeks that followed, Antipas likely wrote more than one letter to the new-Emperor Caius trying to convince him that Aretas was a threat to the Roman Empire. But Antipas' efforts were to no avail. Worse, Caius decided to give Herod Philip's old tetrarchy over to Herod Agrippa to rule. Agrippa was Herodias' arrogant, spendthrift brother and a sworn enemy to Antipas. Less than three years earlier, Antipas and Agrippa had gotten into a heated argument. As a result, Antipas had banished his nephew from Galilee. But with Caius' action, now Agrippa was his equal as a ruler in the Jewish East. Would King Agrippa work against Antipas and seek control over Antipas' own domain? Agrippa was of a younger generation than Antipas, and Caius was of a younger generation still. Antipas was definitely old guard. How long could he hang on to his kingdom? Were his days in power numbered?

As time passed, Antipas had fading hopes that Caius would move against Aretas. Was Agrippa behind Caius' reluctance? As Caius entered his second year as emperor, his erratic and hedonistic behavior was a clear indication to Antipas that a Nabotean military campaign would remain a dead issue. Antipas, too, could not have been anything but pensive and fearful over the rising star of his nephew King Agrippa I.

Agrippa Leaves Rome

Herod Agrippa gained Herod Philip's old kingdom early in A.D. 37, but spent a leisurely year enjoying his Rome palace before deciding to actually inspect his land. Caius enjoyed the company of Agrippa and that was reason enough for Agrippa to stay in Rome. The parties and extravagant events that Agrippa and Caius gave during the first year of Caius' reign were not to be missed.

> Now, in the second year of the reign of Caius Caesar, Agrippa desired leave to be given him to sail home and settle the affairs of his government; and he promised to return again, when he had put the rest in order, as it ought to be put. (*Antiq* XVIII 6:11)

Agrippa might have decided to leave Rome because of his developing fear of Caius. More and more, Caius was executing important people for the express purpose of seizing their estates, or because of jealousy over their power and prestige, or for no reason at all.

Agrippa also had a wife, Cypros, and children to consider. There is no record that Cypros and her children returned to Rome to be with Agrippa during his first year in power. When the two had parted in Alexandria early in A.D. 36, Cypros expected that Emperor Tiberius would welcome her husband's return to Italia by throwing him into debtor's prison. Agrippa was, indeed, eventually imprisoned by Tiberius, but for later treasonous statements and not for his debts to Caesar.

But there is every indication that Cypros, despite Agrippa's sudden rise to wealth and power, decided to remain in the safety of Jerusalem with their three young children instead of joining her husband in Rome. But Agrippa apparently still had affection for his wife despite their long separation. After his arrival in Jerusalem the couple's fourth child was conceived. Drusilla was born late in A.D. 38.

Vitellius Escapes Death

In A.D. 38, Vitellius reached a solid truce with King Artabanus of Parthia, brought about by a series of brilliant diplomatic maneuvers. As a result of conference between Artabanus and Vitellius, Rome received at least two sons of Artabanus as hostages along with a sworn alliance. Artabanus justified his capitulation to his Parthian nobles by saying that while he hated Tiberius, he had no problem with Caius. Artabanus had been an unabashed Germanicus supporter and Emperor Caius was Germanicus' son, after all. Tiberius was widely considered to be complicit in the presumed poisoning of Germanicus.

That Artabanus gave up two sons as hostages, and Rome none, was not as one-sided at it appears on the surface. Artabanus had already been deposed once by internal rebellion. If another revolution occurred and he himself was killed, his sons would be safe in Rome and ready to avenge his death and rule Parthia.

The Roman people greeted the news of an advantageous peace with Parthia with great enthusiasm. Did Caius then begin to look upon Vitellius with an envious eye–and as a rival for the throne?

Late in A.D. 38, Lucius Vitellius was summoned to Rome by Caius. Vitellius was aware of Caius' ill intentions, perhaps so alerted by friends in Rome, or maybe forewarned by King Agrippa I himself. In Agrippa's extended trip to the East earlier in the year, he would have certainly conferred with Vitellius in Antioch. Agrippa knew that Vitellius had powerful friends in Rome–most being a part of the old guard of Tiberius. Vitellius also might have had the loyalty of the generals of foreign-based Roman legions where Caius did not. If Caius executed Vitellius — or tried to—, it could well mean the beginning of another civil war. And how would the family of Herod fare in the chaos that would follow? Agrippa had every reason to surreptitiously warn Vitellius about Caius' murderous intentions.

Vitellius was as insightful as any man in the empire, and he had probably known Caius since he was a small boy. Had Vitellius seen in Caius, at that young age, a potential for venom and cruelty? Too, Flaccus of Egypt may have been a friend of Vitellius', and Flaccus had been recently executed at Caius' command for no good reason.

For these reasons, Vitellius devised a brilliant plan for dealing with the emperor. When he finally met him in Rome, Vitellius presented himself humbly, without pretension, and with a veil covering his face. Prostrating himself before Caius like a common slave, Vitellius addressed him as god and pledged his undying allegiance to him–with complete servility.

> (Lucius Vitellius) had also a wonderful gift for flattery and was the first to begin to worship Gaius Caesar as a god; for on his return from Syria he did not presume to approach the emperor except with veiled head, turning himself about and then prostrating himself. (Sue *Vitellius* 2:5)

Caius was surprised, but pleased, with this unexpected behavior from the great Roman general so fresh from a diplomatic triumph in the East. Caius spared Vitellius' life and from that moment on, Vitellius became a steadfast friend and confidant of the young emperor.

> The case of Lucius Vitellius is in point. This man was neither of low birth nor lacking in intelligence, but, on the contrary, had made a name for himself by his governorship of Syria. For, in addition to his other brilliant achievements during his term of office, he forestalled Artabanus, who was planning an attack on that province also, since he had suffered no punishment for his invasion of Armenia. He terrified the Parthian by coming upon him suddenly when he was already close to the Euphrates and then induced him to come to a conference, compelled him to sacrifice to the images of Augustus and Gaius and made a peace with him that was advantageous to the Romans, even securing his sons as hostages. This Vitellius, now, was summoned by Gaius to be put to death. The complaint against him was the same as the Parthians had against their king when they expelled him; for jealousy made him the object of hatred and fear the object of plots. Gaius, of course, hated all who were stronger than himself and he was suspicious of all who were successful, feeling sure that they would attack him. Yet Vitellius managed to save his life. He arrayed himself in a manner beneath his rank, then fell at the emperor's feet with tears and lamentations, all the while calling him many divine names and paying him worship; and at last vowed that if he were allowed to live he would offer sacrifice to him. By this behaviour he so mollified and soothed Gaius, that he not only managed to survive but even came to be regarded as one of Gaius' most intimate friends. On one occasion, when Gaius claimed to be enjoying converse with the Moon and asked Vitellius if he could see the goddess with him, the other, trembling as in awe, kept his eyes fixed on the ground and answered in a half whisper: "Only you gods, master, may behold one another." So Vitellius, from this beginning, came later to surpass all others in adulation. (Dio 59:27)

With his new-found but necessary servility, Vitellius not only survived but thrived during the reign of Caius. Vitellius went on to serve honorably in various high positions for Emperor Claudius, and remained one of the most powerful men in the empire until his death in A.D. 51.

But Vitellius' escaping of execution and his sudden inclusion in Caius' inner circle may have doomed the Tetrarch Herod Antipas. Vitellius had no time for Antipas, the son of Herod the Great who still harbored faint hopes of obtaining his late brother Herod Philip's kingdom.

The Jealousy of Herodias

Herodias, the wife of Herod Antipas and the sister of King Agrippa, was particularly enraged at the phoenix-like rise of her formerly debt-ridden and arrogant brother. In late A.D. 33, Herodias had gone out of her way to help him, to her detriment. Now Agrippa controlled a kingdom that she had coveted and wanted for her daughter. Arguably, Agrippa now had more power than her husband. Certainly, Agrippa had the ear of Caius where Antipas did not.

Herod Agrippa had married Cypros, who was his own cousin and, of course, Herodias' cousin as well. During his ill-fated journey to the East in A.D. 33, Agrippa found himself being hounded by bill collectors and forced into semi-hiding in Idumea with his family. Cypros appealed directly to her cousin Herodias for help. Herodias had then talked her new husband Herod Antipas into giving Agrippa protection from creditors and a position in Tiberias. Agrippa accepted the invitation and his family moved to Tiberias in Galilee. There, for almost a year they lived in luxury and Agrippa served as a magistrate. Cypros felt comfortable enough in Tiberias to conceive another child; Mariamne was born in A.D. 34. But Agrippa's arrogance eventually got him into a verbal fight with Antipas and as a result Agrippa and his family were forced to leave Galilee.

Three years later Agrippa gained the kingdom that his uncle Herod Philip had once ruled, given to him by his friend and now-Emperor Caius. Herodias had managed to keep her jealousy under control until one day she saw her brother Agrippa marching along dressed in Royal purple robes and enjoying all the trappings of a king.

> She was therefore grieved and much displeased at so great a mutation of his affairs; and chiefly when she saw him marching among the multitude with the usual ensigns of royal authority, she was not able to conceal how miserable she was, by reason of the envy she had towards him; (*Antiq* XVIII 7:1)

This could have taken place in Galilee in A.D. 38. Agrippa had to pass through that country on the way to his own kingdom further to the east.

Herodias could sense her own star falling and did not like it. Eventually, she badgered her aging husband Antipas to the point where he, against his better judgment, acquiesced. The Royal couple personally traveled to Rome to meet with Caius and directly petition him for control of Herod Philip's kingdom.

> .. but she excited her husband and desired him that he would sail to Rome, to court honors equal to his; for she said that she could not bear to live any longer, while Agrippa, the son of that Aristobulus who was condemned to die by his father, one that came to her husband in such extreme poverty, that the necessaries of life were forced to be entirely supplied him day by day; and when he fled away from his creditors by sea, he now returned a king; while he was himself the son of a king and while the near relation he bare to royal authority called upon him to gain the like dignity, he sat still and was contented with a privater life. "But then, Herod, although thou wast formerly not concerned to be in a lower condition than thy father from whom thou wast derived had been, yet do thou now seek after the dignity which thy kinsman hath attained to; and do not thou bear this contempt, that a man who admired thy riches should he in greater honor than thyself, nor suffer his poverty to show itself able to purchase greater things than our abundance; nor do thou esteem it other than a shameful thing to be inferior to one who, the other day, lived upon thy charity. But let us go to Rome and let us spare no pains nor expenses, either of silver or gold, since they cannot be kept for any better use than for the obtaining of a kingdom."
>
> But for Herod, he opposed her request at this time, out of the love of ease and having a suspicion of the trouble he should have at Rome; so he tried to instruct her better. But the more she saw him draw back, the

more she pressed him to it and desired him to leave no stone unturned in order to be king; and at last she left not off till she engaged him, whether he would or not, to be of her sentiments, because he could no otherwise avoid her importunity. So he got all things ready, after as sumptuous a manner as he was able and spared for nothing and went up to Rome and took Herodias along with him. But Agrippa, when he was made sensible of their intentions and preparations, he also prepared to go thither; and as soon as he heard they set sail, he sent Fortunatus, one of his freed-men, to Rome, to carry presents to the emperor and letters against Herod and to give Caius a particular account of those matters, if he should have any opportunity. This man followed Herod so quick and had so prosperous a voyage and came so little after Herod, that while Herod was with Caius, he came himself and delivered his letters; for they both sailed to Dicearchia and found Caius at Bairn which is itself a little city of Campania, at the distance of about five furlongs from Dicearchia. There are in that place royal palaces, with sumptuous apartments, every emperor still endeavoring to outdo his predecessor's magnificence; the place ,also affords warm baths, that spring out of the ground of their own accord which are of advantage for the recovery of the health of those that make use of them; and, besides, they minister to men's luxury also. Now Caius saluted Herod, for he first met with him and then looked upon the letters which Agrippa had sent him and which were written in order to accuse Herod; wherein he accused him, that he had been in confederacy with Sejanus against Tiberius's and that he was now confederate with Artabanus, the king of Parthia, in opposition to the government of Caius; as a demonstration of which he alleged, that he had armor sufficient for seventy thousand men ready in his armory. Caius was moved at this information and asked Herod whether what was said about the armor was true; and when he confessed there was such armor there, for he could not deny the same, the truth of it being too notorious, Caius took that to be a sufficient proof of the accusation, that he intended to revolt. So he took away from him his tetrarchy and gave it by way of addition to Agrippa's kingdom; he also gave Herod's money to Agrippa and, by way of punishment, awarded him a perpetual banishment and appointed Lyons, a city of Gaul, to be his place of habitation. But when he was informed that Herodias was Agrippa's sister, he made her a present of what money was her own and told her that it was her brother who prevented her being put under the same calamity with her husband. But she made this reply: "Thou, indeed, O emperor! actest after a magnificent manner and as becomes thyself in what thou offerest me; but the kindness which I have for my husband hinders me from partaking of the favor of thy gift; for it is not just that I, who have been made a partner in his prosperity, should forsake him in his misfortunes." Hereupon Caius was angry at her and sent her with Herod into banishment and gave her estate to

Agrippa. And thus did God punish Herodias for her envy at her brother and Herod also for giving ear to the vain discourses of a woman. (*Antiq* XVIII 7:1-2)

When exactly was Antipas banished? Josephus provides further evidence.

..for he (Agrippa) reigned four years under Caius Caesar, three of them were over Philip's tetrarchy only and on the fourth he had that of Herod added to it; and he reigned, besides those, three years under the reign of Claudius Caesar; (*Antiq* XIX 8:2)

So Agrippa I gained Herod Antipas' kingdom in late A.D. 39. This fits with the limitations imposed on Mediterranean Sea travel by the usually stormy winter season. Antipas and Herodias probably appeared before Emperor Caius in the fall of A.D. 39.

But no matter when the fateful trip occurred, it brought an amazing end to the political life of Herod Antipas. Certainly, the trip to Rome was a complete disaster for the tetrarch, who, at that time, would have been approaching 65 years of age. When he planned his trip to Rome to petition Emperor Caius, Antipas initially might have had hopes of not only getting control of Philip's old kingdom, but also Jerusalem and the former kingdom of Archelaus, now administered by a Roman prefect of no reputation named Marcellus. What a shock it must have been when Caius took everything away and banished both Antipas and his wife Herodias to the provincial city of Lyons in Gaul! And imagine how how full of venom Agrippa had to have been to accuse his uncle of not only being in league with the hated Sejanus, but also in alliance with Artabanus, the formerly renegade king of Parthia. Clearly, Agrippa hated Antipas with a passion. In the banishment of Herod Antipas, King Agrippa gained a most savage revenge on Antipas–his own uncle–for ejecting him from Galilee four years earlier.

But Antipas helped to seal his own fate. Agrippa also accused Herod of having a stockpile of armor and weapons, enough for 70,000 men (probably more like 7,000 men), something Antipas could not deny. Agrippa claimed that Antipas himself was preparing to revolt against Rome and was in league with King Artabanus of Parthia for this purpose. Emperor Caius could not ignore such a serious charge.

In all likelihood, however, the armor was a legacy from Antipas' disastrous military campaign against Nabotea four years previously, or military stores laid up two years ago when Antipas thought Vitellius was going to march on Petra. When Antipas brought up these very reasonable explanations, Caius perhaps turned to Lucius Vitellius for confirmation.

Lucius Vitellius was then less than a year in Rome after his successful tenure as president of Syria. Vitellius' acknowledgment of Caius' greatness and divine origins not only saved his life and that of his family's, but immediately placed him in Caius' inner circle of confidantes and advisers. Did Vitellius have a role in Caius' decision to banish Herod Antipas? Indeed, while in the East, Vitellius had long grown tired of being put upon by Antipas' airs and demands. If Caius asked his opinion in the matter of Herod Antipas versus Herod Agrippa, Vitellius would not have been supportive of Antipas–the increasingly irrelevant and aging son of Herod the Great.

The final decision for Caius was probably simple and straightforward: Herod Agrippa was a personal friend and Herod Antipas was not; Antipas was from an older generation, while Agrippa represented new blood. To add proverbial insult to injury, Caius not only denied Antipas Philip's old kingdom, but removed him from his own. Caius then gave it and Antipas' fortune, over to King Agrippa.

Interestingly, when Emperor Caius first banished the couple he did not realize that Herodias was the sister of Agrippa. When this was brought to his attention, Emperor Caius then offered Herodias back her personal fortune and clemency as a show of his respect for Agrippa. Herodias rejected both.

"I, who have been made a partner in his (Antipas') prosperity, should (not) forsake him in his misfortunes." (*Antiq* XVIII 7:2).

Thus Herod Antipas was banished from the East in late A.D. 39–this the man who ordered John the Baptist beheaded and interrogated Jesus on Jesus' last day on earth. So, too, banished was Herodias, his wife, who was still beautiful, although she had no doubt aged considerably from her seven stressful years in the East. Stripped of their money and property, the famous couple was sent to Lyons, a then-remote area of Gaul that lay across the Alps from Italy, and became lost to history.

King Aretas of Nabotea

Aretas IV was the powerful king of Nabotea (Arabia) whose daughter had been the first wife of Herod Antipas–a marriage that had lasted more than 25 years. But Herod Antipas had divorced her in order to marry Herodias in A.D. 32. The scorned queen, Pharaelis, fled in fear back to her father. Thus started the deadly vendetta of Aretas towards Antipas which was only partially satisfied when Aretas' Nabotean army destroyed Antipas' army of Galilee in the fall of A.D. 35.

Dio reports that the nation of Arabia was divided up by Caius in A.D. 38 and another ruler was brought in to administer at least an eastern section of it. Perhaps this division was to serve as a *de facto* punishment for Aretas for causing trouble, although the particulars were undisclosed. Certainly, it diminished Aretas' power in the region and made him less of a potential threat to Rome–if he ever was one to begin with.

> Meanwhile he (Caius) granted to Sohaemus the land of the Ituraean Arabians, to Cotys Lesser Armenia and later parts of Arabia, to Rhoemetalces the possessions of Cotys and to Polemon, the son of Polemon, his ancestral domain, all upon the vote of the senate. (Dio 59:12)

Ituraea is a territory north of Caesarea Philippi and roughly 20 miles west of Damascus. A "King Sohemus" is mentioned as fighting alongside General Titus and the Roman army in A.D. 70. The name Sohemus was known among the family of Herod the

Great, so this Sohemus might have been of the Herodian line and a relative of Agrippa I, and controlled some eastern territories.

Nothing is recorded in Josephus about Aretas after Vitellius' retreat from Jerusalem in A.D. 37. In the New Testament, however, the Second Letter from Paul the Apostle to the Church in Corinthians mentions Aretas.

> In Damascus the governor under Aretas the king guarded the city of the Damascenes in order to take me: (II Corinthians 11:32)

Saul (the future Paul) had his Christian epiphany in Damascus in late A.D. 36. According to his Letter to the Church in Galatia, Saul very soon left Damascus for an evangelizing trip into Arabia proper. So it is safe to assume that Aretas was in power for at least three more years after his defeat of Herod Antipas in the fall of A.D. 35.

King Aretas gloated over his victory against Antipas and the Roman Empire then and especially over the subsequent death of Tiberius and retreat of Vitellius in A.D. 37.

> It was also reported, that when Aretas heard of the coming of Vitellius to fight him, he said, upon his consulting the diviners, that it was impossible that this army of Vitellius's could enter Petra; for that one of the rulers would die, either he that gave orders for the war, or he that was marching at the other's desire, in order to be subservient to his will, or else he against whom this army is prepared. (*Antiq* XVIII 5:3)

Time proved the seers to be correct. The leader whom God had deemed to die turned out to be Emperor Tiberius. And when Tiberius' successor, Caius, banished Herod Antipas not three years later and seized his fortune, Aretas was a happy and satisfied man, indeed. His honor had now been satisfied against the damnable family of Herods—who had so disgraced his daughter seven years before. In all likelihood, the Nabotean king remained within his borders and savored his victory—wisely demonstrating no more aggressive actions against Rome or the family of Herod. In A.D. 49, Tacitus refers to Acbarus as the king of Arabia (*Annuls* 12:11), so it can be inferred that Aretas was out of power by that time.

Aristobulos, the Brother of Agrippa I

Earlier, in A.D. 34, Aristobulos was a magistrate in Antioch along with his brother, the future King Agrippa I. At that time, Josephus noted that a history of bad blood existed between them. In fact, Aristobulos was very happy to see Agrippa leave Syria under a cloud of suspicion in early A.D. 34 (*Antiq* XVIII 6:3), and he might have even helped Syrian President Pomponius Flaccus prosecute him.

Surprisingly, however, in the years after being made king by Caius in A.D. 37, Agrippa and his older brother Aristobulos apparently became fully reconciled. How did this come about? Simple expediency was likely a major factor. With so much territory to administer and with few real friends in the East, it would only make sense for Agrippa to put away his differences with his brother and make him a virtual ruling partner. Aristobulos by all accounts was a very capable and dependable man. Lucius Vitellius, who knew Aristobulos well, might have helped smooth over the differences between the two brothers when Agrippa was first named king before Vitellius' own recall from the East by Caius in A.D. 38.

As for Aristobulos, he had to resign himself to the fact that his younger brother had the ear and support of the Royal court, even though Aristobulos had vastly more experience in administration. An element of fear may have also driven Aristobulos' conciliatory demeanor towards his brother. During the banishment of Antipas and Herodias, Agrippa had displayed a dark and vengeful side that respected no family boundaries. Aristobulos knew would be best for him to forget the past and cultivate the man!

Aristobulos, along with his wife Jotape and a deaf daughter of the same name (*Antiq* XVIII 5:4) was probably ordered by King Agrippa to leave Antioch and return south to Tiberias in order to administer Galilee. To be fair, Agrippa wasn't totally ignoring his kingly duties. In Rome, King Agrippa I could keep a close eye on the unstable Caius and look out for the interests of not only the Herod family, but of all the Jews of the Roman Empire.

Josephus mentions Aristobulos in a passage on Caius vexing the Jews late in his reign. Caius was attempting to place a statue of himself in the Second Temple in Jerusalem. The new Syrian President Petronius, who had replaced Lucius Vitellius in A.D. 38, called a meeting of all the important people in Tiberias to discuss options. Aristobulos was one of those summoned.

> ..Petronius..hasted to Tiberias, as wanting to know in what posture the affairs of the Jews were; and many ten thousands of the Jews met Petronius again, when he was come to Tiberias ... When matters were in this state, Aristobulus, king Agrippa's brother and Heleias the Great and the other principal men of that family with them, went in unto Petronius and besought him (*Antiq* XVIII 8:3-4)

No more is heard of Aristobulos, the brother of Agrippa I.

Salome and Aristobulos

At some point after the Passover of A.D. 36, and at her mother Herodias' urging, the young widow Salome married her cousin Aristobulos, who was the son of Herod, the king of Chalcis. Herod was one of Herodias' older brothers.

Salome was likely securely married to Aristobulos when Herodias convinced Antipas to travel to Rome in late A.D. 39 to petition Caius for Agrippa I's kingdom, as Herodias expressed no concern for Salome when she learned her fate. When Salome heard about the shocking banishment of her mother and Antipas, did she fear for her own safety, even though she was safely ensconced in Galilee?

Salome had been a queen for a short time while married to the much-older Tetrarch Herod Philip before his death in A.D. 34. In the marriage to her cousin Aristobulos, she was to again achieve Royal status. In A.D. 53, Emperor Claudius in shuffling kingdoms about took Chalcis away from Agrippa II gave it to the late Herod's son Aristobulos to administer (*Antiq* XX 7:1). In A.D. 54, this same son of Herod, whose mother was Agrippa I's daughter Bernice, was appointed by the new Emperor Nero to be the ruler of Lesser Armenia.

Of all the people involved in the drama of those times, it was perhaps Salome who was the most victimized. Despite the provocative dance that had so enraptured Herod Antipas and led to the death of John the Baptist, Salome was undeniably a young girl caught up in events not of her own making. It can be assumed that she lived out her live in Royal splendor.

The Prefecture of Judea

Soon after he first assumed powers as Emperor in A.D. 37, Caius affirmed Vitellius' choice, Marcellus, to serve as the prefect of Judea. Little else is known about Marcellus, except that he was a high ranking officer on Vitellius' personal staff.

> So Vitellius sent Marcellus, a friend of his, to take care of the affairs of Judea and ordered Pilate to go to Rome (*Antiq* XVIII 4:2)

However, Josephus also indicates that Marcellus served only a few weeks as prefect.

> He (Caius) also sent Marullus to be procurator of Judea. (*Antiq* XVIII 6:10).

Little information exists about either Marcellus or Marullus. It is entirely possible, however, that they are one and the same individual; a new historical character being created through inaccurate copying.

In late A.D. 38, Caius replaced Vitellius with Petronius.

> Hereupon Caius, taking it very heinously that he should be thus despised by the Jews alone, sent Petronius to be president of Syria and successor in the government to Vitellius, (*Antiq* XVIII 8:2)

The prefecture of Judea was relatively peaceful during the reign of Emperor Caius, but an incident did occur which drove the Jews to the brink of war–a problem that was intentionally created by Caius.

Caius the God

Caius' delusional belief that he was a god caused him to flood the empire with statues of himself. These were to be placed in all the houses and temples of worship no matter what the religion. The only people who dared object to this–that we know of–were the Jews, whose religion strictly forbade any graven images in their houses, temples, or anywhere within the holy city of Jerusalem.

> all who were subject to the Roman empire built altars and temples to Caius and in other regards universally received him as they received the gods, these Jews alone thought it a dishonorable thing for them to erect statues in honor of him, as well as to swear by his name (*Antiq* XVIII 8:1)

The Jews maintained a higher profile than most ethnic groups within the Roman Empire. With his friendship with Agrippa, Caius was well aware of the Jews' history and beliefs, but yet he persisted in his plan to desecrate Jewish temples.

Eusebius quotes from Philo on this subject and that paragraph along with the original paragraph from "modern" copies of Philo are reproduced below. Reference copies of Philo used today are at least 500 years later than the source works used by Eusebius. What Eusebius called *Mission* is known today as *Embassy*. Bishop Eusebius possibly had access to a first-generation copy of Philo's writings, so the differences between the two are of interest. Philo wrote five books in total on Caius and the Jews, most of which are lost.

> So incalculable was the behavior of Caius towards everyone, especially the Jewish race. He hated them so bitterly that in city after city, beginning with Alexandria, he seized the synagogues and filled them with images and statues of himself–for as he gave permission for them to be erected, it was really he who put them there–and in the Holy City he tried to change the sanctuary which was still untouched and regarded as inviolate and transform it into a temple of his own, to be called the Temple of Jupiter the Glorious–the Younger Gaius. (Eusebius *History* 2:6 from Philo *Mission*)

So great therefore was his inequality of temper towards every one and most especially towards the nation of the Jews to which he was most bitterly hostile and accordingly beginning in Alexandria he took from them all their synagogues there and in the other cities and filled them all with images and statues of his own form; for not caring about any other erection of any kind, he set up his own statue every where by main force; and the great temple in the holy city which was left untouched to the last, having been thought worthy of all possible respect and preservation, he altered and transformed into a temple of his own, that he might call it the temple of the new Jupiter, the illustrious Gaius. (Philo *Embassy* XLIII 346)

Most conquered people of the Roman Empire at least pretended to recognize Roman culture and paid a token deference to the Roman pantheon of gods and goddesses. The Jews, however, continued to practice their religion to the exclusion of all others, holding fast to their traditional ways. This behavior grated on Caius. Perhaps most irritating to Caius was the Jewish belief of being God's "chosen people," which unavoidably implies that the Roman people were not only inferior to the Jews, but somehow ungodly.

Indeed, Caius must have taken perverted pleasure in forcing the Jews to place his graven likeness in their most holy sanctuaries. But Caius' action drove the Jews perilously close to rebellion. Only quick work by King Agrippa averted an outright empire-wide Jewish insurrection.

But when the Jews were ordered by Caligula to set up his statue in the temple, they preferred the alternative of war. The death of the Emperor put an end to the disturbance. (Eusebius *Histories* 5:9)

For the physical placement of his statue in the Second Temple in Jerusalem, the most holy city of the Jews, Caius relied upon Gaius Petronius, the Syrian president and bypassed the Judean prefect–presumably still Marcellus. But Petronius, after meeting with important Jewish leaders in Tiberias in Galilee in A.D. 40, saw the danger in it. His first action was to send instructions to the artificers of the statue in Sidon telling them to take their time, hoping that Caius might change his mind before the statue was finished.

Then Petronius allowed a delegation to travel from Jerusalem to Rome in protest of Caius' actions. After some thought, Petronius wrote a letter to Caius explaining the delay in the placement of the statue. Petronius blamed it on the artificers but also on the need to collect the harvest before its placement. Petronius' convoluted reasoning to Caius was that the statue in the Temple would so antagonize the Jews that they might sabotage the crops, resulting in famine.

While Petronius was wrestling with the problem in the East as best he could, King Agrippa, too, realized that the Jews would revolt if Caius' gigantic statue ever found its way to the gates of Jerusalem (*Antiq* XVIII 8:2). Agrippa might have known that Caius had, in fact, already ordered Petronius to make war upon the Jews if they did not accede to his request and accept the statue.

King Agrippa decided upon a bold course of action. He put on a great party for Caius where spectacular entertainment was offered, exotic food prepared, and heavy drinking encouraged. After the feast, Caius was so impressed that he promised Agrippa anything he wished in return. Agrippa expected this, perhaps because this was the usual way of Caius.

> Toward those to whom he (Caius) was devoted his partiality became madness. (Sue *Caius* 55)

Agrippa took a great chance and requested of Caius that he not proceed with his plan to place his statue in the Jerusalem Second Temple.

> ..my petition is this, that thou wilt no longer think of the dedication of that statue which thou hast ordered to be set up in the Jewish temple by Petronius." (*Antiq* XVIII 8:7)

Fortunately for Agrippa, Caius acquiesced, albeit reluctantly. True to his word, Caius then sent a letter to Petronius telling him to not proceed with the statue placement.

But Petronius had already sent Caius his own letter. When Caius received it, he was enraged that Petronius circumvented a direct order of his and for such transparent reasons. Caius sent a letter back to Petronius and commanded him to commit suicide. But Caius' second letter arrived in the East after Caius himself had been assassinated. Petronius had only just barely escaped death!

Both Josephus and Philo suggest that Caius had only temporarily lost his enthusiasm for the subversion of the Jewish religion. Philo writes that Caius started plans for another huge bronze statue of himself at Rome destined for placement at the Second Temple.

> Gaius was not quiet; but he had already repented of the favour which he had showed to Agrippa and had re-kindled the desires which he had entertained a little while before; for he commanded another statue to be made, of colossal size, of brass gilt over, in Rome, no longer moving the one which had been made in Sidon, in order that the people might not be excited by its being moved, but that while they remained in a state of tranquillity and felt released from their suspicions, it might in a period of peace be suddenly brought to the country in a ship and be suddenly erected without the multitude being aware of what was going on. (Philo *Embassy* XLII 337)

But before Caius could put this other plan into play he was assassinated in January of A.D. 41.

Caius' death was met with relief by the Jewish nation. But the Jews now fully realized how vulnerable they were to the whims and fancies of the Roman emperor, whoever that might be.

> It is true that the Jews had shown symptoms of commotion in a seditious outbreak and when they had heard of the assassination of Caius, there was no hearty submission, as a fear still lingered that any of the emperors might impose the same orders. (*Annuls* 12:54)

With the death of Caius, King Agrippa had lost a friend, but the Jewish nation had narrowly averted rebellion. Still, though Caius' intended actions against the Jews were ultimately aborted, the Jewish zealots gained a political capital under Caius that they never were able to under Tiberius.

Chapter 12   Emperor Claudius

(Claudius)..was encouraged [to claim the government] partly by the boldness of the soldiers and partly by the persuasion of king Agrippa (*Antiq* XVIV 4:1)

Emperor Caius was well aware toward the end of his reign that he had numerous enemies. As the possibility of his assassination grew, Caius catered to the Praetorian guard to a greater and greater degree. The Praetorian soldiers were Teutonic by intent and harbored no political allegiance but to Caesar. With every additional outrageous action of Caius', his situation became more and more precarious. In fact, in his final months, several different Roman factions vied for the honor of killing him.

Now this Caius did not demonstrate his madness in offering injuries only to the Jews at Jerusalem, or to those that dwelt in the neighborhood; but suffered it to extend itself through all the earth and sea, so far as was in subjection to the Romans and filled it with ten thousand mischiefs; so many indeed in number as no former history relates. (*Antiq* XIX 1:1)

But when he (Caius) had filled the whole habitable world which he governed with false accusations and miseries and had occasioned the greatest insults of slaves against their masters, who indeed in a great measure ruled them, there were many secret plots now laid against him; some in anger and in order for men to revenge themselves, on account of the miseries they had already undergone from him; and others made attempts upon him, in order to take him off before they should fall into such great miseries, (*Antiq* XIX 1:2)

The privilege was won by the tribune of the Praetorian guard, Cherea Cassius, who hated Caius with a visceral passion. Caius had taken to entertaining the Praetorians by mocking Cherea, who had a lisp and other seemingly unmanly characteristics. Interestingly, Cherea was one of the men Caius would turn to if he needed someone tortured. Caius' favorite method of torture was the "death by a thousand cuts," and Cherea was a master of its execution. But despite this singular Imperial honor, Cherea wanted Caius dead.

Those in-the-know about Cherea's intention–a considerable number of people–began to wear their armor about the city expecting the murder at any time. Cherea finally acted on a day where Caius had been enjoying the theater, in January of A.D. 41. After watching the play, Caius left the theater hall for the palace baths at about three in the afternoon. On a narrow passageway in the Royal palace, Cherea and several other conspirators confronted Caius. Cherea delivered the first blow with his sword. The others followed suit and struck until Caius was dead.

> Thus Gaius, after doing in three years, nine months and twenty-eight days all that has been related, learned by actual experience that he was not a god. (Dio 59:30)

The Praetorian guard, horrified at their failure, regrouped to consider their options. As facilitators to Caius' brutality and madness, they were now in great danger.

The Praetorians' Choice

Claudius was with Caius in the theater on the day of the assassination. He had left the theater for the main palace shortly before Caius left for the baths. Learning of the killing, the terrified Claudius fled to an upstairs room in the Royal palace and hid behind a set of curtains. There, he hoped to survive the mayhem that would certainly follow. But Claudius was quickly found by a member of the Praetorian guard who was searching for booty in the chaotic aftermath of Caius' murder. The Praetorian realized his prize and abandoned his search for further treasure. Claudius was worth far more to him than gold! The quivering and fearful Claudius was triumphantly brought before the main body of the Praetorians.

> When, therefore, these German guards understood that Caius was slain, they were very sorry for it, because they did not use their reason in judging about public affairs, but measured all by the advantages themselves received, Caius being beloved by them because of the money he gave them, (*Antiq* XIX 1:1)

> ..for the soldiers had a meeting together; and when they had debated about what was to be done, they saw that a democracy was incapable of managing such a vast weight of public affairs; and that if it should be set up, it would not be for their advantage; and in case any one of those already in the government should obtain the supreme power, it would in all respects be to their grief, if they were not assisting to him in this advancement; (*Antiq* XVIV 2:1)

The Praetorians knew that there was no force in the city of Rome was a match for their power. The closest Roman legion of the main line was days away–and that by fleet transport. The Praetorians now had Claudius in safekeeping. Not only was Claudius a Caesar, but he was the brother of Germanicus! The Praetorians were fully prepared to fight the senate and whatever army the senate could muster on short notice in order to make Claudius emperor.

Agrippa the Power Broker

King Agrippa was in Rome at the time of the assassination. He was relieved that Claudius was found alive and being protected by the Praetorians. The resourceful Agrippa handled the assassination of his friend Caius with a verve and alacrity born out of sheer desperation. Agrippa knew this was an absolutely critical time for the family of Herod the Great. If there was no Caesar in power, who would support the rule of the Herods in the East? They would be in danger of losing not only their powerful positions, but their wealth and possibly their lives. Agrippa knew he had the most to lose, controlling the largest territory in the Jewish lands. He was also fully aware that there were many ambitious Romans anxiously waiting in the wings more than ready to carve up his kingdom — and him.

The Roman Senate was in complete disarray after the assassination. Realizing this, Agrippa boldly decided to seize the moment. He stepped forth and addressed the senate, presenting himself as an impartial arbitrator of Rome's future. Agrippa eloquently and forcefully argued that Claudius should be installed as emperor–and as expeditiously as possible (*Antiq* XIX 4:1-2). But many in the senate wanted a return to Republican rule. A number of these senators displayed a clear readiness to form their own army and fight Claudius and the Praetorians.

Agrippa warned against this, arguing that any army formed in haste by the senate would be no match for the well-trained Praetorians. But the senate had suffered through years of humiliation and diminution of powers under Caius, and many senators stubbornly held their ground. King Agrippa, appreciating their resolve, then pretended to acquiesce. He volunteered to become the liaison between the senate and Claudius in this matter and vowed to try to convince Claudius to abandon any claim to the throne. The senate approved and Agrippa left the senate house ostensibly for that purpose.

But in a meeting later that day with Claudius, Agrippa did the exact opposite, arguing to Claudius that he should act fearlessly and claim absolute power.

> (Claudius)..was encouraged [to claim the government] partly by the boldness of the soldiers and partly by the persuasion of king Agrippa, who exhorted him not to let such a dominion slip out of his hands, when it came thus to him of its own accord. (*Antiq* XVIV 4:1)

Claudius was insightful enough to understand the fears of the senate and through emissaries assuaged them with a promise of concessions.

> ..but that they should taste of an equitable government under him and moderate times, while he should only he their ruler in name, but the authority should be equally common to them all; and since he had

passed through many and various scenes of life before their eyes, it would be good for them not to distrust him. (*Antiq* XIX 4:2)

But the senate had additional incentive to crown Claudius as emperor. The Praetorian guard–hardened soldiers all–threatened to slaughter the entire senate body if they did not confirm Claudius. Fear of the Praetorians had caused some senators to already flee Rome to the relative safety of their country estates.

Thus it was that Tiberius Claudius Nero Germanicus, the son of Drusus the son of Livia, obtained the imperial power without having been previously tested at all in any position of authority, except for the fact that he had been consul. He was in his fiftieth year. (Dio 60:1)

Soon Claudius was confirmed as emperor by a senate that had no other choice. Claudius subsequently ruled for 13 years and, defying his inauspicious beginning, became one of Rome's most popular emperors.

It should be noted that the Roman historian Suetonius barely mentions Agrippa as a factor in the transition of power from Caius to Claudius, and the books of Tacitus that deal with Caius' assassination are lost. But both Josephus and Dio (Dio 60:8) document that Agrippa played a key role in Claudius' ascension. As has been noted, Josephus displays a consistent positive bias toward King Agrippa and his family, but in this case Josephus' narratives are probably accurate.

Caius' Legacy

It is possible that Caius' darker nature was amplified out of proportion by later historians who had a bias against the Caesars. Even Josephus admits that Caius' first two years were exemplary. Philo lauds Caius' first eight months as emperor, after which a severe encephalitis caused him to go mad–at least in Philo's estimation.

Plutarch was a historian who wrote an entire history of the Caesars that was published in the late first century A.D. It would have been a boon to Roman historical researchers, but the work has been lost. In another of his major works that survived, *Lives of the Romans*, Plutarch refers tangentially to Emperor Caius in his biography *Antony and Cleopatra*.

> Caius, after a reign of distinction, was killed with his wife and child;
> (*Plutarch Lives: Antony and Cleopatra*)

Somewhat surprisingly, Plutarch, a legitimate Roman historian, lauded the reign of Emperor Caius.

After his assassination, Caius' body was buried in a shallow grave with no ceremony and no honors. Weeks later, when Caius' sisters were returned from exile by Claudius, they removed Caius from his hastily-prepared grave and interred his remains in a tomb with some measure of dignity and ceremony—even though it had been Caius who exiled them to Pandataria in the first place.

Claudius as Emperor

A more unlikely emperor than Claudius from the Royal family would be hard to imagine. In his favor, Claudius was the brother of the wildly popular Germanicus—an iconic and beloved Roman figure who died under mysterious circumstances in A.D. 19. Claudius was also the son of Drusus the Great, the lionized brother of Tiberius who also suffered an early and untimely death.

But Claudius himself was afflicted with a club foot, a bad stutter, and unpredictable nervous tics and tremblings. Claudius also had a disturbing tendency to drool whenever he happened to speak—especially noticeable when he was excited. Those neurological abnormalities, taken together with Claudius' natural timidity, had led most Romans to think that he was a complete idiot. In fact, before the assassination of Caius, the Royal court and the Roman Senate had paid only token deference to the Royal Claudius. Most times, Claudius was teased and mocked. Emperor Caius, in fact, encouraged guests at feasts to throw food at Claudius, who had a habit of dozing off after a good meal.

For much of his life, the Royal outcast Claudius had turned to bookish pursuits to pass the time, and his friends were freedmen for the most part. But when the improbable occurred and Claudius became emperor late in life by default, his ingrained humble demeanor instantly resonated with the Roman people. They had been used to suffering under arrogant and cruel rulers. Claudius was an unexpected and refreshing change. The even-handed and fair Claudius was beloved by the Roman people and an unqualified success as emperor.

> (Claudius)..possessed majesty and dignity of appearance, but only when he was standing still or sitting and especially when he was lying down; for he was tall but not slender, with an attractive face, becoming white hair and a full neck. But when he walked, his weak knees gave way under him and he had many disagreeable traits both in his lighter moments and when he was engaged in business; his laughter was unseemly and his anger still more disgusting, for he would foam at the mouth and trickle at the nose; he stammered besides and his head was very shaky at all times, but especially when he made the least exertion. (Sue *Claudius* 30)

Claudius knew his place early in life. He pretended to take little interest in politics and encouraged others to think he was, in fact, something of an idiot. Emperor Tiberius, when he was considering who his successor would be, quickly concluded that Claudius was unfit for any role of power.

> Tiberius had even thought of Claudius, as he was of sedate age and had a taste for liberal culture, but a weak intellect was against him. (*Annuls* 6:46)

But given the bloody history of Caius, it is amazing that Claudius survived at all, idiot or not.

> ..indeed, he (Caius) would have killed Claudius, had he not felt contempt for him, inasmuch as the latter, partly by his nature and partly by deliberate intent, gave the impression of great stupidity. (Dio 59:23)

It was Caius' twisted sense of humor that likely preserved Claudius' life. Under Caius, Claudius became a Royal buffoon and the butt of jokes and a source of entertainment at Royal feasts.

> As for his uncle Claudius, he (Caius) spared him merely as a laughingstock. (Sue *Caius* XXIII)

With his physical ailments and speech difficulties, and an intellect that Claudius himself encouraged others to think as dull and retarded, Caius dismissed him completely as a serious rival for power.

Suetonius quotes from a letter Emperor Augustus wrote to his wife Livia concerning Claudius in Claudius' younger years.

> But if we realize that he (Claudius) is wanting and defective in soundness of body and mind, we must not furnish the means of ridiculing both him and us to a public which is wont to scoff at and deride such things. (Sue *Claudius* 4:2)

Claudius' Reign

Claudius' humble affect had been caused by years of mistreatment and having to deal with his socially debilitating physical afflictions. For this reason, unlike Caius, Claudius had no illusions about his divinity. In those days, physical ailments were considered curses from the gods, and a sick body reflected a sick intellect and spirit. Claudius likely believed this as well and so his ego was well-tethered to a harsh reality.

> Besides his moderation in this respect, he further forbade any one to worship him or to offer him any sacrifice; (Dio 60:5)

Also, as a former Royal outcast, Claudius' companions had been freedmen and servants. Claudius learned to trust them and, when he became emperor, the most capable of them were brought into his administration and given great authority. This proved to be much to the benefit of the empire. Emperor

Claudius was also attentive in his work and fair-minded. The Roman people soon realized that Claudius was no idiot.

But for all his diligence, Claudius was a weak and vacillating man. Claudius could be easily talked into any particular course of action by trusted administrators. For this reason, too, the women in his life–to whom Claudius was slavishly devoted–held great power over him.

> Wholly under the control of these and of his wives, as I have said,he played the part, not of a prince, but of a servant lavishing honours, the command of armies, pardons or punishments, according to the interests of each of them, or even their wish or whim; and that too for the most part in ignorance and blindly. (Sue *Claudius* 29:1)

> But no difficulty seemed to be presented by the temper of a sovereign who had neither partialities nor dislikes, but such as were suggested and dictated to him. (*Annuls* 12:3)

But Claudius' advisers were able men and they kept their level of graft and corruption to a minimum. The empire prospered during the reign of Claudius.

Character

Claudius' character and tastes were refreshingly normal for an emperor, given the murderous excesses of Caius.

> He was immoderate in his passion for women, but wholly free from unnatural vice. (Sue *Claudius* 33)

Claudius did have a darker side, but he was not an inordinately cruel man considering the times and the legacy of his predecessors.

> That he was of a cruel and bloodthirsty disposition was shown in matters great and small. He always exacted examination by torture.. (Sue *Claudius* 34)

Claudius was studious as a magistrate, but at times erratic and unpredictable.

> But in hearing and deciding cases he showed strange inconsistency of temper, for he was now careful and shrewd, sometimes hasty and inconsiderate, occasionally silly and like a crazy man. (Sue *Claudius* 15)

In regards to money, Claudius lacked the greed of Caius or the tight-fistedness of Tiberius.

> Moreover, his attitude toward money was remarkable. For he forbade any one to bring him contributions, as had been the practice under Augustus and Gaius and ordered that no one who had any relatives at all should name him as his heir; he furthermore gave back the sums that had previously been confiscated under Tiberius and Gaius, either to the victims themselves, if they still survived, or otherwise to their children. (Dio 60:6)

Claudius also had a literary bent which he had pursued in solitude over his decades spent as a Royal cast-off. This scholarly interest continued after Claudius became emperor, and he spent much time writing various histories of Rome and the Roman people. Interestingly, Claudius also invented three new letters for the Latin alphabet.

> Even while he was emperor he wrote a good deal and gave constant recitals through a professional reader...Besides this he invented three new letters and added them to the alphabet, maintaining that they were greatly needed...These characters may still be seen in numerous Books, in the daily gazette and in inscriptions on public buildings. (Sue *Claudius* 41)

Whether deserved or not, the library at Alexandria in Egypt devoted an entire room to the writings of Emperor Claudius (Sue *Claudius* 42), where public readings were held on a regular basis.

Claudius and Agrippina

When he was first crowned Emperor, Claudius promptly brought back Caius' sisters Agrippina and Julia from exile, making him all the more popular with the Roman people. The two women were his nieces being the daughters of his brother Germanicus.

> He also brought back those whom Gaius had unjustly exiled, including the latter's sisters Agrippina and Julia and restored to them their property. (Dio 60:4)

Exiled to the Pontine islands in their twenties, the two women were forced to live austere lives. At times they had to dive for sponges to sell in order to support themselves. To augment their diets, they likely also dove for clams and oysters as well. This skill at swimming later saved Agrippina's life – albeit for a short period of time – during the reign of her son Nero. Agrippina, who inherited her mother's imperious airs, had become a fit and confident woman during her exile. She soon became a favorite of several several of Claudius' closest advisers.

Claudius had already had two unsuccessful marriages by the time he became emperor at the age of 50. Soon after his ascension to power, Claudius married the most beautiful woman in Rome, Messalina, who was the daughter of one of Claudius' cousins. She turned out to be a notorious profligate, however. Eventually, she was forced to commit suicide, but not before she bore Claudius a son, Britannicus and a daughter, Octavia.

After Messalina's death in A.D. 48, a top priority for Claudius' advisers was to find a suitable woman to be queen. Claudius was a weak man in all respects and never truly made a decision on his own. General Lucius Vitellius, the former president of Syria under Tiberius and Caius, had made a smooth transition from Caius to become one of Claudius' main counselors. Vitellius thought that Agrippina should be Claudius' next wife. He knew that Claudius favored strong women. If the emperor was to be dominated, let it be by the proper woman–a woman from the Augustan line and whose interests were solidly aligned with the best interests of the empire.

Vitellius was the former hero of Armenia who had survived a plot against him by Emperor Caius to become Caius' fast friend and confidante. This was the same man who had removed the

High Priest Joseph Caiaphas from office in Jerusalem 12 years before–likely for Caiaphas' unwarranted actions against Jesus of Nazareth. Vitellius removed the High Priest Jonathan the next year for his actions against the Nazarenes–most notably the stoning of Stephen. Now in Rome, Vitellius had abandoned any further military ambitions–if he had any in the first place–and enjoyed a luxurious if servile life in the Royal courts of Caius and Claudius.

Agrippina the Younger was pretty and at 34 years of age relatively young, even though she had had a son, Lucius Domitius, by her deceased husband Domitius Ahenobarbus. While Claudius' marriage to Agrippina made sense in many ways, it was considered incest which was against Roman custom. Vitellius was no stranger to incestuous marriages from his days with the Herod family in the East. Thinking that incest should not be a barrier to the union, Vitellius argued before the Roman Senate to legalize such marriages between uncles and nieces and to pass a resolution that Claudius should, in fact, marry Agrippina. Claudius had beforehand agreed to abide by whatever the Roman Senate would decree. Tacitus quotes Vitellius before the Senate:

> "But, it will be said, marriage with a brother's daughter is with us a novelty. True; but it is common in other countries and there is no law to forbid it. Marriages of cousins were long unknown, but after a time they became frequent. Custom adapts itself to expediency and this novelty will hereafter take its place among recognized usages." (*Annuls* 12:6)

The Senate passed the edict and, in true Herodian fashion, Claudius married his niece Agrippina in A.D. 49. But it would prove to be a blunder by any measure; Claudius might as well have signed his own death decree.

The next year, in A.D. 50, after much urging by his new wife Agrippina, Emperor Claudius formally adopted Agrippina's son Nero (then known as Domitius) as his own son, making him heir to the empire (*Annuls* 12:26). This was a shocking act, as Claudius already had a blood son, by his late wife Messalina, who was only two years younger than Nero. Agrippina, along with

Vitellius and Claudius' other key advisers, had argued that Britannicus–by all reports a capable and intelligent person and without the physical drawbacks of Claudius–lacked the blood connection with the family of Augustus that Nero enjoyed and that Rome would demand in a successor. Agrippina was the great-granddaughter of the late Emperor Augustus.

Four years afterward, Agrippina would manage to poison Claudius. A year after Claudius' murder, the new Emperor Nero would in turn poison Britannicus, Claudius' natural son (*Annuls* 13:15).

British Campaign

Aside from the usual rumblings from Parthia in the East, there were no real outside threats to the Roman Empire during the reign of Claudius. This was a fortunate situation for Claudius. For the years of Claudius' rule, Rome didn't need strength and military genius in an emperor, just competence and a nominal amount of due diligence. Aside from a single exception, Claudius didn't feel the need to prove himself on the battlefield, for he was a peaceful man. Tacitus quotes Claudius in an A.D. 49 speech.

Rome, sated with her glory, had reached such a height that, she wished even foreign nations to enjoy repose (*Annuls* 12:11)

Early in his reign, however, Claudius did seek his share of military glory. At that time Claudius thought that, in order to be taken seriously as emperor, he had to lead at least one military campaign. So in A.D. 43, Claudius made a foray into Britain at the head of the Roman army.

The British campaign turned out to be largely uneventful. After minimal contact with the enemy–who were wretched and ill-equipped northern tribesmen–Claudius returned to the comfort of Rome in six months. Of course, a great triumph was celebrated.

..without any battle or bloodshed received the submission of a part of the island, returned to Rome within six months after leaving the city and celebrated a triumph of great splendour. (Sue *Claudius* 17:2)

Of note is the fact that during his time away, Claudius designated Lucius Vitellius as the emperor in his absence. This represented the high point of Vitellius' illustrious career.

Caractacus

Some mention should be made of the later capture of the wily Celtic general Caractacus in A.D. 50. The enchained Caractacus was paraded through Rome amid great fanfare–the Roman citizens cheering the brilliance of a man who had been for nine years their greatest foe.

The people were summoned as to a grand spectacle; the praetorian cohorts were drawn up under arms in the plain in front of their camp; then came a procession of the royal vassals and the ornaments and neck-chains and the spoils which the king had won in wars with other tribes, were displayed. Next were to be seen his brothers, his wife and daughter; last of all, Caractacus himself. All the rest stooped in their fear to abject supplication; not so the king, who neither by humble look nor speech sought compassion. (*Annuls* 12:36)

Caractacus then gave a noble speech requesting mercy from Claudius–and Claudius' wife Agrippina.

Upon this the emperor granted pardon to Caractacus, to his wife and to his brothers. Released from their bonds, they did homage also to Agrippina who sat near, conspicuous on another throne, in the same language of praise and gratitude. It was indeed a novelty, quite alien to ancient manners, for a woman to sit in front of Roman standards. In fact, Agrippina boasted that she was herself a partner in the empire which her ancestors had won. (*Annuls* 12:37)

Agrippina was now accepted as co-ruler ruler of the empire, and Claudius became expendable.

Claudius and the Christians

Claudius was less tolerant than Augustus had been in matters of religion. His attitude and actions toward the Druids of Gaul might be indicative of how he felt toward the Christians and their unusual ceremony of the communion.

> (Claudius)..utterly abolished the cruel and inhuman religion of the Druids among the Gauls which under Augustus had merely been prohibited to Roman citizens; (Sue *Claudius* 25:5)

One of Claudius' most consequential acts for both the Christians and the Jews came early in his reign. Then, Claudius transferred the countries of Samaria and Judea to the rule of Agrippa I, the grandson of Herod the Great. King Agrippa now had authority over all of the territories that had composed Herod the Great's old kingdom. Though King Agrippa ruled Judea for only three years before his death in A.D. 44, his effect on Emperor Claudius, the Jewish East, and the Nazarenes cannot be overestimated.

According to Dio, Emperor Claudius addressed the "problem" of the Jews in A.D. 41, his first year in power.

> As for the Jews, who had again increased so greatly that by reason of their multitude it would have been hard without raising a tumult to bar them from the city, he did not drive them out, but ordered them, while continuing their traditional mode of life, not to hold meetings. (Dio 60:6)

But Dio might not be totally accurate. Was he referring to the Christians and not the Jews? Josephus reproduces an edict from Claudius that is favorable to the Jews which was made in A.D. 41.

> Upon the petition of king Agrippa and king Herod, who are persons very dear to me, that I would grant the same rights and privileges should be preserved to the Jews which are in all the Roman empire which I have granted to those of Alexandria... It will therefore be fit to permit the Jews, who are in all the world under us, to keep their ancient customs without being hindered so to do. (*Antiq* XIX 5:3)

The King Herod referenced by Claudius would have been Herod, the older brother of Agrippa I, who was the king of Chalcis.

Suetonius mentions the Christians when writing about Claudius.

> Since the Jews constantly made disturbances at the instigation of Chrestus,he expelled them from Rome. (Sue *Claudius* 25:4)

Here, the Christians are referred to as Jews, indicating that Dio, too, might have been referring to Christians when he referred to "Jews." This action of Claudius is also referenced in a passage in Acts and in the context of the Apostle Paul's visit to Corinth around A.D. 56, some 15 years later.

> And he found a certain Jew named Aquila, a man of Pontus by race, lately come from Italy, with his wife Priscilla, because Claudius had commanded all the Jews to depart from Rome: and he came unto them (Acts 18:2)

In Acts, it is unclear whether the Christians were targeted exclusively by Claudius, or whether they were forced out of Rome along with the greater population of its Jews. Agrippa I was Jewish and enjoyed the great respect of Emperor Claudius. If the Jews were causing trouble in Rome, would Agrippa I have defended them, or recommended punishment? And what problems could the Jews have caused? Certainly the Christians, on the other hand, were known for their irritating ways and dark ceremonies.

Dio wrote in the early third century A.D. Then, the Christians were a major force and it is not likely he would have confused the Christians with the Jews. It is possible, however, that the earlier sources Dio relied on did make this error. So more than likely, giving credence to Suetonius in this regard and considering Claudius' loyalty and respect for Agrippa I, it was the Christians–not the complaining Jews–who were banished from Rome early in Claudius' reign.

As will be seen in the next chapter, King Agrippa would later wreak havoc upon the Christians in his new domain of Judea. It is likely, too, that Agrippa would have urged Emperor Claudius to have a similar disposition toward the Nazarenes who had settled in Rome. Claudius was an indecisive man in this respect and could be persuaded to almost any action upon the strong urging of a trusted confidante.

Chapter 13   Agrippa I and the Judean Procurators

Now about that time Herod the king put forth his hands to afflict certain of the church. (Acts 12:1)

Agrippa I was an important figure in Emperor Claudius' gaining the throne after Caius' assassination. One of grateful Claudius' first acts in A.D. 41 was to place Judea and Samaria, formerly Roman provinces, under Agrippa's control as kingdoms. Upon Agrippa's urging, Claudius gave Agrippa's older brother Herod the domain of Chalcis to rule, and so he became a king as well.

(Claudius)..enlarged the domain of Agrippa of Palestine, who, happening to be in Rome, had helped him to become emperor and bestowed on him the rank of consul; and to his brother Herod he gave the rank of praetor and a principality. And he permitted them to enter the senate and to express their thanks to him in Greek. (Dio 60:8)

It had been almost 45 years since Emperor Augustus had split up Herod the Great's old kingdom and divided it among Herod's sons. Now, under Agrippa, Herod's grandson, the kingdom was reunified. Agrippa also was the great grandson of Hyrcanus II, one of the last true Jewish kings of the Maccabean line. Thus, through Agrippa's elevation, the Asamoneans also regained a measure of their lost authority.

With this prize in hand, Agrippa wasted no time in moving with his family to Jerusalem and taking up residence in the palace of Herod. One of his first acts was to remove Theophilis from the High Priest's position.

And when Agrippa had entirely finished all the duties of the Divine worship, he removed Theophilus, the son of Ananus, from the high priesthood and bestowed that honor of his on Simon the son of Boethus, whose name was also Cantheras whose daughter king Herod married, as I have related above. (*Antiq* XVIV 6:2)

How did this change in High Priests and in the Judean ruler affect the Christians? Jonathan had been brutal in his persecution of the Nazarenes, but had been removed by Vitellius after only a year in power. Theophilis was certainly no friend of the Christians–he was the brother to both Jonathan and Caiaphas, after all–but the message from Rome to tolerate the Christians was clear. Additionally, by that time many of the Apostles had already left Judea to preach and establish churches in other areas of the Roman Empire. Those who remained in Jerusalem kept a low profile and followed Temple Jewish ritual as much as possible.

Most probably, the Second Temple High Priesthood was jubilant over Emperor Claudius and his appointment of Agrippa as king. Caius was dead and he harbored a great contempt for Judaism despite his friendship with Agrippa. Caius' actions were intentionally provocative, and it was obvious that Caius was fully prepared to deal with a Jewish revolt–perhaps he wanted one to combat his boredom.

Claudius, however, was of an older generation and appeared to be liberal, intellectual and tolerant. Now, with Marcellus gone and Agrippa in place, the High Priesthood was very satisfied. After all, Agrippa came from a long line of Asamonean High Priests—he was one of their own. In fact, Agrippa I's appointment was bad news, indeed, for the Jerusalem Nazarenes.

Agrippa's Reign

The Jewish East was a prosperous land for the last three years of Agrippa's reign. Magnanimous in that respect, Agrippa I spent huge sums of money on construction projects, especially in Jerusalem. A third north wall was built around the upper city of Jerusalem. A Royal tower, called Psephinus, was constructed at the new outer wall's northwest corner (*Wars* V 4:1-2). Though living in Jerusalem, Agrippa never lost his taste for Roman culture. In Berytus, he built an ornate theater and an arena for gladiatorial contests. In the true Roman style, he sponsored many games and spectacles (*Antiq* XIX 7:5).

Late in his reign, Agrippa held a summit meeting in the Galilean city of Tiberias for the various kings in that region, including Cotys of Lesser Armenia, and his brother King Herod of Chalcis. The purpose was apparently above board with the kings discussing common issues and problems. But the president of Syria, Marcus, when he arrived for the meeting, was very suspicious. Was Agrippa's secret purpose to lay the groundwork for an eastern-based revolution against Rome? Marcus ordered the meeting disbanded and the kings back to their home countries. Marcus also recommended to Claudius that Agrippa be ordered to stop his fortification of Jerusalem (*Antiq* XIX 7:2,8:1) which Claudius did. This explains why Agrippa's wall didn't extend south to include the lower city of Jerusalem, or why it never reached its full height. Agrippa agreed to stop building the wall, but as a condition requested of Claudius that Marcus stay out of his domain.

Herod Agrippa came from a long line of Royal Asamonean rulers. In fact, his ancestors were High Priests first and became kings later only out of necessity. When Agrippa gained control of Judea and Jerusalem in A.D. 41, he remained true to his heritage by unequivocally supporting the Second Temple High Priesthood.

Virtuous Agrippa?

Unfortunately for Agrippa, he only lived to enjoy his vast kingdom for three more years, dying in A.D. 44. During that time, he lived in Jerusalem in Herod's palace and adopted–according to Josephus–a virtuous lifestyle. Agrippa I sacrificed at the Second Temple almost every day, followed Jewish law scrupulously, and generally kept himself pure in the eyes of God.

But Agrippa's temper was mild and equally liberal to all men. He was humane to foreigners and made them sensible of his liberality. He was in like manner rather of a gentle and compassionate temper. Accordingly, he loved to live continually at Jerusalem and was exactly careful in the observance of the laws of his country. He therefore kept himself entirely pure; nor did any day pass over his head without its appointed sacrifice. (*Antiq* XIX 7:3)

Agrippa also strove to endear himself to the Jewish people.

Now this king was by nature very beneficent and liberal in his gifts and very ambitious to oblige people with such large donations; and he made himself very illustrious by the many chargeable presents he made them. He took delight in giving and rejoiced in living with good reputation. (*Antiq* XIX 7:3)

Agrippa even paid homage to the ancient Jewish acetic sect of the Nazorites.

(Agrippa I)..also came to Jerusalem and offered all the sacrifices that belonged to him and omitted nothing which the law required; on which account he ordained that many of the Nazarites should have their heads shorn. (*Antiq* XIX 6:1)

Apparently, some of those Jews who took the vows of the Nazorites neglected out of convenience to have their hair cut off. Agrippa I saw to it that these temporary ascetics followed strictly the Old Testament law in this regard.

Agrippa's Dark Side

The virtuous picture of Agrippa that Josephus paints is in contrast to the Agrippa seen under Caius' reign. Then, Agrippa had enjoyed life to the fullest in the decadent Royal court of the freewheeling, short-lived emperor. Although Agrippa ruled Herod Philip's old kingdom 1,000 miles away, he kept a palace in Rome and stayed there for much of the time. Under Claudius, however, with his newly-enlarged kingdom Agrippa moved to Jerusalem and, according to Josephus, became a paradigm of goodness and virtue, following the austere rules and practices of devout Jews of the time.

Which Agrippa was the real one?

Agrippa was 20 years older than Caius, and the young emperor likely looked up to Agrippa, at least initially. Was Caius dependent upon Agrippa through a complex emotional dynamic–a dependency that Agrippa recognized and used to his own advantage? When Caius began to consider himself a living god and systematically started executing the most powerful men in the empire, what did Agrippa think? Agrippa at first probably felt it wiser to stay close to the emperor and try to control him rather than retreating to the East. But certainly during the last two years of Caius' reign, Agrippa couldn't help but be nervous for his own safety. In that respect, Agrippa had to be relieved at Caius' assassination, although that brought on an entirely new set of problems.

Agrippa I and the Christians

Agrippa's deference to the Second Temple High Priesthood during this period did not bode well for the early Christians. While Josephus consistently portrays Agrippa I in his writings as having a "great" soul and as a man favored by God, clearly Agrippa was no friend of the fledgling Nazarene sect. Early in his reign over Judea, Agrippa slew James, one of the sons of Zebedee and an original Disciple. In the Passover of A.D. 42, Agrippa I then arrested the Disciple Peter and brought him to trial. Peter was saved from certain execution only by the act of an Angel. In the following selection from Acts, King Agrippa I is referred to as Herod the King.

> [12:1]Now about that time Herod the king put forth his hands to afflict certain of the church. [12:2]And he killed James the brother of John with the sword. [12:3]And when he saw that it pleased the Jews, he proceeded to seize Peter also. And *those* were the days of unleavened bread. (Acts)

It is not surprising that Agrippa took the side of the Jerusalem High Priesthood against the Christians. Even in the works of Josephus, who was a great defender of everything Agrippa did, Agrippa's rougher edges are apparent. Only two years before, Agrippa, when he felt threatened, was quick to accuse his uncle Herod Antipas of being in league with the hated Sejanus and even conspiring with the Parthian King Artabanus (*Antiq* XVIII 7:2). Earlier, Agrippa had flare-ups with his older brother Aristobulos–later an ally–as well as with his sister Herodias and probably unnamed others in the Jewish East during his visit there around A.D. 32-35.

In A.D. 23, a prescient recognition of this darker nature of Agrippa perhaps caused Emperor Tiberius to banish him from his court after the death of his own son Drusus. More than a decade later, Tiberius, after a brief reconciliation, again turned against Agrippa, throwing him into prison in A.D. 36. What did Tiberius see in Agrippa that was so distasteful?!

Roman historian Dio suggests that, while Caius was alive and Agrippa his companion, Agrippa I was every bit as dissolute and evil as Caius had been–even acting as Caius' teacher in that respect.

> All this, however, did not distress the people so much as did their expectation that Gaius' cruelty and licentiousness would go to still greater lengths. And they were particularly troubled on ascertaining that King Agrippa and King Antiochus were with him, like two tyrant-trainers. (Dio 59:24)

The historical record is clear that Agrippa the Great lent his powers to the disruption of the growing Christian movement–and not without enthusiasm.

The Apostles Flee Jerusalem

As a partial consequence of Agrippa's actions, some of the Apostles who had previously reached a truce of sorts with the High Priesthood abandoned Jerusalem. This was no small sacrifice for them, as Angels had promised that Jesus would return on the Mount of Olives across the Kidron Valley from the great city (Acts 1:11). But as the violence against the Christians escalated, the prospect of witnessing Jesus' return lost its immediacy to considerations of sheer survival. Many of the Apostles came to the sobering realization that if they did not leave Jerusalem and Judea they would be killed off one by one. In fact, by the time Agrippa died in A.D. 44, few core disciples remained in Jerusalem at all; most had fled to churches in other parts of the eastern Roman Empire and beyond. Many of these churches had originally been established by Nazarenes who had been hounded out of Jerusalem by the High Priest Jonathan some four years earlier.

Death of Agrippa I

Josephus writes that just before Agrippa died, he vomited up copious amounts of blood (*Antiq* XVII 8:2). In Acts, "Herod the King" is said to have died from being consumed by worms. These are descriptions most likely of the same underlying medical condition–bleeding caused by consumption.

> [12:21]And upon a set day Herod arrayed himself in royal apparel and sat on the throne and made an oration unto them. [12:22]And the people shouted, *saying*, The voice of a god and not of a man. [12:23]And immediately an angel of the Lord smote him, because he gave not God the glory: and he was eaten of worms and gave up the ghost. (Acts)

Immediately after Agrippa died in A.D. 44, his subjects celebrated. This suggests that the Agrippa depicted in Acts is closer to reality than the Agrippa portrayed in Josephus' works.

> But when it was known that Agrippa was departed this life, the inhabitants of Cesarea and of Sebaste forgot the kindnesses he had bestowed on them and acted the part of the bitterest enemies; for they cast such reproaches upon the deceased as are not fit to be spoken of; (*Antiq* XIX 9:1)

King Agrippa left behind four children.

And thus did king Agrippa depart this life. But he left behind him a son, Agrippa by name, a youth in the seventeenth year of his age and three daughters; one of which, Bernice, was married to Herod, his father's brother and was sixteen years old; the other two, Mariamne and Drusilla, were still virgins; the former was ten years old and Drusilla six. (*Antiq* XIX 9:1)

Agrippa the younger (the future Agrippa II) was born in A.D. 27, Bernice in A.D. 28, Mariamne in A.D. 34 and Drusilla in A.D. 38. An eldest son, Drusus, died in childhood, presumably in Rome. The younger Agrippa would eventually assume much of his father's power, but not for years. The daughters would likewise lead illustrious lives. Notably, Drusilla would become the wife of Procurator Antonius Felix, who would imprison Paul the Apostle in A.D. 58. Later, as documented in Acts, Paul the Apostle would preach before Agrippa II and his sister Bernice in Caesarea in A.D. 60. Bernice would become the long-time paramour of future Emperor Titus, but never to the point of marriage. When Agrippa I died, Bernice was married to her uncle, King Herod of Chalcis. Her first marriage was to Marcus, a son of the wealthy and powerful Alexander the alabarch.

Herod, King of Chalcis

The children of Bernice and the executed Prince Aristobulos all received their measure of fame. Agrippa became King of Judea. Aristobulos became a powerful man in Syria. Herodias married the ruler of Galilee. The eldest daughter Mariamne was likely the first wife of Archelaus, Herod the Great's son (*Wars* II 7:4), although this is not certain. A fifth child, Herod, also became a king.

When Claudius became emperor in A.D. 41, Agrippa successfully petitioned to Claudius that his older brother, Herod, be given the kingdom of Chalcis which was a territory north of Galilee in Syria. This Herod had just married Agrippa's own daughter Bernice–incest in true Herodian style. Bernice at the time was 13 years of age. Even at that young age, she had been married previously! Agrippa had wisely arranged an early marriage for her to Marcus, the son of the very wealthy Alexander the alabarch. So at the very least Herod needed his own kingdom to keep Bernice in the luxury to which she was accustomed.

> But when Marcus, Alexander's son, was dead, who had married her when she was a virgin, Agrippa gave her (Bernice) in marriage to his brother Herod and begged for him of Claudius the kingdom of Chalcis. (*Antiq* XIX 5:1)

After Agrippa's death in A.D. 44, Judea and Samaria again reverted to Roman provincial status. Agrippa's son, the future Agrippa II, was seen by Claudius as being too young to assume his father's powers. To preserve a measure of Jewish authority in the area, Herod, now the King of Chalcis, requested that Claudius give him special authority over the Second Temple in Jerusalem, in particular the power to appoint the High Priest. Claudius granted Herod's request.

> Herod also, the brother of the deceased Agrippa, who was then possessed of the royal authority over Chalcis, petitioned Claudius Caesar for the authority over the temple and the money of the sacred treasure and the choice of the high priests and obtained all that he petitioned for. So that after that time this authority continued among all his descendants till the end of the war. Accordingly, Herod removed the last high priest, called Cimtheras and bestowed that dignity on his successor Joseph, the son of Cantos. (*Antiq* XX 1:3)

Josephus reports that King Herod of Chalcis died in A.D. 49, in the eighth year of Claudius' reign. His kingdom was then passed on to Agrippa II (*Antiq* XX 5:2).

In A.D. 53, Claudius gave Agrippa II Herod Philip's old tetrarchy and other territories to go along with it. In kind, Claudius took Chalcis away from Agrippa II and gave it to Herod's son Aristobulos to administer (*Antiq* XX 7:1). In A.D. 54, this same son of Herod was appointed by the new Emperor Nero to be the ruler of Lesser Armenia. Aristobulos' wife was Salome, the daughter of Herodias, who had danced so provocatively for Antipas and brought about the death of John the Baptist.

Return of the Equestrians

When Agrippa the Great died unexpectedly in A.D. 44, Roman equestrians were again appointed to govern much of the Jewish East. Instead of being called prefects, Claudius used the term procurator.

> (Claudius).. was therefore disposed to send Agrippa, junior, away presently to succeed his father in the kingdom and was willing to confirm him in it by his oath. But those freed-men and friends of his, who had the greatest authority with him, dissuaded him from it and said that it was a dangerous experiment to permit so large a kingdom to come under the government of so very young a man and one hardly yet arrived at years of discretion, who would not be able to take sufficient care of its administration; while the weight of a kingdom is heavy enough to a grown man. So Caesar thought what they said to be reasonable. Accordingly he sent Cuspins Fadus to be procurator of Judea and of the entire kingdom and paid that respect to the deceased as not to introduce Marcus, who had been at variance with him, into his kingdom. (*Antiq* XIX 9:2)

This is an interesting paragraph for two reasons. It shows the power of the freedmen in Claudius' administration. The post of procurator in any area was a *de facto* license to steal and the Claudian freedmen wanted it for their own benefit. However, it is probable that with all the violence in Judea that was to come Claudius regretted not instating Agrippa's young son, also named Agrippa, as king–as was his initial inclination.

Cuspius Fadus

The first of these procurators was Cuspius Fadus, whose tenure was A.D. 44-6. Fadus was typical of most of those appointed to rule Judea after Agrippa I. He had no qualms about using deadly force to thwart any hint of religious conflict. Fadus also acted decisively against the robbers and criminals who had taken root in Judea during Agrippa's brief reign.

Fadus also petitioned Claudius to regain Roman control over the High Priest's holy vestments. Fadus wanted to return them to the tower of Antonia and not let them become a potential symbol of sedition to the Jews. The younger Agrippa (the future Agrippa II), who now lived in Rome as a part of Claudius' Royal court, strongly disagreed and expressed this opinion to Claudius. Deferring to Agrippa, Claudius wrote an edict that the Jerusalem priests would retain control of the holy garb (*Antiq* XX 1:2).

While Procurator Fadus was in office, a prophet arose and stirred up the masses. Fadus put down the movement decisively.

> Now it came to pass, while Fadus was procurator of Judea, that a certain magician, whose name was Theudas, persuaded a great part of the people to take their effects with them and follow him to the river Jordan; for he told them he was a prophet and that he would, by his own command, divide the river and afford them an easy passage over it; and many were deluded by his words. However, Fadus did not permit them to make any advantage of his wild attempt, but sent a troop of horsemen out against them; who, falling upon them unexpectedly, slew many of them and took many of them alive. They also took Theudas alive and cut off his head and carried it to Jerusalem. This was what befell the Jews in the time of Cuspius Fadus' government. (*Antiq* XX 5:1)

Theudas' use of the Jordan River in his ministry could have meant that he was a Nazarene or possibly a devotee of John the Baptist. But Theudas could also have been trying to emulate Moses by demonstrating his God-given power over flowing water and the Jordan was simply the closest river available. Fadus' Theudas should not be confused with a troublemaker of the same name to whom Gamaliel made reference in Acts–an "impostor" who was active before the days of the enrollment in A.D. 6 (Acts 5:36).

Tiberius Alexander

Tiberius Alexander was procurator from A.D. 46-8. He came from a famous and wealthy Jewish family and rose to become, arguably, more powerful that King Agrippa II during the time of the Jewish revolt. Alexander was the nephew of the philosopher and historian Philo Judaeus and was the son of Alexander the alabarch. As his name suggests, Tiberius Alexander was a very Romanized—he was not a practicing Jew at all.

> Then came Tiberius Alexander as successor to Fadus; he was the son of Alexander the alabarch of Alexandria which Alexander was a principal person among all his contemporaries, both for his family and wealth: he was also more eminent for his piety than this his son Alexander, for he did not continue in the religion of his country. (*Antiq* XX 5:2)

An "alabarch" was a Roman–designated official, somewhat along the lines of a prefect, who had magisterial powers within a particular ethnic community; in Alexander's case the Jewish community was within Alexandria, Egypt. Earlier in his life, he served first as the steward and later the freedman of Antonia, the honored widow of Drusus the Great, Tiberius' brother, and had lived in Rome.

Alexander the alabarch played a key role in the saga of Herod Agrippa, the future Agrippa I. In Alexandria, in early A.D. 36, he lent the spendthrift Agrippa a substantial amount of money.

> (Agrippa)..went off and sailed to Alexandria, where he desired Alexander the alabarch to lend him two hundred thousand drachmae; but he said he would not lend it to him, but would not refuse it to Cypros, as greatly astonished at her affection to her husband and at the other instances of her virtue; so she undertook to repay it. Accordingly, Alexander paid them five talents at Alexandria and promised to pay them the rest of that sum at Dicearchia [Puteoli]; (*Antiq* XVIII 6:3)

Later, Herod Agrippa, as Agrippa I, would give Alexander's son Marcus his eldest daughter, Bernice, in marriage.

Under Emperor Caius, any freedman of wealth and power became a target. Soon, Caius found a way to place Alexander the alabarch in prison, but details in the historical record are lacking. King Agrippa I apparently wasn't powerful enough–or foolhardy enough–to defend his former benefactor, but was probably key in preventing Caius from executing the man. When Claudius came into power in A.D. 41, Agrippa I was likely the main force behind Alexander's release.

(Claudius).. also set Alexander Lysimachus, the alabarch, at liberty, who had been his old friend and steward to his mother Antonia, but had been imprisoned by Caius, whose son [Marcus] married Bernice, the daughter of Agrippa. (*Antiq* XIX 5:1)

King Agrippa I was probably important in the young Tiberius Alexander's attainment of powerful positions within Claudius' administration. Though Jewish, Tiberius Alexander fully embraced the Roman way of life and so Claudius greatly favored him.

A famine in the Jewish East began during the tenure of Fadus and continued through the term of Tiberius Alexander, including the years A.D. 44-48. This particular famine had been famously predicted by the Christian disciple Agabus.

And there stood up one of them named Agabus and signified by the Spirit that there should be a great famine over all the world: which came to pass in the days of Claudius. (Acts 11:28)

In anticipation of the natural disaster, many of the Apostles in Antioch and other Churches in Asia Minor began to bring relief supplies to their Christian brothers in Jerusalem.

The famine also precipitated a violent Jewish insurrection. Interestingly, the rebel leaders whom Procurator Tiberius Alexander battled were two of the sons of Judas the Galilean, the original zealot who had caused such great trouble in Judea more than 40 years earlier (*Antiq* XVIII 1:8). Tiberius Alexander not only put down the revolt, but had these sons of Judas, James and Simon, both crucified.

The names of those sons were James and Simon, whom Alexander commanded to be crucified. (*Antiq* XX 5:2)

Much later in A.D. 66, Emperor Nero appointed Tiberius Alexander as the procurator of Egypt. This position placed Alexander on a level with King Agrippa II in the empire hierarchy, an amazing achievement for a Jew. The year A.D. 66 is also when the Jewish revolt began in Judea.

Ever since the time of the Divine Augustus Roman Knights have ruled Egypt as kings and the forces by which it has to be kept in subjection. It has been thought expedient thus to keep under home control a province so difficult of access, so productive of corn, ever distracted, excitable and restless through the superstition and licentiousness of its inhabitants, knowing nothing of laws and unused to civil rule. Its governor was at this time Tiberius Alexander, a native of the country. (Tacitus *Histories* 1:11)

About this very time king Agrippa was going to Alexandria, to congratulate Alexander upon his having obtained the government of Egypt from Nero; (*Wars* II 15:1)

As Egyptian procurator, Alexander had control over two Roman legions. Alexander was not hesitant to use his authority. At one time he brutally put down a sedition in the Jewish "quarter" in Alexandria, called Delta, killing 50,000 (according to Josephus). At the time, the Jews in Judea and parts of Galilee had declared their independence from Rome and many Jews in Alexandria revolted as well. Tiberius Alexander made short work of their ambition.

..Tiberius Alexander, the governor of the city,.... perceived that those who were for innovations would not be pacified till some great calamity should overtake them, he sent out upon them those two Roman legions that were in the city and together with them five thousand other soldiers, who, by chance, were come together out of Libya, to the ruin of the Jews. They were also permitted not only to kill them, but to plunder them of what they had and to set fire to their houses. These soldiers rushed violently into that part of the city that was called Delta, where the Jewish people lived together and did as they were bidden, though not without bloodshed on their own side also; for the Jews got together and set those that were the best armed among them in the forefront and made a resistance for a great while; but when once they gave back, they were destroyed unmercifully; and this their destruction was complete, some being caught in the open field and others forced into their houses which houses were first plundered of what was in them and then set on fire by the Romans; wherein no mercy was shown to the infants and no regard had to the aged; but they went on in the slaughter of persons of every age, till all the place was overflowed with blood and fifty thousand of them lay dead upon heaps; nor had the remainder been preserved, had they not be-taken themselves to supplication. So Alexander commiserated their condition and gave orders to the Romans to retire; accordingly, these being accustomed to obey orders, left off killing at the first intimation; but the populace of Alexandria bare so very great hatred to the Jews, that it was difficult to recall them and it was a hard thing to make them leave their dead bodies. (*Wars* II 18:7-8)

During the year of the four emperors in A.D. 69, Alexander was an early supporter of Vespasian. Alexander even made his own legions swear allegiance to "Emperor" Vespasian.

The initiative in transferring the Empire to Vespasian was taken at Alexandria under the prompt direction of Tiberius Alexander, who on the 1st of July made the legions swear allegiance to him. (*Histories* 2:79)

When the initially reluctant Vespasian decided to claim the empire, Alexander committed to Vespasian his two legions for that purpose. Subsequently, when Vespasian achieved the supreme power in December A.D. 69, Tiberius Alexander was assigned to assist Vespasian's son Titus in the final siege and subjugation of Jerusalem. Alexander's legions comprised a significant part of the forces that Titus had at his disposal. Alexander then became second in command of the Roman army, outranking even King Agrippa II (*Wars* VI 4:3).

as also there came Tiberius Alexander, who was a friend of his, most valuable, both for his good-will to him and for his prudence. He had formerly been governor of Alexandria, but was now thought worthy to be general of the army [under Titus]. The reason of this was, that he had been the first who encouraged Vespasian very lately to accept this his new dominion and joined himself to him with great fidelity, when things were uncertain and fortune had not yet declared for him. He also followed Titus as a counselor, very useful to him in this war, both by his age and skill in such affairs. (*Wars* V 1:6)

So Alexander had a memorable career ahead of him when he was relieved of his provincial powers by Claudius in Judea in A.D. 48. As a Roman general in the siege of Jerusalem in A.D. 70, it can be assumed that the historian Flavius Josephus personally knew the man.

Ventidius Cumanus

Tacitus reports an administrative change in Judea after the tenure of Procurator Alexander. In the year A.D. 49, he writes:

> Ituraea and Judaea, on the death of their kings, Sohaemus and Agrippa, were annexed to the province of Syria. (*Annuls* 12:23)

This might help explain the confusion over who had control over what in the Jewish East for the years A.D. 48-52. Two major sources–Tacitus and Josephus–are not in agreement.

Tacitus writes that Judea became a part of Syria after Agrippa died. But Agrippa died in A.D. 44, and Josephus details the activities of both Fadus and Alexander as procurators of Judea in the interval up to A.D. 49. Of course, Judea and Ituraea, to the west of Damascus, were both technically under the ultimate control of Syria.

One way to interpret this is that in A.D. 49 the political situation in Judea was so volatile that Claudius wanted the president of Syria to assume direct control, so the power of the procurator was minimized. The president of Syria at the time was Gaius Cassius. Not long afterward, in A.D. 51, Ummidus Quadratus replaced Cassius in that high post.

However, when Tacitus' narrative moves into A.D. 52, it is stated that Felix had been governor of Judea for "some time" (*Annuls* 12:54). It is possible that in A.D. 49, when President Cassius was given more of a direct role in the affairs of Judea, Felix was appointed to a lessor position in Judea with the job of also supervising the affairs of Samaria. Perhaps this realignment was also associated with the shifting of a number of Cassius' Roman troops from Syria to Judea.

The entire passage from Tacitus is reproduced.

> Not equally moderate was his (Pallas') brother, surnamed Felix, who had for some time been governor of Judaea and thought that he could do any evil act with impunity, backed up as he was by such power. It is true that the Jews had shown symptoms of commotion in a seditious outbreak and when they had heard of the assassination of Caius, there

was no hearty submission, as a fear still lingered that any of the emperors might impose the same orders. Felix meanwhile, by ill-timed remedies, stimulated disloyal acts; while he had, as a rival in the worst wickedness, Ventidius Cumanus, who held a part of the province which was so divided that Galilea was governed by Cumanus, Samaria by Felix. The two peoples had long been at feud and now less than ever restrained their enmity, from contempt of their rulers. And accordingly they plundered each other, letting loose bands of robbers, forming ambuscades and occasionally fighting battles and carrying the spoil and booty to the two procurators, who at first rejoiced at all this, but, as the mischief grew, they interposed with an armed force which was cut to pieces. The flame of war would have spread through the province, but it was saved by Quadratus, governor of Syria. In dealing with the Jews, who had been daring enough to slay our soldiers, there was little hesitation about their being capitally punished. Some delay indeed was occasioned by Cumanus and Felix; for Claudius on hearing the causes of the rebellion had given authority for deciding also the case of these procurators. Quadratus, however, exhibited Felix as one of the judges, admitting him to the bench with the view of cowing the ardour of the prosecutors. And so Cumanus was condemned for the crimes which the two had committed and tranquillity was restored to the province. (*Annuls* 12:54)

Here, the territory of the Galilee is specifically mentioned. For the years A.D. 48-52, the land was apparently under the control of Cumanus, with Felix having control of Samaria and possibly some ancillary authority in Judea under Quadratus. But this accounting clearly contradicts Josephus.

In the Jewish East at that time, sporadic conflicts arose among all three political Jewish sub-groups–the Judeans, the Galileans, and the Samaritans. The Syrian Greeks were also at odds with these Jewish groups at various times. The Syrian Greek conflicts usually occurred either in or around Caesarea, where the Syrian Greeks had a large population. The Procurator Felix, being a Greek freedman himself, would usually side with the Greeks against the Jews. Add to the situation bands of robbers and criminals who abounded in the countryside, and it is easy to appreciate how incendiary and dangerous the entire territory was.

Felix and Cumanus took advantage of the these different factions for criminal profit in the usual custom of the day. When

Quadratus had enough of the complaints from the Jewish groups, he brought both Felix and Cumanus to trial before Claudius in A.D. 52. Felix had the better political connections; his brother Pallas was the secretary of the Roman Treasury! Antonius Felix not only survived unscathed, but Emperor Claudius decided to give Felix complete control of Judea, Samaria and Galilee as a reward–this according to Tacitus.

Battles Between the Jews

In the writings of Josephus, however, the political situation is described differently. Ventidius Cumanus is stated to be the sole procurator of Judea from A.D. 48-52, taking over from Tiberius Alexander. Antonius Felix does not come into the picture until A.D. 52. While Tacitus is presumed to be working directly off the official records kept in the Royal library in Rome, it is hard to dispute Josephus' version–Josephus was actually living in Judea for most of those years.

During Cumanus' tenure, Josephus reports a widespread Passover riot in Jerusalem which resulted in the deaths of 10,000 people (perhaps 1,000 in "real" numbers). Many of them were crush victims as panicked Jews fled the Second Temple and Jerusalem. The riot started after a Roman soldier showed a bawdy disrespect for Temple protocol by displaying his genitals to the gathered Temple crowd. Jewish outrage escalated quickly to physical confrontation, causing Cumanus to mobilize and unleash his soldiers (*Wars* II 12:1).

Also under Cumanus, armed conflict broke out between the Samaritan and Galilean Jews, with some involvement of the Judean Jews. While walking through Samaria from Jerusalem to their home country in Galilee, a group of Galilean Jews was attacked. Not getting any satisfaction when they appealed to Cumanus in Caesarea, the Galilean Jews organized their own militia and attacked the Samaritans.

Cumanus had allegedly been bribed by the Samaritans, so the Roman forces were used against the Galilean Jews, as well as the Judean Jews who joined the Galileans. Josephus does not give us an exact number of fatalities, but they were significant. After their capture by the Romans, some of these Jews were also crucified.

Quadratus to Judea–Trial in Rome

Regardless of which historian is the more accurate, Syrian President Quadratus did decide to visit the Jewish East from Antioch in A.D. 52 to sort out the situation. Quadratus first ordered a number of obviously guilty Samaritan Jews crucified for sedition. As Quadratus investigated further and traveled through the Jewish territories, he likely became more and more confused. He finally decided to send the principal men from all sides–Samaritan, Galilean and Judean–to Rome for a trial in front of Claudius. Also sent to Rome was Ananias, the Temple High Priest and Ananus, the commander of the Temple. Josephus does not tell us whether or not this particular Ananus was the elder former High Priest.

An Imperial trial is an extraordinary event which speaks to the level of Cumanus' cruelty and criminality. But the procurator had many supportive friends in Rome and the trial was a contentious one. However, through the arguments and oratory of King Agrippa II, Cumanus was convicted by Claudius. Cumanus was then formally removed from office and banished (*Antiq* XX 5-6). Claudius also ordered that Cumanus' chief military officer, a man called Celer, be executed, but only after he was sent back to Jerusalem for purposes of public humiliation.

For all the trouble in the Jewish East that occurred after King Agrippa I's death, the younger Agrippa could hardly have done worse if placed in power. But Claudius was a weak and vacillating man, and in that respect was dominated by his advisers and freedmen, all of whom wanted "true" Romans to rule and profit in the East.

Chapter 14   Travels of Paul the Apostle

And when he (Paul) was come to Jerusalem, he assayed to join himself to the disciples: and they were all afraid of him, not believing that he was a disciple.(Acts 9:26)

From the Book of Acts, Paul's Letter to the Galatians, and from other clues in Josephus, a time line of Paul's activities after his epiphany in A.D. 36 can be constructed.

1:13For ye have heard of my manner of life in time past in the Jews' religion, how that beyond measure I persecuted the church of God and made havoc of it: 1:14and I advanced in the Jews' religion beyond many of mine own age among my countrymen, being more exceedingly zealous for the traditions of my fathers. 1:15But when it was the good pleasure of God, who separated me, *even* from my mother's womb and called me through his grace, 1:16to reveal his Son in me, that I might preach him among the Gentiles; straightway I conferred not with flesh and blood: 1:17neither went I up to Jerusalem to them that were apostles before me: but I went away into Arabia; and again I returned unto Damascus. 1:18Then after three years I went up to Jerusalem to visit Cephas and tarried with him fifteen days. 1:19But other of the apostles saw I none, save James the Lord's brother. 1:20Now touching the things which I write unto you, behold, before God, I lie not. (Gal)

2:1Then after the space of fourteen years I went up again to Jerusalem with Barnabas, taking Titus also with me. 2:2And I went up by revelation; and I laid before them the gospel which I preach among the Gentiles but privately before them who were of repute, lest by any means I should be running, or had run, in vain. (Gal)

These are key passages. One of Paul's purposes in writing the Letter to the Galatians was to emphasize his independence from the Jerusalem-based Apostles. Many who remained in Jerusalem, including James, the brother of Jesus and the leader of the Christian Church, adhered closely to the ceremony of Temple Judaism. This deference was in part necessary to keep them safe from the antagonism of the High Priesthood. This was probably looked on with suspicion by the Christian Galatian Church. In emphasizing the few times he had been to Jerusalem Paul gives time structure to what is written in Acts concerning his travels.

Galatia is an area in modern-day Turkey, just to the north of Cilicia and Cappadocia. In his Epistle to the Galatians, Paul writes that his return to Jerusalem was three years after Stephen's stoning and Paul's own roadside epiphany. Much of this time was spent in Damascus as well as Arabia. He returned to Jerusalem 14 years later for a summit meeting concerning protocols for the admission of Gentiles into the Church. Working from the date of Saul's epiphany in late A.D. 36, Paul would have returned to Jerusalem briefly in A.D. 39 and, years later, attend the Jerusalem Christian Church summit meeting in A.D. 53. Archeological evidence also generally supports this and will be presented later in the chapter.

Acts provides us with a critical and linchpin date in the saga of Paul and the early Christians. According to Acts, Paul was imprisoned in Caesarea by Procurator Antonius Felix after being arrested at the Pentecost celebration in Jerusalem. Paul remained imprisoned for two years until Porcius Festus replaced Felix (Acts 24:27). Roman sources are clear that Festus assumed power in Judea in A.D. 60. It can then be derived that Paul was in Jerusalem for the Pentecost celebration of A.D. 58 which would have taken place in late June.

Acts documents enough details about Paul's travels from the time of the Jerusalem Church summit meeting to the Pentecost of A.D. 58 to conclude that about five years had passed which roughly confirms the A.D. 53 date which was calculated from the year of Jesus' crucifixion, A.D. 36 and Paul's Letter to the Galatians.

It should be noted that between Paul's visits to Jerusalem in A.D. 53 and A.D. 58, he apparently made another quick visit to Jerusalem–this after his letter to the Galatians. While Jerusalem is not specifically mentioned, the city can be inferred.

18:22 And when he had landed at Caesarea, he went up and saluted the church and went down to Antioch.(Acts)

Paul in Damascus

In his Letter to the Galatians, Paul writes that after his conversion he didn't immediately return to Jerusalem–his first visit to Jerusalem as a Christian was three years later. During that time in Damascus, he proselytized in the area and also took time out to visit Arabia–and decided to change his name to Paul.

In his new role as evangelist Paul's usual method was to enter Jewish Synagogues and verbally challenge the beliefs of the Jews in attendance. Apparently, during the typical ancient Sabbath service time was set aside for comments and observations from those attending. Acts later describes one such service held years later in a synagogue in Antioch of Pisidia.

13:15 And after the reading of the law and the prophets the rulers of the synagogue sent unto them, saying, Brethren, if ye have any word of exhortation for the people, say on. 13:16 And Paul stood up and beckoning with the hand said, Men of Israel and ye that fear God, hearken.. (Acts)

As Paul admits later in Acts, he was not above going from door to door in his evangelical activities. This is the sanctioned activity of some Christian groups today.

20:20 how I shrank not from declaring unto you anything that was profitable and teaching you publicly and from house to house, 20:21 testifying both to Jews and to Greeks repentance toward God and faith toward our Lord Jesus Christ. (Acts)

Paul soon angered the Damascus Jews, who then began to plot against him. For this purpose, the Jews enlisted help from the soldiers of the governor of Damascus. The Jews and the Damascan soldiers watched the house where Paul was staying, as well as the city gates, in order to catch him when he tried to leave. But Paul escaped the house in a basket that was lowered through an open second-story window. With the help of his new-found Christian friends, Paul made his way to the city wall and climbed over it to safety.

> 9:22But Saul increased the more in strength and confounded the Jews that dwelt at Damascus, proving that this is the Christ. 9:23And when many days were fulfilled, the Jews took counsel together to kill him: 9:24but their plot became known to Saul. And they watched the gates also day and night that they might kill him: 9:25but his disciples took him by night and let him down through the wall, lowering him in a basket. (Acts)

> 11:32In Damascus the governor under Aretas the king guarded the city of the Damascenes in order to take me: 11:33and through a window was I let down in a basket by the wall and escaped his hands. (II Cor)

Damascus at the time was under the rule of King Aretas IV of Nabotea and had a relatively small Jewish population. Damascus was well beyond the reach of the Jerusalem High Priesthood. Remember that Saul had to bring quasi-diplomatic letters from the High Priest Jonathan to Damascus in order to take Christian captives back to the Second Temple for discipline. Remember, too, that in late A.D. 36 the Naboteans were preparing for a Roman invasion by Vitellius, so anyone from Jerusalem would have been treated with suspicion.

Paul's return to Jerusalem

In A.D. 39, Paul returned to Jerusalem. His former mentor High Priest Jonathan had been removed by Vitellius two years previously. It is likely that the stoning of Stephen and the persecutions of the Christians initiated by Jonathan (and carried out by Saul and his friends) were major factors in Vitellius' decision. But the new High Priest Theophilis was the brother of Jonathan, so Paul knew that he was still taking a chance in returning.

Paul's abrasive style of preaching soon made him more enemies in Jerusalem and most of the established Apostles there avoided him. Paul stayed with Peter the Apostle for a little more than two weeks, perhaps the entire length of his visit. Apart from Peter, in Jerusalem Paul conferred with no other Apostle except for James, Jesus' brother and the leader of the Jerusalem Church.

> [1:18]Then after three years I went up to Jerusalem to visit Cephas and tarried with him fifteen days. [1:19]But other of the apostles saw I none, save James the Lord's brother. (Gal 1:18-19)

In Paul's Letter to the Galatian Church, it is suggested that, when Paul returned to Jerusalem in A.D. 39, most of the other Apostles had already left the city due to the persecutions by the Temple-based Jews. Peter (Cephas) was one of the few who remained of the original Disciples.

Paul traveled to Jerusalem to get acquainted with the Christian brothers as well as to see his family. The Christians, however, did not welcome Paul enthusiastically. Many of the Nazarenes knew him only as the brutal Jewish Priest Saul of Tarsus. The Jewish priests would naturally also be antagonistic.

> And when he was come to Jerusalem, he assayed to join himself to the disciples: and they were all afraid of him, not believing that he was a disciple. (Acts 9:26)

The Apostle Barnabas

Joseph Barnabas was to become Paul's defender and advocate, at times his traveling companion, and his greatest friend. In A.D. 39 Barnabas personally stood up for Paul in Jerusalem when no one else would. Barnabas had apparently previously been familiar with Paul in Damascus and knew what a great and positive force he could be for the incipient Christian Church.

..Barnabas took him and brought him to the apostles and declared unto them how he had seen the Lord in the way and that he had spoken to him and how at Damascus he had preached boldly in the name of Jesus (Acts 9:27)

Barnabas was one of the 70 who worked for Jesus late in his ministry, and who became disciples after his crucifixion.

James the Righteous, John and Peter were entrusted by the Lord after his resurrection with their higher knowledge. They imparted it to the other apostles and the other apostles to the Seventy, one of which was Barnabas. (Eusebius *History* 2:1 from Clement *Outlines* Book VIII)

Originally, Barnabas was from Cyprus, where he had been a wealthy landowner.

4:36 And Joseph, who by the apostles was surnamed Barnabas (which is, being interpreted, Son of exhortation), a Levite, a man of Cyprus by race, 4:37 having a field, sold it and brought the money and laid it at the apostles' feet. (Acts)

..for he was a good man and full of the Holy Spirit and of faith: and much people was added unto the Lord. (Acts 11:24)

Exile from Jerusalem

Thanks to the efforts of Barnabas, Paul was reluctantly accepted into the Jerusalem Christian brotherhood. But the Christian leaders were not used to Paul's aggressive manner of preaching. The Nazarenes had be careful of what they did and said.

Paul, for his part, paid little heed to Christian convention. He staked out public areas of Jerusalem–at the various gates of the city, for instance–and evangelized about Jesus. Acts also indicates that Paul might have gone door-to-door spreading the word about Jesus' promise of salvation.

So it was not many days before the Jews–the Grecian Jews in particular–became tired of Paul's aggressive style. The Jerusalem

Christians had spent years convincing the High Priesthood that they were a non-threatening and non-confrontational group; Paul was destroying all that goodwill in just a couple weeks.

> And he was with them going in and going out at Jerusalem, preaching boldly in the name of the Lord: and he spake and disputed against the Grecian Jews; but they were seeking to kill him (Acts 9:28-29).

According to Paul's Letter to the Galatians, he left Judea on his own initiative to return to Tarsus. But according to Acts, the Church elders invited Paul to leave Judea because of the trouble he was causing.

> And when the brethren knew it, they brought him down to Caesarea and sent him forth to Tarsus. So the church throughout all Judaea and Galilee and Samaria had peace, being edified; (Acts 9:30-31)

Most likely, the Christian brothers forced Paul out out of the Jewish lands in no uncertain terms. Paul was ordered away to his home city of Tarsus in Cilicia. He had no choice but to obey.

> Now touching the things which I write unto you, behold, before God, I lie not. Then I came unto the regions of Syria and Cilicia. And I was still unknown by face unto the churches of Judaea which were in Christ: but they only heard say, He that once persecuted us now preacheth the faith of which he once made havoc; and they glorified God in me. (Gal 1:20-24)

In Cilicia, unrecognized as a former persecutor of the Christians, Paul continued to evangelize. According to Paul, his next return to Jerusalem would be 14 years later.

> Then after the space of fourteen years I went up again to Jerusalem with Barnabas, taking Titus also with me. (Gal 1:2:1)

Barnabas Joins Paul

Shortly following Paul's departure, the Church elders sent out the Apostle Barnabas on a special assignment. The Jerusalem

Church leaders had been receiving reports that certain of the Apostles, mainly those from Cyprus and Cyrene, were converting non-Jews to Christianity without requiring them first to be circumcised. Since Barnabas was from Cyprus he was the logical choice to undertake the investigation. He first traveled to Antioch where the practice was gaining a foothold.

> And the report concerning them came to the ears of the church which was in Jerusalem: and they sent forth Barnabas as far as Antioch: (Acts 11:22)

But Barnabas found nothing to fault in the practice and, in fact, was impressed with the Christian Church in Antioch. Barnabas then took the opportunity to travel from Antioch to nearby Tarsus to see his friend Paul, who had been benevolently banished to there by the Church leaders. Barnabas wanted to return him into the Christian evangelical fold. In the opinion of Barnabas, Paul was too great a force to be kept hidden away in Tarsus. Once in Tarsus, Barnabas was able to talk Paul into returning with him to Antioch.

Paul in Antioch

Antioch was then the capital of the eastern Roman Empire with a population between 50,000-100,000 people. Barnabas and Paul stayed there for a full year proselytizing. It was at that time the followers of Jesus first were called "Christians" instead of "Nazarenes."

> And it came to pass, that even for a whole year they were gathered together with the church and taught much people and that the disciples were called Christians first in Antioch. (Acts 11:26)

Also in Antioch at the time was the prophet Agabus who predicted that a great famine would afflict the entire world sometime during the reign of Claudius. Agabus' prophecy would have been made around A.D. 41. A famine lasting several years did, in fact, plague the Jewish East during the period A.D. 44-48.

> Now in these days there came down prophets from Jerusalem unto Antioch. And there stood up one of them named Agabus and signified by the Spirit that there should be a great famine over all the world: which came to pass in the days of Claudius. And the disciples, every man according to his ability, determined to send relief unto the brethren that dwelt in Judea: which also they did, sending it to the elders by the hand of Barnabas and Saul. (Acts 11:27-30)

It was this famine that initiated the tradition of Christians sending alms and supplies to Jerusalem, comparable to the Jews' tithing to the Second Temple.

Inconsistency in Acts

Acts suggests that Barnabas and Paul brought "relief" to Jerusalem either in anticipation of the famine that began in A.D. 44 or early in the course of it. But this is contrary to what Paul himself wrote in his Letter to the Galatians, indicating that his second visit to Jerusalem after his epiphany was years later, in A.D. 53.

Another interesting sentence is found at the end of the 12th chapter in Acts.

> And Barnabas and Saul returned from Jerusalem, when they had fulfilled their ministration, taking with them John whose surname was Mark. (Acts 12:25)

Paul made only three trips to Jerusalem after his epiphany in A.D. 36–one each in early A.D. 39, A.D. 53, and A.D. 58 — according to Paul's Letter to the Church in Galatia. But these verses in Acts suggest that Barnabas and Paul might have made a brief trip to Jerusalem with donations for the Church brothers sometime in A.D. 43 or 44. According to Acts 12:25, John Mark joined the two men on the return journey to Antioch. At that time, John Mark might have been especially anxious to leave Jerusalem. As will be seen, John Mark's mother had housed the fugitive Peter the Apostle after Peter had escaped from the prison of King Agrippa I (Acts 12:12).

Paul might also have made a brief trip to Jerusalem in either late A.D. 55 or early A.D. 56 from Caesarea, though the city of Jerusalem is not mentioned specifically (Acts 18:22).

Agrippa I and the Christians

While Barnabas was in Antioch with Paul in A.D. 40-41 proselytizing, events of great consequence were occurring in the Jewish lands. Caius was attempting to undermine the Second Temple High Priesthood by desecrating the Sanctuary grounds with a statue of himself. This drove the Jews perilously close to rebellion. Only Caius' death in January of A.D. 41 prevented placement of the statue—and probable rebellion. Claudius assumed power after Caius' assassination and turned Judea and Samaria over to the control of King Agrippa I after removing Prefect Marcellus from power.

King Agrippa promptly moved into Herod's palace in Jerusalem. This was unusual. Usually, the Roman prefects stayed at Herod's palace in the cosmopolitan city of Caesarea. Agrippa also removed the High Priest Theophilis from power and appointed to that position Simon, the son of Boethus who was not of the family of Ananus. Was Agrippa issuing a not-so-subtle challenge to the powerful Simon Ananus, who had controlled the Second Temple for at least the last 15 years through his sons?

Worse, Agrippa I proved himself to be no friend of the Christians. Agrippa I found reason to kill James, one of the original Disciples. Details are lacking, but likely a trumped-up charge was brought against James by the High Priesthood. For this act, Agrippa was lauded by the High Priesthood. Encouraged, it did not take Agrippa long to arrest the Apostle Peter, who was in Jerusalem for the Passover–likely the Passover of A.D. 42.

12:4And when he had taken him, he put him in prison and delivered him to four quaternions of soldiers to guard him; intending after the

Passover to bring him forth to the people. ^{12:5}Peter therefore was kept in the prison: but prayer was made earnestly of the church unto God for him. ^{12:6}And when Herod was about to bring him forth, the same night Peter was sleeping between two soldiers, bound with two chains: and guards before the door kept the prison. ^{12:7}And behold, an angel of the Lord stood by him and a light shined in the cell: and he smote Peter on the side and awoke him, saying, Rise up quickly. And his chains fell off from his hands. ^{12:8}And the angel said unto him, Gird thyself and bind on thy sandals. And he did so. And he saith unto him, Cast thy garment about thee and follow me. ^{12:9}And he went out and followed; and he knew not that it was true which was done by the angel, but thought he saw a vision. ^{12:10}And when they were past the first and the second guard, they came unto the iron gate that leadeth into the city; which opened to them of its own accord: and they went out and passed on through one street; and straightway the angel departed from him. ^{12:11}And when Peter was come to himself, he said, Now I know of a truth, that the Lord hath sent forth his angel and delivered me out of the hand of Herod and from all the expectation of the people of the Jews. ^{12:12}And when he had considered *the thing*, he came to the house of Mary the mother of John whose surname was Mark; where many were gathered together and were praying. ^{12:13}And when he knocked at the door of the gate, a maid came to answer, named Rhoda. ^{12:14}And when she knew Peter's voice, she opened not the gate for joy, but ran in and told that Peter stood before the gate. ^{12:15}And they said unto her, Thou art mad. But she confidently affirmed that it was even so. And they said, It is his angel. ^{12:16}But Peter continued knocking: and when they had opened, they saw him and were amazed. ^{12:17}But he, beckoning unto them with the hand to hold their peace, declared unto them how the Lord had brought him forth out of the prison. And he said, Tell these things unto James and to the brethren. And he departed and went to another place. ^{12:18}Now as soon as it was day, there was no small stir among the soldiers, what was become of Peter. ^{12:19}And when Herod had sought for him and found him not, he examined the guards and commanded that they should be put to death. And he went down from Judaea to Caesarea and tarried there. (Acts)

The Apostle Peter was imprisoned by King Agrippa I outside the city at a remote location. It was the Passover and Agrippa did not want to inflame the Christians by keeping Peter in the prison at the tower of Antonia, or anyplace in Jerusalem. In his cell, Peter was chained to not just one but two guards. When

Peter and the Roman guards were sleeping, an Angel appeared and woke Peter up. Peter's chains were loosened. The Angel then led Peter out of the prison and to the walls of Jerusalem. After leading Peter through several gates into the city and past several guards, the Angel left Peter to his own devices. Peter then sought refuge in the Jerusalem home of John Mark, a Christian brother who would later become Peter's greatest disciple, and who would, according to legend, write the Gospel of Mark.

When King Agrippa discovered Peter had escaped, he put all 16 of the prison soldiers assigned to guard Peter to death. There the story ends: another black mark against Agrippa I, a ruler whom Josephus so extols!

Further Travels of Paul

After spending at least three years in Antioch and after a trip back to Jerusalem to give donations to the Christian brothers, the Holy Spirit moved Barnabas and Paul to further travel and evangelize. John Mark initially accompanied them.

> [13:2]And as they ministered to the Lord and fasted, the Holy Spirit said, Separate me Barnabas and Saul for the work whereunto I have called them. [13:3]Then, when they had fasted and prayed and laid their hands on them, they sent them away. (Acts)

Chapter 13 in Acts details these early journeys. From Antioch, Paul and Barnabas and their band of Christians went to Cyprus. In Cyprus, they first stayed at Salamis and then traveled across the island to the city of Paphos, where Paul blinded an evil false-prophet named Elymas. Then they were off to Perga in Pamphylia, where John Mark left them to return to his home in Jerusalem. From Perga, the Christian group traveled to Antioch of Pisidia, where Paul challenged those who attended a Jewish Synagogue service. The Jews became jealous of Paul's popularity and threw Paul and Barnabas out of town.

As chapter 14 opens, Paul and his group are in Iconium where they evangelized for a "long time" (Acts 14:3). That ended when both the Gentiles and the Jews of the town got together to "treat them shamefully and to stone them" (Acts 14:5). Paul and Barnabas then fled to several other cities–Lycaonia, Lystra and Derbe, where they preached for a considerable time. Eventually, when they were in Lycaonia, angry Jews from Antioch and Iconium found them and stoned Paul to the point of death. Paul's disciples, however, managed to revive him and bring him to a place of safety.

Not one to accept defeat easily, Paul then returned to Derbe and Lystra to proselytize. He went from there to Antioch and Iconium. Paul and Barnabas then returned to Perga in Pamphylia and on to Attalia, and then back again to Antioch. These evangelical adventures took roughly 11 years to complete, according to Paul's Letter to the Galatians.

Jerusalem Summit Meeting of A.D. 53

Chapter 15 in Acts deals with the Jerusalem summit meeting of A.D. 53. A number of Christian brothers from Jerusalem were shocked at the Church practices they found in Antioch. The Jerusalem-based Christians wanted all non-Jews who sought acceptance into the Christian Church to first be circumcised. Barnabas and Paul in Antioch, however, had not been preaching this or requiring it in their converts. From a practical standpoint, adult circumcision was extraordinarily painful. If it were required of converts, few would become Christians. Paul and Barnabas considered this requirement a means by which the Jerusalem Christian Church hoped to keep out non-Jews which was antithetical to Jesus' last request before his ascension.

Eventually, it was agreed to send a delegation from Antioch to Jerusalem to determine the proper method of conversion. Paul and Barnabas were part of that group.

> And when Paul and Barnabas had no small dissension and questioning with them, *the brethren* appointed that Paul and Barnabas and certain other of them, should go up to Jerusalem unto the apostles and elders about this question. (Acts 15:2)

The Apostle Peter, who had been criticized for socializing with the uncircumcised, was also in Jerusalem at this meeting.

> ¹¹:¹Now the apostles and the brethren that were in Judaea heard that the Gentiles also had received the word of God. ¹¹:²And when Peter was come up to Jerusalem, they that were of the circumcision contended with him, ¹¹:³saying, Thou wentest in to men uncircumcised and didst eat with them. (Acts)

Not surprisingly, Peter advocated that circumcision should not be necessary for converts. James the Just, the brother of Jesus, was in charge of the proceedings. After several days of discussion, James proposed a compromise; the Gentiles would not be required to be circumcised, but they would have to take special vows regarding specific laws.

> that they abstain from the pollutions of idols and from fornication and from what is strangled and from blood. (Acts 15:20)

There was general agreement to this compromise and the conference ended on a harmonious note. The Jerusalem Church elders then sent two of their most capable evangelists along with Barnabas and Paul back to Antioch. Their names were Judas, called Barsabbas, and Silas (Acts 15:22).

After the Jerusalem Conference

After returning to Antioch, Paul soon grew bored and tried to talk Barnabas into traveling with him again.

> And after some days Paul said unto Barnabas, Let us return now and visit the brethren in every city wherein we proclaimed the word of the Lord and *see* how they fare. (Acts 15:36)

But Barnabas wanted to include John Mark, who also was in Antioch.

> ¹⁵:³⁷And Barnabas was minded to take with them John also, who was called Mark. ¹⁵:³⁸But Paul thought not good to take with them him who

withdrew from them from Pamphylia and went not with them to the work. [15:39] And there arose a sharp contention, so that they parted asunder one from the other and Barnabas took Mark with him and sailed away unto Cyprus; (Acts)

A "rejected" Paul then enlisted Silas as his companion and left Antioch later in A.D. 53. This second set of evangelical adventures took place over the course of perhaps five years. In Acts, Paul's travels with Silas are much better documented than Paul's earlier travels with Barnabas, suggesting that Luke, the Macedonian physician who wrote both the Gospel of Luke and Acts, was a traveling companion and eyewitness to the latter journeys. Paul's adventures ended when he arrived in Jerusalem for the Pentecost celebration of A.D. 58 which would have been in early summer.

Chapter 16 of Acts starts with Paul revisiting the Churches in Derbe and Lystra, after "confirming" the Churches in Syria and Cilicia (Acts 15:41). Paul was spreading the word that new converts did not have to be circumcised which was understandably very good news to these men. Paul and his Christian disciples then traveled through the region of Phrygia and Galatia without preaching, since a vision from the Holy Spirit (Acts 16:6) had instructed Paul not to preach there. The group also avoided Mysia for the same reason. In Troas, Paul had another vision that he was to go to Macedon. He did so, first going to Samothrace, later to Neopolis, and then on to Philippi in Macedonia.

In Philippi, a slave woman with the spirit of divination, was harassing Paul to such a great extent that Paul finally ordered the spirit to leave her. However, her masters were making money from her spiritual talents. With the demon gone, she had lost her value (Acts 16:19). Because the Christians were thought responsible, Paul and Silas had their garments ripped up, were beaten with rods, and then were imprisoned. After being freed by an understanding magistrate, they traveled on to Lydia, where they rested from their adventures in Philippi for a time.

Chapter 17 finds Paul and Silas traveling through Amphipolis, Apollonia, and then coming to Thessalonica. After preaching in Thessalonica for a while, Paul and Silas so inflamed the Jews against them that the Christian brothers in Thessalonica, fearing for their lives, sent Paul and his group by night to Beroea.

But the Jews of Thessalonica found out where Paul and his group were and traveled to Beroea to attack them. The Christian brothers in Beroea then sent Paul to Athens immediately for his own safety, with the promise of sending Silas (and Timothy, who had joined the group in Macedon) later. In Athens, Paul debated doubters vigorously in the Agora and gained many converts.

Corinth

Chapter 18 in Acts has Paul moving on to Corinth. There he met two Christian converts who apparently been expelled from Rome by Claudius. They were tentmakers which was Paul's background, and Paul stayed with them. Silas and Timothy traveled down from Macedonia to join them.

Paul stayed in Corinth, a famously corrupt city, for more than 18 months. During that time, he so angered the Jews that he was brought before Achaean Proconsul Junio Gallio for his religious crimes—who dismissed them.

18:1 After these things he departed from Athens, and came to Corinth. 18:2 And he found a certain Jew named Aquila, a man of Pontus by race, lately come from Italy, with his wife Priscilla, because Claudius had commanded all the Jews to depart from Rome: and he came unto them; 18:3 and because he was of the same trade, he abode with them, and they wrought, for by their trade they were tentmakers. 18:4 And he reasoned in the synagogue every sabbath, and persuaded Jews and Greeks. 18:5 But when Silas and Timothy came down from Macedonia, Paul was constrained by the word, testifying to the Jews that Jesus was the Christ. 18:6 And when they opposed themselves and blasphemed, he shook out his raiment and said unto them, Your blood *be* upon your own heads; I am clean: from henceforth I will go unto the Gentiles....
18:11 And he dwelt *there* a year and six months, teaching the word of God among them. 18:12 But when Gallio was proconsul of Achaia, the Jews

with one accord rose up against Paul and brought him before the judgment-seat, 18:13saying, This man persuadeth men to worship God contrary to the law. 18:14But when Paul was about to open his mouth, Gallio said unto the Jews, If indeed it were a matter of wrong or of wicked villany, O ye Jews, reason would that I should bear with you: 18:15but if they are questions about words and names and your own law, look to it yourselves; I am not minded to be a judge of these matters. 18:16And he drove them from the judgment-seat. 18:17And they all laid hold on Sosthenes, the ruler of the synagogue, and beat him before the judgment-seat. And Gallio cared for none of these things.

Gallio and the Delphic Inscription

Fragments of a temple inscription from Emperor Claudius to honor Apollo were found in 1905 at Delphi. When deciphered, Gallio's tenure as proconsul of Achaea can be linked to a rough time period within Claudius' reign. The inscription was probably made in honor of the week-long Pythian Games that took place in the summer of A.D. 52. The games included music and play competitions as well as athletic contests. The fragments make it indisputable that Gallio was the Achaean Proconsul in the summer of A.D. 52.

They read:

Tiber[ius Claudius C]aes[ar August]us G[ermanicus, great high priest (Pontifex maximus), in the 12th (year) of his tribunican power, (acclaimed) [absolute ruler for the] 26th time, fa[ther of the cou]ntry counsel for the 5th time, Censor, to the city of Delphi, greetings.

For a long [time] have I been devoted to the city of Delphi and well-disposed from the beg inning, [and] I have always observ[ed th]e worsh[ip of the Pythian] Apo[llo.

But now as for what is said about tho[se qu]arrels among the [cit]izens, of wh[ich Lucius Ju]nius Gallio, my f[riend] and [proco]nsul [of Achaia], ... still to maintain the previous decree.

The twelfth year of Claudius' reign and his fifth year as Censor would have been A.D. 52.

According to our time line the summit meeting in Jerusalem was still one year away. Paul's stay in Corinth occurred after that which means that the short-lived trial in front of Gallio had to occur in A.D. 54.

Is that reasonable to assume? Proconsuls in foreign provinces were appointed to yearly terms by the Senate Consuls, who took office in January and themselves served only a single year. Did Gallio then leave office at the end of A.D. 52—rendering our chronology untenable?

However, taking a broader look at contemporaneous Roman history, our hypothesized time line is actually strengthened.

The Ambition of Agrippina

The Proconsul position of Achaea was a new creation and Gallio was apparently the first to serve in that capacity. Gallio was the full brother of the famous philosopher and writer Lucius Seneca, who served as the tutor of Nero and later his political confident. In A.D. 41, Seneca was exiled to Corsica by Claudius at the request of Claudius' profligate wife Messalina. Gallio was almost certainly exiled along with him.

But Messalina was executed in A.D. 48 for supposedly conspiring against Claudius. Claudius now needed a Queen of unquestioned pedigree. General Lucius Vitellius, Claudius' right hand man, was instrumental in getting the Senate to relax its laws against incest so that Claudius could marry his niece Agrippina the Younger. The marriage took place in A.D. 49.

Agrippina quickly persuaded Claudius to return Seneca from exile, presumably along with Gallio. Agrippina was especially keen that Seneca be the tutor to her son Domitius, the future Emperor Nero, who was then 12 years of age. Claudius also succumbed to the urging of Agrippina on another important issue—Domitius was adopted as his legal heir in A.D. 50. The previous heir was Britannicus who was Claudius' son by Messalina. Then at the age of nine, Britannicus demonstrated none of the physical disabilities of his father. Likely Agrippina planned on killing Claudius at her convenience after her son

Domitius became heir. But Agrippina had enemies of her own, and many powerful Romans were impressed with the young Britannicus and still favored him over Domitius.

The death of Lucius Vitellius in A.D. 51 might have emboldened Agrippina in her plan to kill Claudius. By this time, thanks to Agrippina's influrnce Seneca had risen to become one of Claudius' top advisors. To insure a smooth transition of power from Claudius to Domitius after the murder, Agrippina and Seneca placed partisans in positions of power throughout the empire. One of these partisons was Junius Gallio, Seneca's brother, who was appointed to the new position of Proconsul of Achaea in A.D. 52.

Marcus Pallas was another member of Claudius' inner circle, as well as being Agrippina's paramour. Pallas' brother Felix was appointed the Procurator of Judea in the same year, A.D. 52.

To have Gallio serve only one year would not make political sense. Even if he did not enjoy the position, which other ancient writings suggest, Gallio would not have been allowed to resign until after Nero had assumed power in late A.D. 54 and demonstrated that he was firmly in control.

Further Travels

[18:18]And Paul, having tarried after this yet many days, took his leave of the brethren, and sailed thence for Syria, and with him Priscilla and Aquila: having shorn his head in Cenchreae; for he had a vow.

Paul then traveled to Ephesus in Syria and continued to preach. From Ephesus, Paul sailed to Caesarea, where he made a quick trip to Jerusalem (possibly) to pay his respects to the Church (Acts 18:22) and then moved on to Antioch.

Chapter 19 in Acts marks the start of Paul's "third" journey. From Antioch, Paul traveled to the region of Galatia, and then Phrygia, beginning in early A.D. 56, or possibly late A.D. 55. From Phrygia Paul traveled to Achaia in Greece. Paul passed from Achaia through the "upper country" (Acts 19:1) to get back to Ephesus. Paul stayed in Ephesus, "reasoning daily in the school of Tyrannus" (Acts 19:9) for two years. Paul and his disciples became so successful that certain businessmen who made money off tourists visiting the temple of Diana felt threatened. The temple was said to be a wonder of the ancient world and was a huge attraction for religious pilgrims of all faiths.

Chapter 20 in Acts has Paul leaving Ephesus to return to Macedonia. From Macedonia, he traveled into Greece proper, where he spent three months (Acts 20:3). Returning through Macedonia, Paul made his way to Philippi, where Paul celebrated the Passover of A.D. 58.

> And we sailed away from Philippi after the days of unleavened bread and came unto them to Troas in five days, where we tarried seven days. (Acts 20:6)

In Troas, Paul successfully ministered to a young man who had suffered a severe fall, bringing him back to life. Paul then moved on to Assos, where he spent some time and then boarded a sailing vessel, traveling first to Mitylene, then Chios, Samos and Miletus.

Paul wanted to be in Jerusalem for the Pentecost of A.D. 58, where he had planned to meet up with his old friend Barnabas. Paul also had been collecting alms for the brothers in Jerusalem and after more than two years he likely had quite a sum. His family was in Jerusalem as well and Paul had not seen them in years.

Now in Miletus, Paul decided to bypass a planned visit to Ephesus. Paul did, however, meet the Church elders from Ephesus on that island (Acts 20:25).

Chapter 21 finds Paul sailing from Miletus to Cos, then to Rhodes, and then to the Patara. From there, Paul sailed past Cyprus and on to Tyre. After a time spent in Tyre, the ship sailed on to Ptolemais and then to Caesarea. At Caesarea, Paul stayed with Philip the Evangelist (Acts 21:8).

> . [21:8]And on the morrow we departed and came unto Caesarea: and entering into the house of Philip the evangelist, who was one of the

seven, we abode with him. [21:9]Now this man had four virgin daughters, who prophesied. (ActsPhilip was one of the seven disciples that had been ordained over twenty years previously in Jerusalem, along with the long-martyred and now legendary Stephen. As an aside, Philip must have had interesting family dinner conversations, having four daughters who all prophesied!

In Caesarea, Paul met up again with the prophet Agabus, who predicted that Paul would soon be arrested in Jerusalem and given up to the Romans (Acts 21:11).

[21:15]And after these days we took up our baggage and went up to Jerusalem...[21:17]And when we were come to Jerusalem, the brethren received us gladly. [21:18]And the day following Paul went in with us unto James; and all the elders were present. (Acts)

Acts does not mention a reunion in Jerusalem between Paul and Barnabas. It would have been very disappointing to Paul to make such a great effort to be in Jerusalem for the Pentecost to see his friend Barnabas, only to find that he wasn't there.

Paul's various travels took years and covered the duration of Emperor Claudius' reign to well into Nero's. By the time of their end in mid-A.D. 58, King Agrippa I had been dead for 14 years and Antonius Felix had been procurator of Judea for four years. As will be dealt with in a future chapter, only two years previous to Paul's arrival in Jerusalem, Felix arranged for the assassination of the High Priest Jonathan in the Second Temple courtyard — the same Jonathan who encouraged Saul of Tarsus to be a thug.

Nero's horrific persecution of the Christians in Rome was six years in the future. It would be at that time in Rome that he would be martyred, but in A.D. 58 many adventures still lay ahead for Paul the Apostle.

Chapter 15   Emperor Nero

...Nero acted like a madman..and..used his good fortune to the injury of others; and after what manner he slew his brother and wife and mother... at last, he was so distracted that he became an actor in the scenes and upon the theater, ... (*Wars* II 13:1)

Emperor Claudius was a weak man in many respects. In the later years of his reign, his wife Agrippina dominated him along with key advisers like Vitellius, Pallas, Narcissus, and others. Agrippina (the younger) worked closely with Claudius' aides to get men loyal only to her appointed to powerful Roman civil administrative positions. Undeniably, Agrippina's greatest coup was getting Claudius to adopt her son Domitius (Nero) as his heir. This put not only Claudius but his natural son Britannicus in a dangerous position.

Nero's Ascension

Emperor Claudius was murdered on October 13th, A.D. 54–dying after ingesting a poisoned mushroom that Agrippina had lovingly prepared for him. The black-hearted Agrippina had made sure that her son Domitius, now Nero, who was then 16 years old, would face little opposition in gaining the throne. Suspicions of her complicity in Claudius' death were dismissed by the men she had placed in power and the senators she had so assiduously cultivated over the years.

In fact, Nero was accepted by the Roman Senate and the citizens with little dissent. Only a year later, in A.D. 55, Nero arranged to poison Britannicus, Claudius' natural son by Messalina. Britannicus was 14 years old at the time and coming into his own. He had none of the physical deficiencies of his father. Britannicus also had his supporters within the Roman aristocracy — who were driven by their suspicion of Agrippina. But the Roman people did not question this Royal fratricide. If Nero had not killed Britannicus, it was a given that eventually Britannicus would have killed Nero. In the minds of the common Roman citizens it did not matter. The death of either in individual contest was vastly preferable to a long, drawn-out civil war.

To Nero's advantage, Claudius and the other prior ruling Caesars had established a superbly functioning military and civilian bureaucracy. Despite the endemic corruption, the Roman Empire practically ran itself, thus there was little need for bold action or inspired leadership. This was fortunate for the young Emperor Nero, for his interests lay not in conquest and administration but in sport and the arts.

Emperor Nero

Born Lucius Domitius Ahenobarbus (Domitius), Nero had an undeniable Royal pedigree. He was the nephew of assassinated Emperor Caius (A.D. 37-41) and the grandson of Roman political icon Germanicus. Nero's great-grandfather was Drusus, the brother of Emperor Tiberius. His mother was Julia Agrippina, also called Agrippina the Younger. Agrippina was the daughter of Germanicus, sister to Caius, and the great-granddaughter of Augustus through her mother Agrippina the Elder.

In A.D. 28, from the island of Capri the reclusive Emperor Tiberius personally chose the husband for Julia Agrippina. He was vigorous man of Royal blood named Cneius Domitius and would become Nero's father.

> Tiberius meanwhile having himself in person bestowed the hand of his granddaughter Agrippina, Germanicus's daughter, on Cneius Domitius, directed the marriage to be celebrated at Rome. In selecting Domitius he looked not only to his ancient lineage, but also to his alliance with the

blood of the Caesars, for he could point to Octavia as his grandmother and through her to Augustus as his great-uncle. (*Annuls* 4:75).

Nero was born to Agrippina and Domitius in December of A.D. 37, the same year that Tiberius died and Caius gained the empire. Coincidentally, A.D. 37 was also the birth year of Jewish historian Flavius Josephus. Nero and Josephus likely met face-to-face a quarter century later, though Josephus never admitted to it.

Suetonius gives an unflattering portrait of Nero–possibly out of bias.

> In stature he (Nero) was a little below the common height; his skin was foul and spotted; his hair inclined to yellow; his features were agreeable, rather than handsome; his eyes grey and dull, his neck was thick, his belly prominent, his legs very slender, his constitution sound. For, though excessively luxurious in his mode of living, he had, in the course of fourteen years, only three fits of sickness; which were so slight, that he neither forbore the use of wine, nor made any alteration in his usual diet. In his dress and the care of his person, he was so careless, that he had his hair cut in rings, one above another; and when in Achaia, he let it grow long behind; and he generally appeared in public in the loose dress which he used at table, with a handkerchief about his neck and without either a girdle or shoes. (Sue *Nero* LI)

Young Nero had the usual military training of the day for someone of his station, but otherwise his education was neglectful and spotty. During the dark years that his mother Agrippina had been banished to Pandataria by her brother Emperor Caius, Nero was reared by his great-grandmother Antonia. His only tutors were a dancing instructor and a barber. As an adolescent, Nero grew to love the arts and music; he even composed his own verses. Nero also enjoyed wrestling, horses, and chariot racing.

A revealing incident occurred early in the course of his education. When Nero's mother Agrippina returned from banishment in A.D. 41, she instituted a policy against the four-year-old Nero from ever studying philosophy. Agrippina believed that it was a useless discipline for one destined to rule.

Philosophy, according to Agrippina, was a sop and opiate for mortals — and not for a god.

Nero's Advisers

The fact that Emperor Claudius had been a weak and vacillating ruler now benefited Nero. Claudius had surrounded himself with strong and capable administrators; many of them had been recommended by the late Lucius Vitellius — who died in A.D. 51 —, or his mother Agrippina. The new Emperor Nero found little reason to change them. At 16 years of age, Nero, now with absolute power and with no distracting outside threats to the empire, was free to devote himself to his true passions- chariot racing, singing, lyre-playing, and acting.

In the early years of his reign, Nero's mother Agrippina asserted herself in running the empire. But as Nero matured he eased the overbearing Agrippina out of power, eventually killing her. Rising to dominance as Agrippina's star fell were Nero's boyhood teacher, Lucius Seneca, and the captain of the Praetorian guard, Sextus Burrus. Marcus Pallas, a freedman and the older brother of Judean Procurator Antonius Felix, was also kept in power as the secretary of the Roman treasury. Pallas' adept handling of Rome's finances was a key factor in Rome's stability and prosperity during those years. Pallas' own prosperity proved to be his downfall, however. Nero executed Pallas in A.D. 65 in order to gain Pallas' estimated 400-million sesterce fortune.

Seneca was a learned and literary man who had written most of Nero's early speeches. Little is recorded about him which is unfortunate because he appears to have been one of the most interesting men of that era. Fifteen years before Nero gained power, in A.D. 39, Seneca had come close to be being put to death by then-Emperor Caius. His crime was arguing a case before the Senate too well! Caius was jealous of any orator who seemed to be better than he was.

On the other hand, Lucius Annaeus Seneca, who was superior in wisdom to all the Romans of his day and to many others as well, came near being destroyed, though he had neither done any wrong nor had the appearance of doing so, but merely because he pleaded a case well in the senate while the emperor was present. Gaius ordered him to be put to death, but afterwards let him off because he believed the statement of one of his female associates, to the effect that Seneca had a consumption in an advanced stage and would die before a great while. (Dio 58:19)

Seneca's troubles did not stop with Caius' assassination. In A.D. 41, Seneca was banished by Emperor Claudius for adultery because he had earned the distaste of Claudius' wife Messalina. After eight years of exile, Seneca was called back by Agrippina, who herself had been exiled by Caius in A.D. 39. Agrippina wanted Seneca to be the tutor for her son Nero.

Seneca was also a playwright of some note and a philosopher (though he was instructed to avoid teaching it to the young Nero). Seneca was also a libertine who taught Nero much in that regard. Through uncertain means, possibly criminal, Seneca became a wealthy man as well.

Nor was this the only instance in which his conduct was seen to be diametrically opposed to the teachings of his philosophy. For while denouncing tyranny, he was making himself the teacher of a tyrant; while inveighing against the associates of the powerful, he did not hold aloof from the palace itself; and though he had nothing good to say of flatterers, he himself had constantly fawned upon Messalina and the freedmen of Claudius, to such an extent, in fact, as actually to send them from the island of his exile a Book containing their praises—a Book that he afterwards suppressed out of shame. Though finding fault with the rich, he himself acquired a fortune of 300,000,000 sesterces; and though he censured the extravagances of others, he had five hundred tables of citrus wood with legs of ivory, all identically alike and he served banquets on them. In stating thus much I have also made clear what naturally went with it—the licentiousness in which he indulged at the very time that he contracted a most brilliant marriage and the delight that he took in boys past their prime, a practice which he also taught Nero to follow.(Dio 61:10)

Seneca managed to survive much of the reign of Nero only to die by his own hand in A.D. 65, accused by Nero of being a conspirator along with Piso (*Annuls* 15:64).

General Sextus Burrus had been placed in control of the Praetorian guard in A.D. 51, largely through the efforts of Agrippina. Agrippina wanted someone in that position who would unequivocally support her after her planned murder of Claudius. By that time, Vitellius was dead, who might well have been the voice of restraint to Agrippina in her plans to kill Claudius if he had lived. Burrus remained as Praetorian general for almost 10 years after Nero attained power, playing a key role in shaping Nero's foreign policy. But Nero found reason to poison Burrus in early A.D. 62. The general unwisely persisted in criticizing Nero's divorce and subsequent execution of the unfortunate Octavia, Claudius' daughter.

Nero and the Provinces

With Nero's inattention, the Roman East and parts of Britain sank into a mild chaos over the years, culminating with the Jewish rebellion of A.D. 66. Earlier in his reign, in A.D. 55, the Parthians had tested Nero's resolve by appointing their own puppet ruler in Armenia in defiance of a long-standing treaty with Rome. Parthia had tried the same ploy against Tiberius 20 years earlier when Artabanus ruled. Then, Lucius Vitellius' brilliant diplomacy carried the day. But this time Nero's emissaries failed, and Parthia invaded Armenia in A.D. 58.

Roman General Gnaeus Corbula and his legions repelled the Parthian invaders, and another treaty was made that was acceptable to both sides. But in time, the Rome-appointed king of Armenia decided on his own to invade Parthia. General Corbula, now the president of Syria, then recommended that Nero seize the moment and order his legions to invade Parthia as well. To conquer the Parthian Empire would be a great laudatory feat for both Corbula and Nero!

But Nero (likely with Seneca's input) decided to remove the offending king of Armenia instead and put in his place someone more to Parthia's liking. The Armenian troops that had crossed over the Euphrates River were expeditiously withdrawn. Wisely, Nero knew that Rome depended upon the East for trade and food supplies, and a full-scale war with Parthia would greatly disrupt this commerce. Political peace was consummated in A.D. 63, much to Nero's credit.

Boudica

Other parts of the Roman Empire were also experiencing disturbances. Rome even suffered military losses through a minor rebellion in Britain around A.D. 59. Because of the trouble Britain was causing and the long supply lines, Nero considered abandoning the island province. Ultimately, he decided that such a retreat would be unbecoming for a Roman emperor. Besides, the late Emperor Claudius, whom the Romans still revered, had placed a great importance on the northern province; Nero would honor his memory by defending and maintaining Roman positions there.

The leader of the Celts at that time was a remarkable woman named Boudica. Tall and red-haired, she is arguably the most famous female warrior in history.

> But the person who was chiefly instrumental in rousing the natives and persuading them to fight the Romans, the person who was thought worthy to be their leader and who directed the conduct of the entire war, was Buduica, a Briton woman of the royal family and possessed of greater intelligence than often belongs to women. This woman assembled her army, to the number of some 120,000 and then ascended a tribunal which had been constructed of earth in the Roman fashion. In stature she was very tall, in appearance most terrifying, in the glance of her eye most fierce and her voice was harsh; a great mass of the tawniest hair fell to her hips; around her neck was a large golden necklace; and she wore a tunic of divers colours over which a thick mantle was fastened with a brooch. This was her invariable attire. She now grasped a spear to aid her in terrifying all beholders.. (Dio 62:2)

Roman General Paulinus had been away on a remote island in Britain while Boudica had first organized her troops and made initial attacks upon Roman positions. Boudica's Celtic army overran two Roman towns, inflicting much damage and death. However, even with inferior numbers, the Roman armies of General Paulinus managed to eventually defeat the Celts. Boudica herself died not long afterward of natural causes.

Nero as an Artist

Nero never thought of himself as a general or a great leader, but rather as an artist. When Nero gained power at 16 years of age, he devoted himself to music. He enjoyed singing, lyre playing, and the performing public recitals. Nero also composed his own verses that he would set to music. In this regard, Nero was no dilettante; he took lessons from professionals and went through all the disciplined exercises and ritual that were a part of the artist's life in those times. Reports that Nero was an abominable singer are at least exaggerated and probably false. Interestingly, at the rare times when people were publicly critical of his work, Nero accepted their words without retaliation, feeling that the true artist must accept criticism as well as accolades.

> But, above all things, (Nero) most eagerly coveted popularity, being the rival of every man who obtained the applause of the people for any thing he did. (Sue *Nero* LIII)

Gladiatorial Shows

Nero realized early in his reign that one way to ensure popularity was to keep the people entertained. Perhaps Nero had learned that from Emperor Claudius, who enjoyed putting on gladiatorial contests. Nero himself loved chariot races and wrestling competitions as well as singing, music competitions, and theatrical productions. Nero sponsored such events ceaselessly and with gusto. Rome did not yet have the Coliseum which would be completed by Emperor Titus 20 years later in

A.D. 80. Instead, Nero used the massive Circus Maximus–just down the hill south of the Palatine–for many of his spectacles.

> (Nero) presented the people with a great number and variety of spectacles, as the Juvenal and Circensian games, stage-plays and an exhibition of gladiators. In the Juvenal, he even admitted senators and aged matrons to perform parts. In the Circensian games, he assigned the equestrian order seats apart from the rest of the people and had races performed by chariots drawn each by four camels. In the games which he instituted for the eternal duration of the empire and therefore ordered to be called Maximi, many of the senatorian and equestrian order, of both sexes, performed. A distinguished Roman knight descended on the stage by a rope, mounted on an elephant. A Roman play, likewise, composed by Afranius, was brought upon the stage. It was entitled, "The Fire;" and in it the performers were allowed to carry off and to keep to themselves, the furniture of the house which, as the plot of the play required, was burnt down in the theatre. Every day during the solemnity, many thousand articles of all descriptions were thrown amongst the people to scramble for; such as fowls of different kinds, tickets for corn, clothes, gold, silver, gems, pearls, pictures, slaves, beasts of burden, wild beasts that had been tamed; at last, ships, lots of houses and lands, were offered as prizes in a lottery. (Sue *Nero* XI)

Nero also made a habit of giving gifts to favored citizens in order to buy their support. Just as Emperor Caius had squandered his predecessor Tiberius' amassed fortune, so did Nero freely spend the wealth of Claudius. After Nero's forced suicide in late A.D. 68, the short-lived Emperor Galba sponsored an action to retrieve much of Nero's largess.

> On a general inquiry it seemed the fairest course to demand restitution from those who had caused the public poverty. Nero had squandered in presents two thousand two hundred million sesterces. It was ordered that each recipient should be sued, but should be permitted to retain a tenth part of the bounty. (Tacitus *Histories* I-20)

Nero's Palace

Nero had many large and ornate buildings constructed during his reign; he probably had a hand in their design as well. With boundless   ambition, Nero had dreams of constructing an entirely new capital city for the empire which he planned to call "Neropolis." But in overbuilt Rome, what could be done to make way for Nero's vision?

Nero's architectural dream might partially explain the fires of A.D. 64. Perhaps after an accidental fire erupted in Rome in a propitious location, Nero instructed his men to help the fire along and direct its course with the intention of clearing out all seven hills of Rome. Despite Nero's best (or worst!) efforts, much of the city still remained after the fires. Nero continued with his building plans, but was forced to scale down his ambitions and settle for a still-amazing construction–the Golden Palace (Domus Aurea). The ruins of the palace can still be seen today in Rome, underground near the baths of Trajan.

> the porch was so high that there stood in it a colossal statue of himself a hundred and twenty feet in height; and the space included in it was so ample, that it had triple porticos a mile in length and a lake like a sea, surrounded with buildings which had the appearance of a city. Within its area were corn fields, vineyards, pastures and woods, containing a vast number of animals of various kinds, both wild and tame. In other parts it was entirely over-laid with gold and adorned with jewels and mother of pearl. (Sue *Nero* XXXI)

The palace complex covered parts of three hills of Rome that had been devastated in the fires of A.D. 64–the Caelian, Esquiline and Palatine. That Nero needed huge sums of money to complete his palace likely explains the executions of Seneca and Pallas on specious charges of treason. Together they had close to a billion sesterces–all of which went to Nero.

Octavia and Acte

Nero had married his stepsister, Octavia, in A.D. 53 when he was sixteen. Nero's mother, Agrippina the Younger, had arranged the marriage, undoubtedly thinking ahead to Claudius' murder. Nero's marriage to Claudius' daughter would help to legitimize his claim to the throne. Agrippina would successfully poison Emperor Claudius less than a year later.

Once in power, Nero soon tired of Octavia and took up with a slave girl named Acte. Acte would remain Nero's companion and confidante for the next 14 years, until Nero's suicide in A.D. 68. After his suicide it would be Acte who would see to it that Nero had a proper funeral. Despite this apparent devotion to a slave girl, Nero, at his core, was a libertine, indulging and debauching himself at every opportunity — although the accounts of his excesses might be exaggerated.

> Petulancy, lewdness, luxury, avarice and cruelty, he practised at first with reserve and in private, as if prompted to them only by the folly of youth; but, even then, the world was of opinion that they were the faults of his nature and not of his age. (Sue *Nero* XXVI)

> Nero..polluted himself by every lawful or lawless indulgence, (*Annuls* 15:37)

Early in his reign, as a teenager Nero followed the lead of his progenitor Marc Antony and roamed around Rome at night incognito getting into mischief.

> In the consulship of Quintus Volusius and Publius Scipio (A.D. 56), there was peace abroad, but a disgusting licentiousness at home on the part of Nero, who in a slave's disguise, so as to be unrecognized, would wander through the streets of Rome, to brothels and taverns, with comrades, who seized on goods exposed for sale and inflicted wounds on any whom they encountered, some of these last knowing him so little that he even received blows himself and showed the marks of them in his face. When it was notorious that the emperor was the assailant and the insults on men and women of distinction were multiplied, other persons too on the strength of a licence once granted under Nero's name, ventured with impunity on the same practices and had gangs of their own, till night presented the scenes of a captured city. (*Annuls* 13:25)

Soon, however, Poppea Sabina would enter Nero's life. Seven years his senior, Poppea would become his second wife and the mother to his only child.

Poppea Sabina

Poppea Sabina was a beautiful but reputedly heartless Roman aristocrat. As the paramour and later wife of Emperor Nero, she was known for ruthlessly murdering or sending into exile anyone who dared to challenge her. Born in A.D. 30, Poppea used her amours with several key men to finally become, through a liaison with Nero, the most powerful woman in the empire.

> Wherever there was a prospect of advantage, there she transferred her favours.(*Annuls* 13:45)

> For she (Poppea) bestowed the greatest pains on the beauty and brilliancy of her person, (Dio 62:28)

Poppea had an interesting if not laudable pedigree. Her mother, of the same name, was just as beautiful and alluring. She, however, unfortunately had incurred the wrath of Claudius' second wife Messalina. Messalina was jealous of not only the elder Poppea's beauty, but of the number and quality of her alleged paramours. In A.D. 47, Empress Messalina forced Poppea's mother into suicide.

> She hastened herself to effect Poppaea's destruction and hired agents to drive her to suicide by the terrors of a prison. (*Annuls* 11:2)

The father of the younger Poppea was Titus Ollius, who served as a quaestor in Rome. A quaestor was an individual who supervised the financial affairs of the empire at a high level. Ollius, however, was a confidante of the conspirator Lucius Sejanus and died in late A.D. 31 after being named in Tiberius' proscriptions. This association was to the disadvantage of the elder Poppea as well.

Tacitus describes Poppea Sabina.

> This Poppea had everything but a right mind. Her mother, who surpassed in personal attractions all the ladies of her day, had bequeathed to her alike fame and beauty. Her fortune adequately

corresponded to the nobility of her descent. Her conversation was charming and her wit anything but dull. She professed virtue, while she practised laxity. Seldom did she appear in public and it was always with her face partly veiled, either to disappoint men's gaze or to set off her beauty. Her character she never spared, making no distinction between a husband and a paramour, while she was never a slave to her own passion or to that of her lover. (*Annuls* 13:45)

Poppea the younger, born wealthy and famous, moved easily within the highest circles of Roman society. She first married Rufius Crispinus, a Roman knight, but she soon became bored with him and his relatively inferior position. In A.D. 58, Poppea divorced Crispinus after having attracted the eye of the younger Nero. Nero knew that he had to be delicate in his handling of Poppea in light of his marriage to Octavia. Agrippina, Nero's mother, did not approve of the older woman, and the Roman Senate held Octavia in high esteem. To circumvent any problems, Nero arranged that his friend Marcus Otho be Poppea's ostensible escort to Royal court affairs until Nero could sort things out.

Otho was an easy-going aristocratic profligate who had become the fast friend of the similarly inclined Nero. Nero, however, soon realized that Poppea provided too great a temptation for Otho. A jealous Nero soon found reason to assign his erstwhile friend to a remote post in Germany which Otho accepted without guile.

The soul of Otho was not effeminate like his person. (Tacitus *Histories* 1:22)

For Otho's had been a neglected boyhood and a riotous youth and he had made himself agreeable to Nero by emulating his profligacy. For this reason the Emperor had entrusted to him, as being the confidant of his amours, Poppaea Sabina, the imperial favourite, until he could rid himself of his wife Octavia. Soon suspecting him with regard to this same Poppaea, he sent him out of the way to the province of Lusitania, ostensibly to be its governor. (Ibid 1:13)

Concerning Otho and Poppea, there is a rare internal contradiction in Tacitus. In *Annuls*, Tacitus wrote that Otho had actually wed Poppea, contrary to what he wrote in *Histories*.

> Once having gained admission, Poppea won her way by artful blandishments, pretending that she could not resist her passion and that she was captivated by Nero's person. Soon, as the emperor's love grew ardent, she would change and be supercilious and, if she were detained more than one or two nights, would say again and again that she was a married woman and could not give up her husband attached as she was to Otho by a manner of life which no one equalled. (*Annuls* 13:46)

Dio suggests that Otho and Nero enjoyed Poppea together (Dio 61:10), with no marriage between Otho and Poppea.

At any rate, Otho achieved later fame as one of four emperors who temporarily attained power in the politically unstable year of A.D. 69, after Nero's forced suicide in the summer of A.D. 68.

Obstacle to Marriage

Poppea wanted marriage, as did Nero, but a divorce from Octavia first had to have the approval of the senate. That would be difficult, since Octavia was very popular in Rome. Also, Nero's overbearing mother Agrippina would be unlikely to approve.

> In the year of the consulship of Caius Vipstanus and Caius Fonteius (A.D. 59), Nero deferred no more a long meditated crime. Length of power had matured his daring and his passion for Poppaea daily grew more ardent. As the woman had no hope of marriage for herself or of Octavia's divorce while Agrippina lived, she would reproach the emperor with incessant vituperation and sometimes call him in jest a mere ward who was under the rule of others and was so far from having empire that he had not even his liberty. "Why," she asked, "was her marriage put off? Was it, forsooth, her beauty and her ancestors, with their triumphal honours, that failed to please, or her being a mother and her sincere heart? No; the fear was that as a wife at least she would divulge the wrongs of the Senate and the wrath of the people at the arrogance and rapacity of his mother. If the only daughter-in-law Agrippina could bear was one who wished evil to her son, let her be restored to her union with Otho. She would go anywhere in the world,

where she might hear of the insults heaped on the emperor, rather than witness them and be also involved in his perils." These and the like complaints, rendered impressive by tears and by the cunning of an adulteress, no one checked, as all longed to see the mother's power broken, while not a person believed that the son's hatred would steel his heart to her murder. (*Annuls* 14:1)

Nero realized that to marry Poppea and have children who could inherit the empire, he had no choice but to execute his own mother. Without Agrippina, Octavia would then be an easily remedied problem.

Death of Agrippina

As much of an artist as Nero might have been, his sensitive nature didn't preclude him from murder when it served a purpose. The list of Nero's victims in Suetonius is long and impressive, including Nero's own mother. Agrippina at first occupied a powerful position in Nero's court, but Nero quickly became tired of her overbearing sense of entitlement.

But while losing sway over Nero as he grew into manhood, Agrippina the Younger was becoming increasingly iconic and revered by the citizens of Rome in her own right. Aware of her power over the masses and that her son would not dare to act against the wishes of the Roman people, Agrippina continued to assert herself–most significantly by disapproving of a divorce between Nero and Octavia. But Poppea had cast a powerful spell over Nero, and she wanted nothing less than to be queen of the empire. Finally, in A.D. 59, Nero decided to act.

By that time, Nero had a more than casual knowledge of various poisons. Still, he was no match for the skills of Agrippina. Agrippina–canny and suspicious–strongly suspected Nero's intentions toward her and had gotten into the habit of ingesting protective antidotes before eating anything.

After the failure of various other murder attempts, Anicetus, the commander of the Royal fleet and one of Nero's boyhood tutors, suggested that a death at sea would be an appropriate end for Agrippina. He volunteered to rig up a booby-trapped sailing vessel for just that purpose.

> An ingenious suggestion was offered by Anicetus, a freedman, commander of the fleet at Misenum, who had been tutor to Nero in boyhood and had a hatred of Agrippina which she reciprocated. He explained that a vessel could be constructed, from which a part might by a contrivance be detached, when out at sea, so as to plunge her unawares into the water. (*Annuls* 14:3)

The vessel was commissioned and built. A beautiful craft, Agrippina was easily enticed to sail upon it once finished. One night, she and her attendants were sailing blithely unawares in the vessel upon the sea of Sorrentum (*Annuls* 14:8). The self-destruct mechanism was triggered and the beams and timbers of the vessel split asunder at the seams. Agrippina fell into the dark sea along with her attendants.

Agrippina, however, was not your typical Roman aristocrat softened by a life of wealth and ease. Exiled by Emperor Caius, her own brother, to the Pontine islands in her twenties, of necessity Agrippina had turned herself into an expert clam and sponge gatherer. She had maintained this fit state and was an excellent swimmer with great endurance. After the ship fell apart off the coast of Misenum, Agrippina swam to shore in the darkness without difficulty, finding refuge in a beach house. However, Nero quickly learned of the plan's failure and sent Anicetus and the Imperial guard to finish the job without pretension. Later that night, Agrippina was forced to commit suicide under their watchful eye.

Nero probably expected severe repercussions from the senate and the common people after his murder of Agrippina, but, surprisingly, there were none. This proved to be a watershed atrocity for Nero. Even though his conscience bothered him for a long time afterward and he had trouble sleeping, the murder of his mother emboldened Nero to attempt future murders. Nero now realized the full extent of his powers: the Roman people would allow him do anything!

Marriage to Poppea

Nero waited a full three years to marry Poppea after he had forced Agrippina into suicide. This suggests that the Roman Senate and the people proved more of a stumbling block than he originally figured, though details are lacking. Nero's legal wife Octavia was a much-beloved figure to the people of Rome, and she was difficult to set aside politically. But finally in A.D. 62 Nero felt secure enough in his power to act against his step-sister and wife. Nero accused Octavia of infidelity, summarily divorced her and banished her to Campania. Only days later, he married Poppea. Public remonstrations against Nero over this act, however, were much stronger than over his murder of Agrippina! Nero was forced to restore Octavia as his wife. The people rejoiced when he did so.

> Then people in their joy went up to the Capitol and, at last, gave thanks to the gods. They threw down the statues of Poppaea; they bore on their shoulders the images of Octavia, covering them with flowers and setting them up in the forum and in the temples.(*Annuls* 14:61)

Poppea, now realizing the extent of her unpopularity, was disturbed at this reaction. Nero quickly had his soldiers disperse the mob and restore her statues. Poppea, now fearing the mob, pushed even harder for marriage and additional security.

> Ever relentless in her hatred, she was now enraged by the fear that either the violence of the mob would burst on her with yet fiercer fury, or that Nero would be swayed by the popular bias, (*Annuls* 14:61)

Poppea convinced Nero that something bold had to be done about Octavia. Nero agreed and arranged for Anicetus to falsely admit to indiscretions and treason with Octavia – the very man who had overseen the forced suicide of Nero's mother Agrippina.

> Consequently it was decided to procure a confession from some one on whom could also be fastened a charge of revolutionary designs. Fittest for this seemed the perpetrator of the mother's murder, Anicetus,

commander, as I have already mentioned, of the fleet at Misenum, who got but scant gratitude after that atrocious deed and subsequently all the more vehement hatred, inasmuch as men look on their instruments in crime as a sort of standing reproach to them. The emperor accordingly sent for Anicetus and reminded him of his former service. (*Annuls* 14:62)

To get the loyal Anicetus to destroy his own reputation by admitting to treason, Nero had promised to pay him well. Nero assured his fleet commander that his banishment would be to some pleasant island. Anicetus had no choice but to agree, for the alternative that Nero offered was death. This solution would also serve as double duty for Nero, because the conspirator in the murder of his mother would now be out of the way.

As the charges were leveled publicly against Octavia, Nero additionally declared that Octavia had recently aborted their royal child against his wishes. The unfortunate Octavia was summarily executed; she was only 20 years old. Poppea was now satisfied (Sue *Nero* XXXV) and savored her moment of victory in a gruesome way.

To this was added the yet more appalling horror of Poppaea beholding the severed head which was conveyed to Rome.(*Annuls* 14:64)

Poppea–Queen of the Empire

Finally married to Nero in A.D. 62, Poppea was now truly the most powerful woman in Rome and her ambition was satisfied. Early in A.D. 63, Poppea delivered Nero a daughter, Claudia. Then, perhaps the Royal couple were at the height of their marital bliss. However, Poppea's exalted position would last only two more years; she would die in A.D. 65. But in their three-year marriage, and in the years previously when Poppea had been his paramour, the beautiful but heartless woman held great sway over Nero and Rome, which did not bode well for the fledgling Christian sect.

Chapter 16   Felix and the Sicarii

Felix also bore an ill-will to Jonathan, the high priest, because he frequently gave him admonitions about governing the Jewish affairs..And this seems to me to have been the reason why God, out of his hatred of these men's wickedness..but brought the Romans upon us and threw a fire upon the city to purge it; and brought upon us, our wives and children, slavery, as desirous to make us wiser by our calamities. (*Antiq* XX 8:5)

Judean Procurator Antonius Felix was one of the worst of all of the Judean governors, serving from A.D. 52-60. Felix's audacious behavior was virtually unassailable, however, because he came from a powerful Roman family. Felix's brother was Marcus Pallas, the secretary of the Roman treasury and one of the wealthiest men in the empire. Both men rose to power under Emperor Claudius, and Emperor Nero continued their appointments. In A.D. 58, it was Felix who placed the arrested Paul the Apostle in his Caesarean palace "prison" where Paul was to stay for two years.

During Felix's tenure, the Jewish East was as tumultuous and fractious as ever. This presented the ambitious and avaricious Felix with many criminal opportunities. Pallas likely arranged for his brother's appointment to Judea for just that reason–there was much money to be made in the Jewish East. Agrippina the Younger, the wife of Claudius, was also a strong supporter of Felix and so Felix was kept in power when Nero became emperor. As with previous Roman governors, Felix chose to live in the Mediterranean port city of Caesarea, three days' journey northwest of Jerusalem.

Caesarea was a far more liberal and cosmopolitan city than was Jerusalem. Most of the major cities of the eastern empire had sizable populations of Syrian Greeks, but that was especially the case in Caesarea. Caesarea had started out as the Greek city of Strato's Tower before being rebuilt and expanded by Herod the Great, who then renamed it after Caesar Augustus. In Caesarea, Felix would have been isolated from the everyday conflict that occurred in Jerusalem between the High Priesthood and the Christians. More of a concern to Felix would have been the disturbances between the Samaritans, the Judean Jews, and the Syrian Greeks. Through bribes and the illegal use of his Roman forces in settling the constant conflicts that arose between these groups, Felix profited greatly.

> ..Antonius Felix, played the tyrant with the spirit of a slave, plunging into all manner of cruelty and lust and marrying Drusilla, grand-daughter of Cleopatra and Antony. (Tacitus *Histories* V:9)

Felix had "the spirit of a slave" for a good reason–he had been born one. And when fortune brought Felix into a position of wealth and power, he did not hesitate to indulge himself. Tacitus is in error, however, concerning Felix's wife Drusilla. Born in A.D. 38, Drusilla was the sister of Bernice and King Agrippa II, but was not the granddaughter of Cleopatra and Antony.

Felix's Wives

An interesting aspect of Felix were his wives.

> He (Claudius) was equally fond of Felix, giving him the command of cohorts and of troops of horse, as well as of the province of Judaea; and he became the husband of three queens..(Sue *Claudius* 28)

An earlier wife of Felix was also named Drusilla; she was a distant relation of Claudius and had formerly been married to a minor king of the Roman Empire. The second Drusilla, the previously-mentioned sister of Agrippa II, divorced Felix presumably after his disgrace in Judea in A.D. 60. Felix then married another woman with Royal pretension, of whom little is recorded. So Felix would be a notable figure in ancient history if just for his marriages alone. Born a Greek slave in Rome, over the course of his life Felix not only gained his freedom and great wealth, but managed to marry three legitimate queens in the process. Being a slave to the Caesar family was not without opportunity!

Felix's wife Drusilla, the daughter of Agrippa I, was reputedly one of the most stunningly beautiful women of her time. Her sister Bernice, however, who was 10 years older, gave Drusilla stiff competition for that honor. A jealous rivalry developed between the two high-born Asamonean sisters. When Felix was first attracted to Drusilla, she was already married to a king, albeit a minor one. Undeterred, Felix employed a magician and, through the power of the occult arts, successfully managed to persuade Drusilla to divorce the king and become his wife. In time, Drusilla bore Felix a son, who was named–not surprisingly–Agrippa. This Agrippa, the nephew of King Agrippa II, perished in the A.D. 79 eruption of Mount Vesuvius (*Antiq* XX 7:2).

Marcus Pallas

Felix's powerful older brother was named Marcus Pallas. Pallas served as the secretary of the treasury for the entire Roman Empire and was Emperor Claudius' right-hand man in many important matters. Claudius was remarkably egalitarian in that respect. If a man demonstrated competence, he was advanced despite the circumstances of his birth. A Royal outsider himself for most of his life, Claudius had no qualms about associating with slaves and freedmen.

> But most of all he (Claudius) was devoted to his secretary Narcissus and his treasurer Pallas and he gladly allowed them to be honoured in addition by a decree of the senate, not only with immense gifts, but even with the insignia of quaestors and praetors. Besides this he permitted them to amass such wealth by plunder...(Sue *Claudius* 28)

Born a slave, Pallas was freed by Antonia, the widow of Drusus the Great, soon after the Sejanus conspiracy was crushed. Presumably, Antonia also arranged to free Pallas' brother Felix at the same time and probably others of the Greek family. Emperor Tiberius' sister-in-law Antonia warned Tiberius about Sejanus' evil intentions in A.D. 31. Her then-slave Pallas was given the responsibility of delivering the incriminating letters to the reclusive Tiberius.

> Now Sejanus had certainly gained his point, had not Antonia's boldness been more wisely conducted than Sejanus's malice; for when she had discovered his designs against Tiberius, she wrote him an exact account of the whole and gave the letter to Pallas, the most faithful of her servants and sent him to Caprere to Tiberius, who, when he understood it, slew Sejanus and his confederates; (*Antiq* XVIII 6:6)

Interestingly, Alexander the alabarch earlier had also served as the steward of Antonia. While working for Antonia, Alexander amassed a great fortune and eventually was appointed an alabarch with authority within the large Jewish community in Alexandrian Egypt.

When Nero assumed the throne, he recognized the competence of Claudius' appointees. Most, if not all, of Claudius' later appointments had been engineered by Agrippina, Nero's mother. Agrippina, in fact, was Pallas' paramour! Nero was far more interested in his own artistic endeavors anyway and so he retained Claudius' administrators to run the empire–at least for the first part of his reign. Nero also owed Pallas a tremendous debt as Pallas had been instrumental in persuading Claudius to adopt him as his heir.

> ..the adoption of Domitius was hastened on by the influence of Pallas. Bound to Agrippina, first as the promoter of her marriage, then as her paramour, he still urged Claudius to think of the interests of the State (*Annuls* 12:25)

So it was only natural and expected that Marcus Pallas came to his brother Felix's aid when Felix was on trial before Nero in A.D. 60.

.. the principal of the Jewish inhabitants of Cesarea went up to Rome to accuse Felix; and he had certainly been brought to punishment, unless Nero had yielded to the importunate solicitations of his brother Pallas, who was at that time had in the greatest honor by him. (*Antiq* XX 8:9)

The Murder of Jonathan

Felix was appointed to his position in A.D. 52. Prior to that time, there was considerable unrest in Judea that required the Syrian president to move his legions south to settle the land. Several men were placed on trial before Claudius in Rome, and as a result the prior procurator, Cumanus, was removed. Felix barely was exonerated of criminality through the efforts of his powerful brother Marcus.

The High Priest Ananias was also sent to Rome for trial, but apparently escaped the wrath of Claudius and returned to Jerusalem with his position intact. Details are scant, but apparently the High Priesthood was angry over Felix's appointment and continued criminal activity. The elder High Priest at that time was Jonathan, who took a lead role in criticizing the Greek procurator.

Jonathan had been the High Priest for a single year in A.D. 36-37 , and was the first persecutor of the Nazarenes — endorsing the stoning of Stephen and other atrocities with Saul of Tarsus, later Paul the Apostle, acting on his instructions. Agrippa II had offered him the High Priest position earlier in A.D. 49, but he declined saying that having once held the honor was enough.

Jonathan was openly critical of Felix for being too lenient in dealing with the criminals and impostors that were plaguing Judea at that time. Indirectly, Jonathan was accusing Felix of being in collusion with them which, in most instances, was the case.

Felix grew tired of Jonathan's invectives and paid a gang of Jewish knife-wielding assassins–the Sicarii–to murder him in A.D. 56. The killing was accomplished in the courtyard of the Second Temple itself–holy ground! The historian Josephus believed that this murder was a major reason for the Jewish nation losing favor with God. With Jonathan's murder in A.D. 56, the stage was now being set for the divine destruction of Jerusalem and the enslavement of the Jewish people.

> Felix also bore an ill-will to Jonathan, the high priest, because he frequently gave him admonitions about governing the Jewish affairs better than he did, lest he should himself have complaints made of him by the multitude, since he it was who had desired Caesar to send him as procurator of Judea. So Felix contrived a method whereby he might get rid of him, now he was become so continually troublesome to him; for such continual admonitions are grievous to those who are disposed to act unjustly. Wherefore Felix persuaded one of Jonathan's most faithful friends, a citizen of Jerusalem, whose name was Doras, to bring the robbers upon Jonathan, in order to kill him; and this he did by promising to give him a great deal of money for so doing. Doras complied with the proposal and contrived matters so, that the robbers might murder him after the following manner: Certain of those robbers went up to the city, as if they were going to worship God, while they had daggers under their garments and by thus mingling themselves among the multitude they slew Jonathan and as this murder was never avenged, the robbers went up with the greatest security at the festivals after this time; and having weapons concealed in like manner as before and mingling themselves among the multitude, they slew certain of their own enemies and were subservient to other men for money; and slew others, not only in remote parts of the city, but in the temple itself also; for they had the boldness to murder men there, without thinking of the impiety of which they were guilty. And this seems to me to have been the reason why God, out of his hatred of these men's wickedness, rejected our city; and as for the temple, he no longer esteemed it sufficiently pure for him to inhabit therein, but brought the Romans upon us and threw a fire upon the city to purge it; and brought upon us, our wives and children, slavery, as desirous to make us wiser by our calamities. (*Antiq* XX 8:5)

In A.D. 36, it can be speculated that the Prefect Pontius Pilate had no choice but to crucify Jesus, as he was beholden to the High Priesthood for all the bribe money he had received. In A.D. 56, the arrogance of Felix suggests that he had sources of income far more lucrative than what he received from Second Temple operations.

Felix and the Egyptian

Feeding off the discontent of the Jewish people, several self-styled prophets emerged during Felix's tenure.

> Now as for the affairs of the Jews, they grew worse and worse continually, for the country was again filled with robbers and impostors, who deluded the multitude. (*Antiq* XX 8:5)

One of the most successful of these impostors was a Messiah-like figure simply called the "Egyptian." This "prophet" co-opted Christian-style dogma and was able to sway the masses. Possibly this Egyptian was, in fact, an unrecorded fringe leader of the early Christians. The Egyptian was mentioned in both *Antiquities* and *Wars* by Josephus, and Acts also references him.

In the following passages, note how the Egyptian gathered his followers on the Mount of Olives and talked about bringing down the walls of the Second Temple–familiar words to the Christian.

> But there was an Egyptian false prophet that did the Jews more mischief than the former; for he was a cheat and pretended to be a prophet also and got together thirty thousand men that were deluded by him; these he led round about from the wilderness to the mount which was called the Mount of Olives and was ready to break into Jerusalem by force from that place; and if he could but once conquer the Roman garrison and the people, he intended to domineer over them by the assistance of those guards of his that were to break into the city with him. But Felix prevented his attempt and met him with his Roman soldiers, while all the people assisted him in his attack upon them, insomuch that when it came to a battle, the Egyptian ran away, with a few others, while the greatest part of those that were with him were either destroyed or taken alive; but the rest of the multitude were dispersed every one to their own homes and there concealed themselves. (*Wars* II 13:5)

> And now these impostors and deceivers persuaded the multitude to follow them into the wilderness and pretended that they would exhibit manifest wonders and signs, that should be performed by the providence of God. And many that were prevailed on by them suffered the punishments of their folly; for Felix brought them back and then punished them. Moreover, there came out of Egypt about this time to

Jerusalem one that said he was a prophet and advised the multitude of the common people to go along with him to the Mount of Olives, as it was called which lay over against the city and at the distance of five furlongs. He said further, that he would show them from hence how, at his command, the walls of Jerusalem would fall down; and he promised them that he would procure them an entrance into the city through those walls, when they were fallen down. Now when Felix was informed of these things, he ordered his soldiers to take their weapons and came against them with a great number of horsemen and footmen from Jerusalem and attacked the Egyptian and the people that were with him. He also slew four hundred of them and took two hundred alive. But the Egyptian himself escaped out of the fight, but did not appear any more. (*Antiq* XX 8:6)

Josephus mentions nothing of the role of the Temple High Priesthood in this incident. It is likely, however, that the priests approved strongly of Felix's attack upon the Egyptian and his supporters, since the priests disapproved of all perceived heretics.

Later, in A.D. 58, when the Apostle Paul caused problems in the Second Temple courtyard, the Roman captain in charge at first thought Paul was this same Egyptian.

Art thou not then the Egyptian, who before these days stirred up to sedition and led out into the wilderness the four thousand men of the Assassins? (Acts 21:38)

The same passage in Acts is quoted by Eusebius, with a slightly different translation.

"Then you're not the Egyptian who a little while back started a revolt and led the 4,000 sicarii out in the wilds?" (Eusebius *History* 2-21)

The murder of Jonathan and the slaughter of Egyptian's army are just two violent incidents Josephus documents that occurred during Felix's tenure–there were likely many others. It was into this unsettled and dangerous climate that Paul the Apostle would arrive for the Pentecost celebration of A.D. 58. He might have planned his trip there knowing that his arch-enemy, the High Priest Jonathan, had been previously murdered.

Paul's adventures in Jerusalem will be detailed in the next chapter, but eventually the Apostle was brought to trial in front of Felix in Caesarea. Felix found no fault with Paul, but imprisoned him anyway, hoping to gain a substantial ransom for his release.

Felix Removed

For the two years that Paul was in "prison", criminal activity and political tumult in Judea continued with Felix playing a central and controlling role. Finally, in A.D. 59 a delegation of Jews from Caesarea petitioned Nero directly for the removal of Felix for his many crimes against them. In particular, they alleged that Felix had been bribed by the Syrian Greeks of Caesarea to take sides against the Jews. The conflict in question had escalated into pitched battles between the Greek and Jewish forces, when Felix entered the fray — using his Roman army against the Jews with devastating results. Like Procurator Cumanus before him, Felix was recalled to Rome to answer these charges of corruption, this time by Nero.

That the Imperial trial even occurred is curious in itself, as Pallas was still the secretary of the Roman treasury. But remember that Nero had just arranged the forced suicide of his mother Agrippina, and Agrippina had been Pallas' paramour. Felix's Roman trial and removal as procurator could well have been the first step in Nero's planned execution of Marcus Pallas and the seizure of Pallas' sizable fortune.

At Felix's trial, Pallas supported his brother Felix unequivocally and Nero acquiesced, to a degree. Still, Felix lost his position in the East and never again returned to Caesarea. Porcius Festus was sent out as Felix's replacement (*Antiq* XX8:9) in A.D. 60.

Porcius Festus

Procurator Porcius Festus proved to be a much milder administrator of Judea and Samaria than his predecessor Felix.

Festus is famous today for his politic and even sagacious disposition of the Apostle Paul in late A.D. 60 which irritated the High Priesthood. Festus as well had to deal with charismatic, seditious leaders and the infamous Sicarii assassins.

> Upon Festus's coming into Judea, it happened that Judea was afflicted by the robbers, while all the villages were set on fire and plundered by them. And then it was that the sicarii, as they were called, who were robbers, grew numerous... So Festus sent forces, both horsemen and footmen, to fall upon those that had been seduced by a certain impostor, who promised them deliverance and freedom from the miseries they were under, if they would but follow him as far as the wilderness. Accordingly, those forces that were sent destroyed both him that had deluded them and those that were his followers also. (*Antiq* XX 8:10)

Festus died in office in A.D. 62. His death was unexpected and unexplained. Logistically, it took at least several weeks for a replacement to be found and sent out from Rome to Judea. The Second Temple High Priesthood took full advantage of this power vacuum to assert their sadly-eroded authority. This resulted in the execution of Jesus' brother, James the Just, and other Jerusalem Christians, as will be seen.

Chapter 17   Trials of Paul

Now as for the affairs of the Jews, they grew worse and worse continually, for the country was again filled with robbers and impostors, who deluded the multitude. (*Antiq* XX 8:5)

The Apostle Paul was taking a huge risk by attending the Jerusalem Pentecost celebration of A.D. 58. While in Caesarea just before leaving for Jerusalem, Agabus, the Christian prophet, even warned Paul about it. Agabus had gained fame 15 years earlier by predicting that a great famine would soon afflict the Jewish East (Acts 11:28) which came to pass.

21:10 And as we tarried there some days, there came down from Judaea a certain prophet, named Agabus. 21:11 And coming to us and taking Paul's girdle, he bound his own feet and hands and said, Thus saith the Holy Spirit, So shall the Jews at Jerusalem bind the man that owneth this girdle and shall deliver him into the hands of the Gentiles. 21:12 And when we heard these things, both we and they of that place besought him not to go up to Jerusalem. (Acts)

The Jerusalem Christian Church had managed to survive in the shadow of the Second Temple for two decades by keeping a low profile. By far most of the evangelistic activity of the Christians was happening outside of Judea, centering around Asia Minor and Greece. In fact, considering the hostility of the Jerusalem High Priesthood toward the Christians, likely the only reason they remained in Jerusalem at all was to maintain ceremony at the place of Jesus' crucifixion and to await his promised return. James the Just, the brother of Jesus and the leader of the Church, scrupulously adhered to Judaic law so the High Priesthood could find no fault with him. Interestingly, according to Hegesippus, James the Just drank no wine, despite being a Christian and presumably an endorser of the communion ceremony.

> ...the Lord's brother James...drank no wine or intoxicating liquor and ate no animal food; no razor came near his head..(Eusebius *History* 2:23– Hegesippus Book V)

James the Just might also have gained a measure of respect from the Second Temple High Priesthood by taking the vows of the Nazorites upon occasion. But while James drank no wine as is consistent with the vows of the Nazorite, he also did not shave his head which is required by those same vows.

As always, the Jerusalem High Priesthood was primed and ready to strike at anyone who threatened to cause trouble during the Pentecost festival, just as they were at all the festivals throughout the year. Was Paul prepared to rein in his enthusiasm for Christianity while worshiping at the Second Temple?

Previously, the Apostles Paul and Barnabas had made arrangements to meet in Jerusalem for the Pentecost of A.D. 58 (Acts 20:16). Paul was looking forward to seeing his old friend and also members of his own family who still lived there. On his way to Jerusalem, Paul stayed for a few days in Caesarea at the home Philip the Evangelist, one of the seven who had been appointed a special disciple of the Church in A.D. 36. Another of the seven had been Stephen, who was to become the first Christian martyr (Acts 6:5). Aiding in Stephen's murder was Paul, then known as Saul. No one could say that Philip didn't have a forgiving nature! Philip had four virgin daughters living with him in Caesarea at the time (Acts 21:8-9); all were recognized as prophetesses.

> 21:17And when we were come to Jerusalem, the brethren received us gladly. 21:18And the day following Paul went in with us unto James; and all the elders were present. (Acts)

The author of Acts of the Apostles is presumed to be Luke, the author of the Gospel of that name and Paul's companion for a portion of his later travels. The years Paul had spent evangelizing in Greece and Asia since his epiphany were adventurous and dangerous times for the former Judean priest. As Paul himself relates in his Second Letter to the Church of Corinth:

> [11:24]Of the Jews five times received I forty *stripes* save one. [11:25]Thrice was I beaten with rods, once was I stoned, thrice I suffered shipwreck, a night and a day have I been in the deep; [11:26]*in* journeyings often, *in* perils of rivers, *in* perils of robbers, *in* perils from *my* countrymen, *in* perils from the Gentiles, *in* perils in the city, *in* perils in the wilderness, *in* perils in the sea, *in* perils among false brethren; [11:27]*in* labor and travail, in watchings often, in hunger and thirst, in fastings often, in cold and nakedness. (II Corin)

But now in Jerusalem, Paul was about to face his most dangerous adversary to date–the High Priest of the Second Temple.

Paul in the Second Temple

In A.D. 39, the Judean Jews had plotted to kill Paul for his proselytizing words. The Jerusalem Church elders had no choice but to order Paul to leave Jerusalem, not only for his own safety but also in the interest of keeping the peace. Would the passage of 19 years have softened the stance of the Jerusalem Jews? Whatever the situation, however, Paul was not one to back down when his beliefs were challenged. Paul also came with donations for James the Just and his Christian brothers–who continued to steadfastly maintain the watch in anticipation of Jesus' return on the Mount of Olives.

> [15:25]but now, I *say*, I go unto Jerusalem, ministering unto the saints. [15:26]For it hath been the good pleasure of Macedonia and Achaia to make a certain contribution for the poor among the saints that are at Jerusalem. [15:27]Yea, it hath been their good pleasure; and their debtors they are. For if the Gentiles have been made partakers of their spiritual things, they owe it *to them* also to minister unto them in carnal things. [15:28]When therefore I have accomplished this and have sealed to them this fruit, I will go on by you unto Spain. (Romans)

At the time, the Pentecost was being celebrated and the Temple courtyard was filled with worshipers. While the Pentecost did not draw the number of pilgrims that the Passover did, certainly at least 100,000 worshipers were in Jerusalem for the celebration. A significant fraction of them gathered in the Temple's outer courtyard at any one time during the daylight hours.

Arrest

The Jerusalem Christian brothers, including James the Just, warned Paul when he arrived in Jerusalem to worship at the Second Temple that he was a famous man for his anti-Judaic proselytizing.

> 21:21and they have been informed concerning thee, that thou teachest all the Jews who are among the Gentiles to forsake Moses, telling them not to circumcise their children neither to walk after the customs. 21:22What is it therefore? They will certainly hear that thou art come. (Acts)

They suggested that he go to the Temple and worship with a group of four men who had taken the Nazorite vows. The Nazorites as a matter of course shave their heads. Paul being with them (perhaps he was naturally bald himself) would not arouse suspicions.

The popular Nazorite vows then involved staying overnight for seven days in the inner courtyards and performing certain rituals and offerings. But Paul was recognized there, and, worse, the men with him were assumed to be Greek. A non-Jew was not allowed in the inner sanctuary courtyards upon pain of death, nor could a Jew knowingly allow in a non-Jew.

> 21:27And when the seven days were almost completed, the Jews from Asia, when they saw him in the temple, stirred up all the multitude and laid hands on him, 21:28crying out, Men of Israel, help: This is the man that teacheth all men everywhere against the people, and the law, and this place; and moreover he brought Greeks also into the temple, and

hath defiled this holy place. $^{21:29}$For they had before seen with him in the city Trophimus the Ephesian, whom they supposed that Paul had brought into the temple. $^{21:30}$And all the city was moved, and the people ran together; and they laid hold on Paul, and dragged him out of the temple: and straightway the doors were shut. $^{21:31}$And as they were seeking to kill him, tidings came up to the chief captain of the band, that all Jerusalem was in confusion. $^{21:32}$And forthwith he took soldiers and centurions, and ran down upon them: and they, when they saw the chief captain and the soldiers, left off beating Paul. (Acts)

The Roman chief guard, whom Acts identifies as Captain Claudius Lysias, saw the commotion and quickly mobilized a few of his men. Paul was rescued from the mob and taken to the nearby tower of Antonia not only for his own safety but also for further questioning.

Only two years previously, the Temple courtyard had been the site of the bold slaying of the High Priest Jonathan–arranged by the Procurator Felix. Felix had also recently ordered the destruction of the citizen army of a crypto-Christian leader simply called the "Egyptian." The worshipers in the Temple courtyard and the Temple guards themselves were understandably edgy.

During the interrogation by the Roman soldiers, Paul was not cooperative. About to be flogged for insolence, Paul protested that he was a Roman citizen and could not be punished without a proper trial. Paul had many run-ins with authorities during his travels and knew his rights as a Roman. Apparently, Paul carried documentation attesting to his Roman civil status.

That gave Lysias pause. He knew that Paul was absolutely correct, so in deference to Paul's Roman citizenship, Captain Lysias set up a hearing the next day in front of the High Priest Ananias and the Sanhedrin. As Paul's supposed crime was of a religious nature, it fell under the jurisdiction of the Sanhedrin; Roman law would then not have to be invoked. But Lysias had to know that this was only a temporary solution, even a pointless one. If the Sanhedrin found him guilty of a crime, Paul could again hide behind his Roman citizenship.

It is interesting to note that the Roman captain had the power to convene the Jewish Sanhedrin. Josephus does not mention this power anywhere else. It also indicates that Lysias was probably the ranking Roman official in Jerusalem at that time, since Procurator Felix was in Caesarea.

Sanhedrin Trial

The next day, a hearing before the Sanhedrin was held. It was contentious from the start and Paul gave no quarter to the powerful High Priest and his inquisitors. After decades of preaching and debating doubters and defending himself against accusers and nay-sayers, Paul's Christian rhetoric was smooth and polished.

> [23:1]And Paul, looking stedfastly on the council, said, Brethren, I have lived before God in all good conscience until this day. [23:2]And the high priest Ananias commanded them that stood by him to smite him on the mouth. [23:3]Then said Paul unto him, God shall smite thee, thou whited wall: and sittest thou to judge me according to the law and commandest me to be smitten contrary to the law? [23:4]And they that stood by said, Revilest thou God's high priest? (Acts)

The High Priest Ananias had ordered Paul to be struck for his presumed insolence. In retaliation, Paul insulted the High Priest by comparing him to a "whited wall." "Whited wall" likely referred to a wall soiled by bird droppings.

Bird pollution was a huge and continuous problem at the lofty Second Temple complex, where the height of the Sanctuary building birds found particularly attractive. As a practical solution, the roof of the Temple Sanctuary was studded with spear-like projections to prevent birds from perching upon it and causing pollution.

> On its top it had spikes with sharp points, to prevent any pollution of it by birds sitting upon it. (*Wars* V 5:6)

The High Priest was a semi-divine figure to the Jews, so Paul had spoken deadly, words indeed!

Within the Sanhedrin itself, Paul likely had his supporters. Many members probably did not want to prosecute Paul, fearing he might be speaking with the power of Angels. More than 20 years previously, Jesus had his secret disciples who were members of the priesthood and the principal men of Jerusalem. Were any secret Christian disciples still among the Sanhedrin that had assembled to judge Paul? Also, previously Paul had lived in Jerusalem. Then known as Saul, many members of his family still lived in the city. Perhaps several in the Sanhedrin knew him from those early days, or were at least familiar with Paul's family.

Because of these factors, the hypothesis can be made that many of the Sanhedrin members were not inclined to be aggressive toward Paul, even though he was undeniably a heretic under Jewish law. Perhaps a Sanhedrin member or two hid smiles, or even laughed out loud, when Paul compared Ananias to bird droppings on a stone wall.

As the trial progressed, Paul continued to evangelize about Jesus and discourse upon his own religious visions. Perhaps some Sanhedrin members showed an interest. Ananias began to realize that conviction was not a certainty—or even probable.

In the course of the trial, Paul skillfully managed to set the Pharisees and Sadducees at odds with each other, igniting a heated argument between the members of the two sects. The trial degenerated first into an unruly shouting match and then into physical violence. Amidst the fighting and chaos, the captain of the Roman guard spirited Paul off to the safety of the tower of Antonia.

> And when there arose a great dissension, the chief captain, fearing lest Paul should be torn in pieces by them, commanded the soldiers to go down and take him by force from among them and bring him into the castle. (Acts 23:10)

The High Priest Ananias had to be enraged at the intentional and artful obfuscation that Paul generated at that first day's hearing and how he controlled the direction of the questioning and led the trial into chaos.

Plan to Murder

Ananias then resorted to another approach to eliminate Paul. Following the deadly example of Procurator Felix, who had two years before arranged to have the High Priest Jonathan murdered, the High Priest endorsed a plan to have Paul killed before the next session of the Sanhedrin convened.

> 23:12And when it was day, the Jews banded together and bound themselves under a curse, saying that they would neither eat nor drink till they had killed Paul. 23:13And they were more than forty that made this conspiracy. 23:14And they came to the chief priests and the elders and said, We have bound ourselves under a great curse, to taste nothing until we have killed Paul. 23:15Now therefore do ye with the council signify to the chief captain that he bring him down unto you, as though ye would judge of his case more exactly: and we, before he comes near, are ready to slay him. (Acts)

But Paul's sister, who lived in Jerusalem, heard of the plot and sent her son to warn Paul in prison. After hearing what was planned for him, Paul sent his nephew directly tell the Roman Captain Lysias of the conspiracy.

> 23:16But Paul's sister's son heard of their lying in wait and he came and entered into the castle and told Paul. 23:17And Paul called unto him one of the centurions and said, Bring this young man unto the chief captain; for he hath something to tell him. 23:18So he took him and brought him to the chief captain and saith, Paul the prisoner called me unto him and asked me to bring this young man unto thee, who hath something to say to thee. 23:19And the chief captain took him by the hand and going aside asked him privately, What is it that thou hast to tell me? 23:20And he said, The Jews have agreed to ask thee to bring down Paul tomorrow unto the council, as though thou wouldest inquire somewhat more exactly concerning him. 23:21Do not thou therefore yield unto them: for there lie in wait for him of them more than forty men, who have bound themselves under a curse, neither to eat nor to drink till they have slain him: and now are they ready, looking for the promise from thee. (Acts)

Lysias did not want to be a party to Paul's murder. A mob killing of a Roman citizen was unacceptable. Lysias knew he had to get Paul out of Jerusalem expeditiously.

The next night, Paul was taken to Caesarea. There, Paul, as a Roman citizen, would be judged by the presumably more fair-minded Felix. The population in Caesarea also was less likely to be whipped into a frenzy by edicts from the High Priesthood. So under the cover of darkness, the trip to Caesarea was made. Lysias provided Paul with an escort of over 200 Roman soldiers, 70 horsemen and 200 pikemen–a formidable force by any measure.

Imprisonment in Caesarea

Five days later in Caesarea, Paul's new trial in front of Felix began. Present also was Felix's beautiful wife, Drusilla, the daughter of Agrippa I and not yet 20 years of age. The High Priest and others had been forced to travel to Caesarea in order to confront Paul again. They were angry at this, but they had arranged to indict Paul with energy and gusto. Ananias was taking no chances. An advocate named Tertullus spoke for the High Priesthood and the Second Temple.

> For we have found this man a pestilent fellow and a mover of insurrections among all the Jews throughout the world and a ringleader of the sect of the Nazarenes: who moreover assayed to profane the temple: on whom also we laid hold: and we would have judged him according to our law. (Acts 24:5-6).

The usual penalty for religious sedition was death by stoning which had happened to the Apostle Stephen 20 years before. In his role as magistrate, Felix was sitting on the judgment seat that represented his authority. Was this ornate chair the same one that Pilate had sat upon when judging Jesus two decades earlier?!

The accusations against Paul were probably many, varied and venomous, but Paul defended himself with all the considerable skill he could muster. Procurator Felix, after hearing the evidence, decided to not execute Paul. Paul was a Roman citizen after all, and to execute a citizen for a provincial religious crime was unthinkable. But Felix knew that the Jerusalem High Priesthood could be troublesome and so he had Paul thrown in jail. Ultimate judgment against Paul would now be deferred.

> But after certain days, Felix came with Drusilla, his wife, who was a Jewess and sent for Paul and heard him concerning the faith in Christ Jesus. [24:25]And as he reasoned of righteousness and self-control and the judgment to come, Felix was terrified and answered, Go thy way for this time; and when I have a convenient season, I will call thee unto me. He hoped withal that money would be given him of Paul: wherefore also he sent for him the oftener and communed with him. (Acts 24:24-26)

Felix also had ulterior motives in doing this. Felix knew that Paul came from a family of tent makers in Jerusalem. Perhaps Felix suspected–or knew–that these were wealthy people who would pay a large ransom to Felix for Paul's release. Or perhaps Felix thought that the Jerusalem Christian brothers were wealthy enough to pay the ransom themselves.

Another factor might have been the simple fact that Paul was half-Greek and Felix was a full-blooded Greek. Drusilla, Felix's wife, could have also played a role in influencing his decision. Drusilla was the sister of Agrippa II (*Antiq* XX 7:1) and the daughter of Agrippa I. But remember that Agrippa I had been no friend of the Christians, so her bias could have gone either way. Did she intervene on Paul's behalf, lobby for a more severe punishment for him–or simply remain silent?

For the next two years, Paul remained a prisoner in Herod's palace in Caesarea. Did that really represent a punishment, or was this a relatively pleasant "out" that Felix graciously provided for a fellow Greek? In Herod's palace, Paul was safe from the Jerusalem assassins, the Sicarii, who had already been paid by the High Priest to kill him. Over time, Felix got to like Paul and "communed" with him often. Like Paul, Antonius Felix had lived his early life as an outsider–a slave, in his case–and could probably sympathize with the animosity the Jews had shown toward Paul. Additionally, both men were Roman citizens with no small amount of formal education. It is very likely that soon Paul had quite a bit of freedom in Caesarea, although still under the loose supervision of a Roman guard or two. Paul's own companions visited with him as often as they liked. Life could have been worse for the Apostle!

Festus' Trial

When Porcius Festus assumed power as the Judean procurator in A.D. 60 after Felix's recall, Paul had been in imprisoned for two years in Caesarea. Festus, however, didn't want any holdover prisoners from Felix's administration. After reviewing the case against Paul, Festus saw no real crime and sought to have him released.

The Jerusalem High Priesthood got word of Festus' plan and strongly objected. Even after two years, the priests saw Paul as enough of a threat to merit execution. For the two years that he was incarcerated, Paul had likely preached to the Jews in Caesarea, or to those Jews who were journeying on to the Second Temple for the different festivals, during his numerous periods of supervised freedom. Felix could have intentionally let him out when large passenger ships docked for that purpose, just to irritate the High Priesthood. Reports of Paul's evangelizing were probably received frequently from these pilgrims by members of the Jerusalem High Priesthood.

> 25:1Festus therefore, having come into the province, after three days went up to Jerusalem from Caesarea. 25:2And the chief priests and the principal men of the Jews informed him against Paul; and they besought him, 25:3asking a favor against him, that he would send for him to Jerusalem; laying a plot to kill him on the way. . (Acts)

But Festus wanted no part of this plot to murder the prisoner he had inherited from Felix. Festus, too, respected the fact that Paul was a Roman citizen. Festus then arranged for a trial back in Caesarea.

> 25:5Let them therefore, saith he, that are of power among you go down with me and if there is anything amiss in the man, let them accuse him.

^{25:6}And when he had tarried among them not more than eight or ten days, he went down unto Caesarea; and on the morrow he sat on the judgment-seat and commanded Paul to be brought. ^{25:7}And when he was come, the Jews that had come down from Jerusalem stood round about him, bringing against him many and grievous charges which they could not prove; ^{25:8}while Paul said in his defense, Neither against the law of the Jews, nor against the temple, nor against Caesar, have I sinned at all. ^{25:9}But Festus, desiring to gain favor with the Jews, answered Paul and said, Wilt thou go up to Jerusalem and there be judged of these things before me? ^{25:10}But Paul said, I am standing before Caesar's judgment-seat, where I ought to be judged: to the Jews have I done no wrong, as thou also very well knowest. ^{25:11}If then I am a wrong-doer and have committed anything worthy of death, I refuse not to die; but if none of those things is *true* whereof these accuse me, no man can give me up unto them. I appeal unto Caesar. ^{25:12}Then Festus, when he had conferred with the council, answered, Thou hast appealed unto Caesar: unto Caesar shalt thou go. (Acts)

Festus put Paul up for trial again in front of his accusers. But instead of resolution, there was more conflict and accusations, with Paul asserting his right to a trial before Nero. Festus agreed to Paul's demand, seeing in this a way out of a no-win situation. A short time afterward, King Agrippa II and his sister Bernice arrived in Caesarea. Festus asked Agrippa, as the most powerful Jew in the empire, for help in dealing with the problem of Paul.

King Agrippa II and Bernice

At that time, Agrippa II held control over the Second Temple and determined who would serve as the High Priest. If Agrippa decided that Paul should be set free, the Jerusalem High Priesthood could hardly contest it. Agrippa obliged to help Festus out and hear Paul. The sister of Agrippa II and Bernice, Drusilla, only a year previously had been living in Herod's opulent palace in Caesarea as the wife of Antonius Felix with the powers of a virtual queen. It can be speculated that Drusilla in past conversations with her sister and brother, or perhaps in letters, had commented on the odd religious prisoner named Paul that Felix kept in a cell within the palace.

King Agrippa II was the son of Agrippa the Great, or Agrippa I, who had died 16 years previously. In A.D. 60, Agrippa II was 33 years old and Bernice was 32. The younger Agrippa had proven himself to be a capable administrator first to Emperor Claudius and then to Emperor Nero. Agrippa II already had gained control over a portion of his father's former domain. He had hopes of eventually ruling all of it which would include Festus' current territory of Judea, Samaria, and the plum cities of Jerusalem and Caesarea. In fact, Agrippa would indeed gain those territories six years later in A.D. 66. A year after that, in A.D. 67, Agrippa would meet and eventually become great friends with the captured Jewish General Joseph bar Matthias, later known as the Jewish historian Flavius Josephus and our major source.

Queen Bernice was widely acknowledged as one of the most beautiful women in the empire, taking after her aunt Herodias, the former queen of Galilee. Herodias had been banished to Gaul along with her husband Herod Antipas 20 ago and thus disappeared from history. Bernice, born in A.D. 28, had first been married to a son of Alexander the alabarch, named Marcus. Bernice then could not have been more than 10 or 11 and Marcus died relatively soon afterward. In A.D. 41 at the ripe old age of 13, Bernice embarked on her second marriage, this time to her uncle Herod, who would soon become the king of Chalcis. This Herod had died in A.D. 49, leaving Bernice with a son, Hyrcanus (*Antiq* XX 5:2). Bernice was then briefly married to Poleme, the king of Cilicia (*Antiq* XX 7:3).

At the time of the Caesarea trial of Paul the Apostle, Bernice was probably unattached. There were unsubstantiated rumors that she and Agrippa II maintained an incestuous relationship. But the future would be eventful for Bernice, as it usually is for ambitious and beautiful women. Not long after the destruction of Jerusalem in A.D. 70, Bernice would become the paramour of the victorious Roman General Titus, the son of Emperor Vespasian. Bernice was 13 years older than Titus — in A.D. 41, when Titus was born, Bernice had already consummated her second marriage!

Berenice was at the very height of her power and consequently came to Rome along with her brother Agrippa. The latter was given the rank of praetor, while she dwelt in the palace, cohabiting with Titus. She expected to marry him and was already behaving in every respect as if she were his wife; but when he perceived that the Romans were displeased with the situation, he sent her away (Dio 64:15)

Second Trial in Caesarea

In mid-A.D. 60, the Royal siblings arrived in Caesarea after a long sea voyage. They were probably very weary of travel and in no hurry to leave the magnificent and cultured city. Caesarea, formerly Strato's Tower, had been reconstructed at great expense by Herod the Great 70 years before. The city boasted a state-of-art concrete quay and a harbor that could enclose and service 100 vessels. On either side of the north-facing entrance to the harbor, Herod the Great had erected six towering bronze statues set on carved block pedestals in the sea — Venus, Apollo and Roma on the east and Augustus Caesar, Julius Caesar and Jupiter on the west.

Caesarea also boasted a five-mile-long double aqueduct to bring in fresh water from the northeast hills. Along the waterfront was a massive and imposing temple to Augustus. The city also had a circus and an amphitheater along with many other gleaming marble-faced edifices. A large and bustling marketplace behind the circus held most of the goods for sale and trade that the empire had to offer–and in great quantities. The ocean-side palace of Herod lay up against the southern aspect of the circus with a view of the Mediterranean to the west and an open view of the amphitheater to the east. Caesarea then was at the height of its glory. Agrippa and Bernice likely planned to stay a few days to enjoy all the city had to offer.

King Agrippa II knew that, in his powerful position, Imperial Rome expected him to adjudicate major disputes between Jews no matter where in the empire they occurred — if the local Roman administrator requested it. Agrippa was also well aware that religion and to a lesser extent politics were the life's blood of the

Jewish people. A decision from a Jewish Royal would hold far more weight than one from a Roman procurator. Agrippa II fully appreciated the difficult position that Festus found himself in, and knew that in the future it might prove advantageous if he helped Festus out today.

So Agrippa and Bernice agreed to Festus' request for aid in judging the supposed crimes of Paul. In due time, Paul was brought before them and the trial commenced.

> 25:23So on the morrow, when Agrippa was come and Bernice, with great pomp and they were entered into the place of hearing with the chief captains and principal men of the city, at the command of Festus Paul was brought in. 25:24And Festus saith, King Agrippa and all men who are here present with us, ye behold this man, about whom all the multitude of the Jews made suit to me, both at Jerusalem and here, crying that he ought not to live any longer. 25:25But I found that he had committed nothing worthy of death: and as he himself appealed to the emperor I determined to send him. 25:26Of whom I have no certain thing to write unto my lord. Wherefore I have brought him forth before you and specially before thee, king Agrippa, that, after examination had, I may have somewhat to write. 25:27For it seemeth to me unreasonable, in sending a prisoner, not withal to signify the charges against him. (Acts)

Agrippa II and his sister Bernice patiently listened to Paul's arguments. They were impressed by what they heard–or at least out of politeness pretended to be.

> 26:28And Agrippa *said* unto Paul, With but little persuasion thou wouldest fain make me a Christian. 26:29And Paul *said*, I would to God, that whether with little or with much, not thou only, but also all that hear me this day, might become such as I am, except these bonds. 26:30And the king rose up and the governor and Bernice and they that sat with them: 26:31and when they had withdrawn, they spake one to another, saying, This man doeth nothing worthy of death or of bonds. 26:32And Agrippa said unto Festus, This man might have been set at liberty, if he had not appealed unto Caesar. (Acts)

But both Agrippa and Festus realized that if Paul were set free in Caesarea, he would be a target for Jewish assassins–the Sicarii.

Jews killing Jews was one thing, but the killing of a Roman citizen could mean trouble for both Festus and Agrippa. Agrippa II agreed with Festus that the best solution would be to transfer Paul to Rome to be tried before Caesar.

Sea Voyage

So Paul was sent west to Rome. A trusted centurion named Julius was ordered to escort Paul and a few other prisoners on this sea voyage. The author of Acts and the Book of Luke, Luke of Macedon, also was with Paul. During the trip, Paul was treated very well–a low security prisoner if there ever was one. The Roman centurion unchained him frequently and even let Paul visit his friends at various scheduled stops.

> Julius treated Paul kindly and gave him leave to go unto his friends and refresh himself. (Acts 27:3)

But it was late in the shipping season of A.D. 60 and the winter storms were beginning. The transport vessel was caught up in a violent tempest that lasted for two weeks and severely damaged the craft. The crew abandoned the ship in fear and left the passengers on board and fearing for their lives. Luckily for Paul, the ship didn't sink, but drifted for days with its distraught passengers clinging on board. Eventually, the ship broke apart and sank after crashing on the rocky coastline of an island. Paul and Julius and a few others (Luke of Macedon, for one) managed to survive the breakup and made it safely onto the island which was called Melita. Paul and Julius had various other adventures on the island before finally reaching Rome, probably in early A.D. 61.

Paul in Rome

Initially, Paul was locked up in Rome with Julius as his guard. His companions, apparently including Luke of Macedon, were not allowed to be with him.

> And when we entered into Rome, Paul was suffered to abide by himself with the soldier that guarded him. (Acts 28:16)

After languishing for three days, Paul got tired of waiting and forced the issue. He boldly summoned the leader of the Jewish community in Rome and some of the other principal Roman Jews. If these Roman Jews wanted to prosecute him, well then, Paul was ready for it.

> And they said unto him, We neither received letters from Judaea concerning thee, nor did any of the brethren come hither and report or speak any harm of thee. (Acts 28:21)

To Paul's surprise, the Jerusalem High Priesthood had sent no prosecutors to Rome and Festus had sent no indictment. Both Roman and Jewish officials did not know or care who Paul was. The Roman Centurion Julius also had no interest in pressing Paul's prosecution–his job was to be a guard only. Probably with great relief, Julius the Centurion loosened the bonds on Paul and set him free. Julius might have then found his way back to Caesarea on a transport ship, or perhaps joined an Augustan band (Imperial guard) and stayed in Rome.

As for Paul the Apostle, he received enough donations from the Christian brothers in Rome to secure a dwelling for himself, and he stayed there for at least two years preaching the word of Jesus.

> 28:30And he abode two whole years in his own hired dwelling and received all that went in unto him, 28:31preaching the kingdom of God and teaching the things concerning the Lord Jesus Christ with all boldness, none forbidding him. (Acts)

The Book of the Acts of the Apostles — the work of Paul's disciple Luke of Macedon — ends with Paul being a free man in Rome.

Was Paul's unexpected freedom after arriving in Rome the result of a miraculous series of bureaucratic miscues, or did Procurator Festus intentionally not bother to send written indictments ahead to Rome? Festus himself did not know exactly what the charge against Paul should be. Possibly, Festus had sent

Paul to Rome purposefully with no instructions at all just to get rid of him. Paul suffered a shipwreck and a delay in arrival that might have been measured in months. The High Priesthood may have received reports about the shipwreck, assumed Paul was dead, and recalled their prosecutors.

Whatever the truth of the matter, the officials of Rome knew nothing about Paul when he arrived, and they certainly did not care about a foreign religious squabble between Paul and the Jerusalem High Priesthood. Perhaps intentionally, Festus had provided Paul with a free trip to Rome, complete with an armed escort. The year was A.D. 61, and Paul was safely in Rome out of harm's way and free to evangelize.

The Martyrdom of James the Just

Porcius Festus served for a little over two years as procurator before he died suddenly in A.D. 62. There was a delay of weeks if not months before Lucceius Albinus, Nero's choice as Festus' replacement, arrived in Judea to take control. During that interval, the newly-appointed High Priest Ananus, the son of Ananus, called the Sanhedrin to council without Roman consultation. This was an illegal action. Years before, the Romans had taken away the power of convocation from the High Priesthood. Since then, only the Roman procurator or the Jerusalem senior Roman military officer could call the Sanhedrin into session — and only then for a specific purpose.

The new and fiery High Priest Ananus definitely had a specific purpose in mind. Quickly, James the Just, the brother of Jesus and the leader of the Christian Church, was placed on trial by the Sanhedrin, along with other important Jerusalem Christians. All were found guilty of religious crimes and were executed by public stoning. This sudden and deadly attack on the leadership of the Christians by the Jerusalem High Priesthood was shocking.

> And now Caesar, upon hearing the death of Festus, sent Albinus into Judea, as procurator. But the king deprived Joseph of the high priesthood and bestowed the succession to that dignity on the son of Ananus, who was also himself called Ananus.. this younger Ananus,

who, as we have told you already, took the high priesthood, was a bold man in his temper and very insolent; he was also of the sect of the Sadducees, who are very rigid in judging offenders, above all the rest of the Jews, as we have already observed; when, therefore, Ananus was of this disposition, he thought he had now a proper opportunity [to exercise his authority]. Festus was now dead and Albinus was but upon the road; so he assembled the sanhedrim of judges and brought before them the brother of Jesus, who was called Christ, whose name was James and some others, [or, some of his companions]; and when he had formed an accusation against them as breakers of the law, he delivered them to be stoned: but as for those who seemed the most equitable of the citizens and such as were the most uneasy at the breach of the laws, they disliked what was done; they also sent to the king [Agrippa], desiring him to send to Ananus that he should act so no more, for that what he had already done was not to be justified; nay, some of them went also to meet Albinus, as he was upon his journey from Alexandria and informed him that it was not lawful for Ananus to assemble a sanhedrim without his consent. (*Antiq* XX 9:1)

Interestingly, in the previous eight months, the Temple had seen two other men in the High Priest's office. The High Priest Ismael had served from at least A.D. 60 to early A.D. 62 before voluntarily giving up the position to move to Rome. The circumstances of this highly unusual occurrence will be dealt in the next chapter. Ismael's replacement was Joseph (Cabi), but he only served a few months until being replaced by Ananus — who then promptly initiated indictments against James and the Jerusalem Christian leaders.

The appointment of Ananus coincided with the death of Procurator Festus. With the subsequent bold stroke of the Sanhedrin illegally convening to execute the Christians, the question must be raised: Was Festus' death a natural one or was he assassinated on the order of the High Priesthood?

Conspiracy of the High Priesthood

In those years, the Jerusalem High Priesthood was increasingly angry with not only the Christians for eroding their authority, but with their Roman overseers for failing to do anything about it. Josephus also documents friction between the High Priesthood and the principal men of Jerusalem, to the point where the priests had to steal from the wealthy in order to survive — many of the lower-class priests facing starvation (*Antiq* XX 8:8).

In A.D. 58, Procurator Felix declined to convict Paul the Apostle. This had to be infuriating to the Jerusalem Temple priests.

Worse, in A.D. 60 the new Procurator Festus let Paul the Apostle "escape" to Rome. The Temple priests had hoped that Festus, unlike Felix, would let them expeditiously kill the man. When the High Priesthood later learned of Paul thriving in Rome, did the Temple priests finally have enough of Rome's coddling of the Christian sect? It is possible that a daring plan to assassinate Procurator Festus was put into action which resulted in his "sudden" death. With Festus out of the way, the Sanhedrin could then convene unhindered and so eliminate the Jerusalem Christian leadership once and for all.

This is not as speculative as it might sound, as the Roman Procurator Felix had assassinated the High Priest Jonathan only seven years before. A revenge factor could have been a major justification for Festus' murder. With Festus out of the way, Ananus quickly replaced Joseph (Cabi) as High Priest in order to facilitate the execution of the Christians — Joseph perhaps not agreeing with the plan.

But the stonings caused a huge outcry from the Jewish population. Over the years, the common Jews had learned to live with the growing sect of the Christians and likely found them decent enough people. In response, King Agrippa II was forced to remove Ananus as High Priest after only three months in power. But the damage had already been done — James and the other Christian leaders were dead.

The Execution of Paul

In Rome, the Apostle Paul became a leader in the Christian Church soon after his arrival in A.D. 61. Acts ends with Paul still in Rome two years later. According to Christian legend, Paul would die in Nero's persecution of the Christian community after the devastating July A.D. 64 fires in Rome. Peter the Apostle was also in Rome and was executed at roughly the same time. Since Acts does not mention Nero's persecutions, it is reasonable to assume that Luke of Macedon completed writing Acts in A.D. 64 while in Rome with Paul. Luke, in fact, might have been killed along with Paul and Peter—which would account for Acts' somewhat abrupt ending.

Eusebius confirms the martyrdom of both Peter and Paul, though not specifically mentioning Nero's persecutions. Eusebius quotes from a now-lost letter written by the first century Bishop of Corinth, Dionysius, to the Church in Rome.

> In this way by your impressive admonition you have bound together all that has grown from the seed that Peter and Paul sowed in Romans and Corinthians alike. For both of them sowed in Corinth and taught us jointly: in Italy too they taught jointly in the same city and were martyred at the same time. (Eusebius *History* 2:25)

But these facts raise more questions than they answer. Was it just a coincidence that Nero's systematic persecutions of the Christians took place so soon after Paul's arrival in Rome? Or did the abrasive Paul play an incendiary role in what would become one of Christianity's–and Rome's–darkest hours? Two years earlier, the Second Temple High Priesthood had executed the Christian leaders in Jerusalem—to include James, the brother of Jesus.

Did the High Priesthood have a role in the execution of the Christian leaders in Rome as well?

Chapter 18   Poppea's Salon

.. Poppea, Nero's wife.. was a religious woman and had requested these favors of Nero and who gave order to the ten ambassadors to go their way home; but retained Helcias and Ismael as hostages with herself.. (*Antiq* XX 8:11)

Empress Poppea Sabinus was famous for her eclectic Royal court of philosophers, religious leaders, and artists. This stable of talented people would entertain and be a part of discussions with the Royal couple and their friends during feasts and social events. Josephus writes that Poppea had a special interest in religion which is mildly contradictory given her apparently avaricious and immoral nature. Seven years older than Nero, Poppea likely was dominant in determining who was in their social circle and who was excluded.

What sort of people made up her court? Personal friends and family of Nero and Poppea would have been permanent fixtures, of course. Singers and musicians would be invited for their entertainment value; poets, writers, and philosophers for their insightful observations on people, politics, and life; wealthy individuals who sought Imperial favor and foreign dignitaries who happened to be in the city if Nero or Poppea found them interesting enough; Roman generals, Roman administrators, and wealthy merchant travelers depending on the whim of Poppea. Certainly courtesans and beautiful women were always welcome to attend the nightly feasts as long as they were attentive to other male guests and did not pose romantic competition for Poppea.

Apart from the "official" Royal salon, Poppea on her own held secret councils with astrologers, soothsayers and other occult figures. Poppea was especially fascinated by astrology which was popular over much of the ancient world—as it is today. What could be more compelling than divining the unknown future by charting the movements of the mysterious stars and planets across the night sky? But even in those ancient times it was known that many astrologers were charlatans who used the pseudoscience to take advantage of people.

> The astrologers..(are).. a class of men, whom the powerful cannot trust and who deceive the aspiring, a class which will always be proscribed in this country and yet always retained. Many of these men were attached to the secret councils of Poppaea and were the vilest tools in the employ of the imperial household. (Tacitus *Histories* 1:22)

While Tacitus writes that astrology was proscribed in Rome, it was a very loosely enforced regulation. Emperor Tiberius knew the art as well as anyone and the superstitious Herod Antipas was a famous follower of astrology and the occult. Most Royal courts in ancient times had official Astrologers whether admitted to or not.

The people with whom Poppea populated the Royal court could not help but influence Nero's attitude toward the early Christians. At the time of persecutions, Nero would have been only 27 years of age—impressionable still despite his 10 years in power. The Jewish community, then as today, had many accomplished and talented people who would have appealed to Poppea and Nero and been included in Poppea's gatherings. It can be assumed that few of these Jews, if any, would have defended the Christian sect in the early 60's A.D.

Josephus' Embassy to Rome

In his autobiography, Josephus writes about a trip he made to Rome in early A.D. 63. The voyage was not for the purposes of sight-seeing, but a quasi-diplomatic mission of liberation. Several Jerusalem priests had been jailed in Rome by the former

Procurator Antonius Felix years before and apparently had been forgotten by higher Roman authorities. Only a personal pardon by Nero could get them released, and Josephus wanted to facilitate that. Likely, Josephus brought along a large sum of money, as bribery and the paying of ransom was an accepted solution to many political problems in those days.

> But when I was in the twenty-sixth year of my age, it happened that I took a voyage to Rome and this on the occasion which I shall now describe. At the time when Felix was procurator of Judea there were certain priests of my acquaintance and very excellent persons they were, whom on a small and trifling occasion he had put into bonds and sent to Rome to plead their cause before Caesar. These I was desirous to procure deliverance for and that especially because I was informed that they were not unmindful of piety towards God, even under their afflictions, but supported themselves with figs and nuts. (*Life* 3)

Josephus does not say if he was sent by the Jerusalem priesthood or not. Josephus does state that he knew the imprisoned priests personally. Josephus himself came from a wealthy family and his father could well have paid for the trip in order to rescue their friends.

Josephus relates that his trip across the Mediterranean Sea was long and arduous. In the course of it, Josephus' ship floundered in the Adriatic with 600 people on board. After a night spent floating in the sea, Josephus and only 80 others survived to be picked up by a passing ship. They were then dropped off in Campania, a port city on the west coast of Italy. This was also a popular vacation spot for the Roman wealthy and high-born and close by to the island of Capri made famous by Tiberius.

With the luck that was to be with him for all of his life, in Campania Josephus made the acquaintance of a famous Jewish actor named Aliturius. Propitiously, Aliturius was a favorite of Poppea Sabina, the wife of Emperor Nero, and he eventually facilitated a meeting of Josephus with her in Rome. Aliturius, who was Jewish, was probably an occasional guest when Poppea's salon held their functions.

I became acquainted with Aliturius, an actor of plays and much beloved by Nero, but a Jew by birth; and through his interest became known to Poppea, Caesar's wife and took care, as soon as possible, to entreat her to procure that the priests might be set at liberty. And when, besides this favor, I had obtained many presents from Poppea, I returned home again. (*Life* 3)

Josephus states he was 26 when he visited Rome. Obligingly, he also tells us he was born in the year of Tiberius' death which we know to be A.D. 37. This makes the year of his visit A.D. 63. Josephus had many adventures along the way, including the shipwreck, before actually reaching Rome, so his actual arrival was likely sometime in mid-to-late A.D. 63.

This fits in well with another known fact about the Royal couple. Queen Poppea was not in Rome during the first part of A.D. 63–she was in confinement for the last stages of her pregnancy. Emperor Nero was with Poppea as well. After the birth of their daughter, Claudia, the Royal couple returned to Rome and only then would have been able to hear petitioners.

Josephus did eventually see at least Poppea and gain the release of the Jewish prisoners. The mission was a success! Josephus boasts that Poppea gave him many presents, suggesting that she was personally taken by him. This was probably not the idle boast of an arrogant young man–Josephus (then Joseph bar Matthias) likely stayed more than just a few days in Rome.

It can be assumed that Josephus had a mastery of Latin and spoke it fluently–why else would his father have trusted him on the mission? A Judean Jewish priest who spoke conversational Latin would have been a novelty to Poppea. Josephus also had a fabulous memory and knew by rote all the exciting stories of the ancient Jewish nation. It is easy to visualize Josephus captivating the Royal salon with his dramatic recounting of the actions of the great men and prophets in Jewish history.

Interestingly, Josephus does not admit to actually meeting Nero. But considering the nature of his quest, it is unlikely that he could have avoided it. Also, if there ever was a blissful time when the Royal couple would be inseparable, it would have been during this period of time in A.D. 63 after the birth of their first daughter. Then, Nero and Poppea had been formally married for only year.

If Josephus met and socialized with Nero, then why didn't he mention it in his autobiography? But it must be remembered that Josephus' purpose in setting down his life's story was to convince the Jews that he had served the Jewish nation well during the revolt–or at least to the best of his abilities–and that he was no traitor. Disclosing his association with Emperor Nero before the revolt started would have been counter-productive!

Another consideration is that *Life* was written in A.D. 100, almost two generations after the age of the Caesars had ended. By that time, Nero had become, whether deservedly or not, the most hated of all the Caesars–except perhaps for Caius. The Romans themselves would not have been impressed with Josephus' personal interactions with Nero. But the younger Poppea Sabina, on the other hand, was more of a sympathetic figure to both the Jews and the post-Caesar "modern" Roman world. Poppea could be considered to be a victim of Nero — albeit by accident.

Josephus and the Christians

Josephus, in his early life at least, had a disdainful opinion of Christianity. Regarding the Jewish nation, it has been established that later Josephus clearly believed that God had turned his countenance away from the Jews for their evil deeds, and that Jerusalem would deserve its destruction by the Romans. But how did Josephus' later opinion of the fallen Jewish nation translate over to Christians? Did Josephus feel that the Christians were destined to inherit the mantle of God's chosen people that the Jews had lost? Or, with the repugnant occult overtones of the communion ceremony, did Josephus think that Christianity was nothing more than a dark and evil spawn of Judaism?

While Josephus was visiting in the Royal court with Poppea and Nero in A.D. 63, did the subject of the Christians ever come up? Most likely it did. Josephus himself was a Jewish priest and Poppea was interested in religion, after all. What would

Josephus' comments have been if Poppea had asked about the Christians? Very likely Josephus would have expressed a negative opinion of them–perhaps in a jokingly derisive and dismissive manner.

What about King Agrippa II? Acts identifies Agrippa as at least pretending to be sympathetic to the preachings of Paul when Paul stood before him on trial in A.D. 60. Agrippa II in all of Josephus' writings comes across as a reasonable and tolerant man. It seems unlikely that Agrippa would be antagonistic to the Christians and their philosophy within the setting of the Royal court in Rome. But how much of a presence did Agrippa have in the salon of Poppea? Agrippa and his sister Bernice were very close. Bernice was famously beautiful and unattached at that time. Poppea likely would not have wanted Bernice to overshadow her at salon functions.

During that critical time in the early 60's A.D., however, there was another member of Poppea's Royal court that bears careful scrutiny in this matter–the former Second Temple High Priest Ismael.

The High Priest Ismael

In early A.D. 63, Josephus was excited at the prospect of seeing the famous city of Rome and having a chance to meet Emperor Nero. In fact, Josephus had every reason to believe that his mission to free the Jerusalem priests would be a success. Why? By that time, a former High Priest of the Second Temple was an honored member of the Royal court in Rome. His name was Ismael, the son of Fabi. While the dates are not certain, Ismael had likely been the High Priest from A.D. 59 or 60 until his resignation in A.D. 62. Ismael was then in Rome and a personal friend of the queen of the Roman Empire. Josephus had to be confident that Ismael would aid him. In fact, Ismael, in Rome, might had alerted the Jerusalem aristocrats, including Josephus' father, to the existence of the imprisoned priests in the first place.

How Ismael came to reject the High Priesthood for the Roman Royal court is an extraordinary story in itself. To the Jerusalem

Jews, the resignation of a High Priest of the Second Temple would have been an almost incomprehensible event. Josephus documents how it all came about.

> About the same time king Agrippa built himself a very large dining-room in the royal palace at Jerusalem, near to the portico. Now this palace had been erected of old by the children of Asamoneus, and was situate upon an elevation and afforded a most delightful prospect to those that had a mind to take a view of the city which prospect was desired by the king; and there he could lie down and eat and thence observe what was done in the temple; which thing, when the chief men of Jerusalem saw they were very much displeased at it; for it was not agreeable to the institutions of our country or law that what was done in the temple should be viewed by others, especially what belonged to the sacrifices. They therefore erected a wall upon the uppermost building which belonged to the inner court of the temple towards the west which wall when it was built, did not only intercept the prospect of the dining-room in the palace, but also of the western cloisters that belonged to the outer court of the temple also, where it was that the Romans kept guards for the temple at the festivals. At these doings both king Agrippa and principally Festus the procurator, were much displeased; and Festus ordered them to pull the wall down again: but the Jews petitioned him to give them leave to send an embassage about this matter to Nero; for they said they could not endure to live if any part of the temple should be demolished; and when Festus had given them leave so to do, they sent ten of their principal men to Nero, as also Ismael the high priest and Helcias, the keeper of the sacred treasure. And when Nero had heard what they had to say, he not only forgave them what they had already done, but also gave them leave to let the wall they had built stand. This was granted them in order to gratify Poppea, Nero's wife, who was a religious woman and had requested these favors of Nero and who gave order to the ten ambassadors to go their way home; but retained Helcias and Ismael as hostages with herself. As soon as the king heard this news, he gave the high priesthood to Joseph, who was called Cabi, the son of Simon, formerly high priest. (*Antiq* XX 8:11)

To summarize, a conflict arose over a construction at the Second Temple involving the High Priest and Agrippa II. Festus declined to issue a judgment in the matter so either the issue was to be left unresolved or taken up before Nero in Rome. The High Priest was adamant, so off to Rome the principals went to plead their cases.

In the course of waiting for the trial, undoubtedly there were social events at a Royal level that provided Poppea with an opportunity to get to know the High Priest Ismael. In fact, Poppea was so taken by the man that she invited him to stay in Rome as a hostage. She also became an advocate for the High Priesthood's position and, not surprisingly, Nero ruled in priest's favor. Nero's ruling against Agrippa II might have reflected a previous conflict with him, or Poppea's jealous aversion to Agrippa's sister Bernice.

The term "hostage" usually referred to a young member of Royalty from either a conquered nation, or a nation or empire that had a treaty with Rome. The hostage served as blood security to ensure the continued obedience of a client kingdom or neighboring nation. Also, in the event of future trouble, the protected hostage in Rome could be produced and returned to serve as king or ruler of that country if need be.

This situation, however, didn't strictly apply to Ismael, the High Priest of the Second Temple. Did Ismael make the case to Poppea that he feared for his life back in Jerusalem? Perhaps. Josephus hints that Ismael may well have been in danger if he remained in Jerusalem. During Ismael's tenure as High Priest, the High Priesthood hierarchy was at odds with many of the principal men of Jerusalem and not just Procurator Felix.

> About this time king Agrippa gave the high priesthood to Ismael, who was the son of Fabi. And now arose a sedition between the high priests and the principal men of the multitude of Jerusalem; each of which got them a company of the boldest sort of men and of those that loved innovations about them and became leaders to them; and when they struggled together, they did it by casting reproachful words against one another and by throwing stones also. And there was nobody to reprove them; but these disorders were done after a licentious manner in the city, as if it had no government over it. And such was the impudence and boldness that had seized on the high priests, that they had the hardiness to send their servants into the threshing-floors, to take away those tithes that were due to the priests, insomuch that it so fell out that the poorest sort of the priests died for want. To this degree did the violence of the seditious prevail over all right and justice. (*Antiq* XX 8:8)

So self-preservation could have been at least a partial motive in Ismael's abandoning Jerusalem.

Poppea was fascinated by the High Priest Ismael and his demigod status among the Jews. She wanted to keep him in Rome for the amusement and entertainment of herself and her friends. Also appealing to Poppea was that Ismael, like all of the Jewish High Priests, was skillful in astrology — ostensibly a forbidden art in Rome.

Ismael, for his part, was fully aware that he served at the pleasure of the Rome. In Rome's eyes, Ismael knew he was simply an administrator. Did Poppea make the sort of request to Ismael that was impossible to refuse?! Perhaps so, but being at the very center of power in Rome likely had an appeal of its own for   Ismael which trumped the honor of being one of the most respected and powerful men in the Jewish nation.

Ismael and Josephus

Josephus certainly knew High Priest Ismael personally as a young man. For the wealthy and high born in Jerusalem and those who worked in the Second Temple on a daily basis, the world was a small one.

Josephus would have been 23 when Ismael took over Ananias as the Second Temple High Priest in A.D. 59. By all indications, the high-born Josephus was a young priest solidly on the fast track for power within the Temple. Unlike Paul the Apostle, Josephus' bloodlines were pure and impeccable. Josephus would have been known to Ismael, and he likely knew him on a first-name basis.

The year A.D. 62 was an eventful one for the High Priesthood. Ismael resigned early in the year. Joseph Cabi served as High Priest for a few months at most, and then Ananus, the son of Ananus, was appointed to that position for three months late in the year. In fact, if we can be flexible with the dates, it is entirely possible that Josephus was sent on his mission to ransom the imprisoned priests in Rome not by his father, but by the "renegade" High Priest Ananus during his short tenure in late A.D. 62.

Flavius Josephus writes that he was in Rome in A.D. 63 and probably saw the Royal couple in the middle of that year at the earliest. If Ismael was in Rome as well during that time, which by all indications he was, Josephus would have surely socialized with him. The Jewish priest Helcias had also agreed to stay in Rome with Ismael on Poppea's invitation. Probably other Jewish attendants remained in Rome as part of Ismael's entourage as well. How could Josephus have not met them all?! Curiously, however, no meeting of this sort is mentioned by Josephus in his autobiography.

The Succession of High Priests

Ananias had been appointed as High Priest by the brother of Agrippa I, King Herod of Chalcis, in A.D. 48. This was coincident with the appointment of Ventidius Cumanus as Judean procurator by Emperor Claudius.

> But now Herod, king of Chalcis, removed Joseph, the son of Camydus, from the high priesthood and made Ananias, the son of Nebedeu, his successor. And now it was that Cumanus came as successor to Tiberius Alexander; as also that Herod, brother of Agrippa the great king, departed this life, in the eighth year of the reign of Claudius Caesar. (*Antiq* XX 5:2)

In the years A.D. 51-52, a considerable amount of turmoil and dissension erupted in the Jewish East. Events became so serious and widespread that in A.D. 52 the Syrian Governor Quadratus traveled south with a large contingent of soldiers to establish peace. This was the same period of time when Josephus' father decided to send him away from Jerusalem and into the Judean desert for several years of religious training. There, the young Josephus studied under Banus, the ascetic (*Life* 1).

President Quadratus suspected that the Judean Jews were plotting a full-scale revolt against the empire and undoubtedly some were. After determining the perpetrators, Quadratus executed many of them and sent several Jewish leaders back to Rome for trial by Emperor Claudius. Among those sent were two of the Jerusalem Temple High Priesthood, who were placed in bondage for the trip. One of them was Ananias–a High Priest in chains!

> but still he (Quadratus) sent away Ananias the high priest and Ananus the commander [of the temple], in bonds to Rome, to give an account of what they had done to Claudius Caesar. (*Antiq* XX 6:2)

The possibility of such a powerful Temple figure as the elder Ananus also being slapped in chains and sent to Rome for an Imperial interrogation does not sound likely. At that time, Ananus would have been in his seventies. Josephus, in a following verse, does not mention such a humiliating episode occurring in Ananus' life (*Antiq* XX 9:1). However, if Quadratus meant to send the two most powerful members of the Jerusalem High Priesthood to Rome to stand before Claudius, they would certainly have been the current High Priest Ananias and the elder Ananus. But it is possible that it was the younger Ananus, the later High Priest, who was sent to Rome instead.

In *Wars*, Josephus writes about this same incident, but gives slightly different details.

> After which he (Quadratus) went to Cesarea and crucified all those whom Cumanus had taken alive; and when from thence he was come to the city Lydda, he heard the affair of the Samaritans and sent for eighteen of the Jews, whom he had learned to have been concerned in that fight and beheaded them; but he sent two others of those that were of the greatest power among them and both Jonathan and Ananias, the high priests, as also Artanus the son of this Ananias and certain others that were eminent among the Jews, to Caesar (*Wars* II 12:6)

In this selection, Josephus writes that Jonathan accompanies Ananias as well, referring to both of them as High Priests. There were several high-ranking members of the High Priesthood sent to Rome, so this is not an issue of concern. All returned to the East with powers intact.

Back in Judea, Ananias assumed his duties as the actual High Priest. While Josephus is not clear on this return of Ananias, the book of Luke is unequivocal that it was the High Priest Ananias who put Paul the Apostle on trial in A.D. 58.

And while it was Ananias who was the driving force against Paul the Apostle in A.D. 58, the High Priest Ismael was involved two years later. Without question, the High Priest Ismael knew about and endorsed, the third trial of Paul in A.D. 60 in Caesarea. Then, the High Priesthood had lost none of their zeal against Paul—he still had to be executed, even if it meant hiring assassins.

In Josephus, we read about Ananias being sent to Rome A.D. 52, then the High Priest Jonathan being murdered in A.D. 56, and then Ismael, the son of fabi, becoming the High Priest "about that time." This is unusual for Josephus, who is usually very accurate on the dates of High Priest succession.

Jonathan, whether he was the current High Priest or not, took to relentlessly criticizing the new Procurator Antonius Felix for his criminal activity. This boldness was to eventually bring about Jonathan's assassination.

> Certain of those robbers went up to the city, as if they were going to worship God, while they had daggers under their garments and by thus mingling themselves among the multitude they slew Jonathan (*Antiq* XX 8:5)

The year can be fixed by the relative placement of the preceding paragraph in *Antiquities* which deals with Nero's first year as Emperor—A.D. 54.

> For in the first year of the reign of Nero, upon the death of Azizus, king of Emesa, Soemus, his brother, succeeded in his kingdom and Aristobulus, the son of Herod, king of Chalcis, was intrusted by Nero with the government of the Lesser Armenia. Caesar also bestowed on Agrippa a certain part of Galilee, Tiberias and Tarichae and ordered them to submit to his jurisdiction. He gave him also Julias, a city of Perea, with fourteen villages that lay about it. (*Antiq* XX 8:4)

According to Josephus, Ismael, the son of Fadi, was given the High Priest's position by King Agrippa II after the murder of Jonathan by the Sicarii, an act that was orchestrated by Procurator Felix.

> About this time king Agrippa gave the high priesthood to Ismael, who was the son of Fabi.(*Antiq* XX 8:8)

It is unfortunate that Josephus used "about this time" rather than a solid date for Ismael's appointment, or at least linked Ismael's succession to a preceding High Priest.

It is accepted that Porcius Festus became procurator of Judea and Samaria in A.D. 60. How long did the dispute between King Agrippa II and the Temple priests drag on before Festus decided to send the case to Rome? A year or more is a reasonable estimate. In fact, Festus might been so pleased with his seamless disposition earlier of Paul the Apostle in A.D. 60 that he did the same for this dispute. So, in late in A.D. 61 or early A.D. 62, both the High Priest Ismael and King Agrippa II, and their entourages, traveled to Rome to argue before Nero. It should be noted that it was the priests, and not Agrippa II, who requested an Imperial judgment.

In Rome, Poppea requested the Ismael stay in her salon, and he agreed. But did he have an agenda? In Rome, did Ismael discover that Paul the Apostle was not only alive but a free man, and active in the Christian community? And did Ismael plan revenge against the Apostle while in Rome and a member of Poppea's salon?

Or can it be hypothesized that Ismael knew beforehand that Paul was in Rome, and maneuvered the controversy with Agrippa to get his men to Rome to assess the situation with the subversive Christian community and Paul?

Interlude: A Meeting in Rome?

Paul was shipwrecked in A.D. 60 and had many other subsequent adventures before finally reaching Rome. When Paul arrived–still chained to his Roman guard–in A.D. 61, no Roman authority was there to meet him. As has been seen, eventually Paul became a free man and decided to make Rome his home, settling down within the Christian community. Paul was already famous in Christian circles and he would have been immediately regarded as a leader. Acts ends with Paul being in Rome for two years which would bring the narrative in Acts up to A.D. 63.

> ^{28:30}And he abode two whole years in his own hired dwelling and received all that went in unto him, ^{28:31}preaching the kingdom of God and teaching the things concerning the Lord Jesus Christ with all boldness, none forbidding him. (Acts)

Josephus was also in Rome in A.D. 63 and the former High Priest Ismael was in Rome as well. Then, the Jewish and Christian communities were relatively small. It is extraordinary to imagine these three men interacting in some way–even if accidentally meeting on a Roman street.

If anything can be said about Paul the Apostle, it is that he was not shy about preaching the Gospel of Jesus–and aggressively–no matter where he was. Rome was a tolerant city in those times, though admittedly not on the level of an Athens or Ephesus. But Rome had several areas set aside for public discourse and open debate. Years before in Jerusalem, Paul the Apostle had been bold enough to preach around the city gates and in the shadow of the Second Temple where his life had been threatened. Would he have been any less courageous in Rome?

It is known for a surety that Ismael was part of the Royal court of Nero and Poppea in the months and years leading up to the A.D. 64 fires of Rome. Who could deny that the former High Priest Ismael at times discussed the Christians with Poppea and Nero during the frequent feasts of the Royal court? Here was a new religion, originating in Jerusalem, where a man–a miracle worker!–was resurrected from the dead by the power of God, and who promised a form of everlasting life to his followers. And there was a brilliant star that marked the birth of this man, and his followers could perform miracles under this man's authority. Core to this "Christian" religion was a ceremony called the communion which mystically connected the followers with the now-departed prophet, and with undercurrents suggestive of cannibalism and the occult. All this would have been utterly fascinating to Queen Poppea and might have partially explained her attraction to both Josephus and Ismael.

When the subject of Christianity came up in the Royal court of Nero and Poppea, rest assured both Josephus and Ismael–if present–would have been quick to excoriate the Christians for their dark rituals, trick miracles and delusional promises to the masses. The resurrection? The two priests would have asserted that Jesus' dead body was simply stolen from its tomb and then reburied in a secret place by his followers–or worse. The priests would likely go on to say that the intent of the Nazarenes was to fool the gullible Jews into partaking of the communion ceremony–a hideous ritual–which then corrupted them forever. Yes, what a perverse religion Christianity was! The two priests might have then recited stories about the many false Messiahs that had plagued the Jewish East over the centuries and especially in the 100 years since the Roman occupation.

Speculating further, it would not have been out of character for the curious Poppea to arrange for Paul the Apostle to talk before the salon or perhaps at one of her secret gatherings. Paul was a very well educated Roman citizen after all. It is documented that Poppea had "secret councils" with forbidden astrologers (Tacitus *Histories* 1:22). Why not one with a Christian?

For his part, the Apostle Paul would have welcomed the chance to preach before Poppea and Nero. In fact, if Paul happened to find himself within earshot of Emperor Nero (not an impossibility in a city of only a million people), it is easy to envision the Apostle shouting out a proselytizing message about Jesus. Nero considered himself an artist and was fond of giving public performances. Paul the Apostle, a Roman citizen, could have easily planned an encounter with the emperor at one of them.

> ..teaching the things concerning the Lord Jesus Christ with all boldness..
> (Acts 28:31)

Relevant to this possibility, Paul himself made a revealing statement that is reported in Acts. On his way to Rome as a prisoner, Paul was on a ship that was being threatened by one of the worst storms ever to hit the eastern Mediterranean. Paul took comfort by the presence of an Angel.

> For there stood by me this night an angel of the God whose I am, whom also I serve, saying, Fear not, Paul; thou must stand before Caesar: (Acts 27:23-24)

Did Paul fulfill the Angel's prophecy in a literal sense and indeed stand before Nero? If so, such a trial was not recorded in Acts. It is not out of the question that Paul, a Roman citizen after all, had been simply and cordially invited into Poppea's regular salon to give a discourse on Jesus and Christianity.

An exciting prospect, to be sure! In a single opulent chamber would be Nero, Poppea and other luminaries of the Roman Empire, perhaps with Ismael and Josephus there as well, all reclining on gold-framed satin couches and enjoying a Royal feast served by dozens of attendants. If Agrippa II had been in Rome, he would have also been there. Along with him might have been his beautiful sisters Drusilla and Bernice. Did Poppea also invite Peter the Apostle? Peter was known to associate with Gentiles which had gotten him into early trouble with the Jerusalem Church (Acts 11:3), so on that level he would not hesitate to come. If Peter was there as well as Paul, what a Christian *tour de force* it would have been!

If such a gathering occurred, it would have been the high point in Paul the Apostle's ministry. Paul had spent more than 20 years preparing for this. There was not a challenge to Christian dogma that Paul had not heard and did not have a pat answer for. His delivery would have been smooth and polished. Did any of the powerful Romans present rise to debate him? Did the Judean priests challenge him? The imperious Poppea likely encouraged vigorous debate between her guests and was excited by it.

At some point did the skeptical Romans laugh or become derisive at some of Paul's statements? It is easy to see Paul getting angry if he felt he was not being taken seriously. Did the hot-tempered Paul insult Ismael, or insult Nero himself, or even Poppea? If so, Paul may have been the first victim of Nero's wrath against the Christians and the *primus* reason behind Nero's subsequent persecution of all Christians in the aftermath of the fires in Rome that were to come.

In all fairness, however, Josephus never admits to meeting Nero, and Acts never documents a meeting between Paul the Apostle and any of the Royal family of Rome. Tacitus simply ignores Paul the Apostle altogether, although he documents the persecutions in detail and with a measure of sympathy.

As for the former High Priest Ismael, it is reasonable to assume that he was a high-profile member of the Royal court during Josephus' visit and for years afterward, though nothing of that nature is documented. To Poppea, Ismael was very much a "trophy" hostage, and she would have expected him to attend with diligence her social gatherings.

The Death of Ismael

Josephus gives a tantalizing reference to the death of Ismael in *Wars*. During the course of the Jerusalem siege of A.D. 70, General Titus gave refuge to many High Priests and their families.

> Some also there were who, watching a proper opportunity when they might quietly get away, fled to the Romans, of whom were the high priests Joseph and Jesus and of the sons of high priests three, whose father was Ishmael, who was beheaded in Cyrene..(*Wars* VI 2:2)

We learn from Josephus that by at least by A.D. 70, Ismael had died. Beheaded in Cyrene! A very bizarre death, indeed, and in a very strange land for a man of such importance.

Cyrene was a former Greek colony in North Africa that, more than a century before, General Pompey had turned into a Roman possession. Cyrene was located along the southern Mediterranean coastline 500 miles to the west of Alexandria. The population was mostly Greek, but the Jewish population had been steadily growing under Rome's control.

Early in the Jewish revolt in A.D. 66, there was an insurrection in Alexandria that was quickly put down by the Romans. But it resulted in the deaths, according to Josephus, of thousands of Jews. During the Jewish revolt, many of the surviving zealots fled west to Cyrene where they apparently enjoyed a measure of sanctuary in city's remote location. This refugee population — many of them criminal Sicarii — dramatically increased as Rome gained the upper hand in the Jewish wars.

How did Ismael get to Cyrene? It can be speculated that he perhaps grew bored of Nero's Royal court. Early in the course of the revolt, Ismael might have volunteered to be a negotiator in Cyrene and other cities outside of the Jewish East — cities that did not possess their own Jewish prefect or alabarch. As former High Priest, the respected Ismael could have been especially useful to Nero in certain delicate situations.

One can only imagine the sort of disastrous diplomatic mission to zealot-infested Cyrene that resulted in Ismael's own beheading! If, however, Ismael had played a role in Nero's savage conduct towards the Christians years earlier, such a fate would have been justly earned.

Chapter 19   Fires of Rome

..Nero fastened the guilt and inflicted the most exquisite tortures on a class hated for their abominations, called Christians.. (*Annuls* 15:44)

On the 19th of July A.D. 64, a devastating fire erupted in the city of Rome and raged for days, resulting in the destruction of most of the city. Rome then had an estimated population of over a million people. In the fire, thousands of people–if not tens of thousands–lost their lives as a result of the fires, and hundreds of thousands displaced from their homes. It was a catastrophe of the first order and a peacetime disaster on a scale never before seen in the empire.

> Rome ..is divided into fourteen districts, four of which remained uninjured, three were leveled to the ground, while in the other seven were left only a few shattered, half-burnt relics of houses. (*Annuls* 15:40)

The original fire burned for five days. After dying down considerably, it began anew in a different part of the city–a section that Nero coveted for the site of a proposed new palace. Was there a connection? Did agents of Nero "extend" the fire on purpose?

Ancient Rome

In A.D. 64, the established city of Rome was more than 800 years old. Over the centuries as the population grew, Rome's borders had been pushed across the Tiber River and far out into the surrounding hills. It didn't help that Rome had many aqueducts bringing water in from great distances which could be used to fight the fire. The aqueduct system, combined with a sophisticated below-ground sewer system, in a sense made the situation worse. High-density housing was possible with those civic amenities in place. Fire safety then was a minor afterthought to city architects and builders.

Most of Rome's narrow and twisting streets were tightly flanked by towering, three-story, wood-and-brick buildings. Fire breaks were an unknown concept, and many of the buildings shared a common wall. In most homes, cooking fires were maintained, and in the winter fires were necessary for heat.

A century before Nero, Marcus Crassus had ruled the Roman Empire as one of the First Triumvirate, along with Julius Caesar and Sextus Pompey. Best known today as the executioner of the slave-rebel Spartacus, Crassus was the richest man in the Rome and remains as one of the richest men known in all of ancient history. He became wealthy by buying up fire-ravaged properties in Rome and renovating them or rebuilding them completely. The rumor was that agents of Crassus had set many of those fires purposefully, hoping to buy properties cheaply after they had been ravaged. In the fires of A.D. 64, was Nero following the example of Crassus?

Accusations of arson were soon leveled against Nero. Afterward, certainly, Nero wasted no time in building his masterwork, the "Golden Palace," in the area of the three hills where the fires had been the most devastating. Historians tend to agree that Nero at least encouraged the fires to burn in the proper direction after their accidental beginning.

> And he (Nero) acted accordingly: for, pretending to be disgusted with the old buildings and the narrow and winding streets, he set the city on fire so openly, that many of consular rank caught his own household servants on their property with tow and torches in their hands, but durst not meddle with them. (Sue *Nero* XXXVIII)

(Nero).. secretly sent out men who pretended to be drunk or engaged in other kinds of mischief and caused them at first to set fire to one or two or even several buildings in different parts of the city, so that people were at their wits' end, not being able to find any beginning of the trouble nor to put an end to it, (Dio 62:16)

The legend turned aphorism that Nero fiddled as Rome burned is a false one. Suetonius writes that Nero dressed up in "tragic" costume and sang mournfully while the fires raged around him.

..a rumour had gone forth everywhere that, at the very time when the city was in flames, the emperor appeared on a private stage and sang of the destruction of Troy, comparing present misfortunes with the calamities of antiquity. (*Annuls* 15:39)

This fire (Nero) beheld from a tower in the house of Mecaenas and "being greatly delighted," as he said, "with the beautiful effects of the conflagration," he sung a poem on the ruin of Troy, in the tragic dress he used on the stage. (Sue *Nero* XXXVIII)

Nero ascended to the roof of the palace, from which there was the best general view of the greater part of the conflagration and assuming the lyre-player's garb, he sang the "Capture of Troy," as he styled the song himself, though to the enemies of the spectators it was the Capture of Rome. (Dio 62:17)

The Christians as Scapegoats

Nero was keenly aware of the rumors that he had started the fires. When the enormity of the pain, suffering, and loss from the fires became apparent, Nero realized that he had to divert attention away from himself. The fire damage was so widespread that it would not do to blame it on just a single individual. A conspiracy would have to be invented. Nero decided to blame the Christians.

Nero first arranged for several Christians to be tortured into a confession. This accomplished and publicized, excoriation and revenge upon the rest of the Christians followed. The punishment was severe and carried out with a righteous vengeance. At the time, probably no more than a few thousand Christians were living in Rome. Nero knew that the Roman people loved gladiatorial contests. When there was no public outcry over the initial killings, Nero turned the executions of the Christians into public spectacles, thinking that the performances would help improve his tarnished image.

The historian Publius Tacitus had a low opinion of both the Jews and the Christians, but even he was appalled at the tortures Nero chose to inflict upon the religious sect.

> ..Nero fastened the guilt and inflicted the most exquisite tortures on a class hated for their abominations, called Christians by the populace. Christus, from whom the name had its origin, suffered the extreme penalty during the reign of Tiberius at the hands of one of our procurators, Pontius Pilatus and a most mischievous superstition, thus checked for the moment, again broke out not only in Judaea, the first source of the evil, but even in Rome, where all things hideous and shameful from every part of the world find their centre and become popular. Accordingly, an arrest was first made of all who pleaded guilty; then, upon their information, an immense multitude was convicted, not so much of the crime of firing the city, as of hatred against mankind. Mockery of every sort was added to their deaths. Covered with the skins of beasts, they were torn by dogs and perished, or were nailed to crosses, or were doomed to the flames and burnt, to serve as a nightly illumination, when daylight had expired. Nero offered his gardens for the spectacle and was exhibiting a show in the circus, while he mingled with the people in the dress of a charioteer or stood aloft on a car. Hence, even for criminals who deserved extreme and exemplary punishment, there arose a feeling of compassion; for it was not, as it seemed, for the public good, but to glut one man's cruelty, that they were being destroyed. (*Annuls* 15:44)

Two of the most famous early Christians lost their lives in Nero's persecutions. At the time of the fires in A.D. 64, the Apostle Paul was in Rome and likely functioning as a leader of the Christian Church. He had arrived there as a prisoner for trial in front of Nero only three years before, sent by Judean Procurator Porcius Festus. Festus, however, had not sent ahead an indictment and no one in authority in Rome seemed to care about Paul one way or the other. As a result, Paul the Apostle had been living in Rome as a free man.

The Apostle Peter, an original Disciple and possibly Paul's rival for Church leadership, was also in Rome at that time and died with Paul in the same series of persecutions. According to Eusebius, Paul was beheaded by the Romans, and Peter was crucified–upside down by his own request (Eusebius *History* II:25).

Reasons for Persecution

Given what is known of Nero's life and reign, what can be concluded about Nero's sudden actions against the Christians in A.D. 64? After all, the Christians were just one religious sect of many that had found a home and flourished in libertine Rome. At that time, Rome was by far the greatest city in the world and known for its religious tolerance. Roman culture was remarkably accommodating to most indigenous provincial religions and harmless superstitions among the conquered nations of the empire. That policy was one of the keys to the empire's longevity and stability. Additionally, probably no more than a few thousand souls—if that—in Rome called themselves Christians. What caused them to receive Nero's diabolic focus and be accused by him of setting the devastating fires of the great city–a preposterous accusation on its face?

The true causes and inciting events will always be speculative. It is well-documented, however, that Paul the Apostle was an incendiary religious figure wherever he went. Over the course of his 26 year ministry, he became the target of assassins on many occasions in Damascus, Jerusalem, Caesarea, and other places. After Paul's arrival in Rome in A.D. 61, how much of a disruptive force did he eventually become? There is no reason to think that in Rome Paul changed his confrontational style of evangelism. Did the common people of Rome, or the Roman Jews themselves, complain to the authorities about Paul? Did Paul disrupt the Jewish Synagogues? Did he disturb the temple ceremonies of pagan sects?

From the Book of Acts, it is known Paul thought nothing of insulting a Jerusalem High Priest–considered by the Jews to be semi-divine. Would Paul be any less reluctant to publicly malign a Roman emperor–or an empress–under the right circumstances? If so, Paul could have made himself and by proxy his fellow Christians a very convenient and tempting target for blame when Nero needed one.

It is known that the former High Priest Ismael was a part of Nero's social circle in the early 60s A.D. The Christian community of Rome could not have been happy when Ismael relocated to Rome and had the apparent ear of the Royal couple. The fearless Paul himself probably didn't care, ready to be a crusader for Jesus no matter what the circumstances. But remember that it was the High Priest Ismael in A.D. 60 who demanded that Festus either execute Paul, or allow Paul to be murdered by assassins that the High Priesthood would arrange for.

And now Ismael was in Rome.

Indeed, a strong case can be made that Ismael, the priest Helcias, and their attendants at least contributing to whatever anti-Christian feelings were being popularized in the Royal court of Rome just before the great fires of A.D. 64. Josephus, too, in his stay in the Royal salon in A.D. 63 would have expressed negative opinions about the Christians if the subject ever came up.

But a   darker picture can also be painted. If the High Priesthood conspired to eliminate the Christian leaders in Jerusalem two years before, did Ismael somehow engineer the Christian persecutions in Rome with similar foresight?   And were both actions coordinated?

The Death of Poppea

Poppea Sabina died ingloriously not long after the Christian persecutions.   In A.D. 65. Nero kicked her in the stomach, supposedly in a bout of rage. Poppea was again pregnant at the time.

After the conclusion of the games Poppaea died from a casual outburst of rage in her husband, who felled her with a kick when she was pregnant. That there was poison I cannot believe, though some writers so relate, from hatred rather than from belief, for the emperor was desirous of children and wholly swayed by love of his wife. Her body was not consumed by fire according to Roman usage, but after the custom of foreign princes was filled with fragrant spices and embalmed and then consigned to the sepulchre of the Julii. She had, however, a public funeral and Nero himself from the rostra eulogized her beauty, her lot in having been the mother of a deified child and fortune's other gifts, as though they were virtues.

...the death of Poppaea, though a public grief, was a delight to those who recall(ed) the past thought of her shamelessness and cruelty, (*Annuls* 16:6-7)

Dio relates a slightly different story. Nero had leaped upon Poppea when she was prone in an accidentally playful–or malicious–act. Poppea met her end due to internal bleeding.

Sabina also perished at this time through an act of Nero's; either accidentally or intentionally he had leaped upon her with his feet while she was pregnant. The extremes of luxury indulged in by this Sabina I will indicate in the briefest terms. She cause gilded shoes to be put on the mules that drew her and caused five hundred asses that had recently foaled to be milked daily that she might bathe in their milk. For she bestowed the greatest pains on the beauty and brilliancy of her person and this is why, when she noticed in a mirror one day that her appearance was not comely, she prayed that she might die before she passed her prime. Nero missed her..greatly after her death..(Dio 62:27-28).

Nero mourned the death of Poppea and he was never the same afterward. He threw himself into his singing and acting with a delusional intensity born out of grief. Nero later spent much of his time in Greece, perhaps to get away from the memory of Poppea. Dio relates this interesting bit of information.

The masks that he wore were sometimes made to resemble the characters he was portraying and sometimes bore his own likeness; but the women's masks were all fashioned after the features of Sabina, in order that, though dead, she might still take part in the spectacle. (Dio 63:9)

After the death of Poppea, Nero invited Antonia to become his third wife. Antonia was the daughter of Emperor Claudius and Claudius' second wife, Aelia Paetina. Through this, Nero was perhaps attempting to recapture the popularity he had lost through his divorce and execution of Octavia. When Antonia declined his kind invitation, Nero couldn't bear the rejection and had her executed as well.

Nero then decided to marry a slave boy named Sporus! Sporus had the unfortunate luck to look like Poppea, and so he was castrated and did, in fact, legally become Nero's wife.

The Last of the Caesars

Only four years after the beginning of the Christian persecutions, Nero would be forced into suicide. Nero spent much of these delusional later years touring Greece, giving artistic performances and sponsoring shows and gladiatorial contests–all while running the Roman Empire from afar with his usual high level of inattention.

Nero was still in Greece when the Jews revolted in A.D. 66. After the unrelated death of Syrian President Cestius Gallus, General Lucinius Mucianus was sent to replace him and deal with the situation. But Mucianus met with a poorly documented defeat at the hands of the Jews. Realizing the seriousness of the situation, Nero then assigned one of his most experienced generals, Vespasian, to settle the affairs of the Jewish lands.

> While Nero was still in Greece, the Jews revolted openly and he sent Vespasian against them. (Dio 63:1)

Nero's demise began with the boldness of the leader of the Gauls, Julius Vindex, who was also a Roman Senator. Disgusted at Nero's behavior and murderous delusions, he publicly called for revolution. Not wanting the supreme power for himself, he proclaimed Sulpicious Galba as the one best fit to rule.

Vindex's invectives were damning, but popular with many who heard them, as Dio documents.

"he (Nero) has despoiled the whole Roman world, because he has destroyed all the flower of the senate, because he debauched and then killed his mother and does not preserve even the semblance of sovereignty. Many murders, robberies and outrages, it is true, have often been committed by others; but as for the other deeds committed by Nero, how could one find words fittingly to describe them? I have seen him, my friends and allies,— believe me,— I have seen that man (if man he is who has married Sporus and been given in marriage to Pythagoras), in the circle of the theatre, that is, in the orchestra, sometimes holding the lyre and dressed in loose tunic and buskins and again wearing in general-soled shoes and mask..I have often heard him sing, play the herald and act in tragedies. I have seen him in chains, hustled about as a miscreant, heavy with child, aye, in the travail of childbirth..Will anyone, then, style such a person Caesar and emperor and Augustus? Never! Let no one abuse those sacred titles. (Dio 63:22)

Galba was then the governor of Spain, a respected elder Roman with his own strong military force. Vindex's call to revolt was agreeable to the Gauls and to Galba. The soldiers of Gaul and Spain both proclaimed Galba emperor. The governor of Germany, Rufus, ostensibly loyal to the Caesars, then moved his own legions to counter the advancing army of Vindex. Vindex arranged to meet with Rufus and turned Rufus against Nero and into an ally (Dio 63: 22-24). But through a military misunderstanding, some of Rufus' forces slaughtered a number of Gauls, causing Vindex to commit suicide as a result. Seeing opportunity, Rufus' soldiers then wanted Rufus himself to assume the throne, but the German governor refused and continued to support Galba.

As Nero's former colleague Galba led the Spanish provinces in revolt, other ambitious Roman generals maneuvered their own legions into strategic positions in anticipation of Nero's death or abdication. Nero was losing popular support, and there was no other Caesar to turn to–Nero was the last of them.

Nero was driven from power by evil tidings and rumours rather than by the sword. (Tacitus *Histories* 1:89)

Dio writes that the emperor thought of escaping to Alexandria in Egypt. There, Nero had delusions that he could leave his

Imperial past behind and support himself by singing and playing the lyre in public performances.

> Now that he had been abandoned by everybody alike, he began forming plans to kill the senators, burn down the city and sail to Alexandria. He dropped this hint in regard to his future course: "Even though we be driven from our empire, yet this little talent shall support us there." To such a pitch of folly, indeed, had he come as to believe that he could live for a moment as a private citizen and especially as a lyre-player. (Dio 63:27)

The Roman Senate then voted Galba emperor. The Praetorian guard with no more Caesars waiting in the wings also firmly supported Galba. At the time, Nero was in fact preparing to move to Alexandria and abandon Rome.

> He (Nero) was on the point of putting these measures into effect when the senate withdrew the guard that surrounded him and then, entering the camp, declared him an enemy and chose Galba in his place..when he perceived that he had been deserted also by his body-guards (he happened to be sleeping in a certain garden), he undertook to flee. Accordingly, he put on shabby clothing, mounted a horse no better than his attire and with his head covered he rode while it was yet night towards an estate of Phaon, an imperial freedman, in company with Phaon himself, Epaphroditus and Sporus. (Dio 63:27)

With the loss of senate confirmation and the loss of the Praetorians, Nero fled Rome on horseback seeking safety. He later committed suicide in a small village near Rome.

Nero's last words were not about the empire, but about his own cruel fate.

> What an artist is now about to perish! (Sue *Nero* XLIX).

A secretary assisted Nero in his suicide and his wish was granted that he not be beheaded. Nero died in June of A.D. 68, being 31 years of age. Nero's long-time companion Acte and his wife Sporus, attended to his modest funeral.

Nero in History

Both Tacitus and Suetonius wrote their histories about Nero two generations after the fact, and Dio wrote almost 200 years later. All three of these Roman historians used sources largely written during the Flavian period, an era that was openly hostile to the Caesars. In contrast to what these historians suggest, there are indications that Nero was actually quite popular with the Roman people, even up until his suicide. Under Nero, wars were few and corn was plentiful. Nero provided ample and exciting spectacles, contests, and theater for the common people to enjoy. Nero himself even performed publicly for his subjects, an endearing factor that should not be lightly dismissed. While Nero was a murderous brute by modern standards, a sovereign in those days was expected to be such–to a degree. After centuries of enduring pointless civil wars, the common people realized it was far better to have ambitious aristocrats kill each other off rather than to recruit armies and throw the entire empire into the chaos of war.

Flavius Josephus read many if not all of the contemporary biographies of Nero and disapproved of them. Josephus' opinion should carry no small weight, as he lived through Nero's reign. Moreover, in all likelihood Josephus had met Emperor Nero personally while in Rome as a young man.

> ... for there have been a great many who have composed the history of Nero; some of which have departed from the truth..out of hatred to him and the great ill-will which they bare him, (and) have so impudently raved against him with their lies, that they justly deserve to be condemned..(*Antiq* XX 8:3)

Josephus, of course, had little sympathy for the Christians, and did not mention Nero's persecution of them in his own writings.

Chapter 20   The Jewish Revolt

..(Josephus) put up a secret prayer to God and said, "Since it pleaseth thee, who hast created the Jewish nation, to depress the same and since all their good fortune is gone over to the Romans and since thou hast made choice of this soul of mine to foretell what is to come to pass hereafter, I willingly give them my hands and am content to live. And I protest openly that I do not go over to the Romans as a deserter of the Jews, but as a minister from thee." (*Wars* III 8:3)

The final chapters will discuss the Jewish revolt of A.D. 66 and the role that the Jewish General Joseph bar Matthias (later to become Flavius Josephus) played in it. As a captured enemy general, to what extent did Josephus undermine the efforts of the Jewish rebels? Josephus was certainly a traitor to the Jewish people, but did he remain true to the "Jewish" god he originally trained to serve as a priest? The fall of the Jewish East is also interesting in that the early Christians felt this was God's vengeance against the Jews for the crucifixion of Jesus.

Previously, Josephus' early life has been examined with particular focus on his trip to Rome at the age of 26. There, Josephus met with Nero's wife Poppea, and probably Nero, and successfully arranged for several imprisoned Jerusalem priests to be freed. By late A.D. 63, Josephus had returned to Jerusalem, presumably with the priests in tow.

Josephus' stature increased with his successful embassy to Rome, and he was on the fast track to a powerful position within the Jerusalem High Priesthood. But Josephus also returned to a Jerusalem that was now administered by Albinus, a new Roman procurator. Albinus was not nearly as reasonable or as easy to work with as Festus had been—who died suddenly in office and might have been assassinated. Albinus served ingloriously for two years and was then replaced by Flores—who was worse.

> But then Albinus, who succeeded Festus, did not execute his office as the other had done; nor was there any sort of wickedness that could be named but he had a hand in it. ..And although such was the character of Albinus, yet did Gessius Florus who succeeded him, demonstrate him to have been a most excellent person, upon the comparison; (*Wars* II 14:1)

Gessius Florus and Revolt

According to Josephus, Florus gained his position because his wife, Cleopatra, was a friend of Nero's wife Poppea (*Antiq* XX 11:1). Poppea was also a personal friend of Josephus. Likely this connection put Josephus and his family automatically on very good terms with new procurator Florus. At the very least, Florus and his wife probably knew something of the young priest Josephus who so impressed Poppea in Rome two years before.

But if the Jews were expecting a respite under Florus, they were disappointed. Florus' level of avarice, corruption, and personal penchant for violence against the Jews was unmatched. Florus condoned robbery in the Judean countryside as long as he received a portion of the ill-gotten gains. Convicted murders and other dangerous criminals could buy their way out of prison. Florus personally encouraged the gang of assassins called Sicarii–so called because of the small daggers they hid under their cloaks–and financially benefited from their for-hire killings. Murders of principal men were in fact taking place routinely, even in the Temple courtyard. No one in Jerusalem was safe!

In the countryside, outbreaks of sedition were commonplace as the Jews reacted against their new procurator. Eventually, the principal men of Jerusalem openly considered sending a delegation to Rome to petition Nero for Florus' removal. Florus learned of it and became worried, for he knew that he could not count on Nero's support. Nero's wife Poppea had been "accidentally" killed by the emperor only months after Florus' appointment, and she had been his strongest supporter. What would the unpredictable Nero do?

The Jews had similarly petitioned Emperor Claudius 15 years before seeking relief from the corrupt Judean Procurator Cumanus. At that trial, Claudius was sympathetic toward the Jews' pleading. Not only was Cumanus removed from his position and banished from Rome, but Cumanus' tribune and criminal partner, Celer, was sent back to Jerusalem for a public beheading (*Antiq* XX 6:3). And just four years previously, Jewish petitioners had convinced Nero to remove Procurator Felix and bring him to Rome for trial for crimes similar to what Flores was now accused of. Felix escaped conviction, but just barely.

Florus concluded that the only way to save his position was to force the Jews into an outright armed rebellion. Emperor Nero would then have no choice but to send in the Roman army and settle things in his–and Rome's–favor.

In early A.D. 66, Flores found an opportunity to incite the Jews to revolt. There occurred a minor dispute in Caesarea between the Jewish population and the larger population of Syrian Greeks. On a pretext of needing funds to protect the Jews, Florus dispatched a number of horsemen to Jerusalem to steal 18 talents of silver from the Second Temple Corban. This was accomplished despite the Jews' vociferous protests and demonstrations. It was a sacrilege to take God's money out of God's house for any profane purpose!

In response to the unrest, Florus marched into Jerusalem with his auxiliary army and killed nearly 4,000 Jewish citizens (400 if the Josephus "factor" is used). This murderous act inflamed the Jews even more. From that moment onward, there would be no turning back. Florus had achieved his objective, and for the Jews the rebellion had begun.

Early Jewish Victory

The rebellion began with scattered insurrections against Roman officials in the Judean countryside and soon spread to include Jerusalem itself. In A.D. 66, Cestius Gallus was the president of Syria and had ultimate military control over the eastern empire. In the early summer of that year, Florus persuaded him to intervene in Judea and quell the sedition that Florus himself had created. With a single Roman legion and supporting forces, the Syrian governor quickly subdued the Judean countryside. He stopped short, however, of attempting a conquest of Jerusalem. Gallus knew that it would be next to impossible to take the well-fortified city with his relatively small force.

Camped within sight of the north wall of Jerusalem and with the towers of Antonia and the palace towers of Herod dominating the skyline, Gallus hoped that by his decisive actions in the Judean countryside the Jews had learned their lesson and would accept Rome authority. With no small measure of optimism, if not delusion, Gallus ordered his forces to depart from their encampment, satisfied that this show of force had accomplished its objective.

Gallus' retreat, however, was seen as cowardice by the Jews. The seditious elements in Jerusalem and surrounding towns regrouped and went on the attack. Gallus and his retreating legion were assaulted from the rear. The passionate Jewish warriors destroyed the surprised and off-balance Roman legion and gained an unexpected victory.

> But, upon his (Cestius Gallus) coming and fighting, he was beaten and a great many of those that were with him fell. And this disgrace which Gessius [with Cestius] received, became the calamity of our whole nation; for those that were fond of the war were so far elevated with this success, that they had hopes of finally conquering the Romans. (*Life* 6)

This military misadventure humiliated Rome and gave encouragement to the zealots, and even the robbers grew bolder in their crimes.

In the summer of A.D. 66, Nero removed Florus and appointed King Agrippa II to power. Nero hoped that an Asamonean ruler would help short-circuit the incipient nationwide rebellion. King Agrippa, later that year, made an impassioned speech to the people of Jerusalem (*Wars* II 16:4) not to fight Rome, but the idea of Jewish independence had taken too firm a hold. Still, several large cities–Sepphoris, Tiberias, and Scythopolis among them– were unenthusiastic, though ostensibly supporting the revolt. The majority of the Judeans and Galileans supported the revolt with passion. Some cities in Samaria were supportive as well.

After the unrelated death of Cestius Gallus in mid-late A.D. 66, Lucilius Mucianus was appointed the president of Syria. Sources suggest that he, too, was defeated by the Jews in a military action, but the details are poorly documented. Mucianus had marched with General Corbula earlier and could have been present for Gallus' disastrous retreat from Jerusalem, explaining "his" defeat. At any rate, Mucianus was unable to negotiate a peaceful settlement with the Jews.

On Mucianus' recommendation, later in the year Emperor Nero, then on tour in Greece, decided to recall General Vespasian from Gaul and send him to the East. Vespasian went to Antiochus and took over the 15th legion and also joined up with Agrippa II, who had his own legion and was the official procurator/king of the Jewish East. Vespasian's son Titus left Achaia, where he had been with Nero, and traveled to Alexandria. There Titus picked up the 5th and 10th legions and eventually brought them to Ptolemais. By that time, in early spring of A.D. 67, Vespasian and Agrippa were already in Mediterranean port city with their armies.

The Roman forces were formidable, as Josephus describes. One legion was usually 4,800 men. One cohort was 480 men.

> But as to Titus, he sailed over from Achaia to Alexandria, and that sooner than the winter season did usually permit; so he took with him those forces he was sent for, and marching with great expedition, he came suddenly to Ptolemais, and there finding his father, together with the two legions, the fifth and the tenth, which were the most eminent legions of all, he joined them to that fifteenth legion which was with his

father; eighteen cohorts followed these legions; there came also five cohorts from Cesarea, with one troop of horsemen, and five other troops of horsemen from Syria. Now these ten cohorts had severally a thousand footmen, but the other thirteen cohorts had no more than six hundred footmen apiece, with a hundred and twenty horsemen. There were also a considerable number of auxiliaries got together, that came from the kings Antiochus, and Agrippa, and Sohemus, each of them contributing one thousand footmen that were archers, and a thousand horsemen. Malchus also, the king of Arabia, sent a thousand horsemen, besides five thousand footmen, the greatest part of which were archers; so that the whole army, including the auxiliaries sent by the kings, as well horsemen as footmen, when all were united together, amounted to sixty thousand, besides the servants, who, as they followed in vast numbers, so because they had been trained up in war with the rest, ought not to be distinguished from the fighting men; for as they were in their masters' service in times of peace, so did they undergo the like dangers with them in times of war, insomuch that they were inferior to none, either in skill or in strength, only they were subject to their masters. (Wars III 4:2)

The Priests Organize

The defeat of a legion of Roman regulars was a great and unexpected victory for the Jewish rebels. But Josephus and others, who knew of the might and resolve of Rome, saw the event for what it really was: the beginning of a monumental catastrophe for the Jewish nation.

The High Priesthood in Jerusalem had undeniable religious power over all Jews of the East. With rule of Rome in question and in the finest tradition of the ancient Maccabees, the priests now assumed full civil and military authority. With their own Temple-sanctioned military force, it was thought that renegade zealot armies in the countryside might be held in check. Also, the Syrian Greeks, who made up much of the population in not only the cities of the Decapolis but Galilee as well, were becoming a problem. Without the presence of Rome, the Syrian Greeks were preying upon defenseless Jewish enclaves within their cities and villages. For this reason, the Temple High Priesthood appointed capable men as generals, or "legates", to organize and lead armies in order to protect the Jews in the different regions of

Judea and Galilee, as well as to deal with the approaching Roman army.

Not every Jewish city accepted the Temple's authority. Many Jews saw the Second Temple High Priesthood as Roman collaborators, and this belief was well-grounded in reality. How could the same priests who previously served Roman interests now be accepted as leaders of the newly independent Jewish nation? Ambitious Jews from the larger cities outside of Judea formed their own armies to fight the Romans and defend themselves against the Syrian Greeks of the Decapolis–it was they who were the true army of Israel! These local forces resented the Jerusalem High Priesthood's intrusion into their affairs and ignored Temple orders to submit to their generals. At the other extreme, several large cities, most notably Sepphoris and Tiberias in Galilee, only grudgingly recognizing the oversight power of the High Priesthood initially. In fact, these cities would be quick to surrender when the Roman legions arrived.

In Judea and Galilee, the Temple-appointed generals were given broad and somewhat confusing powers. Included was the authority to control sedition, establish armies, fortify the major cities, protect the Jewish population and make to war upon the Romans or to sue for capitulation and peace as the situation might dictate. Josephus was given a generalship over Galilee–a plum assignment.

> ..the principal men of Jerusalem, seeing that the robbers and innovators had arms in great plenty and fearing lest they, while they were unprovided of arms, should be in subjection to their enemies which also came to be the case afterward; and, being informed that all Galilee had not yet revolted from the Romans, but that some part of it was still quiet; they sent me and two others of the priests, who were men of excellent characters, Joazar and Judas, in order to persuade the ill men there to lay down their arms and to teach them this lesson, - That it were better to have those arms reserved for the most courageous men that the nation had [than to be kept there]; for that it had been resolved, That those our best men should always have their arms ready against futurity; but still so, that they should wait to see what the Romans would do. (*Life* 7)

While history regards Josephus as one of the greatest Jewish generals who ever lived, many Jews even today regard him as a despicable traitor to the Jewish people.

General Joseph Ben Matthias

Josephus apparently had no formal military training, but this worked to his advantage — Josephus' defensive strategies were not constrained by traditional military concepts. General Josephus fought a guerrilla-style war against the Romans–his Galilean armies never fought in the open field. This was purposeful, as Josephus realized that the Jewish forces were no match for the Romans under those conditions.

Josephus' appointment also might have been driven by his engineering skills. Siege warfare was the order of the day, and strong stone walls were imperative for any city that hoped to survive a determined attack force. As the points of first contact, the northern cities of Galilee had to have strong walls–and quickly. But the fortifications were in a sad state of repair, for the Romans had occupied the East for over a century during which Galilee had seen only peace.

Josephus was also fluent in Latin and doubtless one of the very few priests who had actually been to Rome. The familiarity with Rome and its language would be very useful if peace negotiations with the Roman army became necessary.

Two other Priests were appointed along with Josephus to administer Galilee, but they were soon caught demanding bribes from the Jews they had authority over in true Roman fashion. Josephus, enraged, immediately sent the men back to Jerusalem to answer to the High Priesthood. Josephus now had sole military authority over the entire Galilee. He expeditiously formed an army and began training the soldiers. Using the Josephus "factor" for very large numbers, his army strength was probably a more believable 10,000 men and not 100,000.

> He (Josephus) also got together an army out of Galilee, of more than a hundred thousand young men, all of which he armed with the old

weapons which he had collected together and prepared for them. (*Wars* II 20:6)

Writing in the third person, Josephus documents his training methods, patterned after the Romans.

> And when he had considered that the Roman power became invincible, chiefly by their readiness in obeying orders and the constant exercise of their arms, he despaired of teaching these his men the use of their arms which was to be obtained by experience; but observing that their readiness in obeying orders was owing to the multitude of their officers, he made his partitions in his army more after the Roman manner and appointed a great many subalterns. He also distributed the soldiers into various classes, whom he put under captains of tens and captains of hundreds and then under captains of thousands; and besides these, he had commanders of larger bodies of men. He also taught them to give the signals one to another and to call and recall the soldiers by the trumpets, how to expand the wings of an army and make them wheel about; and when one wing hath had success, to turn again and assist those that were hard set and to join in the defense of what had most suffered. He also continually instructed them ill what concerned the courage of the soul and the hardiness of the body; and, above all, he exercised them for war, by declaring to them distinctly the good order of the Romans and that they were to fight with men who, both by the strength of their bodies and courage of their souls, had conquered in a manner the whole habitable earth. He told them that he should make trial of the good order they would observe in war, even before it came to any battle, in case they would abstain from the crimes they used to indulge themselves in, such as theft and robbery and rapine and from defrauding their own countrymen and never to esteem the harm done to those that were so near of kin to them to be any advantage to themselves; for that wars are then managed the best when the warriors preserve a good conscience; but that such as are ill men in private life will not only have those for enemies which attack them, but God himself also for their antagonist. (*Wars* II 20:7)

Josephus set his engineers busy repairing the walls of the important northern Galilee cities and building them higher — from Jotapata and Sepphoris in the western hills, to Arbel and Tiberias near the western shores of Lake Gennesareth, to Gamala in the mountains east of the Gennesareth, and in other front line cities.

In his autobiography, Josephus spends much time detailing the military skirmishes early on with the Jews unwilling to accept his authority. Over the course only eight months from late A.D. 66 to early A.D. 67, Josephus and his army had to subdue Sepphoris twice and Tiberias four times! In the case of Sepphoris, Josephus found himself attacking and breaching the very walls that he had reinforced only weeks earlier (*Life* 15,37).

Action against Tiberias

Josephus first showed his military skill in early A.D. 67 during one of these Jewish mini-revolts against his Temple-based authority. Tiberias, a major city on the western shores of the Gennesareth, had been built largely from scratch by Herod Antipas 50 years previously. The capital of Galilee in Antipas' day, Tiberias was still an important city and rivaled the present-day capital city of Sepphoris that lay in the hills to the west.

The city of Tiberias was governed by its own senate, although Nero had given formal administration of the city to King Agrippa II years before. Agrippa II was rarely in Tiberias, however, despite the impressive palace that Antipas had built there. Agrippa arranged for others to collect the taxes and trusted the wisdom of the local senate in handling civil affairs. After the Jewish revolt of A.D. 66, various political factions fought for preeminence in the city — some supported Josephus, some supported Agrippa and the Romans, and others supported various rogue leaders who would occasionally spring up from Tiberias' own population.

One of these leaders in Tiberias, Justus,the son of Pistus, bitterly opposed Josephus and all he represented. Justus survived the revolt to write a history of the Jewish kings. This competed–intentionally–with Josephus' own works. In the now-lost book Justus reportedly excoriated Josephus for his traitorous actions in the Jewish wars.

Initially, the city leaders of Tiberias had assured Josephus that they supported the Jewish Temple alliance. Taking them at their word, Josephus set his men to work fortifying the city walls preparing for Roman attack. But the principal men then secretly wrote to King Agrippa II and asked that he send auxiliary Roman troops to Tiberias in order to protect them from Josephus' men.

Several days after this request, Roman horsemen were spotted not far from the city. The principal men of Tiberias assumed that this was the sentinel forces sent by Agrippa in response to their request. Great joy and commotion broke forth in the population of Tiberias as they prepared for their arrival.

Josephus was resting in the nearby lakeside city of Tarichess, five miles to the north along the same stretch of western Lake Gennesareth shoreline. He was informed that Tiberias was about to surrender to the approaching army of Agrippa II which was now supposedly only hours away in the hills of Galilee. Josephus was surprised and angered. His soldiers were close to finishing the walls that would make Tiberias one of the strongest cities in Galilee. It would be much the worse for the Jewish nation if the Romans were able to use it as a military base. Already, the loyalty of Sepphoris was in question.

As for the approaching troops of Agrippa II, Josephus had strong doubts that was actually the case. He dispatched some of his horsemen into the surrounding hills and mountains for reconnaissance. When they returned and reported seeing no armies, Josephus was satisfied. But he knew he must act quickly in order to preserve Tiberias as a Jewish stronghold.

It was the day before the Sabbath, and unfortunately Josephus had sent most of his army back to their homes in observance of it. Also, it was not lawful to mount an offensive action on the Sabbath day although Jewish law did permit mounting a defense if attacked. Josephus came up with a brilliant stratagem which made use of the short sailing distance between Tiberias and Tarichess.

Enlisting the aid of the people of Tarichess, Josephus and a small band of soldiers commandeered over 200 fishing vessels that were moored at lakeside. The next day, on the Sabbath, Josephus dressed for battle and sailed before dawn with his makeshift war fleet to Tiberias. Only Josephus' boat was packed with battle-ready soldiers, however. The rest of the boats contained only a single man. Josephus instructed these other boats to stay far enough from shore so that the people on Tiberias would not be able to see them clearly. Only Josephus in his "flagship" vessel, full of soldiers, sailed close to the city. Of course, the telescope had not been invented yet!

As expected, in the light of morning the citizens of Tiberias saw the distant fleet and gathered fearfully on the shore, not knowing what to expect. Then a single vessel approached the shore–carrying Josephus and seven soldiers, armed and dressed for battle. Josephus then angrily shouted to the people that the Tiberian senate and perpetrators of the rebellion should be delivered to him immediately, or his force would attack!

Josephus' bold confidence convinced the terrified townspeople that the distant ships were also full of warriors. By then, the citizens knew that the Roman horsemen who had been spotted the previous day were not from Agrippa's army. Indeed, Agrippa might not have even received the message. Now the townspeople were on their own in facing the wrath of Josephus and his marine force.

As Josephus had expected, the people of Tiberias quickly switched loyalties. Ten of the ringleaders were roughly rounded up by the citizens and brought to the shore. Josephus then signaled to a single empty ship from the distant fleet. When it came to shore, Josephus commanded that the troublemakers embark on it and then he instructed the ship's captain to sail with the prisoners back to Tarichess. Repeating the same process over and over again, Josephus removed from Tiberias the members of their senate and most of their principal men, sending them all to Tarichess as prisoners.

The practical citizens of Tiberias now shouted their approval and hailed Josephus as a hero for saving them from these Roman sympathizers. Lastly, the citizens presented to Josephus the prime author of the mini-revolt, a man called Clitus. Deciding that an example had to be made of him, Josephus ordered one of his soldiers to disembark from the sailing craft, go on shore, and cut off Clitus' hands at the wrists–the usual punishment for sedition. But the soldier was fearful that once he was on the shore, the crowd would turn upon him and kill him. Josephus considered this, and then thought up another plan.

> So I called to Clitus himself and said to him, "Since thou deservest to lose both thine hands for thy ingratitude to me, be thou thine own executioner, lest, if thou refusest so to be, thou undergo a worse punishment." And when he earnestly begged of me to spare him one of his hands, it was with difficulty that I granted it. So, in order to prevent the loss of both his hands, he willingly took his sword and cut off his own left hand; and this put an end to the sedition. (*Life* 32-34)

Here we not only see Josephus' inventiveness in quelling the revolt of the Tiberians, but get a glimpse into the dark and vengeful side of this warrior-priest. Also revealing is the rebel Clitus' unhesitating act of horrific self-mutilation on the mere command of Josephus, demonstrating the abject fear that Josephus could instill in his enemies.

Well-satisfied, Josephus then sailed away and returned to Tarichess where his hoard of captives was waiting for him. These traitorous principal men of Tiberias once again changed their stripes and swore allegiance to Josephus and the rebels. Many thanked Josephus for securing the city with so little bloodshed. Josephus accepted their loyalty at face value and made peace with them—he would soon need their support against the Romans.

A great victory for Josephus, but it proved to be only temporary. Months later, when the Roman army did march on Galilee, these same men surrendered Tiberias without a fight, just as the principal men of Sepphoris surrendered their own city.

John of Gischala

John, the son of Levi, was another challenger of Josephus' authority, this time in the city of Gischala. Using another tactic, John traveled to Jerusalem and bribed the High Priesthood– possibly even the former High Priest Ananus himself–to have

Josephus not only removed from power but executed. The High Priesthood seriously considered doing this which means that there is much to this story that Josephus is leaving out. Though Josephus apparently had the support of the common Galileans, it would have likely been the worse for him with the Temple High Priesthood had not the Romans initiated their military actions at roughly the same time. With the war commencing in earnest, the High Priesthood dropped their initiative and let Josephus run the Galilean campaign–such as it was.

Later, in A.D. 68, after the fall of his home city of Gischala, John would show up in Jerusalem as a refugee. Soon, he would attain a leadership position within the defending Jerusalem zealot force. But by then, the long-captured Josephus would be working for the Romans–an adviser and confidant of Vespasian and Titus.

Chapter 21   Jotapata and Josephus

..the women and children, when they saw their city encompassed by a threefold army,..when they also saw, not only the walls thrown down, but their enemies with swords in their hands, as also the hilly country above them shining with their weapons and the darts in the hands of the Arabian archers, they made a final and lamentable outcry of the destruction, as if the misery were not only threatened, but actually come upon them already. (*Wars* III 7:26)

In the spring of A.D. 67, at the same time Josephus was busy organizing his Jewish forces in Galilee, the Roman army–perhaps 50,000 strong under the command of battle-hardened veteran General Titus Flavius Vespasian–was massing in Ptolemais just to the north. Vespasian was Nero's most experienced general, with an unmatched record of victories in Spain, Gaul, Germany, and the British Isles. King Agrippa II was also there with his own force to command–perhaps a legion's worth of men.

Vespasian was an energetic soldier; he could march at the head of his army, choose the place for his camp and bring by night and day his skill, or, if the occasion required, his personal courage to oppose the foe. His food was such as chance offered; his dress and appearance hardly distinguished him from the common soldier; in short, but for his avarice, he was equal to the generals of old. (*Histories* 2-5)

Josephus knew that his triumphs in intra-Jewish squabbles now meant nothing. For the Jews to defeat the Romans, a divine intervention of biblical proportions would be needed. Through his dreams and visions, Josephus knew that would not be a likely occurrence.

In fact, Sepphoris capitulated to the Romans early in A.D. 67 without a fight, despite their contrary promises to Josephus. Emissaries from Sepphoris met the Roman army on its march to Ptolemais and surrendered. Placidus secured Sepphoris and based his army there. Josephus, based out of Garis, not far away from Sepphoris, attacked the city with his forces but was repulsed.

Placidus took this move by Josephus' army as license to ravage the countryside of Galilee, with many Galileans fleeing to the fortified cities in the area. One of those cities was Jotapata. Placidus recognized it as a stronghold and attacked it — unsuccessfully.

Not long afterward Vespasian marched out of Ptolemais to Sepphoris. Most of Josephus' men at Garis (modern Cana) deserted at the news, and Josephus himself retreated with a handful of his men to Tiberias on the shores of the Galilee. There, Josephus wrote a letter to the High Priesthood in Jerusalem and requested that either he be sent more reinforcements, or be allowed to surrender.

Jotapata

The first major confrontation between the two nations occurred at Jotapata which was a few miles to the north of Sepphoris across a plain. There, Josephus would command his first and last siege defense.

> Now Jotapata is almost all of it built on a precipice, having on all the other sides of it every way valleys immensely deep and steep, insomuch that those who would look down would have their sight fail them before it reaches to the bottom. It is only to be come at on the north side, where the utmost part of the city is built on the mountain, as it ends obliquely at a plain. This mountain Josephus had encompassed with a wall when he fortified the city, that its top might not be capable of being seized upon by the enemies. The city is covered all round with other mountains and can no way be seen till a man comes just upon it. And this was the strong situation of Jotapata. (*Wars* III 7:7)

Josephus had recently rebuilt the walls of Jotapata, especially fortifying the northern wall which, unlike the other three sides of the city, was situated on a small plain and the only viable attack point for the Romans. Jotapata provided a convenient base from which the Jews could attack and harass the Romans in true hit-and-run Maccabean style. For that reason, the Romans targeted Jotapata for early destruction.

Jotapata, however, had easily repulsed an earlier Roman assault by the overconfident forces of General Placidus in April. Dismayed and irritated, the veteran General Vespasian then took personal field command over the situation–Jotapata became a priority. In early May of A.D. 67, Vespasian began his troop placement. After widening the access road to the frontal plain on the north which took took four days in itself, three Roman legions–the 5th, 10th, and 15th–, plus auxiliaries, set up camp. Strategic positions were also taken on the low mountains that ringed Jotapata. The mountain ridges proved advantageous for Vespasian's highly trained Arabian archers — the mountain upon which Jotapata was built being within their range and slightly below them.

Josephus knew, however, that a relatively small number of Jews could hold off thousands of Roman soldiers almost indefinitely — if the wall held. Water and food supplies could be a problem, yes, but the city had many underground cisterns and storage caves which had been been filled to capacity. Steep mountain paths to the south could be used to transport in more supplies by night if need be.

Vespasian initially put his soldiers on display for the Jews. Tens of thousands of Roman soldiers in full regalia took offensive positions on the northern plain in front of the walls and also upon the ridges of the surrounding mountains. Hundreds of Roman drums were beaten in unison and the horns sounded. With this thundering display there was much fear instilled in the citizens of Jotapata, as was the intent. Most Jews expected an early defeat and faced the prospect of slavery if not death.

Enter Josphus

In a bold and surprise move, General Josephus himself entered Jotapata one night by means of a mountain trail and assumed personal command of the defense of the city. The Jews became jubilant–with Josephus, they knew they had a chance!

When he learned of it, General Vespasian was also pleased. He knew of Josephus' reputation. If the Jewish general could be killed or captured in this first engagement, it might mean a speedy capitulation to the rest of the Jewish nation.

The initial battles were indecisive. The heavily armored Romans were at a disadvantage to the lightly armored and more mobile Jews. Also, many of the Romans' sophisticated battle formations and preset offensive maneuvers were unworkable on the narrow plain in front of Jotapata's formidable northern wall. The Roman soldiers fought with the usual Roman discipline and pride, but the Jews fought with the desperation of a nation invaded. For the Jews, the lives of their families and loved ones were at stake! The 30-year-old Josephus led many counter-charges against the Romans himself, inspiring his Jewish co-defenders.

Vespasian was surprised at the strength of the Jewish resistance. He decided to modify his tactics. Vespasian continued to assault Jotapata, but he also set thousands of soldiers to work felling trees on nearby mountain slopes and gathering large stones as well. These were placed so as to form a bank against a portion the north wall of Jotapata. The bank would provide a strong foundation so battering rams built within the Roman tower "engines" of war could be set up and pommel the wall's weaker upper portions into dust. While the Jews harassed the Romans from the top of the wall, the raising of the banks proceeded largely unaffected.

When the bank was thought high enough, Vespasian brought out more than 100 of his "machines" of war. These were large wooden crossbow-like devices that launched not arrows but large rocks. Rounded stones up to 70 pounds apiece were set in leather pouches attached to a thick wooden cross member by tensioned ropes. When the ropes were cut, the cross member snapped and the missiles screamed off at great velocity and usually with great accuracy.

With the ramparts of the wall becoming more and more dangerous to his warriors, Josephus countered the Romans by building up the north wall of Jotapata another 30 feet. Josephus protected the wall workers from the stones, arrows and missiles of the enemy with large shields of stretched-out swaths of hide from freshly killed cattle. The hides served to absorb the force of the rocks and missiles and the projectiles would fall harmlessly to the ground after bouncing off the cattle skin.

Faced with Josephus' successful counter-stratagem, and with Jewish defenders' continued successful sallies out from Jotapata, Vespasian modified his tactics once again. Vespasian decided not to lose any more men on direct frontal assaults while the banks were being raised. He would be patient. Surrounded on all sides by Roman forces and with limited supplies, Jotapata would surely fall–eventually.

The Siege

Josephus countered Vespasian's stratagem by having his soldiers sneak out at night for supplies from the countryside. A steep trail on the southern aspect of the mountain of Jotapata was carelessly guarded by the Romans. Josephus had his men cover themselves in sheepskins when they navigated the path in the dark. If they were seen by the Romans, they might think they were grazing livestock. This was a successful ploy and a limited amount of supplies reached the besieged city this way.

Despite these minor victories Josephus knew that Jotapata was a lost cause and Vespasian would prevail. Inevitably, the banks would be raised high enough so the battering rams could be moved into place and breach the walls. Josephus made secret plans to leave the city in order to survive and direct the defense of the other Galilean cities that lay in the Romans' path. But the people of Jotapata discovered his escape plans and became angry. They feared that Josephus once out of the city would betray them to the Romans. Old accusations resurfaced: Josephus was a Roman sympathizer!

Despite his best arguments, Josephus realized that the men of Jotapata would kill him before letting him leave. So Josephus, accepting his fate, agreed to stay to the end. To prove his loyalty in dramatic fashion, Josephus personally led the Jewish defenders in a series of successful raids over the next few days– one raid even pressing the Romans to the edge of their camp.

In time, the banks built by the Romans were high enough to bring out the massive iron-tipped battering rams. To protect the rams and their operators, thousands of Arabian archers positioned on the tops of nearby mountains shot arrows down upon the ramparts of Jotapata. To protect the stone north wall from the battering rams, Josephus had his soldiers fill cloth sacks with chaff and lower them by ropes in front of the walls in order to blunt the force of the log rams. As the Romans moved the rams to avoid the chaff-filled sacks, the Jewish soldiers would sally forth from the gate and set fire to the wooden rams and any catapults in their path.

This stratagem worked successfully for several days. In time, however, the Romans then countered the chaff-filled sacks by simply cutting the suspending ropes with sharpened knives attached to long poles. The sacks fell harmlessly to the ground, and the battering ram could continue its work.

Now, with the battering rams slowly crumbling the walls of Jotapata, large rocks screaming into the besieged city from the Roman machines, and with the arrows from the Arabian archers continuing to rain in from the surrounding mountaintops, Josephus knew that the end was near.

> But still Josephus and those with him, although they fell down dead one upon another by the darts and stones which the engines threw upon them, yet did not they desert the wall, but fell upon those who managed the ram, under the protection of the hurdles, with fire and iron weapons and stones; and these could do little or nothing, but fell themselves perpetually, while they were seen by those whom they could not see, for the light of their own flame shone about them and made them a most visible mark to the enemy, as they were in the day time, while the engines could not be seen at a great distance and so what was thrown at

them was hard to be avoided; for the force with which these engines threw stones and darts made them hurt several at a time and the violent noise of the stones that were cast by the engines was so great, that they carried away the pinnacles of the wall and broke off the corners of the towers; for no body of men could be so strong as not to be overthrown to the last rank by the largeness of the stones. And any one may learn the force of the engines by what happened this very night; for as one of those that stood round about Josephus was near the wall, his head was carried away by such a stone and his skull was flung as far as three furlongs. In the day time also, a woman with child had her belly so violently struck, as she was just come out of her house, that the infant was carried to the distance of half a furlong, so great was the force of that engine. The noise of the instruments themselves was very terrible, the sound of the darts and stones that were thrown by them was so also; of the same sort was that noise the dead bodies made, when they were dashed against the wall; and indeed dreadful was the clamor which these things raised in the women within the city which was echoed back at the same time by the cries of such as were slain; while the whole space of ground whereon they fought ran with blood and the wall might have been ascended over by the bodies of the dead carcasses; the mountains also contributed to increase the noise by their echoes; nor was there on that night any thing of terror wanting that could either affect the hearing or the sight: yet did a great part of those that fought so hard for Jotapata fall manfully, as were a great part of them wounded. However, the morning watch was come ere the wall yielded to the machines employed against it, though it had been battered without intermission. However, those within covered their bodies with their armor and raised works over against that part which was thrown down, before those machines were laid by which the Romans were to ascend into the city. (*Wars* III 7:23)

So with the walls compromised and the final deadly assault by the Romans inevitable, Josephus encouraged his men with these words:

..every one should strive to do his best, in order not to defend his own city, as if it were possible to be preserved, but in order to revenge it, when it was already destroyed; and that they should set before their eyes how their old men were to be slain and their children and wives were to be killed immediately by the enemy; and that they would beforehand spend all their fury, on account of the calamities just coming upon them and pour it out on the actors. (*Wars* III 7:25)

Josephus describes the fear in the city as the Romans positioned themselves for the final assault:

> but then for the useless part of the citizens, the women and children, when they saw their city encompassed by a threefold army, (for none of the usual guards that had been fighting before were removed,) when they also saw, not only the walls thrown down, but their enemies with swords in their hands, as also the hilly country above them shining with their weapons and the darts in the hands of the Arabian archers, they made a final and lamentable outcry of the destruction, as if the misery were not only threatened, but actually come upon them already. But Josephus ordered the women to be shut up in their houses, lest they should render the warlike actions of the men too effeminate, by making them commiserate their condition and commanded them to hold their peace and threatened them if they did not, while he came himself before the breach, where his allotment was; for all those who brought ladders to the other places, he took no notice of them, but earnestly waited for the shower of arrows that was coming. (*Wars* III 7:26)

Stopping up their own ears to deaden the shouts from the invading Romans, the Jewish defenders made what they thought would be their last stand. As the Romans ascended makeshift ladders placed on the outside of the battered north wall, Josephus ordered boiling oil poured upon them from the ramparts. In horrifying fashion, the advance of the Romans was slowed — but not stopped. But Josephus also had prepared large quantities of animal fat grease and his soldiers had applied it to the compromised ramparts. Any Roman who had avoided the oil and made it upon the ramparts slipped and fell. Quickly, they would be slain by the nimble Jewish defenders.

With these extraordinary and desperate strategies, Josephus stymied the Romans once again. Vespasian pulled back his soldiers from the assault, ruining what Vespasian–and likely Josephus himself–thought would be the day of capitulation. Vespasian now directed his efforts to raise the banks to an even higher level and ordered his three major assault towers sheeted with iron, making them fireproof.

Betrayal

Days later, a deserter from Jotapata upon interrogation told Vespasian when the best time to invade the city would be – the hours before sunrise when the guards on the walls were usually sleeping. Even when crucified, the informant did not change his story. Vespasian was satisfied.

By then the bank had been built up to Vespasian's specifications and the protected assault towers were ready as well. Vespasian decided to use the deserter's information and attack Jotapata before dawn with a massive number of his regular soldiers.

This proved successful. The final capitulation took place in an early morning fog on June 17th, A.D. 67. It was virtually a bloodless affair, with General Titus, Vespasian's son, the first man over the walls.

> Now when the citadel was taken and the enemy were in the very midst of the city and when it was already day, yet was not the taking of the city known by those that held it; for a great many of them were fast asleep and a great mist which then by chance fell upon the city, hindered those that got up from distinctly seeing the case they were in, till the whole Roman army was gotten in and they were raised up only to find the miseries they were under; and as they were slaying, they perceived the city was taken. And for the Romans, they so well remembered what they had suffered during the siege, that they spared none, nor pitied any, but drove the people down the precipice from the citadel and slew them as they drove them down; at which time the difficulties of the place hindered those that were still able to fight from defending themselves; for as they were distressed in the narrow streets and could not keep their feet sure along the precipice, they were overpowered with the crowd of those that came fighting them down from the citadel. This provoked a great many, even of those chosen men that were about Josephus, to kill themselves with their own hands; for when they saw that they could kill none of the Romans, they resolved to prevent being killed by the Romans and got together in great numbers in the utmost parts of the city and killed themselves. (*Wars* III 7:34)

So Jotapata was finally taken after a siege of 47 days. In the mayhem that followed, the Roman soldiers murdered or took captive the citizens and ransacked Jotapata for booty. Vespasian then ordered the city razed and the walls torn down. But in all this blood and destruction—and much to Vespasian's great disappointment—, the Romans did not find General Joseph bar Matthias among the living or the dead.

End Game

While thousands were slain and many of the principal men committing suicide and slaying their own families rather than surrender to the Romans, Josephus and 40 others found a secure hiding place in a cave. The entrance was hidden in a deep pit located within the city walls, and so the Romans did not discover it in their ransacking. Conveniently, it was also stocked with provisions—someone had planned ahead!

Josephus and the others lay undiscovered for three days as the city was being methodically razed above them. Josephus, ever resourceful and knowing it was only a matter of time before discovery, would sneak out at night in an attempt to find the best means of escaping from Jotapata completely.

> And now the Romans searched for Josephus, both out of the hatred they bore him and because their general was very desirous to have him taken; for he reckoned that if he were once taken, the greatest part of the war would be over. (*Wars* III 8:1)

Then the Romans captured a woman who not only knew of the cave, but had actually been in it. To gain favor with the Romans, she betrayed its location. Vespasian was delighted at the news. The cave was soon found and through a "tribune" named Nicanor, whom Josephus had known from before. Josephus was offered clemency if he surrendered peacefully, but no guarantees were given the other men. Suspicious, these men were not about to let Josephus go over to the Romans, fearing it would mean their own death. Questions concerning Josephus' true loyalties again were revived. The Jewish men in the cave, armed and angry, threatened to kill Josephus if he tried to leave.

But Josephus, through his persistent dreams and his own convictions, believed that it was God's plan for him to survive and work with the Romans, just as it had been fated for the Romans to destroy the Jewish nation for its wickedness.

> Now as Josephus began to hesitate with himself about Nicanor's proposal, the soldiery were so angry, that they ran hastily to set fire to the den; but the tribune would not permit them so to do, as being very desirous to take the man alive. And now, as Nicanor lay hard at Josephus to comply and he understood how the multitude of the enemies threatened him, he called to mind the dreams which he had dreamed in the night time, whereby God had signified to him beforehand both the future calamities of the Jews and the events that concerned the Roman emperors. Now Josephus was able to give shrewd conjectures about the interpretation of such dreams as have been ambiguously delivered by God. Moreover, he was not unacquainted with the prophecies contained in the sacred Books, as being a priest himself and of the posterity of priests: and just then was he in an ecstasy; and setting before him the tremendous images of the dreams he had lately had, he put up a secret prayer to God and said, "Since it pleaseth thee, who hast created the Jewish nation, to depress the same and since all their good fortune is gone over to the Romans and since thou hast made choice of this soul of mine to foretell what is to come to pass hereafter, I willingly give them my hands and am content to live. And I protest openly that I do not go over to the Romans as a deserter of the Jews, but as a minister from thee." (*Wars* III 8:3)

Well and good that God intended him to survive, but how was Josephus to deal with the other 39 surviving Jews who were with him in the cave—men who would kill him first if he decided to surrender to Vespasian?

> However, in this extreme distress, he (Josephus) was not destitute of his usual sagacity; but trusting himself to the providence of God, he put his life into hazard [in the manner following]: "And now," said he, "since it is resolved among you that you will die, come on, let us commit our mutual deaths to determination by lot. He whom the lot falls to first, let him be killed by him that hath the second lot and thus fortune shall make its progress through us all; nor shall any of us perish by his own right hand, for it would be unfair if, when the rest are gone, somebody should repent and save himself." This proposal appeared to them to be very just; and when he had prevailed with them to determine this matter by lots, he drew one of the lots for himself also. He who had the first lot laid his neck bare to him that had the next, as supposing that the general would die among them immediately; for they thought death, if Josephus

might but die with them, was sweeter than life; yet was he with another left to the last, whether we must say it happened so by chance, or whether by the providence of God. And as he was very desirous neither to be condemned by the lot, nor, if he had been left to the last, to imbrue his right hand in the blood of his countrymen, he persuaded him to trust his fidelity to him and to live as well as himself. (*Wars* III 8:7)

Again, Josephus escaped a dangerous situation. All in the cave agreed to die. The order of death was to be determined by lottery–with Josephus organizing the drawing. To avoid suicide which was forbidden by Jewish law, the loser of the drawing was to be killed by the "second" loser. Whatever the technical particulars of this deadly lottery were, somehow it is not surprising that Josephus drew a "safe" lot 38 straight times. Certainly to Josephus' advantage was the fact that the light within the cave had to be very poor.

But Josephus now had to slay the second to last man which he was loathe to do. Instead, with the bodies of the slain men all around them, Josephus persuaded his co-survivor to surrender with him, perhaps promising him protection from the Romans. The man agreed and together they left the cave.

Vespasian was pleased at the capture of Josephus three days after the capitulation of Jotapata.. At their first meeting, the prisoner Josephus hailed Vespasian as a future emperor of Rome. Was this a true vision from his dreams, or just a form of flattery to gain advantage with Vespasian? Josephus had to know that every Roman general, secretly or otherwise, coveted the Roman Empire. As Josephus hoped, Vespasian was intrigued with him–as perhaps Empress Poppea had been only four years before. Vespasian learned that Josephus had predicted the exact day that the siege would end: 47 days from its beginning. After Vespasian verified this minor but impressive prophecy, he treated Josephus not as rebel but a respected enemy general. Of course, Josephus was fluent in Latin and he was willing to aid the Romans. Additionally, Josephus had actually dined with Nero's late wife Poppea, and Josephus was probably quick to inform Vespasian of that event. Josephus soon found himself safe, out of harm's way, and well accepted into the Roman high command.

Josephus claimed that the total number of dead in Jotapata was 40,000, but that is open to question. The mountaintop site of ancient Jotapata has been identified as Yodefat. However, even if significant site erosion is factored in, it is doubtful that 40,000 people could have even fit into the limited area of the site. The most generous estimate is that ancient Jotapata covered 13 acres. As has been discussed, the very large number could simply be an error in transcription with the real number being closer to 4,000.

Josephus Serving Rome

Josephus proved to be of great value as an adviser to Vespasian. In time, Josephus became a trusted member of the Roman command. During the whole of the Jewish revolt, four future Roman Emperors were involved: Vespasian, Titus, Domitian, and Trajan. Josephus worked closely with them all and gained their trust, thus assuring himself an honored place in Rome's Royal court when the war ended. Additionally, Josephus formed a close relationship with King Agrippa II, who had his own auxiliary army and was actually a distant relative of Josephus[1].

In spite of the honors and respect that the Romans bestowed on Josephus, most Jews have always considered him a traitor. Was this a warranted accusation? In the early stages of the revolt, before he was appointed general, Josephus talked openly and strongly against resisting Rome, for he had been to Rome and had seen Rome's seemingly-invincible power. But Josephus quickly became silent when it was apparent that the majority of the people were bent on revolution. The damage to his reputation, however, had probably already been done.

Years later Josephus wrote his massive historical works partially to tell his side of the story and dispel all rumors that he had betrayed the Jewish nation. But were Josephus' writings self-serving and cleverly constructed to cover up an actual betrayal–a betrayal conceived when Josephus was enjoying life with Nero and Poppea at the court of Rome in A.D. 63?

Josephus acknowledges that during the Jewish revolt he was used for intelligence purposes and to arrange surrenders and communication with the Jewish rebels, but nothing more. Josephus, however, may well have downplayed or ignored instances altogether where he more aggressively aided the Roman army in defeating the Jewish nation.

The Mind of Josephus

In spring of A.D. 63, when Josephus visited Rome, rebellion was fomenting in the Jewish East. Only three years later Jewish discontent would erupt into open insurrection. Though he was apparently proud and diligent in his role as a general, Josephus had to know all along that the Jewish nation would be destroyed. Josephus, in fact, writes about having vivid dreams and visions predicting his future service to Rome.

> But wonderful it was what a dream I saw that very night; for when I had betaken myself to my bed, as grieved and disturbed at the news that had been written to me, it seemed to me, that a certain person stood by me, and said, "O Josephus! leave off to afflict thy soul and put away all fear; for what now grieves thee will render thee very considerable and in all respects most happy; for thou shalt get over not only these difficulties, but many others, with great success. However, be not cast down, but remember that thou art to fight with the Romans." (*Life* 42)

But if Josephus knew that God wanted him to fight "with" the Romans, then why did accept a leadership position in the Jewish Galilean army? It would have been the ultimate suicide mission and against God's will as it was revealed to him in dreams.

Now for some speculation. When Josephus was in Rome, did he have these same prescient dreams? Assuming he did, perhaps there was more to Josephus' visit to Rome than he lets on in his autobiography. Was Josephus recruited as an agent for Rome during his visit? Did Josephus, in fact, volunteer himself to the Roman army to spy for the empire when he returned to Jerusalem? That he was an agent of Rome certainly was the continuing accusation after he was appointed as a general early in the revolt.

When Josephus was trapped in a cave at Jotapata after its fall, Vespasian sent a "familiar acquaintance" to plead for Josephus' surrender.

> Vespasian sent besides these a third tribune, Nicanor, to him; he was one that was well known to Josephus and had been his familiar acquaintance in old time. (*Wars* III 8:2)

Was Nicanor a Jew from Sepphoris, a city that remained loyal to Rome? Or was Nicanor a Roman officer whom Josephus knew from his visit to Rome years earlier? As the only Galilean general, Josephus would not have had any difficulty in arranging his own capture by the Romans. That he was trapped in Jotapata early in the war might have been an unforeseen development that he had to work around. Nicanor shows up later in *Wars* as a companion to the now-freed Josephus when first surveying the formidable walls of Jerusalem in early A.D. 70.

> But at this time, as he was going round about the city, one of his friends, whose name was Nicanor, was wounded with a dart on his left shoulder, as he approached, together with Josephus, too near the wall, (*Wars* V 6:2)

Josephus spent considerable space in *Wars* documenting the siege of Jotapata. Certainly, Josephus was innovative and heroic, but did he embellish his deeds at Jotapata to hide the truth that his plan was to be captured there?

As the revolt progressed, two major actions suggest that Josephus played a key role in Roman victories that he declined to take credit for.

Gamala

The fortress-city of Gamala, located to the northeast of Lake Gennesareth, like Jotapata was situated on a mountain that was surrounded by natural gorges on three sides. A strong wall along its sloping northern perimeter had been reinforced by Josephus only months earlier.

> Josephus, the son of Matthias, (was made General) of both Galilees. Gamala also which was the strongest city in those parts, was put under his command. (*Wars* II 20:4)

> Those of Gamala also wrote to me, desiring me to send them an armed force and workmen to raise up the walls of their city; nor did I reject either of their requests. (*Life* 37)

> and in Gaulonitis he fortified (the walls of) Seleucia and Sogane and Gamala; (*Wars* II 20:6)

> As this city was naturally hard to be taken, so had Josephus, by building a wall about it, made it still stronger, as also by ditches and mines under ground. (*Wars* IV 1:2)

In A.D. 67, Agrippa II had his army initiate what turned out to be a somewhat casual siege to Gamala. Agrippa's auxiliary forces camped outside Gamala's north wall and launched occasional attacks on it for almost seven months; all with minimal effect. Gamala was well fortified and with the added advantage of having a freshwater spring located within the city walls. Thousands of Jews from the fertile surrounding countryside had taken refuge there; many had brought their food stock with them.

On September 8, A.D. 67, Vespasian arrived with his three legions to aid Agrippa and bring about a speedy end to this irritating pocket of resistance. The Romans soon breached the walls of Gamala in an all-out assault. Success seemed assured, but then disaster struck! While the Roman forces were massing on the tops of the closely packed buildings in the northern part of the steeply sloped city, the roofs collapsed. The buildings slid down upon each other and crumbled into rock and stone. Hundreds of invading Roman soldiers were killed or maimed in the dusty cascade of rubble. The Jewish defenders saw this and were heartened. They regrouped and attacked the remaining Roman soldiers with a vengeance and won the battle.

Vespasian and his son Titus were demoralized and discouraged. They both decided to leave Gamala with most of their men and move on to other areas of Galilee pursuing the war, leaving the city still under siege.

Weeks later on October 3rd, the remaining Roman contingent executed a decidedly Josephus-like action against Gamala. Was Josephus–the architect of the walls of Gamala–also the architect of the walls' destruction?

> .. three soldiers of the fifteenth legion, about the morning watch, got under a high tower that was near them and undermined it, without making any noise; nor when they either came to it which was in the night time, nor when they were under it, did those that guarded it perceive them. These soldiers then upon their coming avoided making a noise and when they had rolled away five of its strongest stones, they went away hastily; whereupon the tower fell down on a sudden, with a very great noise and its guard fell headlong with it; so that those that kept guard at other places were under such disturbance, that they ran away; the Romans also slew many of those that ventured to oppose them, among whom was Joseph, who was slain by a dart, as he was running away over that part of the wall that was broken down: but as those that were in the city were greatly aftrighted at the noise, they ran hither and thither and a great consternation fell upon them, as though all the enemy had fallen in at once upon them. (*Wars* IV 1:9)

How did it come about that these five soldiers knew about the weakness of the tower? Most Roman soldiers were simple farmers before joining the army and they would know little of engineering. Josephus doesn't tell us where he was during this particular action, but if anyone would know where the Achilles' heel of the Gamala wall would be, it would have been Josephus.

Conveniently, General Titus son arrived upon the scene only a day after the undermining of the large tower, and Gamala was taken with relative ease. That Titus, a Josephus favorite, was present to co-ordinate the final assault makes it doubly suspicious that Josephus was the author of the plan.

At which time Titus, who was now returned a little ahead of Vespasian, out of the indignation he had at the destruction the Romans had undergone while he was absent, took two hundred chosen horsemen and some footmen with him and entered without noise into the city. (*Wars* IV 1:10)

Josephus, a proud man, would have wanted to see his brilliant plan documented for the sake of history, although he would not have wanted the Jews to know that he had been its author. Interestingly, Titus had also been the first Roman officer through the breached wall in Jotapata when that city fell some months before.

Jerusalem

The final siege of Jerusalem three years later will be dealt with in detail later, but an aspect of it bears mentioning here. At one point in the siege, stones were removed from the base of the tower of Antonia. This was a key event in the taking of Jerusalem and is reminiscent of the final action at Gamala.

> But then, as they were beneath the other and were sadly wounded by the stones thrown down upon them, some of them threw their shields over their bodies and partly with their hands and partly with their bodies and partly with crows, they undermined its foundations and with great pains they removed four of its stones. (*Wars* VI 1:3)

The wall eventually collapsed and Antonia was breached which directly led to the fall of the Second Temple and then Jerusalem. In that instance, it is known for a fact that Josephus was at the siege and advising Titus. Was this action at Josephus' suggestion and direction as well? Josephus was intimately familiar with the defensive walls of Jerusalem.

Justus of Tiberias

Justus of Tiberias, son of Pistus, wrote a book on Jewish history. Justus was also one of Josephus' early rivals for a leadership position during the Jewish revolt. His work, *History of the Jewish Kings,* is now lost, but in the book Justus had questioned Josephus' loyalties. In a section dealing with the

Jewish revolt, he had apparently shown Josephus in a much different light.

Josephus writes about the competing work:

> And now I am come to this part of my narration, I have a mind to say a few things to Justus, who hath himself written a history concerning these affairs, as also to others who profess to write history, but have little regard to truth and are not afraid, either out of ill-will or good-will to some persons, to relate falsehoods. These men do like those who compose forged deeds and conveyances; and because they are not brought to the like punishment with them, they have no regard to truth. (*Life*, 65)

Continuing Accusations

While enjoying life in the Roman Royal court in his later years, Josephus had to constantly defend himself against charges of betrayal leveled by angry Jewish loyalists. Josephus proudly states that whoever the Roman emperor was at the time always supported him and punished the accusers.

> However, the kindness of the emperor (Vespasian) to me continued still the same; for when Vespasian was dead, Titus, who succeeded him in the government, kept up the same respect for me which I had from his father; and when I had frequent accusations laid against me, he would not believe them. And Domitian, who succeeded, still augmented his respects to me; for he punished those Jews that were my accusers and gave command that a servant of mine, who was a eunuch and my accuser, should be punished. He also made that country I had in Judea tax free which is a mark of the greatest honor to him who hath it; nay, Domitia, the wife of Caesar, continued to do me kindnesses. And this is the account of the actions of my whole life; and let others judge of my character by them as they please. (*Life*, 76)

Which version about Josephus is to be believed? Was Josephus' ultimate goal in accepting a Galilean generalship to end up in the Roman army as an honored and worthy prisoner? Did Josephus desire to live in Rome and enjoy the Royal court of Nero which he had visited years before when he was 26? Or was Josephus, as he insists, simply a divine instrument, following his destiny as God defined it to him through dreams and visions?

"..I protest openly that I do not go over to the Romans as a deserter of the Jews, but as a minister from thee (God)." (*Wars* III 8:3)

To be fair, Josephus did work for the Jewish cause fortifying cities and directing early operations with skill and apparent commitment. At the end of the siege in Jotapata, boiling oil was poured upon the Romans–a borderline war crime even in those days. This was hardly an action designed to endear Josephus to General Vespasian.

In any case, Josephus' public reason for his embracing the Romans must have grated on Jewish loyalists, and, based on it alone, how could Josephus not expect the lifelong enmity of the surviving Jews?

Josephus is, in a real way, antithetical to the great Jewish patriarch Moses. Moses believed that the Jews were God's chosen people whereas Josephus believed that the Jews had lost that covenant with God for their wickedness; Moses led the Jews to the "land of milk and honey" but Josephus asserted that God empowered the Romans to take that land away. For the vast majority of Jews to whom religion is everything, Josephus' beliefs were unacceptable and sacrilegious.

Chapter 22   Unsettled Empire

there were all the debaucheries of luxurious peace, all the horrors of a city most cruelly sacked, till one was ready to believe the Country to be mad at once with rage and lust. (Tacitus *Histories* 3:83)

The suppression of the revolt had gone well. Even while Vespasian was laying siege to Jotapata the previous year, General Trajan (the future emperor) of the 10th legion took Japha, and General Cerealis of the 15th secured much of Samaria by taking a stronghold of rebels atop Mount Gerizim—as tepid as the overall Samarian resistance was. When Jotapata finally fell on June 17th of A.D. 69, the Galilean general Josephus was also captured which was a great coup for the Roman forces.

Joppa then fell, and, in August of A.D. 67, the Lake Gennesareth city of Tarichae was taken—this after a particularly ugly sea battle which resulted in 6,500 Jewish dead left floating in the water for days. In September, a rebel outpost on Mount Tabor was taken. In October, Gamala fell to siege, and Gischala was captured after its leader, John, escaped through ruse. Both the latter actions were led by General Titus.

At the end of A.D. 67, General Vespasian, foreseeing civil war in Rome, began to secure and garrison those cities in Galilee and Judea that had already been taken while moving most of his forces to Caesarea and Ptolemais.

Campaign Suspended

When civil discord formally rocked the empire upon the assisted suicide of Nero in June of A.D. 68, Vespasian was prepared and retreated to Caesarea. At that time, Jerusalem was the only major city not controlled by Rome. The southern Herodian fortresses of Herodium, Macherus, and Masada remained held by "robbers" according to Josephus and so were of lesser importance.

> Now as Vespasian was returned to Cesarea and was getting ready with all his army to march directly to Jerusalem, he was informed that Nero was dead, after he had reigned thirteen years and eight days...Wherefore Vespasian put off at first his expedition against Jerusalem and stood waiting whither the empire would be transferred after the death of Nero. (*Wars* IV 9:2)

That Vespasian stopped his campaign for the duration of the uncertainty of Roman leadership was perhaps an indication of the strength of Jerusalem. Did Vespasian plan on requesting more legions in order to subdue to the well-defended city? In a civil war, additional legions to fight the Jews would be hard to come by. Or did Vespasian not want to involve his own forces in siege warfare, when they might be needed to march on Rome when he himself laid claim to the empire?.

In a marvelous and very long sentence, Josephus gives a surprisingly complete summary of the Roman leadership changes in the unsettled years of A.D. 68-69.

> But as to any narration after what manner he (Nero) abused his power in the government and committed the management of affairs to those vile wretches, Nymphidius and Tigellinus, his unworthy freed-men; and how he (Nero) had a plot laid against him by them and was deserted by all his guards and ran away with four of his most trusty freed-men and slew himself in the suburbs of Rome; and how those that occasioned his death were in no long time brought themselves to punishment; how also the war in Gall ended; and how Galba was made emperor and returned out of Spain to Rome; and how he was accused by the soldiers as a pusillanimous person and slain by treachery in the middle of the market-place at Rome and Otho was made emperor; with his expedition

against the commanders of Vitellius and his destruction thereupon; and besides what troubles there were under Vitellius and the fight that was about the capitol; as also how Antonius Primus and Mucianus slew Vitellius and his German legions and thereby put an end to that civil war; - I have omitted to give an exact account of them, because they are well known by all and they are described by a great number of Greek and Roman authors; yet for the sake of the connexion of matters and that my history may not be incoherent, I have just touched upon every thing briefly. (Wars IV 9:2)

Sulpicious Galba

Governor Sulpicious Galba of Spain had been declared emperor by his own troops weeks before Nero's death and, accepting the honor, was preparing to march on Rome to battle the last Caesar for control of the empire. After Nero's convenient suicide in June of A.D. 68, however, that was not necessary; Galba was formally acknowledged by the Roman Senate.

Galba came from a noble family and had a distinguished career. Decades before, in A.D. 41, he had strongly been considered for emperor by the Roman Senate after the assassination of Emperor Caius. Then, however, the Praetorian guard forced Claudius upon the senate under threat of the sword, and Galba lost out.

Vespasian promptly communicated to Galba his support and waited for instructions about the furtherance of the Jewish war. But not all of the generals supported Galba. In the north, General Aulus Vitellius, the governor of Lower Germany, had his ambitions as did General Marcus Otho–ostensibly an ally of Galba's. Over and above their ambition, these generals had legitimate concerns about Galba's ability to adequately serve the needs of the empire.

Galba was now in his early seventies and to some was becoming increasingly feeble-minded. He also had no heir so on his death the future of the empire would again be in question. It was also entirely probable that, in A.D. 68, Emperor Galba was being used as a puppet by more powerful men and was intended to live for only as long as was convenient to their ambition.

To allay one of those concerns, Galba adopted as a son and heir a vigorous young man from an honored and ancient family, Lucius Piso. But General Marcus Otho, at 37 years of age, had supported Galba with the expectation of receiving that honor. Otho, a former dissolute companion of Nero, now plotted Galba's destruction, with the intention of seizing the empire for himself.

Marcus Otho

Vespasian, according to all sources, had no desire to rule and stayed out of the fray far to the east in Caesarea. After several months of hearing little from Galba concerning the Jewish campaign, in January of A.D. 69 Vespasian sent his son Titus to Rome. Accompanied by King Agrippa II, Titus' purpose was to meet with Emperor Galba to address the issue of the eastern insurrection. En route, however, it was learned by Titus that Galba had been killed–assassinated in a Roman marketplace. General Otho had assumed the supreme power and was now emperor.

Moreover, when he heard that Galba was made emperor, he attempted nothing till he also should send him some directions about the war: however, he sent his son Titus to him, to salute him and to receive his commands about the Jews. Upon the very same errand did king Agrippa sail along with Titus to Galba; but as they were sailing in their long ships by the coasts of Achaia, for it was winter time, they heard that Galba was slain, before they could get to him, after he had reigned seven months and as many days. After whom Otho took the government and undertook the management of public affairs. So Agrippa resolved to go on to Rome without any terror; on account of the change in the government; but Titus, by a Divine impulse, sailed back from Greece to Syria and came in great haste to Cesarea, to his father. And now they were both in suspense about the public affairs, the Roman empire being then in a fluctuating condition and did not go on with their expedition against the Jews, but thought that to make any attack upon foreigners was now unseasonable, on account of the solicitude they were in for their own country. (*Wars* IV 9:2)

But General Aulus Vitellius, soon to be the governor of lower Germany, also had his ambitions and had been preparing his forces and forging alliances for months. Vitellius saw Otho as weak and effeminate.

Aulus Vitellius soon gained the loyalty of several northern legions and started marching south to Italia for the purpose of challenging Otho. Otho was aware of what, to him, was a northern rebellion, even as he settled into the city of Rome and governed with authority in late January of A.D. 69. Otho, a former partisan of Nero, though he was supported by the senate, never gained any great popularity with the Roman people.

> Yet he (Otho) did not succeed in winning the attachment of any save a certain few who were like himself. For there were several circumstances, such as his restoration of the images of those under accusation, his life and habits, his intimacy with Sporus and his keeping in his service the rest of Nero's favourites, that alarmed everybody. They hated him most of all, however, because he had shown that the imperial office was for sale and had put the City in the power of the boldest spies; (Dio 63:8)

The two rivals Otho and Vitellius communicated frequently even as they prepared for civil war. Each offered the other personal freedom and an easy life if they abandoned ambition for the throne.

> Meanwhile frequent letters, disfigured by unmanly flatteries, were addressed by Otho to Vitellius, with offers of wealth and favour and any retreat he might select for a life of prodigal indulgence. Vitellius made similar overtures. Their tone was at first pacific; and both exhibited a foolish and undignified hypocrisy. Then they seemed to quarrel, charging each other with debaucheries and the grossest crimes and both spoke truth. (Tacitus *Histories* 1:74)

But with no compromise from either general, war was inevitable. The people of Rome, according to Tacitus, were aghast that a war of such great a magnitude would be waged by two men of such low quality.

Vitellius with his sensuality and gluttony was his own enemy; Otho, with his profligacy, his cruelty and his recklessness, was held to be more dangerous to the Commonwealth. (Tacitus *Histories* 2:31)
Some were speculating on Vespasian and the armies of the East. Vespasian was indeed preferable to either, yet they shuddered at the idea of another war, of other massacres. Even about Vespasian there were doubtful rumours and he, unlike any of his predecessors, was changed for the better by power. (Tacitus *Histories* 1:50)

The civil war was fought on several fronts, with the most important battle being at Bedriacum in Italy. There, 40,000 Romans lost their lives as the forces of Otho were ultimately defeated. When Emperor Otho, who chose to stay in Rome, learned of the debacle, he put his affairs in order and committed a Roman-style suicide, gaining much honor in the process.

Others may have held the throne for a longer time, but no one can have left it with such fortitude.(Ibid 2:47)

Otho had been in power for only three months and died at the age of 37.

Emperor Vitellius

While Aulus Vitellius had a poor personal reputation, he came from one of the most illustrious families of Rome. His father Lucius Vitellius had been consul three times and served under Emperors Tiberius and Caius as the president of Syria. It was widely thought that for years Lucius Vitellius, along with Pallas and secretary Narcissist, dictated Roman foreign policy to Emperor Claudius. Lucius Vitellius died in A.D. 51.

Emperor Vitellius had been consul of the senate in A.D. 48 and proconsul of Africa 10 years later. It was Emperor Galba, in fact, who had appointed Vitellius to the position of governor of lower Germany in A.D. 68. Officially, Vitellius began his rule as emperor in April of A.D. 69.

Vitellius did not immediately learn of Otho's suicide, as he was on a leisurely march south with his German-dominated legions through Italia. In Rome and now as emperor, Vitellius could not control his German soldiers and they began to wreak havoc everywhere—looking for plunder and easy pleasure. The Romans did not like this. Vitellius also apparently had a reputation as a dissolute and glutton.

> (Vitellius)..had a scandalous and insatiable passion for feasts; the provocatives of gluttony were conveyed to him from the capital and from Italy, till the roads from both seas resounded with traffic; the leading men of the various states were ruined by having to furnish his entertainments and the states themselves reduced to beggary; (Tacitus *Histories* 2:62)

> Vitellius, addicted as he was to luxury and licentiousness, no longer cared for anything else either human or divine..Now, when he was in a position of so great authority, his wantonness only increased and he was squandering money most of the day and night alike. He was insatiate in gorging himself and was constantly vomiting up what he ate, being nourished by the mere passage of the food..The entire period of his reign was nothing but a series of carousals and revels. All the most costly viands were brought from as far as the Ocean (not to say farther) and drawn from both land and sea and were prepared in so costly a fashion that even now certain cakes and other dishes are named Vitellian, after him..For example, he once caused a dish to be made that cost a million sesterces, into which he put a mixture of tongues and brains and livers of certain fishes and birds. As it was impossible to make so large a vessel of pottery, it was made of silver and remained in except for some time, being regard somewhat in the light of a votive offering, until Hadrian finally set eyes on it and melted it down. (Dio 64: 2-3)

But the Flavian historians had their biases. In elevating the Flavians, perhaps of necessity Vitellius had to be demonized. Even Dio admits that as emperor, Vitellius demonstrated admirable qualities.

> (Vitellius)..was not entirely without good deeds. For example, he retained the coinage minted under Nero, Galba and Otho, evincing no displeasure at their likenesses; and any gifts that they had bestowed upon any persons he held to be valid and deprived no one of any such possession. He did not collect any sums still owing of former levies and he confiscated nones' property. He put to death but very few of those who had sided with Otho and did not withhold the property of these even from their relatives. Upon the kinsmen of those previously executed he bestowed all their funds that were still to be found in the

public treasury. He did not even find fault with the wills of such as had fought against him and had fallen in the battles. Furthermore he forbade the senators and the knights to fight as gladiators or to perform in any spectacle in the orchestra. For these measures he was commended. (Dio 64:6)

With an inability to form a cohesive and supportive mandate with the Romans, Vitellius' star was falling rapidly. Vespasian, biding his time in Caesarea, was seen as the only viable alternative. Vespasian himself was reluctant to make any claims on the empire, but the rising sentiment supporting him was becoming difficult to ignore. His three legions supported him unequivocally, as did the powerful the eastern Generals Tiberius Alexander and Mucianus–who together controlled six additional legions.

Vespasian Challenges Vitellius

During his hiatus in Caesarea from mid-A.D. 68 to the summer of A.D. 69, Vespasian did not totally neglect the Jewish war. He launched several minor campaigns in Judea keeping the Jewish rebels under control and "boxed in" in certain areas. Only Jerusalem and the southern mountain fortresses of Herodium, Macherus and Masada were left still in a state of revolt and under the control of the zealots. The surrounding countrysides were subdued and ready for the main force and final stroke of the Roman army against Jerusalem, the city that was the soul of the Jewish nation.

Vespasian had all but completed the Jewish war and only the siege of Jerusalem now remained, an operation, the difficulty and arduousness of which was due, rather to the character of its mountain citadel and the perverse obstinacy of the national superstition, than to any sufficient means of enduring extremities left to the besieged. As we have mentioned above, Vespasian himself had three legions inured to war. Mucianus had four under his command in his peaceful province. Emulation, however and the glory won by the neighbouring army had banished all tendency to sloth and unbroken rest and exemption from the hardships of war had given them a vigour equivalent to the hardihood which the others had gained by their perils and their toils.

Each had auxiliary forces of infantry and cavalry, each had fleets and tributary kings and each, though their renown was of a different kind, had a celebrated name. (Tacitus *Histories* 2:4)

As the months passed of Vitellius' only marginally-competent leadership, Rome was sinking further into chaos. Vespasian was urged to seize power. Chief among his supporters was the president of Syria, Licinius Mucianus. Vespasian had actually been sent by Nero to replace Mucianus as the Roman supreme military commander early in the war. Tiberius Alexander, the powerful governor of Egypt–and a Jew–also urged Vespasian to lay claim to the empire.

Vespasian's soldiers, taking a cue from the soldiers of the now-executed Galba, were the first to declare him emperor. Vespasian rejected the mantle. But some of these same soldiers, realizing the chaotic state that Rome was in and fearing for their lives and the lives of their families, threatened Vespasian with the sword if he did not seize control.

> ..but when he refused the empire, the commanders insisted the more earnestly upon his acceptance; and the soldiers came about him, with their drawn swords in their hands and threatened to kill him, unless he would now live according to his dignity. And when he had shown his reluctance a great while and had endeavored to thrust away this dominion from him, he at length, being not able to persuade them, yielded to their solicitations that would salute him emperor. (*Wars* IV 9:4)

Vespasian finally yielded. By the 15th of July, A.D. 69 Vespasian had declared himself. All of the East enthusiastically fell into line and pledged their support–including Agrippa II.

> Before long Agrippa, who had been summoned from the capital by secret despatches from his friends, while as yet Vitellius knew nothing, was crossing the sea with all speed. Queen Berenice too, who was then in the prime of youth and beauty and who had charmed even the old Vespasian by the splendour of her presents, promoted his cause with equal zeal. (Tacitus *Histories* 2:81)

General Titus especially benefited from this. Not only was Titus now heir to the empire, but the famously beautiful Queen Bernice, Agrippa's sister and constant companion, now deemed to become his paramour. Bernice was certainly beautiful, but hardly in the "prime of youth", as Tacitus writes. Bernice, at the age of 41, was 13 years older than Titus.

Vespasian then moved on to Alexandria in Egypt, to confer and council with General Tiberius Alexander, as well as to collect money to fill his war chest. Vespasian also wanted to buy corn and grain to send to a hungry Rome. Apparently, Vitellius' incompetence was affecting food distribution, and Vespasian knew that providing shiploads of corn would gain him much public support. General Mucianus was sent overland with his legions for the purpose of eventually subduing the armies of Vitellius.

> It was arranged that Titus should pursue the war in Judaea, while Vespasian should secure the passes into Egypt. To cope with Vitellius, a portion of the army, the generalship of Mucianus, the prestige of Vespasian's name and the destiny before which all difficulties vanish, seemed sufficient. (Ibid 2:82)

Upon hearing of the commitment of Vespasian, several key generals for Vitellius revolted without waiting for the arrival of Mucianus–many had been generals under Otho. The most important of these was General Antonius Primus of the Pannonian (modern-day Hungary) legion who immediately sent his forces to war against the legions of Vitellius.

A hugely important battle took place at Cremona and Bedriacum, in much the same area where Vitellius' forces had defeated the legions of Otho seven months previously. Many of the opposing combatants knew each other well.

> But what is there surprising about this, considering that when the women of the city in the course of the night brought food and drink to give to the soldiers of Vitellius, the latter, after eating and drinking themselves, passed the supplies on to their antagonists? One of them would call out the name of his adversary (for they practically all knew one another and were well acquainted) and would say: "Comrade, take

and eat this; I give you, not a sword, but bread. Take and drink this; I hold out to you, not a shield, but a cup. Thus, whether you kill me or I you, we shall quit life more comfortably and the hand that slays will not be feeble and nerveless, whether it be yours that smites me or mine that smites you. (Dio 64:13)

With Mucianus still approaching, the victorious legions of Antonius–newly allied with Vespasian–made camp around the city of Rome, waiting for Mucianus. Upon his arrival, Antonius and Mucianus with their soldiers moved in upon Rome in loose coordination. Soon, there was street warfare between the Vespasians and the Vitellians.

It was a terrible and hideous sight that presented itself throughout the city. Here raged battle and death; there the bath and the tavern were crowded. In one spot were pools of blood and heaps of corpses and close by prostitutes and men of character as infamous; there were all the debaucheries of luxurious peace, all the horrors of a city most cruelly sacked, till one was ready to believe the Country to be mad at once with rage and lust. (Tacitus *Histories* 3:83)

The Vitellians were defeated and Vitellius was captured.

Then Vitellius in his fear put on a ragged and filthy tunic and concealed himself in a dark room where dogs were kept, intending to escape during the night to Tarracina and there join his brother. But the soldiers sought and found him; for naturally he could not go entirely unrecognized very long after having been emperor. They seized him, covered as he was with rubbish and blood (for he had been bitten by the dogs) and tearing off his tunic they bound his hands behind his back and put a rope round his neck. (Dio 64:20)

Vitellius was roughly brought to the Rostra in the Imperial Forum, where he was pilloried, abused, and then beheaded.

And thus they led down from the palace the Caesar who had revelled there; along the Sacred Way they dragged the emperor who had often paraded past in his chair of state and they conducted the Augustus to the Forum, where he had often addressed the people. Some buffeted him, some plucked at his beard; all mocked him, all insulted him, making comments especially upon his riotous living, since he had a protuberant belly..(Dio 64:20)

Then (Vitellius) fell under a shower of blows and the mob reviled the dead man with the same heartlessness with which they had flattered him when he was alive. He had nearly completed his 57th year. His consulate, his priesthood, his high reputation, his place among the first men of the State, he owed, not to any energy of his own, but to the renown of his father. (Tacitus *Histories* 3:85-6)

After Vitellius' death, Vespasian's son Domitian, who was in the city and had endured no small measure of peril in escaping the supporters of Vitellius, presented himself to the city elders as a representative of his father and assumed proxy control. Domitian was only 19 and loved to give orders, but he was closely held in check by General Mucianus, who had formal letters of authority from Vespasian.

General Titus and the Jewish Campaign

The Roman Senate formally declared Vespasian emperor in December of A.D. 69, two weeks after Vitellius' beheading. Vespasian would be the fourth emperor in less than a year. Vespasian, however, remained in Alexandria for several months waiting for good sailing weather.

One of the first acts of Vespasian was to designate his son Titus as leader of the Roman forces of the East and to order him to resume the Jewish wars.

So upon this confirmation of Vespasian's entire government which was now settled and upon the unexpected deliverance of the public affairs of the Romans from ruin, Vespasian turned his thoughts to what remained unsubdued in Judea. However, he himself made haste to go to Rome, as the winter was now almost over and soon set the affairs of Alexandria in order, but sent his son Titus, with a select part of his army, to destroy Jerusalem. (*Wars* IV 11:5)

Vespasian had heard of the victory of Cremona and had received favourable tidings from all quarters and he was now informed of the fall of Vitellius by many persons of every rank, who, with a good fortune equal to their courage, risked the perils of the wintry sea. Envoys had come from king Vologesus to offer him 40,000 Parthian cavalry. It was a matter of pride and joy to him to be courted with such splendid offers of help from the allies and not to want them. He thanked Vologesus and recommended him to send ambassadors to the Senate and to learn for himself that peace had been restored. While his thoughts were fixed on Italy and on the state of the Capital, he heard an unfavourable account of Domitian which represented him as overstepping the limits of his age and the privileges of a son. He therefore entrusted Titus with the main strength of the army to complete what had yet to be done in the Jewish war. (Tacitus *Histories* 4:51)

Vespasian wanted to finish the Judean campaign himself, but his son Domitian was in Rome acting the part of emperor, and the senate had already given him the name of Caesar. Also, the true loyalty of General Antonius was a question mark and he was hugely popular with the people.

The loyal Mucianus in Rome skillfully held Antonius and Domitian in check, but still urged Vespasian to leave Jerusalem to Titus and to proceed to Rome as soon as possible.

To finish the Jewish campaign, Vespasian assigned Titus more than twice the number of troops that Nero had given him three years before. Vespasian now fully appreciated the physical defenses of the city of Jerusalem and the tenacity and passion of the Jewish warriors. Also, as the resolution of the Jewish revolt would mark the first major action of his Imperial reign, Vespasian wanted the victory to be as swift and as impressive as possible. Joining the Emperor's eldest son Titus was the Jewish King Agrippa II and his auxiliary forces, and the former Judean and Egyptian governor Alexander Tiberius–a Jew by birth–who commanded two Roman legions.

Conflict Within Jerusalem

During the 18-month hiatus in the Jewish war, zealot refugees from all across the war-torn Jewish East sought sanctuary in Jerusalem. One of these was John of Gischala, Flavius Josephus' old Galilean nemesis. In early A.D. 67, John had convinced the High Priesthood in Jerusalem to not only recall Josephus from Galilee, but to have him executed for treason. That was forgotten, however, when the Romans invaded Galilee some weeks later. Soon after, Josephus was captured and the issue became moot.

When John of Gischala arrived in Jerusalem in A.D. 68 as a refugee, he soon became one of the zealot leaders.

> ..John, the son of a certain man whose name was Levi...was a cunning knave and of a temper that could put on various shapes; very rash in expecting great things and very sagacious in bringing about what he hoped for. It was known to every body that he was fond of war, in order to thrust himself into authority; (*Wars* IV 2:1)

While vastly outnumbered by the "regular" citizens of Jerusalem, the zealots were strong young men willing and anxious to fight. Within Jerusalem, Eleazor, the son of Simon (not the later leader of the Masada Sicarii) had organized the zealots into a quasi-criminal group. The zealots then took over the Second Temple. The walled Second Temple not only boasted the castle of Antonia as a separate fortress, but also had an inner wall as well. This surrounded a 15-acre area that could serve as a final stronghold if needed.

The zealots occasionally raided the city below for food and supplies, though the inner Temple was amply stocked with provisions and possessed its own cisterns. The zealots also tried to sway the common citizens over to their side by spreading the lies that the High Priesthood was making secret capitulation plans with the Romans.

One of the former High Priest leaders was Ananus, the son of the elder Ananus. The younger Ananus was the High Priest for a short time in late A.D. 62. He was responsible for the execution of James the Just, the brother of Jesus and the leader of the Jerusalem Christian Church at that time during his tenure. He might have had a hand in the death of Procurator Festus. The elder Ananus would likely have been in his 80's in A.D. 69. The amount of energy and leadership he would have brought to the defense of Jerusalem is debatable.

At first, when John of Gischala arrived, he supported Ananus. According to Josephus, however, John was actually working to betray the High Priesthood to the zealots.

> Now it was John who, as we told you, ran away from Gischala and was the occasion of all these being destroyed. He was a man of great craft and bore about him in his soul a strong passion after tyranny and at a distance was the adviser in these actions; and indeed at this time he pretended to be of the people's opinion and went all about with Ananus when he consulted the great men every day and in the night time also when he went round the watch; but he divulged their secrets to the zealots, (*Wars* IV 3:13)

Soon it became apparent to the High Priesthood and the citizens that the zealots had to be defeated. The elder Ananus was one of the organizers of the "army" of the High Priesthood.

> And now the multitude were going to rise against them already; for Ananus, the ancientest of the high priests, persuaded them to it. He was a very prudent man and had perhaps saved the city if he could but have escaped the hands of those that plotted against him. (*Wars* IV 3:7)

Symeon, the son of Gamaliel (*Wars* IV 3:9), was also a leader in the citizen army. Gamaliel was the name of an honored family in Jerusalem and Gamaliel himself was the Pharisee who was quoted in Acts (Acts 5:38; 22:3) and was a teacher of Saul of Tarsus (Paul the Apostle).

In the zealot stronghold of the Second Temple dissension developed and the zealots split into two groups. Eleazor and his men controlled the walled and elevated inner courtyard and the Sanctuary building while John of Gischala controlled the outer courtyard, the cloisters, and the tower of Antonia. Both areas were roughly equal in size–approximately 15 acres each. With the priesthood and most of the population against them, the two warring zealot factions, under a siege of sorts, had to settle for an uneasy truce within the Second Temple.

John of Gischala then had a brilliant idea. He sent an invitation to the Idumeans in the south of Judea to come to Jerusalem and help defend the city. The Idumeans quickly responded, well aware of the riches that lay within the great city and happy for an opportunity to gain them–Romans or no Romans. Over 20,000 Idumean men soon arrived outside Jerusalem and demanded entrance. The Temple priests, who controlled the gates, understandably did not want to let them in.

Eventually, the zealots from the Second Temple sneaked down into the main city and sawed open a Jerusalem gate near the Idumean encampment (*Wars* IV 4:7). Thousands of Idumean soldiers poured in and proceeded to ransack the city. In the confusion, the zealots took temporary control of the main city of Jerusalem. The High Priests who were the enemies of the zealots–including the younger Ananus and his father–were slain.

> But the rage of the Idumeans was not satiated by these slaughters; but they now betook themselves to the city and plundered every house and slew every one they met; and for the other multitude, they esteemed it needless to go on with killing them, but they sought for the high priests and the generality went with the greatest zeal against them; and as soon as they caught them they slew them and then standing upon their dead bodies, in way of jest, upbraided Ananus with his kindness to the people and Jesus with his speech made to them from the wall. Nay, they proceeded to that degree of impiety, as to cast away their dead bodies without burial, although the Jews used to take so much care of the burial of men, that they took down those that were condemned and crucified and buried them before the going down of the sun. I should not mistake if I said that the death of Ananus was the beginning of the destruction of the city and that from this very day may be dated the overthrow of her wall and the ruin of her affairs, whereon they saw their high priest and the procurer of their preservation, slain in the midst of their city. (*Wars* IV 5:2)

Most of the Idumeans, having sated themselves, then retired out of the city. The zealots continued to kill those Jerusalem citizens and priests who might provide resistance to their rule. It was during this time that Josephus' family was put in prison.

Simon of Gerasa

Simon was a man of ambition who first made his reputation as a robber working out of the old Herodian mountaintop fortress of Masada. He originally came from Gerasa, or Philadelphia, in the Decapolis. Simon then took criminal control of an area called the Acrabattene. The territory was close enough to Jerusalem, and Simon was perceived as being enough of a threat, that either Ananus the elder or the younger drove him out of it. From this defeat, Simon retreated to the mountain fortress of criminals, Masada.

> And now there arose another war at Jerusalem. There was a son of Giora, one Simon, by birth of Gerasa, a young man, not so cunning indeed as John [of Gisehala], who had already seized upon the city, but superior in strength of body and courage; on which account, when he had been driven away from that Acrabattene toparchy which he once had, by Ananus the high priest, he came to those robbers who had seized upon Masada. (*Wars* IV 9:3)

Simon soon gained the confidence of the Sicarii who controlled Masada and led raids and attacks on the nearby towns and villages of Idumea. The bold and ambitious Simon then left Masada and formed his own small criminal army and became a virtual king with continued successful raids and campaigns in the area. The zealots of Jerusalem fought him on several occasions outside the city walls. Though Simon beat the zealots in every encounter, Simon never dared attempt to breach the walls of Jerusalem itself.

At this time, within Jerusalem the citizens were again battling against the tyranny of Eleazor and John and their zealot armies. Eventually, by their sheer numbers, the citizens managed to force the zealots back up into the Second Temple. That accomplished, he citizens and High Priesthood knew they needed help. Seeing Simon as more an enemy of the zealots than of themselves, the citizens invited him into Jerusalem to become their leader.

> Now it was God who turned their opinions to the worst advice and thence they devised such a remedy to get themselves free as was worse than the disease itself. Accordingly, in order to overthrow John, they determined to admit Simon and earnestly to desire the introduction of a second tyrant into the city; which resolution they brought to perfection and sent Matthias, the high priest, to beseech this Simon to come ill to them, of whom they had so often been afraid. (*Wars* IV 9:11)

> And thus did Simon get possession of Jerusalem, in the third year of the war, in the month Xanthicus [Nisan]; whereupon John, with his

multitude of zealots, as being both prohibited from coming out of the temple and having lost their power in the city, (for Simon and his party had plundered them of what they had,) were in despair of deliverance. (*Wars* IV 9:12)

Simon gained power over the citizens of Jerusalem in March of A.D. 69. One of Simon's first acts was to attack John's zealots who were holed up in the Second Temple, but in this he was unsuccessful. For the next year, these three groups lived in Jerusalem, with occasional battles between them, as they waited for Rome to remount an offensive action against the city.

Passover of A.D. 70

As the Passover of A.D. 70 approached, the Romans were marching toward Jerusalem from several directions. Vespasian was firmly in power and there was no need to delay concluding the Jewish campaign any longer.

Within the walls of Jerusalem, Simon of Gerasa held firm control of the upper and lower cities. Simon himself had settled comfortably in to Herod's walled palace, taking over the tower of Phasaelus for his personal quarters. Outnumbered, the zealots were forced back into their stronghold of the Second Temple and the well-fortified tower of Antonia. As they had done before, the zealot leader Eleazor, the son of Simon, and his faction held the inner Temple courtyards, with John of Gischala and his men holding the outer courtyard, including the tower of Antonia.

For the Passover of A.D. 70, in a gesture of goodwill, Eleazor let the priests and supplicants of the main city into the inner courtyard to perform the usual and necessary sacrificial and ritual functions of the festival. Despite the unsettled and dangerous conditions that existed in Judea at that time, and the approaching legions of Titus, hundreds of thousands of Jewish pilgrims came out of the country and entered the holy city to worship and sacrifice.

Taking advantage of the situation, the zealot leader John of Gischala devised a plan to oust Eleazor and his forces from the inner Temple. John had his men disguise themselves as worshipers and infiltrate the inner courtyard. On cue, John's men attacked the zealots of Eleazor. In the struggle that followed, Eleazor and his men were defeated.

AS now the war abroad ceased for a while, the sedition within was revived; and on the feast of unleavened bread which was now come, it being the fourteenth day of the month Xanthicus, [Nisan,] when it is believed the Jews were first freed from the Egyptians, Eleazar and his party opened the gates of this [inmost court of the] temple and admitted such of the people as were desirous to worship God into it. But John made use of this festival as a cloak for his treacherous designs and armed the most inconsiderable of his own party, the greater part of whom were not purified, with weapons concealed under their garments and sent them with great zeal into the temple, in order to seize upon it; which armed men, when they were gotten in, threw their garments away and presently appeared in their armor. Upon which there was a very great disorder and disturbance about the holy house; while the people, who had no concern in the sedition, supposed that this assault was made against all without distinction, as the zealots thought it was made against themselves only. So these left off guarding the gates any longer and leaped down from their battlements before they came to an engagement and fled away into the subterranean caverns of the temple; while the people that stood trembling at the altar and about the holy house, were rolled on heaps together and trampled upon and were beaten both with wooden and with iron weapons without mercy. Such also as had differences with others slew many persons that were quiet, out of their own private enmity and hatred, as if they were opposite to the seditious; and all those that had formerly offended any of these plotters were now known and were now led away to the slaughter; and when they had done abundance of horrid mischief to the guiltless, they granted a truce to the guilty and let those go off that came cut of the caverns. These followers of John also did now seize upon this inner temple and upon all the warlike engines therein and then ventured to oppose Simon. And thus that sedition which had been divided into three factions, was now reduced to two. (*Wars* V 3:1)

The defeated Eleazor was either killed in this action along with a significant portion of his men, or he was allowed to leave Jerusalem. John of Gischala now held the entire Second Temple. Thus, to fight the Romans now massing outside the walls of Jerusalem, the Jews now had two leaders: Simon of Gerasa and John of Gischala.

Chapter 23   The Fall of Jerusalem

The populace was stationed below in the court, the senators on the steps and the priests in the sanctuary itself. And though they were but a handful fighting against a far superior force, they were not conquered until a part of the temple was set on fire. Then they met death willingly, some throwing themselves on the swords of the Romans, some slaying one another, others taking their own lives and still others leaping into the flames. (Dio 65:6)

At the time of the Passover of A.D. 70, on the 14th of Nisan, or the 3rd of April, Titus had reached Jerusalem with his legions and auxiliaries — well over 60,000 men — and had positioned them around the city. The scores of thousands of Passover celebrants not from Jerusalem were now trapped inside the city. Impregnable from any side but the north, Titus established four main camps around the upper city with the intent of attacking the three north walls.

Jerusalem Divided

Jerusalem was divided between the citizens and the remaining Idumeans on one side and the zealots in the Second Temple on the other. After an initial period of peace between them as the Romans established their siege, friction between the two Jewish factions resurfaced.

But although they had grown wiser at the first onset the Romans made upon them, this lasted but a while; for they returned to their former madness and separated one from another and fought it out and did everything that the besiegers could desire them to do; for they never suffered any thing that was worse from the Romans than they made each other suffer; nor was there any misery endured by the city after these men's actions that could be esteemed new. But it was most of all unhappy before it was overthrown while those that took it did it a greater kindness for I venture to affirm that the sedition destroyed the city and the Romans destroyed the sedition, which it was a much harder thing to do than to destroy the walls; so that we may justly ascribe our misfortunes to our own people and the just vengeance taken on them to the Romans; as to which matter let every one determine by the actions on both sides. (*Wars* V 6:1)

Many of the battles fought between the two Jewish groups took place around the Second Temple. Essential stores of corn and grain were destroyed in these reckless actions which proved to be of the greatest consequence in future months as the siege progressed.

The Attacks Begin

Josephus knew Jerusalem and its people well as did Agrippa II. Fluent in Latin and believing Rome's punishment of the Jews represented the will of God, Josephus became one of Titus' most important advisers. Initially, Titus sent Josephus and his aide/friend Nicanor around the walls of Jerusalem, hoping that Josephus could make contact with someone on the ramparts of the wall. With luck, Titus hoped that given the chaos and violence within the city of Jerusalem a surrender could be arranged expeditiously. But the Jews were not receptive to terms, and the very sight of Josephus was incendiary. In one instance Nicanor was even hit by a dart! And so Titus began the siege.

The rocky and uneven terrain outside the walls had to be made level for the Roman engines, which were basically battering rams mounted in tall, mobile towers. Suburbs of Jerusalem were set on fire and leveled. Trees were felled and placed against the walls. Three vulnerable places on the north wall were identified by Titus (likely aided by Josephus, who knew the wall well). Most of the north wall had been built by Agrippa I but to the west of the tower of Hippicus the wall base had been standing in front of very rough terrain for hundreds of years, though rebuilt and reinforced by both Herod the Great and Agrippa I. The Jews on the ramparts of these walls tried to hinder the mounting of these bulwarks as much as possible. To counter the Jewish darts and stones, the Romans began to use their machines of war — large crossbow-like contrivances that could hurl rocks over distances of a half mile or more. Josephus reports that initially these were of little concern. The rocks were white and when a rampart guard saw one, he would warn the people and cover would be taken. But the Romans then took to painting the rocks black, which made them very difficult to be seen (*Wars* V 6:3).

With the Roman bulwarks against the walls set and finished, and with the engines and machines being put place, Simon and John were again forced to come together and coordinate their counterattacks against the Romans.

> So on both sides they laid aside their hatred and their peculiar quarrels and formed themselves into one body; they then ran round the walls and having a vast number of torches with them, they threw them at the machines and shot darts perpetually upon those that impelled those engines which battered the wall; nay, the bolder sort leaped out by troops upon the hurdles that covered the machines and pulled them to pieces and fell upon those that belonged to them and beat them, not so much by any skill they had, as principally by the boldness of their attacks. (*Wars* V 6:4)

Making sorties from the wall, bands of Jewish defenders tried to set fire to the engines. To counter this, Titus mobilized his horseman and successfully battled the torch-carrying Jews. Josephus reports on Titus' reaction to the Jewish resistance:

> Now it happened at this fight that a certain Jew was taken alive, who, by Titus's order, was crucified before the wall, to see whether the rest of them would be aftrighted and abate of their obstinacy. (*Wars* V 6:5)

But this crucifixion had little effect on the resolve of the Jewish warriors.

Titus positioned 75-foot high iron-clad towers on the bulwarks at three separate places along the expanse of the north wall.

Jerusalem
A.D. 70

Roman camps

350 yards

Agrippa's Wall

Psephinus

Asamonean Wall

Agrippa's Wall

Bezetha

Roman camps

Gennath Gate

Bethso

Wall of Titus

Phasaelus

Antonia

Hippicus

Mariamne

Golgotha

Herod's Palace

Essene Gate

Gabatha

Second Temple

Ancient Wall

Asamonean Palace

Kathros House

Dung Gate

Agrippa's Wall

Tyropean Valley

Wall of Titus

Ancient Wall

Lower City

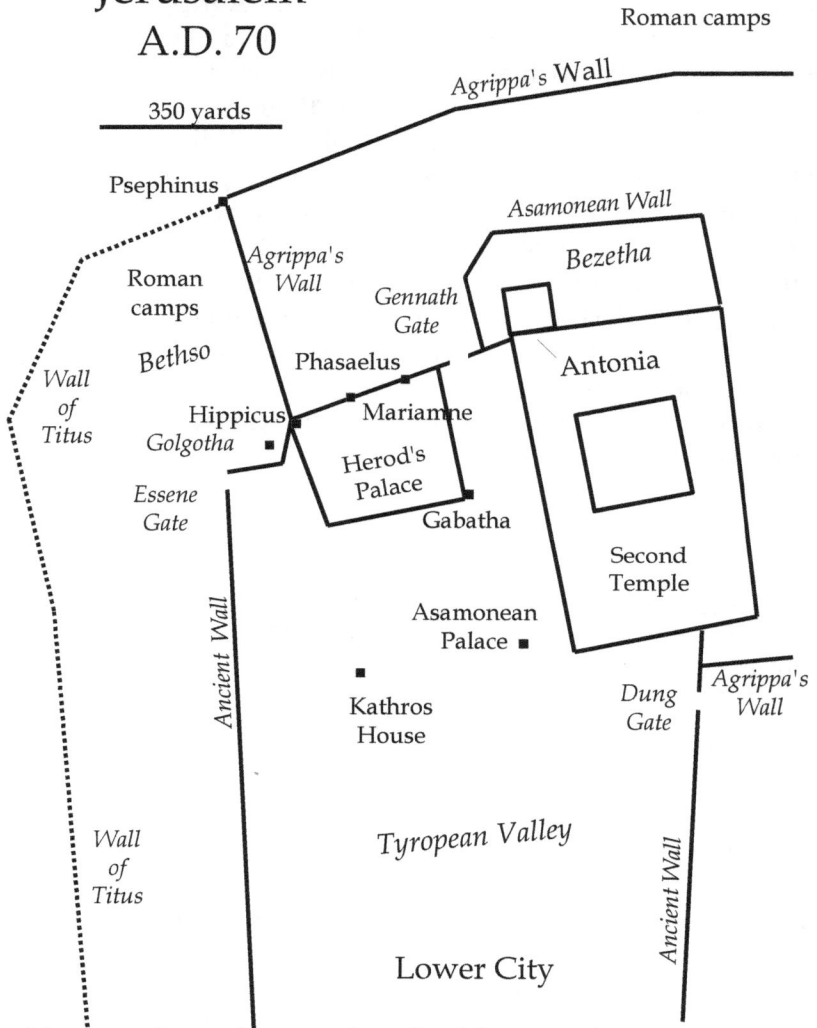

Northern Jerusalem, as described by Josephus, in A.D. 70.
Note the "first" north wall is the "ancient" north wall and forms the
northern wall of Herod's palace. The "second" north wall is the
Asamonean wall, the "third" north wall is Agrippa's wall. The wall of
Titus was built several months into the siege to prevent the escape of the
Jews from the city.

Most of the north wall was less than 50 feet in height, so these were very concerning to the Jewish defenders. The battering rams were set to work.

> Now these towers were very troublesome to the Jews, who otherwise opposed the Romans very courageously; for they shot at them out of their lighter engines from those towers, as they did also by those that threw darts and the archers and those that flung stones. For neither could the Jews reach those that were over them, by reason of their height; and it was not practicable to take them, nor to overturn them, they were so heavy, nor to set them on fire, because they were covered with plates of iron. (*Wars* V 7:2)

The third wall was soon breached, which occurred less that two weeks after the start of the Passover, on the 26th day of April. The engine that did the most damage was one that the Jews themselves gave a name, Nico, because it conquered all things. This northernmost wall had been built by King Agrippa I more than 35 years earlier. It had not been built to its intended height, however, due to an order by Emperor Claudius, who was concerned over Agrippa I's ambition. This lower height worked to the Roman's advantage.

But Jerusalem still had two other walls on the north side that were very formidable and gave the Jews every confidence that they could still withstand the Romans. However, once the war engines had been moved into their new forward positions, the second wall–the wall of the Asamoneans–did not last long. It was breached by the Romans on May 1st.

> NOW Caesar took this wall there on the fifth day after he had taken the first; (*Wars* V 8:1)

In this there was a minor debacle for the Romans. The area enclosed between the second wall and a smaller wall that protected the base of the tower of Antonia was a thriving commercial district full of narrow and obliquely-angled streets and tall buildings. The Romans soldiers that poured through the breach in the second wall were ambushed by the Jews in these narrow confines and forced back out or slain (*Wars* V 8:1). The

Jews also blocked the breach on Roman counter-attack with their own bodies. This success, however, was only temporary.

> (the Jews)..covered themselves with their armor and prevented the Romans, when they were trying to get into the city again and made a wall of their own bodies over against that part of the wall that was cast down. Thus did they valiantly defend themselves for three days; but on the fourth day they could not support themselves against the vehement assaults of Titus..(*Wars* V 8:2)

Two Walls Conquered

With only the most-ancient first wall left, the block-stone northern faces of the tower of Antonia, and the Second Temple, Titus decided to relax the siege in order to give the Jews a chance to contemplate their bleak future and, hopefully, surrender. Behind the remaining wall of Jerusalem were still hundreds of thousands of desperate people. Titus wanted the revolt to end as bloodlessly as possible.

For five days Titus made a great public show of paying all of his soldiers–more than 60,000 men. They dressed in battle regalia and stood in formation a safe but viewable distance from the old north wall. It took more than four full days for all of the men to individually pass before the paymaster (*Wars* V 9:1). During that time the wall ramparts were packed with thousands of Jewish spectators.

But afterward there were no indications that the Jews were considering surrender despite the show of Roman power. Disappointed, Titus resigned himself to the completion of the siege. He then concentrated his bank-building efforts mainly at the tower of Antonia and John's monument. John's monument was likely near the tower of Hippicus where the old wall had already been perceived to be weak. The tower of Antonia held the highest point in the city of Jerusalem, and Titus knew it had to be conquered early. Plus, Antonia would provide the gateway to the Second Temple which was the major stronghold within Jerusalem.

For his part, Flavius Josephus, on several different occasions and from various positions a safe distance away from Jerusalem's wall, reasoned with the Jews to abandon the city. While many Jews did find their way out of Jerusalem and desert, if John or Simon perceived that was the intention of any citizen, their throats were immediately cut (*Wars* V 10:1).

Famine

As the Romans worked on banks against the first wall and the tower of Antonia, famine became widespread within Jerusalem. Great stores of corn and other foodstuff had been thoughtlessly burned months earlier as collateral damage due to Jewish fighting. Now, robbers preyed on those in the city who had any measure of food. Somewhat callously, Josephus believed that the Jerusalem citizens deserved this fate.

> neither did any other city ever suffer such miseries, nor did any age ever breed a generation more fruitful in wickedness than this was, from the beginning of the world. Finally, they brought the Hebrew nation into contempt, that they might themselves appear comparatively less impious with regard to strangers. They confessed what was true, that they were the slaves, the scum and the spurious and abortive offspring of our nation while they overthrew the city themselves and forced the Romans, whether they would or no, to gain a melancholy reputation, (*Wars* V 10:5)

Many Jews would sneak out of the city at night to search for food. Rough chasms surrounded Jerusalem on two of three sides and the prodigious length of the city perimeter made it difficult difficult for the Romans to patrol. Even so, on some days over 500 people would be caught. The prisoners were then beaten and many were crucified before the walls of the city as an example to others (*Wars* V 11:1). This strategy, however, served only to discourage those citizens who were of a mind to desert.

Titus then took to cutting off the hands of those caught outside of the walls searching for food and sent them back into Jerusalem to serve as visual deterrents.

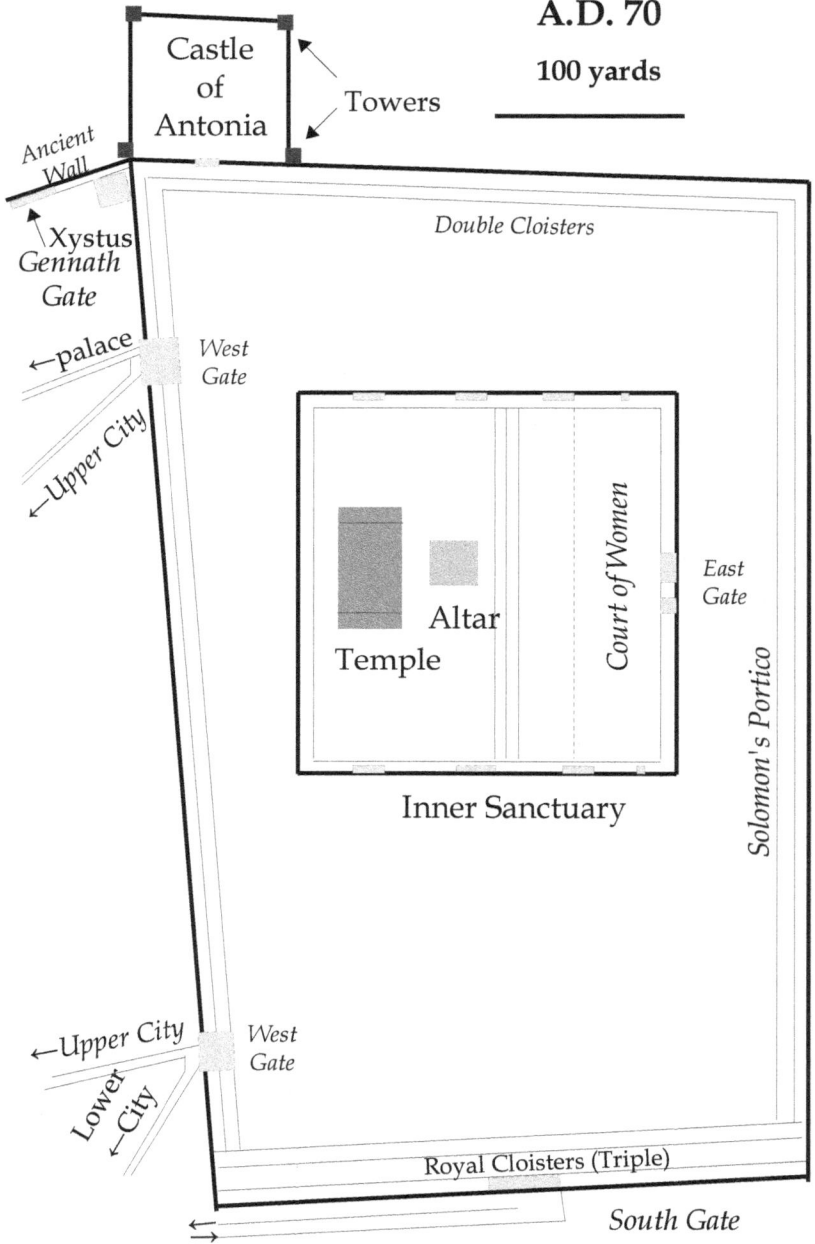

Second Temple
A.D. 70

100 yards
_____

Castle
of
Antonia

Towers

Ancient
Wall

Xystus

Gennath
Gate

←palace

West
Gate

←Upper City

Double Cloisters

Court of Women

Temple

Altar

East
Gate

Inner Sanctuary

Solomon's Portico

←Upper City

West
Gate

Lower
←City

Royal Cloisters (Triple)

South Gate

Engines of War

By the 18th day of May, after more than two weeks of effort by tens of thousands of Roman soldiers, banks had been raised to sufficient height at not two but four separate places.

> For there were now four great banks raised, one of which was at the tower Antonia; this was raised by the fifth legion, over against the middle of that pool which was called Struthius. Another was cast up by the twelfth legion, at the distance of about twenty cubits from the other. But the labors of the tenth legion, which lay a great way off these, were on the north quarter and at the pool called Amygdalon; as was that of the fifteenth legion about thirty cubits from it and at the high priest's monument (*Wars* V 11:4)

The Romans set the ironclad towers with their battering rams in position and prepared to pound the walls of Jerusalem into oblivion. The Jews countered boldly, with warriors carrying quantities of fiery pitch and bitumen outside the walls which they used to burn the massive machines after battling the Romans protecting them.

> The armies also were now mixed one among another and the dust that was raised so far hindered them from seeing one another and the noise that was made so far hindered them from hearing one another, that neither side could discern an enemy from a friend. However, the Jews did not flinch, though not so much from their real strength, as from their despair of deliverance. The Romans also would not yield, by reason of the regard they had to glory and to their reputation in war and because Caesar himself went into the danger (*Wars* V 11:6)

In a stunning setback for the Romans, within a little more than an hour, all four bulwarks of the Romans were destroyed–two weeks of work by 60,000 Roman soldiers up in smoke!

The Wall of Titus

With this debacle and knowing that the people of Jerusalem were starving, a frustrated Titus decided to play a waiting game. With the conditions severe enough, Titus knew that the Jews would eventually surrender–surrender or starve to death. To prevent the mass desertion of Jews and to keep his soldiers busy, Titus decided to build an enclosing wall that would encompass the entire city–no small undertaking.

> That therefore his opinion was, that if they aimed at quickness joined with security, they must build a wall round about the whole city; which was, he thought, the only way to prevent the Jews from coming out any way and that then they would either entirely despair of saving the city and so would surrender it up to him, or be still the more easily conquered when the famine had further weakened them; (*Wars* V 12:1)

> Titus began the wall from the camp of the Assyrians, where his own camp was pitched and drew it down to the lower parts of Cenopolis; thence it went along the valley of Cedron, to the Mount of Olives; it then bent towards the south and encompassed the mountain as far as the rock called Peristereon and that other hill which lies next it and is over the valley which reaches to Siloam; whence it bended again to the west and went down to the valley of the Fountain, beyond which it went up again at the monument of Ananus the high priest and encompassing that mountain where Pompey had formerly pitched his camp, it returned back to the north side of the city and was carried on as far as a certain village called "The House of the Erebinthi;" after which it encompassed Herod's monument and there, on the east, was joined to Titus's own camp, where it began. Now the length of this wall was forty furlongs, one only abated. Now at this wall without were erected thirteen places to keep garrison in, whose circumferences, put together, amounted to ten furlongs; the whole was completed in three days; (*Wars* V 12:2)

The famine continued to intensify. The dead within the city were now thrown over the walls into the adjoining valleys, creating a great stench. This was also a horrible sight to behold for Titus as he made his daily rounds on horseback. But Simon and John were still firmly in control and there was no sign of capitulation–the Jewish leaders killed those who doubted them.

Renewed Assaults

Titus felt increasingly sorry for the people trapped and starving within Jerusalem. He changed tactics — again — and decided to end their miseries as swiftly as possible (*Wars* V 12:4).

Accordingly, he abandoned his wait-and-see strategy and began again to raise banks against the northern wall. Grist for the four banks–chiefly logs and timber–were now scarce. Soldiers had to travel more than 10 miles in order to secure such material to make bulwarks. Titus concentrated his most prodigious bank at the tower of Antonia which was perceived to be the weakest section of the northern wall.

Resigning themselves to the inevitable, more and more Jews began to flee the city at night. Many would swallow their gold fortunes before their attempt, knowing they could retrieve it later after a successful escape. But the Arabians and Greek Syrians of the Roman army were also aware of this.

> But when this contrivance was discovered in one instance, the fame of it filled their several camps, that the deserters came to them full of gold. So the multitude of the Arabians, with the Syrians, cut up those that came as supplicants and searched their bellies. Nor does it seem to me that any misery befell the Jews that was more terrible than this, since in one night's time about two thousand of these deserters were thus dissected. (*Wars* V 13:4)

Titus was aghast when he learned of this gruesome procedure and promised to put to death any soldier caught doing it, but it continued anyway.

> these barbarians would go out still and meet those that ran away before any saw them and looking about them to see that no Roman spied them, they dissected them and pulled this polluted money out of their bowels; which money was still found in a few of them while yet a great many were destroyed by the bare hope there was of thus getting by them, which miserable treatment made many that were deserting to return back again into the city. (*Wars* V 13:5)

During this time, Simon began to systematically slaughter those of the High Priesthood and their families. The most prominent of these was Matthias, the son of Boethus, along with three of his sons (a fourth escaped to desert to Titus). Ironically, Matthias was the High Priest who was the most supportive of opening the city gates to Simon in the first place (*Wars* V 13:1).

The grim end of Jerusalem was coming.

some of the deserters, having no other way, leaped down from the wall immediately while others of them went out of the city with stones, as if they would fight them; but thereupon they fled away to the Romans. But here a worse fate accompanied these than what they had found within the city; and they met with a quicker despatch from the too great abundance they had among the Romans, than they could have done from the famine among the Jews; for when they came first to the Romans, they were puffed up by the famine and swelled like men in a dropsy; after which they all on the sudden overfilled those bodies that were before empty and so burst asunder, excepting such only as were skillful enough to restrain their appetites and by degrees took in their food into bodies unaccustomed thereto. (*Wars* V 13:4)

..Manneus, the son of Lazarus, came running to Titus at this very time and told him that there had been carried out through that one gate, which was intrusted to his care, no fewer than a hundred and fifteen thousand eight hundred and eighty dead bodies, in the interval between the fourteenth day of the month Xanthieus, [Nisan,] when the Romans pitched their camp by the city and the first day of the month Panemus [Tamuz]. This was itself a prodigious multitude; and though this man was not himself set as a governor at that gate, yet was he appointed to pay the public stipend for carrying these bodies out and so was obliged of necessity to number them while the rest were buried by their relations; though all their burial was but this, to bring them away and cast them out of the city. After this man there ran away to Titus many of the eminent citizens and told him the entire number of the poor that were dead and that no fewer than six hundred thousand were thrown out at the gates, though still the number of the rest could not be discovered; and they told him further, that when they were no longer able to carry out the dead bodies of the poor, they laid their corpses on heaps in very large houses and shut them up therein; as also that a medimnus of wheat was sold for a talent; and that when, a while afterward, it was not possible to gather herbs, by reason the city was all walled about, some persons were driven to that terrible distress as to search the common sewers and old dunghills of cattle and to eat the dung which they got there; and what they of old could not endure so much as to see they now used for food. When the Romans barely heard all this, they commiserated their case; while the seditious, who saw it also, did not repent, but suffered the same distress to come upon themselves; for they were blinded by that fate which was already coming upon the city and upon themselves also. (*Wars* V 13:7)

Antonia breached

An adequate bank was raised against the tower of Antonia in 21 days, constructed with tree trunks and materials brought in from long distances. The Romans suspected, or perhaps they had been informed by Josephus, that Antonia's north "wall was but weak and its foundations rotten" (*Wars* VI 1-3). On the 17th of June, the Jews realized that the Romans had found their Achilles Heel and attacked the bulwarks with desperation. The Jewish actions, however, were repulsed by the Romans without difficulty. A solid defensive front was maintained around the banks and the engine of war — tower of war! — and so the Jewish incendiary devices and flaming bitumen were useless.

But the wall of Antonia did not yield easily to the blows of the Roman engines, and the Romans operating them were exposed to the zealous attacks and dart-throwing of the Jews on high. Then, in a brilliant action that is strongly suggests Josephus' involvement, four Roman soldiers, while under fire, managed to dislodge four large foundation stones of Antonia's base. Initially, there was no effect and the Romans fought the Jews to a stalemate that day. Later that night, however, the wall collapsed upon itself (*Wars* VI 1:3). John and his zealot soldiers hastily built another wall behind it, but it proved no match for the Romans, who now fought on ensuing days with renewed energy.

Sensing a major victory was at hand, Titus extorted his soldiers to disdain death for eternal glory.

> For what man of virtue is there who does not know, that those souls which are severed from their fleshly bodies in battles by the sword are received by the ether, that purest of elements and joined to that company which are placed among the stars; that they become good demons and propitious heroes and show themselves as such to their posterity afterwards? (*Wars* VI 1:5)

Titus' speech resulted in an unsuccessful solo foray by an inspired Roman soldier on the 19th of June. Two days later while Titus was planning his final strategy, a band of Roman night watchmen decided to make a sneak attack on Antonia. They slit the throats of the nearest guards at the ninth hour of the night (3 a.m.) and then had a Roman trumpeter sound the horn. The rest of the Jewish night guards thought a full-scale Roman attack was underway and fled. Titus heard the horn in his camp and ordered an attack by the Roman forces closest to Antonia.

Antonia was soon taken and the Roman soldiers could now move up through the Antonia passageways to the cloisters. The fighting now shifted to the stepped portico between the tiled courtyard of the Second Temple and the castle of Antonia.

As the darkness turned into day, Titus observed the battle in one of Antonia's southern towers.

> (The Jews)..esteemed themselves entirely ruined if once the Romans got into the temple, as did the Romans look upon the same thing as the beginning of their entire conquest. So a terrible battle was fought at the entrance of the temple..Great slaughter was now made on both sides and the combatants trod upon the bodies and the armor of those that were dead and dashed them to pieces." (*Wars* VI 1:7)

The battle lasted through to the seventh hour of the next day (1 p.m.), with the Romans failing to gain the Temple. Satisfied with their progress, however, they retreated into their prize of Antonia and began to secure it.

On July 4th, Titus ordered Antonia destroyed. Seven days later, the area was sufficiently reduced to make a broad and steeply angled ramp up the 95 feet to the outer courtyard of the Second Temple. Now the main force of the Roman army, including horses and machines of war, could enter into the Temple courtyard. With this irresistible force, the Jews were forced to retreat. The zealots abandoned the outer courtyard of the Temple completely and holed up in the elevated inner courtyard where the Temple was located. The 15-acre inner courtyards were protected by 60-foot walls of no mean thickness.

The Famine Continues

While battles were being for control of the Second Temple, in the rest of Jerusalem the Jews fought each other over food.

their hunger was so intolerable, that it obliged them to chew every thing while they gathered such things as the most sordid animals would not touch and endured to eat them; nor did they at length abstain from girdles and shoes; and the very leather which belonged to their shields they pulled off and gnawed: (*Wars* VI 3:3)

Josephus then reports a case of a woman driven by hunger to cannibalism.

That, however, this horrid action of eating an own child ought to be covered with the overthrow of their very country itself and men ought not to leave such a city upon the habitable earth to be seen by the sun, (*Wars* VI 3:5)

It should be noted that the Romans had their own problems with supplies–namely ensuring an adequate supply of fresh water. The Jews while lacking for corn, had their own freshwater supply channeled into the lower city courtesy of King Hezekiah hundreds of years before. The Romans had to transport their water from great distances and the Jews did everything they could to sabotage the transport of it.

But the Romans suffered most hardship from the lack of water; for their supply was of poor quality and had to be brought from a distance. The Jews found in their underground passages a source of strength; for they had these tunnels dug from inside the city and extending out under the walls to distant points in the country and going out through them, they would attack the Romans' water-carriers and harass any scattered detachments. But Titus stopped up all these passages. (Dio 65:4)

Sanctuary in Flames

The outer courtyard secured, now the walls of the inner courtyard had to be breached. Titus assigned two legions at two different points to raise banks against them. Material from the first wall was brought up into the Second Temple and placed. On the 22nd of July the work was completed and the engines were positioned. For six days the battering rams pounded the 60-foot high walls, but to no avail. In the battles in the outer courtyard that followed, the Jews actually got control of some of these engines and destroyed them.

> But when Titus perceived that his endeavors to spare a foreign temple turned to the damage of his soldiers and then be killed, he gave order to set the gates on fire. (*Wars* VI 4:1)

> And now the soldiers had already put fire to the gates and the silver that was over them quickly carried the flames to the wood that was within it, whence it spread itself all on the sudden and caught hold on the cloisters. Upon the Jews seeing this fire all about them, their spirits sunk together with their bodies and they were under such astonishment, that not one of them made any haste, either to defend himself or to quench the fire, but they stood as mute spectators of it only. (*Wars* VI 4:2)

Titus set the gates to the inner sanctuary "fortress" on fire and let the fires spread to the cloisters and burn for two days. On the third day, he prepared a select force for the final assault at the wall's weakest section. One of the six leaders was to be a Jew — General Tiberius Alexander, who was "the commander [under the general] of the whole army" (*Wars* VI 4:3).

Before the assault, Titus told his men That the Temple building should be preserved.

> But Titus said, that "although the Jews should get upon that holy house and fight us thence, yet ought we not to revenge ourselves on things that are inanimate, instead of the men themselves;" and that he was not in any case for burning down so vast a work as that was, because this would be a mischief to the Romans themselves, as it would be an ornament to their government while it continued. (*Wars* VI 4:3)

Titus divided the select force up into units, each entering the breach at separate times and reuniting on the inside at a predetermined place. The initial invaders met with stiff resistance by the Jews. Titus, seeing this from his usual tower position, ordered horseman inside to support the soldiers. This temporarily gave the Romans the advantage, but the Jews managed to regroup and prevail that day.

The next day, July 25th, Titus resolved to burn the inner courtyard completely, save the Temple itself.

The early morning attack was successful, but the Temple building was set fire by an overzealous Roman soldier ignoring orders. He threw burning material though a "golden window" of the sanctuary.

> As the flames went upward, the Jews made a great clamor, such as so mighty an affliction required and ran together to prevent it; and now they spared not their lives any longer, nor suffered any thing to restrain their force, since that holy house was perishing, for whose sake it was that they kept such a guard about it. (*Wars* VI 4:6)

> Then the Jews defended themselves much more vigorously than before, as if they had discovered a piece of rare good fortune in being able to fight near the temple and fall in its defence. The populace was stationed below in the court, the senators on the steps and the priests in the sanctuary itself. And though they were but a handful fighting against a far superior force, they were not conquered until a part of the temple was set on fire. Then they met death willingly, some throwing themselves on the swords of the Romans, some slaying one another, others taking their own lives and still others leaping into the flames. And it seemed to everybody and especially to them, that so far from being destruction, it was victory and salvation and happiness to them that they perished along with the temple. (Dio 65:6)

The Jews battled furiously, but were defeated as their most-holy Sanctuary burned behind them.

Titus was dismayed to learn that the Temple building had been set on fire. He personally left the tower and ran into the battle scene hoping to get his men to put out the raging fire, but his soldiers paid him no heed. The Romans were storming into the burning building, hoping to find its legendary riches inside.

> Moreover, the hope of plunder induced many to go on, as having this opinion, that all the places within were full of money and as seeing that all round about it was made of gold. (*Wars* VI 4:7)

> And now, since Caesar was no way able to restrain the enthusiastic fury of the soldiers and the fire proceeded on more and more, he went into the holy place of the temple, with his commanders and saw it, with what was in it, which he found to be far superior to what the relations of foreigners contained and not inferior to what we ourselves boasted of and believed about it. But as the flame had not as yet reached to its

inward parts, but was still consuming the rooms that were about the holy house and Titus supposing what the fact was, that the house itself might yet he saved, he came in haste and endeavored to persuade the soldiers to quench the fire..(*Wars* VI 4:7)

But the fire continued as the soldiers sought plunder and so the holy house of the Jews burnt down.

Now although any one would justly lament the destruction of such a work as this was, since it was the most admirable of all the works that we have seen or heard of, both for its curious structure and its magnitude and also for the vast wealth bestowed upon it, as well as for the glorious reputation it had for its holiness; yet might such a one comfort himself with this thought, that it was fate that decreed it so to be, which is inevitable, both as to living creatures and as to works and places also. (*Wars* VI 4:8)

Negotiation

With the seditious escaping into the city from the Temple, and the Temple itself in flames, the Romans took a respite and celebrated their hard-fought victory. The upper and lower cities remained to be taken, and Herod's palace in the upper city was protected by 40 foot walls, but the Roman conquest of the Second Temple and Antonia were huge milestones. The legion ensigns were brought up into the Temple and sacrifices offered. Titus was acclaimed.

Several days later the Jewish leaders of the revolt, Simon and John, realized that Titus' five-mile long wall surrounding Jerusalem was a strong one. It was also well guarded and so they had little hope of escaping over it. The two men and their remaining forces requested a pardon from Titus.

In response, Titus was accusatory toward the rebel leaders, for he had always offered what he thought were fair terms of surrender.

You have been the men that have never left off rebelling since Pompey first conquered you and have, since that time, made open war with the Romans..After every victory I persuaded you to peace, as though I had been myself conquered. When I came near your temple, I again departed from the laws of war and exhorted you to spare your own sanctuary and to preserve your holy house to yourselves. I allowed you a quiet exit out of it and security for your preservation; (*Wars* VI 6:2)

Titus then made his final offer:

If you throw down your arms and deliver up your bodies to me, I grant you your lives; and I will act like a mild master of a family; what cannot be healed shall be punished and the rest I will preserve for my own use. (Ibid)

But John and Simon refused. They wanted to be let through the wall surrounding Jerusalem and be allowed to leave for the desert with their wives and children–abandoning the city to the Romans.

Titus was outraged at this and rejected the proposal. He replied that he would now take no more deserters, but fight the remaining Jewish warriors to the last man. And so the negotiation ended badly for the Jews.

So he (Titus) gave orders to the soldiers both to burn and to plunder the city; who did nothing indeed that day; but on the next day they set fire to the repository of the archives, to Acra, to the council-house and to the place called Ophlas; at which time the fire proceeded as far as the palace of queen Helena, which was in the middle of Acra; the lanes also were burnt down, as were also those houses that were full of the dead bodies of such as were destroyed by famine. (*Wars* VI 6:3)

The Zealots' Final Stand

The zealots knew it would be the worse for them if they made a stand in the lower city. It was a different situation in the upper city, where the walled palace of Herod, near the Second Temple, was a mighty stronghold. Thousands of followers of Simon had already taken refuge there. Also, many valuables looted from Jerusalem had been stored within the 40-foot high walls of the palace.

The zealots of John, now displaced from the Second Temple, decided on refuge there as well and battled the Jewish citizens who had already established themselves within. According to Josephus, the zealots slew 8,400 of these citizen Jews and "secured" the palace (*Wars* VI 7:1).

Over the next several days, the Romans took the lower city of Jerusalem with little difficulty. They set the area on fire to its southern apex at the pool of Siloam. The Romans then again took time off to celebrate, though they were angry that the zealots had escaped to Herod's palace with much of the booty they thought was rightfully theirs.

> Nor was there any place in the city that had no dead bodies in it, but what was entirely covered with those that were killed either by the famine or the rebellion; and all was full of the dead bodies of such as had perished, either by that sedition or by that famine. (*Wars* VI 7:2)

Eschewing the palace of Herod, some of the zealots and certain members of the citizen army–Simon of Gerasa among them–decided to hide in the extensive system of caves and tunnels that lay under the upper city. There, they hoped to wait for the departure of the Romans and then emerge with their lives and loot intact. To hasten the departure of the Romans, Josephus writes that some zealots even set fire to parts of the upper city themselves (*Wars* VI 7:3).

On August 6th, Titus decided to raise banks against the palace walls. It is likely that when Josephus is referring to the upper city, he actually is referring to the palace of Herod. The old banks were dismantled from the Second Temple and sections of the north wall–large tree trunks, mostly–and relocated to the palace walls a few hundred feet away.

> The works that belonged to the four legions were erected on the west side of the city, over against the royal palace; but the whole body of the auxiliary troops, with the rest of the multitude that were with them, [erected their banks] at the Xystus, whence they reached to the bridge and that tower of Simon which he had built as a citadel for himself against John, when they were at war one with another. (*Wars* VI 8:1)

By 22nd day of August, the banks to the upper city (the palace) were finished and the Titus set his engines to work. The walls were quickly broken down and the defenders fled.

> Now as soon as a part of the wall was battered down and certain of the towers yielded to the impression of the battering rams, those that opposed themselves fled away and such a terror fell upon the tyrants, as was much greater than the occasion required; for before the enemy got over the breach they were quite stunned and were immediately for flying away. (*Wars* VI 8:4)

Victory

On August 23rd, A.D. 70, Titus and the Roman army now had possession of the entire city of Jerusalem, after a five month siege. In the smoldering aftermath, Titus had nothing but admiration for the constructions in Herod's palace, even as burned out as they were. Titus decided to spare two of the palace towers, along with a portion of the western city wall. Then Titus then ordered the rest of Jerusalem totally demolished.

There were still many Jews left alive, however and what was Titus to do with them?

> Caesar gave orders that they should kill none but those that were in arms and opposed them, but should take the rest alive. But, together with those whom they had orders to slay, they slew the aged and the infirm; but for those that were in their flourishing age and who might be useful to them, they drove them together into the temple and shut them up within the walls of the court of the women; (*Wars* VI 9:2)

Those of "flourishing age" who were the best physical specimens were saved for the anticipated Roman triumph. The rest over 17 years of age were placed in bonds and many were sent to work in the Egyptian mines. Thousands were sent to the provinces to serve as gladiators. Titus himself kept almost 3,000 for a similar purpose. Those under 17 were sold as slaves.

> Now the number of those that were carried captive during this whole war was collected to be ninety-seven thousand; as was the number of those that perished during the whole siege eleven hundred thousand, the greater part of whom were indeed of the same nation [with the citizens of Jerusalem], but not belonging to the city itself; for they were come up from all the country to the feast of unleavened bread..(*Wars* VI 9:3)

Hundreds of thousands of Jews had died in the course of the siege, with a considerable number being those inadvertently caught in the city due to their presence at that year's Passover.

Captured Rebels

The tyrants John and Simon had escaped to the underground caverns, but did not stay there long. Simon and a few of his men and a number of expert stone carvers hid in the caves that honeycombed the upper city and interconnected with the foundation of the Second Temple. They were hoping to tunnel through to an elevated area whereby there could easily elude the Romans and escape into the desert. But this proved to be impossible, and so Simon devised another stratagem.

> And now Simon, thinking he might be able to astonish and elude the Romans, put on a white frock and buttoned upon him a purple cloak and appeared out of the ground in the place where the temple had formerly been. (*Wars* VII 1:1)

> ..many captives were taken, among them Bargiora, their leader; and he was the only one to be executed in connexion with the triumphal celebration. (Dio 65:6)

Simon thought that the superstitious Romans would think him a god and flee, giving him a chance to escape to safety. Instead, he was captured without incident. Simon was then sent in chains to Caesarea to await transport to Rome for the triumph.

John of Gischala was also captured alive. Instead of being sent to Rome to face beheading, however, John spent the rest of his life in a Roman prison– probably at hard labor. This is somewhat curious, as John was every bit the Jewish leader as Simon was — and even more so in some respects. John was fighting the Romans at the very outset of the rebellion while Simon came on the scene more than two years later as a mercenary general. But it must be remembered that John was Josephus' old nemesis from early in the war. John of Gischala even convinced the Jerusalem High Priesthood to recall General Josephus from Galilee to face probable execution in early A.D. 67 for undisclosed crimes.

But now Josephus had the upper hand. Having the ear of Emperor Vespasian and General Titus, and being a vengeful man at heart, Josephus must have thought that a swift and honorable death was too good for John.

> AND thus was Jerusalem taken, in the second year of the reign of Vespasian, on the eighth day of the month Gorpeius [Elul] (August twenty-third)....It was demolished entirely by the Babylonians, four hundred and seventy-seven years and six months after (King David). And from king David, who was the first of the Jews who reigned therein, to this destruction under Titus, were one thousand one hundred and seventy-nine years; but from its first building, till this last destruction, were two thousand one hundred and seventy-seven years; yet hath not its great antiquity, nor its vast riches, nor the diffusion of its nation over all the habitable earth, nor the greatness of the veneration paid to it on a religious account, been sufficient to preserve it from being destroyed. And thus ended the siege of Jerusalem. (*Wars* 6 10:1)

But while Jerusalem was crushed and most of its constructions dismantled and destroyed, and its people either slain in battle, dead from starvation, executed for crimes against Rome, or sold into slavery, there were still rebel Jewish enclaves in the Jewish East. Titus, however, chose to ignore them, as he was tired of war.

Chapter 24   End of the Revolt

..so that as now all the places were taken, excepting Herodium and Masada and Macherus which were in the possession of the robbers.. (*Wars* IV 9:9)

By September of A.D. 70, Jerusalem had been captured and the surviving Jews either executed or enslaved. Jerusalem itself was physically leveled, save for a few structures of strategic or symbolic importance. Titus then spent the next few months relaxing in the Jewish East with his new love Bernice, waiting for favorable sailing weather for his return to Rome. During that time, he visited the major cities in the region, such as Antioch, Caesarea, and Caesarea Philippi, — giving gladiatorial shows, receiving accolades, and enjoying his hard-earned triumph.

But the Jewish nation had not been totally subjugated. There were still three strong mountain fortresses to the south that remained under the control of the Jewish zealots and Sicarii. This is somewhat puzzling because at the end of the Jerusalem siege Titus had the equivalent of nine battle-hardened legions at his command. Why not immediately march south and eliminate these strongholds? Titus probably reasoned that, without Jerusalem, the southern fortresses posed little threat to Roman interests. But that Titus was tired of war was certainly a factor.

In the course of the siege of Jerusalem, according to Josephus over a million Jews had perished — either by the sword or through famine. How many had Titus either killed or seen killed? How many dead bodies had he seen over the past four years?

Bernice might have also have played a role along with the anticipation of the exciting life that awaited him in Rome. Not only would a great triumph be celebrated in his — and his father's — honor, but he would be introduced to the Roman people as heir-apparent to Emperor Vespasian.

> Titus himself had Rome with all its wealth and pleasures before his eyes. (*Histories* 5:11)

Titus knew that Herodium–only five miles south of Jerusalem– could be overrun easily, but then he would be obligated to move on to the vastly stronger mountaintop fortresses of Macherus and Masada. From his recent hellish experience with Jerusalem, Titus knew that the subjugation of them could take many months.

Certainly, Titus' Jerusalem experience extinguished whatever natural passion for war he had. This could explain why, when Titus became emperor 10 years later, he became known as one of Rome's most reasonable and humane rulers — never executing anyone out of anger or jealousy.

> Titus after becoming ruler committed no act of murder or of amatory passion, but showed himself upright, though plotted against and self-controlled, though Berenice came to Rome again. This may have been because he had really undergone a change.. Titus.. ruled with mildness and died at the height of his glory..(Dio 66 18)

Vespasian had hoped that Titus would bring about a speedy resolution to the Jewish revolt. To that end, he assigned his son Titus almost double the number of Roman legions that Nero had assigned to him in A.D. 66. Partially for that reason, Emperor Vespasian stayed in Alexandria for months before finally returning to Rome in the late spring of A.D. 70; Vespasian was hoping that a victorious Titus could make a triumphant return to Rome with him.

The siege of Jerusalem dragged on, however, and with other pressing matters needing his personal attention, Vespasian left the East for Rome without Titus. Did Titus feel like he had let his father down by not overrunning Jerusalem quickly? That also might have been part of the reason why, after the destruction of Jerusalem, Titus declared a premature end to the Jewish wars.

Now in late A.D. 70, winter was fast upon the East and the weather did not favor a wholesale transfer of prisoners and loot to Rome by sea. And there was a lot of both. In the months that Titus stayed in the East, a portion of this booty found its way to the markets in Syria. So much gold was taken from Jerusalem in its defeat that, in Syrian markets, that the price of the precious metal was halved!

As the Roman force waited out the winter, King Agrippa II invited Titus and his entourage to Caesarea Philippi. This was the capital of Agrippa II's own kingdom and, even in winter and though at altitude, it was a very pleasant place. The beautiful Queen Bernice claimed the palace in Caesarea Philippi as her part-time home as well — an added attraction for Titus.

> But as for Titus, he marched from that Cesarea which lay by the sea-side and came to that which is named Cesarea Philippi and staid there a considerable time and exhibited all sorts of shows there. And here a great number of the captives were destroyed, some being thrown to wild beasts and others in multitudes forced to kill one another, as if they were their enemies. (*Wars* VII 1:1)

From Caesarea Philippi, Titus proceeded to move across the Jewish East as his inclination dictated, receiving the accolades of the people and exhibiting his prisoners and having many perform and die in gladiatorial contests.

> While Titus was at Cesarea, he solemnized the birthday of his brother Domitian] after a splendid manner and inflicted a great deal of the punishment intended for the Jews in honor of him; for the number of those that were now slain in fighting with the beasts and were burnt and fought with one another, exceeded two thousand five hundred. Yet did all this seem to the Romans, when they were thus destroyed ten thousand several ways, to be a punishment beneath their deserts. (*Wars* VII 2:1)

Titus traveled north to Antioch exhibiting "magnificent" shows wherever he went. He continued east across the expanse of Syria and on to the Euphrates River. There, a delegation of Parthians brought him a crown of gold in honor of his victory over the Jews. Returning to Antioch, Titus then traveled by land to Alexandria in Egypt. From Alexandria, he and the army finally traveled by sea to Rome in the early spring of A.D. 71.

Triumph in Rome

A Roman triumphal celebration was always an amazing spectacle. As this was Vespasian's first major military success as emperor, great plans were made for it to be memorable. It was also a celebration of a new age for Rome, recently freed from the yoke of the Caesars.

Josephus describes the triumph in colorful detail. As with all Roman triumphs throughout history, it ended with the slaying of one of the leaders of the enemy nation. In the case of the Jewish revolt, the leader presented was Simon of Gerasa, the son of Giora. Simon was ritually beheaded at the base of the Capitoline Hill, below the magnificent temple of Jupiter Capitolinus on the hill's top, to the cheers of the mob.

Josephus, an eyewitness, describes that day of celebration.

> And as soon as ever it was day, Vespasian and Titus came out crowned with laurel and clothed in those ancient purple habits which were proper to their family and then went as far as Octavian's Walks; for there it was that the senate and the principal rulers and those that had been recorded as of the equestrian order, waited for them. Now a tribunal had been erected before the cloisters and ivory chairs had been set upon it, when they came and sat down upon them. Whereupon the soldiery made an acclamation of joy to them immediately and all gave them attestations of their valor; while they were themselves without their arms and only in their silken garments and crowned with laurel: then Vespasian accepted of these shouts of theirs; but while they were still disposed to go on in such acclamations, he gave them a signal of silence. And when every body entirely held their peace, he stood up and covering the greatest part of his head with his cloak, he put up the accustomed solemn prayers; the like prayers did Titus put up also; after which prayers Vespasian made a short speech to all the people and then

sent away the soldiers to a dinner prepared for them by the emperors. Then did he retire to that gate which was called the Gate of the Pomp, because pompous shows do always go through that gate; there it was that they tasted some food and when they had put on their triumphal garments and had offered sacrifices to the gods that were placed at the gate, they sent the triumph forward and marched through the theatres, that they might be the more easily seen by the multitudes. (*Wars* VII 5:4)

Now it is impossible to describe the multitude of the shows as they deserve and the magnificence of them all; such indeed as a man could not easily think of as performed, either by the labor of workmen, or the variety of riches, or the rarities of nature; for almost all such curiosities as the most happy men ever get by piece-meal were here one heaped on another and those both admirable and costly in their nature; and all brought together on that day demonstrated the vastness of the dominions of the Romans; for there was here to be seen a mighty quantity of silver and gold and ivory, contrived into all sorts of things and did not appear as carried along in pompous show only, but, as a man may say, running along like a river. Some parts were composed of the rarest purple hangings and so carried along; and others accurately represented to the life what was embroidered by the arts of the Babylonians. There were also precious stones that were transparent, some set in crowns of gold and some in other ouches, as the workmen pleased; and of these such a vast number were brought, that we could not but thence learn how vainly we imagined any of them to be rarities. The images of the gods were also carried, being as well wonderful for their largeness, as made very artificially and with great skill of the workmen; nor were any of these images of any other than very costly materials; and many species of animals were brought, every one in their own natural ornaments. The men also who brought every one of these shows were great multitudes and adorned with purple garments, all over interwoven with gold; those that were chosen for carrying these pompous shows having also about them such magnificent ornaments as were both extraordinary and surprising. Besides these, one might see that even the great number of the captives was not unadorned, while the variety that was in their garments and their fine texture, concealed from the sight the deformity of their bodies. But what afforded the greatest surprise of all was the structure of the pageants that were borne along; for indeed he that met them could not but be afraid that the bearers would not be able firmly enough to support them, such was their magnitude; for many of them were so made, that they were on three or even four stories, one above another. The magnificence also of their structure afforded one both pleasure and surprise; for upon many of them were laid carpets of gold. There was also wrought gold and ivory fastened about them all; and many resemblances of the war and those in several ways and variety of contrivances, affording a most lively portraiture of itself. For there was to be seen a happy country laid waste and entire squadrons of enemies slain; while some of them ran away and some were carried into captivity; with walls of great altitude and magnitude overthrown and ruined by machines; with the strongest fortifications taken and the walls of most populous cities upon the tops of hills seized on and an army pouring itself within the walls; as also every place full of slaughter and supplications of the enemies, when they were no longer able to lift up their hands in way of opposition. Fire also sent upon temples was here represented and houses overthrown and falling upon their owners: rivers also, after they came out of a large and melancholy desert, ran down, not into a land cultivated, nor as drink for men, or for cattle, but through a land still on fire upon every side; for the Jews related that such a thing they had undergone during this war. Now the workmanship of these representations was so magnificent and lively in the construction of the things, that it exhibited what had been done to such as did not see it, as if they had been there really present. On the top of every one of these pageants was placed the commander of the city that was taken and the manner wherein he was taken. Moreover, there followed those pageants a great number of ships; and for the other spoils, they were carried in great plenty. But for those that were taken in the temple of Jerusalem, they made the greatest figure of them all; that is, the golden table, of the weight of many talents; the candlestick also, that was made of gold, though its construction were now changed from that which we made use of; for its middle shaft was fixed upon a basis and the small branches were produced out of it to a great length, having the likeness of a trident in their position and had every one a socket made of brass for a lamp at the tops of them. These lamps were in number seven and represented the dignity of the number seven among the Jews; and the last of all the spoils, was carried the Law of the Jews. After these spoils passed by a great many men, carrying the images of Victory, whose structure was entirely either of ivory or of gold. After which Vespasian marched in the first place and Titus followed him; Domitian also rode along with them and made a glorious appearance and rode on a horse that was worthy of admiration. (*Wars* VII 5:5)

Now the last part of this pompous show was at the temple of Jupiter Capitolinus, whither when they were come, they stood still; for it was the Romans' ancient custom to stay till somebody brought the news that the general of the enemy was slain. This general was Simon, the son of Gioras, who had then been led in this triumph among the captives; a rope had also been put upon his head and he had been drawn into a proper place in the forum and had withal been tormented by those that drew him along; and the law of the Romans required that malefactors condemned to die should be slain there. Accordingly, when it was related that there was an end of him and all the people had set up a shout for joy, they then began to offer those sacrifices which they had consecrated, in the prayers used in such solemnities; which when they had finished, they went away to the palace. And as for some of the spectators, the emperors entertained them at their own feast; and for all the rest there were noble preparations made for feasting at home; for this was a festival day to the city of Rome, as celebrated for the victory obtained by their army over their enemies, for the end that was now put to their civil miseries and for the commencement of their hopes of future prosperity and happiness. (*Wars* VII 5:6)

Vespasian later built a sumptuous and ornate temple to Peace (Pax) in the hope that the entire empire would remain in peace forever (*Wars* VII 5:7).

Macherus and Herodium

General Lucilius Bassus became the legate of Judea after the departure of Titus in A.D. 71. Formerly, Bassus had been prefect of the Roman fleet at Ravenna under the short-lived reign of Aulus Vitellius. In a fortuitous move, Bassus half-heartedly revolted from Vitellius and gave his support to Vespasian in A.D. 69. Vespasian now rewarded his loyalty with control over Judea.

Lucilius Bassus, prefect of the Ravenna fleet, finding that the troops wavered in purpose, from the fact that many were natives of Dalmatia and Pannonia, provinces held for Vespasian, had attached them to the Flavianist party. The night-time was chosen for accomplishing the treason, because then, unknown to all the rest, the ringleaders alone might assemble at head-quarters. Bassus, moved by shame, or perhaps by fear, awaited the issue in his house. The captains of the triremes rushed with a great outcry on the images of Vitellius; a few, who attempted to resist, were cut down; the great majority, with the usual love of change, were ready to join Vespasian. Then Bassus came forward and openly sanctioned the movement. (Tacitus Histories 3:12)

General Bassus had the governorship of Judea and the command of the 10th legion. Vespasian, perhaps disappointed that Titus had left the Jewish campaign unfinished, ordered Bassus to subjugate the remaining Jewish strongholds.

The Roman legate first set his sights on Macherus, a very formidable mountain-top city in nearby Perea. Macherus was the site where, 35 years before, John the Baptist had been imprisoned and executed. It was in the high palace of Macherus where the daughter of Herodias danced seductively before Antipas and his generals, and then made her deadly request.

Macherus was situated on a mountain close to the eastern shores of Lake Asphaltitis and surrounded by deep chasms. On the north and south aspects of Macherus, two of these canyons descended westwards to the inhospitable and briny Asphaltitis. A lesser chasm existed to the east of Macherus. There, a steep and narrow trail was the only access route to the fortress.

Macherus was close to Nabotea, and so King Alexander Jannaeus developed it as a military base 150 years before. On it he constructed a two-tiered city. Herod the Great rebuilt Macherus 50 years later and it became a key part of his southern command strategy. His son Herod Antipas anticipated using it as a jump-off point for his planned invasion of Arabia in A.D. 35.

Macherus was now one of the strongholds for the remaining Jewish zealots and Sicarii, but it also held a considerable number of non-Jews. Upon arrival and after assessing the situation, Bassus decided to use the manpower of the army to fill in the chasm to the east (*Wars* VII 6:4). In turn, the zealot Jews prepared for battle by claiming the palace on the upper portion of the mountain for themselves and sending all the non-Jews down to the lower city. From the high palace, the Jews also sent out sorties to battle the laboring Roman soldiers who were filling in the eastern chasm.

Though the Jews had considerable success in hampering the Roman efforts, Macherus soon fell to Bassus without a fight. According to Josephus, the Romans captured the bold young son of a prominent family. After seeing him publicly tortured and hearing the Romans threaten to crucify the young man, the Jews of Macherus decided to surrender in order to save his life.

But this story might be doubted. The site of Macherus has been identified in Jordan on the east side of the Dead Sea. It is now known as "Mukavir." A thick spine does indeed exist on the east side of the mountain which connects it with the nearest substantive land mass across a narrow canyon. This could well have been created by the Romans in their initial actions against the city, as Josephus reports. But higher up on the mountain there is another assault "bank" made up of loose rocks–a ramp that leads up from the west to the east, and to the ruins of an ancient palace on top of the mountain. This evidence would fit a scenario of the Romans first gaining the lower city and then having to build a second bank to breech the strong walls of the upper city palace.

At any rate, many of the most extreme of the Jewish rebels managed to escape Macherus before the final capitulation. Josephus reports that a great number sought refuge in a nearby forest (!) where Bassus pursued them and eventually killed 3,000 in battle (*Wars* VII 6:5).

Bassus then took the 10th legion and marched back around the Asphaltitis north towards Jerusalem. His intention was to subdue the zealot stronghold of Herodium which was five miles south of the city. Then from there Bassus intended to follow the western shore of the Asphaltitis south to Masada and subdue it.

Herodium was the site of a large and fortified summertime palace that Herod the Great had constructed on the top of an artificially heightened hill. Herodium was filled with subterranean chambers and passageways. Herod had enjoyed it there so much that he designated it as the site of his burial tomb. Archaeological evidence suggests that only months after Herod's interment there in 4 B.C., it was looted. Bassus had little difficulty in dislodging the zealot refugees ensconced in Herodium and conquering it.

Masada—The Last Fortress

On the way to the last fortress, Masada, with his 10th legion, Lucilius Bassus died. This occurred in late A.D. 72. Bassus' successor, General Flavius Silva, continued on with the Masada campaign.

WHEN Bassus was dead in Judea, Flavius Silva succeeded him as procurator there; who, when he saw that all the rest of the country was subdued in this war and that there was but one only strong hold that was still in rebellion, he got all his army together that lay in different places and made an expedition against it. This fortress was called Masada. (*Wars* VII 8:1)

Masada was under the control of the Sicarii leader Eleazor– who was no relation to Eleazor, the son of Simon, who was a leader of zealots early during the course of the siege of Jerusalem. This Eleazor, however, boasted quite a resume of his own. He was descended from the very Judas the Galilean who started a fourth sect of the Jews (to join the Pharisees, Sadducees and Essenes) which was based on resistance to Roman authority and Roman-mandated taxes. Judas came to the fore during the enrollment period ordered by Emperor Augustus in A.D. 6. Two of Judas' sons decades later would play key roles in the initiation of the revolt against Rome in A.D. 66.

The fortress was virtually impregnable and for decades served as a base for criminal raids into the surrounding Idumean countryside. The Masada Sicarii were so feared that the neighboring Idumeans established a 25,000 man army to protect themselves (*Wars* IV 9:5). One of the "alumni" of the Masada Sicarii, in fact, was the eventual leader of Jerusalem's defense in the Jewish revolt, Simon, son of Giora (*Wars* IV 9:3). Simon had only recently been publicly beheaded in Rome as the leader of the rebel Jews to the cheers of tens of thousands of Romans.

And now a fourth misfortune arose, in order to bring our nation to destruction. There was a fortress of very great strength not far from Jerusalem which had been built by our ancient kings, both as a repository for their effects in the hazards of war and for the preservation of their bodies at the same time. It was called Masada. Those that were called *sicarii* had taken possession of it formerly, but at this time they overran the neighboring countries, aiming only to procure to themselves necessaries; for the fear they were then in prevented their further ravages. But when once they were informed that the Roman army lay still and that the Jews were divided between sedition and tyranny, they boldly undertook greater matters; and at the feast of unleavened bread which the Jews celebrate in memory of their deliverance from the

Egyptian bondage, when they were sent back into the country of their forefathers, they came down by night, without being discovered by those that could have prevented them and overran a certain small city called Engaddi:--in which expedition they prevented those citizens that could have stopped them, before they could arm themselves and fight them. They also dispersed them and cast them out of the city. As for such as could not run away, being women and children, they slew of them above seven hundred. Afterward, when they had carried every thing out of their houses and had seized upon all the fruits that were in a flourishing condition, they brought them into Masada. And indeed these men laid all the villages that were about the fortress waste and made the whole country desolate; while there came to them every day, from all parts, not a few men as corrupt as themselves. *Wars* IV 6:3)

The Masada Sicarii also held in subjugation many nearby villages. General Silva soon subdued all of the surrounding countryside with many of the inhabitants escaping to Masada. Taking a cue from Titus' actions in Jerusalem, Silva had his soldiers build a wall around the base of Masada so that no one could escape the Romans. Three Roman camps were also constructed–the outlines of which can be seen to this day–and the siege commenced.

Masada

Only two passages led to the top of Masada. On the east, there existed a steep trail that switchbacked up to the mountain's plateau-like summit. This trail still exists. On the west side of the mountain, there was another ascent, but not as precipitous — as the surrounding land is higher than on the east. It is here where the Romans concentrated their efforts and constructed a thick bank to access the heights of Masada.

There was a rock, not small in circumference and very high. It was encompassed with valleys of such vast depth downward, that the eye could not reach their bottoms; they were abrupt and such as no animal could walk upon, excepting at two places of the rock, where it subsides, in order to afford a passage for ascent, though not without difficulty. (*Wars* VII 8:3)
Upon this top of the hill, Jonathan the high priest first of all built a fortress and called it Masada: after which the rebuilding of this place

> employed the care of king Herod to a great degree; he also built a wall round about the entire top of the hill, seven furlongs long; it was composed of white stone; its height was twelve and its breadth eight cubits; there were also erected upon that wall thirty-eight towers, each of them fifty cubits high; out of which you might pass into lesser edifices which were built on the inside, round the entire wall; (*Wars* VII 8:3)

Seven furlongs corresponds to 1500 yards which is roughly the modern measured length of the wall perimeter. Much of the ground at the top of Masada was composed of fertile soil. In the case of an extensive siege, food could conceivably have been grown there, with the proper amount of irrigation. Cisterns had also been cut into the rock, where rainwater could be collected.

Herod the Great build a palace on the northern inclination of Masada.

> Now the wall of this palace was very high and strong and had at its four corners towers sixty cubits high. The furniture also of the edifices and of the cloisters and of the baths, was of great variety and very costly; and these buildings were supported by pillars of single stones on every side; the walls and also the floors of the edifices were paved with stones of several colors. He also had cut many and great pits, as reservoirs for water, out of the rocks, at every one of the places that were inhabited, both above and round about the palace and before the wall; and by this contrivance he endeavored to have water for several uses, as if there had been fountains there. Here was also a road digged from the palace and leading to the very top of the mountain which yet could not be seen by such as were without [the walls]; nor indeed could enemies easily make use of the plain roads; for the road on the east side, as we have already taken notice, could not be walked upon, by reason of its nature; and for the western road, he built a large tower at its narrowest place, at no less a distance from the top of the hill than a thousand cubits; which tower could not possibly be passed by, nor could it be easily taken; nor indeed could those that walked along it without any fear (such was its contrivance) easily get to the end of it; and after such a manner was this citadel fortified, both by nature and by the hands of men, in order to frustrate the attacks of enemies. (*Wars* VII 8:3)

When Herod the Great was defeated by the Parthians and the Asamonean King Antigonus in 41 B.C., it was in Masada where he hid much of his treasures before leaving the East to seek help in Rome. This included his beautiful wife Mariamne I and her entourage and guards.

Even after the Parthians had been defeated by Herod in 37 B.C., the prescient if not paranoid king took to keeping the fortress well-supplied with food and supplies. Herod the Great not only feared being deposed by his subject Jews, but also Queen Cleopatra of Egypt. Cleopatra had the ear of Antony and it was no secret that she coveted the Jewish East. Herod did not plan on giving up his kingdom without a fight.

The desert air made the long-term preservation of so-called perishable goods possible. In fact, when Eleazor and his Sicarii removed themselves to Masada 100 years later, they found a veritable cornucopia of supplies dating from the age of Herod the Great. Some of the foodstuffs were still edible.

> ..for here was laid up corn in large quantities and such as would subsist men for a long time; here was also wine and oil in abundance, with all kinds of pulse and dates heaped up together; all which Eleazar found there, when he and his sicarii got possession of the fortress by treachery. These fruits were also fresh and full ripe and no way inferior to such fruits newly laid in, although they were little short of a hundred years from the laying in these provisions [by Herod], till the place was taken by the Romans; nay, indeed, when the Romans got possession of those fruits that were left, they found them not corrupted all that while; (*Wars* VII 8:4)

Herod the Great also had stored enough weapons at Masada to equip an army of 10,000 men!

The Siege of Masada

Roman General Silva began to raise a bank on the west side of Masada up to the lower wall of the palace of Herod. On this west side existed a large rock formation called the White Promontory which was next to the mountain of Masada. This was easily accessed by the Roman army and only 500 feet from Masada's summit. Soon, the bank had been raised to the height of the lower defensive walls. The massive Roman engines of war were then assembled and moved into place.

Through the pummeling of the iron-tipped log rams, a portion of the lower wall on the western side collapsed. The Masada defenders quickly rushed in to fortify the secondary walls behind it as they succeeded in pushing the Romans back. The Jews then ingeniously made a replacement wall of large timbers with dirt sandwiched between them. This configuration blunted much of the power of the ram; in fact the percussive force of the battering ram served to compact the soil and make the wall even stronger.

To combat this, General Silva simply ordered the wooden wall set on fire. That strategy initially backfired as a north wind blew the flames back upon the Romans, but then the wind changed to the south and spread the fire all along the length wooden wall, destroying much of it. With a solid breach in hand and the fall of Masada in sight, the Romans retreated to their camps. Silva planned to assault Masada in proper fashion early the next morning. Extra guards were placed around Masada to make extra sure no Jews escaped.

Eleazor saw that defeat was inevitable, but he had no thoughts of escape. Instead, he wanted the Jews to join him in a suicide pact, preferring death to surrender.

> "Since we, long ago, my generous friends, resolved never to be servants to the Romans, nor to any other than to God himself, who alone is the true and just Lord of mankind, the time is now come that obliges us to make that resolution true in practice.. Let our wives die before they are abused and our children before they have tasted of slavery; and after we have slain them, let us bestow that glorious benefit upon one another mutually and preserve ourselves in freedom, as an excellent funeral monument for us. But first let us destroy our money and the fortress by fire; for I am well assured that this will be a great grief to the Romans, that they shall not be able to seize upon our bodies and shall fall of our wealth also; and let us spare nothing but our provisions; for they will be a testimonial when we are dead that we were not subdued for want of necessaries, but that, according to our original resolution, we have preferred death before slavery." (*Wars* VII 8:6)

Eleazor's passionate speech persuaded most all of the people in Masada agree to his plan (*Wars* VII 8:7). But suicide was against

Jewish law. All the people on Masada had to be killed in a systematic and "orthodox" way.

They decided on a plan reminiscent of Josephus' "end game" at Jotapata. The Sicarii men gathered their families around them and tearful goodbyes were said. Then the men killed them all. Next, by lottery 10 men were selected out of the remaining hundreds. Those 10 then killed the rest of the Sicarii. That bloody deed accomplished, another lottery was held amongst the 10. The "winner" then slew the other nine, and then committed suicide — the only one to be guilty of the sacrilege.

> ..for a conclusion, the nine offered their necks to the executioner and he who was the last of all took a view of all the other bodies, lest perchance some or other among so many that were slain should want his assistance to be quite despatched and when he perceived that they were all slain, he set fire to the palace and with the great force of his hand ran his sword entirely through himself and fell down dead near to his own relations. (*Wars* VII 9:1)

In all, 960 were executed in this fashion. The mass "suicide" happened on the 15th day of Nisan (April fourth) in A.D. 73.

Early the next morning at first light, the Roman soldiers entered Masada through the breach. The soldiers were fully armed, battle-ready and prepared for a furious and deadly fight with hardened Jewish warriors. The Romans were also fully aware that Masada held many Jewish women and children which would make the men fight with all the more desperation.

But, to their surprise and amazement, the Roman soldiers were greeted with an eerie silence at the top of the smoke-filled plateau. To the north, Herod's palace was in flames and in the broad plain front of them was the grisly spectacle of a nearly 1,000 dead men, women and children scattered about.

> Now for the Romans, they expected that they should be fought in the morning, when, accordingly, they put on their armor and laid bridges of planks upon their ladders from their banks, to make an assault upon the fortress which they did; but saw nobody as an enemy, but a terrible solitude on every side, with a fire within the place, as well as a perfect silence. (*Wars* VII 9:2)

How did Josephus learn the details of this horrific action if everyone died? A woman learned of the plan beforehand, and hid herself and her five children in one of Masada's underground caverns–taking with her enough water to drink and food to last her family for several days.

After Masada

Many of the defeated Sicarii, zealots, and other seditious Jews over the last years of the revolt had escaped the Jewish East to find refuge in Egypt and points west. These refugees, however, were not content to live out their lives in peace and accept Roman dominance. They continued to rebel against the Romans and their Jewish collaborators. The Romanized Alexandrian Jews were forced to take action against them and hundreds of zealots were captured and brought to Roman justice (*Wars* VII 10:1). The governor of Alexandria subsequently reported on these events to Emperor Vespasian, who was so alarmed that he ordered that the Jewish temple near Alexandria in Onias be destroyed which was a smaller version of the former Temple in Jerusalem.

The Sicarii refugees of Cyrene, 500 miles to the west of Alexandria, also caused trouble. Roman retribution ordered by Vespasian resulted in the deaths of over 3,000 zealot Jews (*Wars* VII 11 1-4).

And so, with the putting down of the Cyrenian uprising, Josephus brings to an end his recounting of the Jewish wars.

> And here we shall put an end to this our history; wherein we formerly promised to deliver the same with all accuracy, to such as should be desirous of understanding after what manner this war of the Romans with the Jews was managed. Of which history, how good the style is, must be left to the determination of the readers; but as for its agreement with the facts, I shall not scruple to say and that boldly, that truth hath been what I have alone aimed at through its entire composition. (*Wars* VII 11:5)

Chapter 25   Epilogue

What can be learned about Christianity from the conclusions of our journey through the world of 2,000 years ago? Most significantly, the key crucifixion year of A.D. 36 gives new importance to the actions of Syrian president Lucius Vitellius as documented by Josephus and validates the political realities that Paul the Apostle faced a quarter-century later as recounted in Acts of the Apostles and the Epistles.

The Jerusalem Second Temple dominated Jewish life religiously and politically in the three decades before and after Jesus' crucifixion. The Temple operation itself developed into a vast economic profit center through carefully crafted religious rituals, tithing requirements, and a procession of yearly major and minor festivals. In fact, the Temple supported the economy of Jerusalem as well as making several High Priesthood families very wealthy.

The subjugating Romans were aware of the complexity of the Jewish religion and the all-encompassing nature of Jewish law. For this reason, the Romans allowed the Jewish High Priests to serve as *de facto* Roman administrators, with minimal oversight by appointed Roman prefects and procurators—who usually lived in Caesarea. Corruption was endemic to Roman provincial rule and bribes were expected. In Judea, the appointed Romans were certainly paid large sums of money by the priesthood not to interfere with lucrative Temple operations.

As the decades passed, the common Jews increasingly resented the presence of Rome and the collaboration with Rome of their High Priesthood. This caused many Jews to embrace zealotry, a quasi-religious movement that called for a return to Jewish independence. Unrest in the Jewish East became widespread and minor outbreaks of violence were frequent. Splinter religious sects antagonistic to the Second Temple priests also took root. Jesus headed up one of these movements— ultimately the most successful of them.

With the situation in the Jewish East deteriorating, Rome began to question whether the High Priesthood was truly supported by the common Jews. Did they deserve the powers Rome had given them? The High Priesthood, fully aware of Rome's concerns, aggressively moved to protect their position. Jewish troublemakers were dealt with severely using any means possible.

The Gospels are clear that the Jerusalem High Priesthood was the driving force behind Jesus' crucifixion. Today, this tends to be downplayed in favor of a more antagonistic view of Rome; after all, the Judean Prefect Pontius Pilate ordered the crucifixion of Jesus by Roman soldiers. Also, it was Emperor Nero who ordered the persecution of the early Christians—much to the disgust of Roman historian Tacitus.

But the Roman Empire throughout its history displayed a policy of tolerance toward all religions. Nowhere is it recorded that any conquered nations were forced to worship Jupiter—or Augustus. Then why would Rome suddenly change their policy and target the Christian sect?

The answer is that Rome didn't. A more disciplined look at history not only supports the Gospels' view, but shows that in several situations the Romans, far from being antagonistic, protected the Christians from the Second Temple priests as much as was possible.

In Pontius Pilate, we see a corrupt provincial governor, bribed by the High Priesthood, executing Jesus on the order of Caiaphas in A.D. 36. Syrian President Lucius Vitellius, new to the Jewish East and in Jerusalem for the Passover, removed Caiaphas probably for this reason. He was likely very close to removing Pilate as well. Vitellius knew that Emperor Tiberius and Rome did not approve of their appointed rulers—religious or otherwise—abusing the power of Caesar to settle religious conflicts or oppress their own people.

After the crucifixion, the followers of Jesus began to organize and proselytize. In response, the new High Priest Jonathan sanctioned their harassment to the point of assault and murder. When Vitellius returned to Jerusalem in A.D. 37, Jonathan was removed—likely for this reason. Pontius Pilate had been removed weeks earlier by Vitellius for similar acts on a larger scale against the Samaritans.

Two decades later, we see the Roman authorities turning even further against the High Priesthood, with Judean Procurator Felix openly challenging them—something Pilate never would have done. Felix, in fact, arranged for the murder of High Priest Jonathan in A.D. 56 for Jonathan's relentless criticism of him.

Later, in A.D. 58, Felix protected Paul the Apostle from the hostility of the Jerusalem High Priesthood. Felix imprisoned Paul in his palace at Caesarea but let him move about the city freely as Paul preached about Jesus and against the High Priesthood. This further enraged the Jerusalem priests—if that were possible!

When Festus replaced Felix in A.D. 60, the High Priesthood, now led by High Priest Ismael, quickly requested that the still-imprisoned Paul be turned over to them for trial—meaning execution. Festus not only refused, but eventually sent Paul away to Rome on pretext for Paul's own safety.

For this act, Festus might have paid with his life. Festus' untimely and unexplained death in A.D. 62 was closely followed by the illegal convening of the Jerusalem Sanhedrin by the High Priesthood. The execution of James the Just and other Christian leaders quickly followed.

It was only two years later, in A.D. 64, that the unstable young Emperor Nero began his infamous persecutions of the Christians in Rome. Executed were the Apostles Paul and Peter as well as a large number of Christians. Suspiciously, in Rome at the time as a part of Nero's Royal court was former High Priest Ismael—the same Ismael who four years earlier was demanding Procurator Festus execute Paul.

In A.D. 66 the Jewish revolt began in earnest. In this, the politics involved are muddy but clearly the zealots had gained enough popular support to throw the Jewish East into widespread rebellion. Given its position, the High Priesthood had no choice but to try to ride herd over the unsettled and fractious nation. They appointed generals to at least protect the Jews from their Greek Syrian neighbors and hopefully control the independent zealot armies that had formed in several cities.

The revolt proved to be a complete disaster for the Jewish nation with hundreds of thousands of Jews perishing and an even greater number enslaved. In A.D. 70 Jerusalem and the Second Temple were destroyed to their foundations and the Jews were banned from ever living in the city again. The ritual and hierarchy of the Jewish High Priesthood was outlawed by an angry Roman Senate.

Christianity survived, however. This was ironically due to the antagonism they faced early on from the Jerusalem High Priesthood. By the time of the revolt in A.D. 66 most of the Christian centers were well out of harm's way having been long-established in Italia, Greece, Egypt, and Asia Minor.

Later Christians believed that the destruction of the Jewish nation was God's revenge for the crucifixion of Jesus. Events subsequent to the crucifixion do little to counter this belief. Within days, Joseph Caiaphas had been removed as High Priest. Within a year, the Prefect Pontius Pilate lost his office, and the High Priest Jonathan, Caiaphas' replacement, was himself dismissed — to be murdered 20 years later by Felix.

Within four years of Jesus' crucifixion, the Tetrarch Herod Antipas lost his kingdom and his fortune, and was banished in disgrace to Gaul along with his wife, Herodias. Within 40 years, the dynasty of the Caesars ended with the forced suicide of Nero.

And what of Vitellius, who protected the Christians to the extent that he could? After engineering a brilliant triumph in Syria, in Rome Vitellius artfully turned the dangerous Emperor Caius from his potential executioner into a fast friend. He subsequently was a key adviser to both Emperors Caius and

Claudius, and served two more senate consulships. Vitellius even ran the empire for six months while Claudius was away in Britain fighting the Celts.

Judaism managed to survive the first revolt with the Jews regrouping and centering their religion—without a High Priest —in the Galilean city of Tiberias. But in A.D. 132 the Jews revolted again, only to be crushed—again!—by the Romans, and further dispersed throughout the ancient world.

As for the Church, despite enduring episodic periods of persecution, it grew steadily over the centuries with its base now in Rome. In A.D. 325 Christianity became the state-sanctioned religion of the Roman Empire.

Author John Hagan is a medical physician, with a special interest in ancient history. Non-fiction works include *Year of the Passover, Fires of Rome,* and *The Essene Diet.*

Bibliography

The New Testament; American Standard Version 1901

The Works of Flavius Josephus; translated by William Whiston 1737

The Complete Works of Tacitus; translated by Alfred John Church and William Jackson Brodribb 1942

The Works of Philo Judaeus; translated by C.D. Yonge 1854

Eusebius: The History of the Church; translated by G.A. Williamson Penguin Classics 1965

Cassius Dio: History of Rome; Loeb Classical Library, 9 volumes, Greek texts and facing English translation: Harvard University Press, 1914-1927. Translation by Earnest Cary.

Suetonius: The Lives of the Twelve Caesars; translated by J. C. Rolfe 1914

Pliny the Elder: The Natural History; translation by John Bostock and H. T. Riley 1855

Index

www.ingramcontent.com/pod-product-compliance
Lightning Source LLC
Chambersburg PA
CBHW031227090426
42742CB00007B/111